His Redeeming Love

His Redeeming Love

Matthew Robert Payne

"His Redeeming Love" a Memoir of Matthew Robert Payne

Editing and proofreading done by www.odesk.com freelance workers

Cover Design Bjarki Clausen
Internet www.merkiverk.is
Email: merkiverk@merkiverk.is

The cover is a picture of Jesus' tomb. It is through the resurrection power of Jesus was can overcome all things, and our lives can be redeemed and used for good.

Revival Waves of Glory Books & Publishing
PO Box 596
Litchfield, IL 62056
United States of America
www.revivalwavesofgloryministries.com

Revival Waves of Glory Books & Publishing is committed to excellence in the publishing industry.

Published in the United States of America

Ebook: 978-1-312-58758-8
Paperback: 978-1-63443-247-4
Hardcover: 978-1-312-58757-1

1. Religion / Christian Life / Spiritual Growth
2. Religion / Christian Life / Personal Growth

How to contact Matthew:

Email: survivors.sanctuary@gmail.com
Website: www.matthewrobertpayneministries.net
Facebook: www.facebook.com/people/Matthew-Robert-Payne/585589458
YouTube: www.youtube.com/user/MatthewRobertPayne1

You can also find me as the creator and lead admin on a group called "Open Heavens and Intimacy with Jesus" on Facebook at this link

https://www.facebook.com/groups/OpenHeavensGroup/

Table of Contents

Acknowledgments

First and foremost, I have to give thanks to Jesus the Messiah, for coming into my life and persevering with me for so long. You have been my friend for a very long time; You have loved me much; You have forgiven me much; and with your tenderness, You have been healing me day by day and year by year. You directed me to write this book; You have sustained me to get this book done; and you have brought me the friends that have encouraged me to be bold enough to put it into print. You are the One that sets people free. You are the One that could rightly judge, but never looks at me with guilt or condemnation. You have been with me all these years, and You have cried tears with me as I have cried them. Over the years, I have learned to walk by Your Holy Spirit, and He is precious to me and orders my days and puts words in my mouth. You, Jesus, introduced me to My Father in Heaven when the time was right, and You are holding me by the right hand and walking with me through this treacherous life I have been living. It is You that deserves all the Glory, Honor and Praise. May this work of ours encourage others to open up and confess their sins before their brethren, so they can be healed.

Secondly, I would like to thank my mother June Payne, and my father Bob Payne, for bringing me into this world. As an unplanned child, I suffered for many years under this knowledge, and yet your love and giving to my life has shown me that I was born to be an encouragement to others. Dad, I thank you for reading your Bible and repenting of your anger issues and becoming a new man that I no longer have to fear. I thank you from the bottom of my heart for that day on the Sydney ferry when you apologized for the life you gave us with your anger. A part of me healed that day. Mom, I want to thank you for the hundreds of hours that you have prayed for me, all those years in addiction. I want to thank you for never giving up on me and for keeping everyone that asks about me up-to-speed about how I am. I want to thank both of you, mom and dad, for the gift of hospitality that you showed me how to express. I am not sure how I could have survived my personal breakdowns, my marriage breakdown, and my tumultuous life, if it had not been for you both.

Thirdly, I want to thank my brother Rodney, who has now had a breakdown and has been diagnosed with Bipolar Disorder, like me. I want to thank you for listening to me and being my best friend all of these years, as I have grown up. Only Heaven seems to know how great a brother you have been to me. I pray that, one day, the whole world might know what a champion you are.

Fourthly, I want to thank Sarah Moulds for loving the legalistic, religious fool that I was, and loving me so much as to poke holes in my beliefs and, through prayer and books, convert me into a strong believer in God's grace. I want to thank you for the many hours you just listened to me, as I talked and talked and talked. You are a "*little Jesus*" to me . Though I have not seen you much this year, I will always love you, and when this book comes out, people who you don't even know will want to friend request you on Facebook! I wish that every Christian out there would have the balance of their life right between the world and Jesus' as I see you do.

And to all of you who read the acknowledgments, I want to thank you for choosing to download or buy this book. It is a big decision to buy a book and commit to reading it. I pray that my story shows you that you too can be honest and share with another person your secret sins. I have gone to the expense of making both a paperback and Kindle edition of this book, so that I might bless you who read it. Please take the time to write to me and tell me how my book affected you. I have gone to all this effort only for you, and for that reason, I want to acknowledge you as people who helped me get this story out there. Please give it or share it with the worst people you know.

This book would not be possible without Maria, who transcribed the videos. I would like to thank her for her many hours of work. If anyone wants to use a good editor or transcriptionist/typist, please email me for their contact details.

A heartfelt thanks goes out to my copy editor Melanie for her wonderful job with re-creating my words and polishing what I say so that I seem smarter then what I really am. She does a magical job with what I give to her and yet after all her changes my words retain my character and truth.

Melanie also wrote the back cover blurb for this book. Melanie can be contacted though www.Odesk.com , a freelance website and can weave her magic on your words also if you are a student, or want to venture into book writing yourself. She is great fun to work with, a committed Christian and very professional.

I want to thank my good friend Bjarki Clausen for his time for making the cover for this book. He took time out of his 90 hour working week to make sure the cover for this book. You can contact him at
www.merkiverk.is

I would also like to thank my publisher Revival Waves of Glory ministries~ Books and Publishing for taking the time and effort to publish my book. I recommend them to people wanting to get published.

Love Matthew

Dedications

June Payne

Mom, I want to thank you for giving birth to me, for nurturing me, for praying for me and for being my friend and mother. You are precious to me, and although some parts of this book will be too graphic for you to read, please know that without you in my life, I could have never had the courage to be so honest.

Chloe

You might never get to read this book, as we have not seen each other for over twenty years, but I will never forget you as someone that really loved me for who I was inside. You will be forever immortalized on these pages before, what I hope to be, thousands of people, and I pray that all the working girls are loved through what I said about you. Thank you for loving me and thank you for letting me go.

Mitchell Evans.

Thank you for being my friend and my pastor. You never judge me or make me feel bad. You always encourage and build me up and put a smile on my face. You let me into your personal world; you let me come and shoot the breeze in your office anytime; and you ask me my advice on songs and other things close to your heart. Sometimes, even for me, it is hard to get a grasp on Jesus, and yet I know if He is anything like you, than my sins are fine with him. You are a great leader, a great friend, and someone that I admire greatly. You even wouldn't have a problem with me dedicating this book to you, one that is full of vile sins of my past. Like Jesus, you love the sinner and love him even with him sinning in your midst. I think you have only ever given me pastoral counsel once; all the rest of the times, it was two best friends speaking. I praise God that you are my pastor, and I will cry a bucket load if I ever have to part your company.

Paul Moulds

You are one of only a couple of people that have every book of mine, and the only one that has read them and given me feedback. You were a great pastor to me and fathered the almighty Sarah Moulds. You have given of your time, reading my books, and have been honest with me in your sharing of feedback. You also are a living expression of Jesus Christ on earth to me. Everyone wants to speak to you when you come to church to visit, and like Jesus, I wish I could get you all to myself for a few hours. I guess seeing as you are going to read this book of mine, I will have you all to myself. I dedicated the parables book to your wife, Robbin, my prophetic book I dedicated to Sarah, your daughter, and today, your name gets a mention, as you are strong and mighty in battle, a valiant soldier of the Lord of Hosts.

Themes of this book - things to ponder as you read

"That I may know Him and the power of His resurrection, and the fellowship of His sufferings, being conformed to His death" (Philippians 3:10 Bible).

"You'll never know how great God's love is, how great His forgiveness is, until you've been as guilty as me." ~ Joshua Graham in his book BEYOND JUSTICE

Therefore I say to you, her sins, which are many, are forgiven, for she loved much. But to whom little is forgiven, the same loves little." (Luke 7:37 Bible)

Other Books by Matthew Robert Payne

The Musings of Mad Prophet
The Parables of Jesus Made Simple
The Prophetic Supernatural Experience
Prophetic Evangelism Made Simple
Your identity in Christ
Kingdom Nuggets

Chapter 1

The Early Years

I was born into a family of few children. I had an older sister, Carmen - three years senior to me – an older brother, Rodney – eighteen months senior to me – and a younger brother, Tony, born three years after my arrival in the family.

Now I am forty-six, my siblings are alive and well, and maintaining the age difference at a constant level – growing older happens to all of us. My father used to work 12-hour shifts when I was born so he would leave before I was up in the morning. Well, as a baby, I probably would have been up, but as a younger child I was still in bed at 6:00am when he left and by the time he travelled home at night, I was already asleep. Consequently, I began to miss my father, and this put an emotional need in me.

Some children manage to cope better with an absent father. However, in my case, I think what happened was that I felt as if my father did not love me. Until some emotional healing much later, a strong sense developed through my life that my father had indeed rejected me. I felt that he did not like me or appreciate me as much as my older siblings. This mistaken feeling of rejection became very real to me. It manifested itself in many ways in my life, and as my story unfolds, you will begin to realize that rejection is a powerful and potentially harmful human emotion.

When someone you know feels rejected, whether by you, or by other loved ones in their life, it becomes a real thing – something that Satan can grab hold of and control. Evil spirits or demons just relish the thought of latching on to the feeling of rejection. This evil spirit of rejection is a difficult thing to break, but everything is possible through the cleansing blood of Jesus Christ and the power of the Holy Spirit. With the right help, everything can be broken.

My older brother, only a toddler himself, didn't appreciate my intrusion into the family. He had been happy receiving the baby's share of attention from my mother, but when I came on the scene, he was upset with me. Apparently, he asked one day where I came from, and my mother said that I came from the hospital. My brother quickly replied: "Take him back!"

That incident may not have happened straight after my birth, but in later years he did make that statement. His verbal resentment towards me was one of the foundation stones of my feeling of rejection. He often made it very clear that he did not want me in his family. My mother had to admit that she could not leave my older brother unattended in the same room as me because he often tried to upset me or to physically hurt me.

Of course, these things have long been forgiven. My older brother is one of my very best friends. I could not imagine moving forward in life without having an older brother to run things past, to listen to and to have as a close friend. However, it is important in my story to establish that as a child, I felt rejected by my father. Whether this was real or intentional on his part, I don't know, but quite definitely, my older brother picked on me. He had a serious case of sibling rivalry and jealousy about my very existence.

In reflection, my older brother was just plain difficult to handle!

At pre-school, it was discovered that Rod had probably had an inner ear problem from birth. Ear wax would move around and cause him endless pain and frustration. This condition irritated him so much, that "*any disappointment*" would cause him to repeatedly bang his head against the wall or floor in frustration. For the vital informative years of his young life, my mother had simply presumed that she had an uncontrollable child. To add to Rod's continual frustration, his distorted hearing caused a serious speech problem. His school teacher in First Class would sometimes ask me to interpret what he was saying. This both humiliated and infuriated him and it certainly didn't endear him towards me!

Rod was a child whose mind could not be consoled. He habitually misbehaved at every opportunity. For my mother, my brother was uncontrollable – and this created in her mind a feeling of insecurity, worthlessness, and of not being a capable mother. All she understood was that she could not even control her own children, especially my brother.

At one stage, all four children were under the age of five and this placed a heavy burden on mom. She was desperately lonely for adult company but hated leaving the house with all of us. As I grew, I was happy that we were all living, but sometimes I would wish we had not been born so mom would not have to struggle the way she did. It is important that mothers obtain a sense of identity from the job they are doing, and having an unruly child or irresponsible children upset my mother and increased her sense of insecurity and unworthiness in the world.

It was difficult for her to go fourteen hours every day without a husband – without the one who really appreciated and loved her, but as bread-winner dad needed to travel a long way to earn a living for the family. There was no social security in those days. Eventually, my mother was befriended by a next-door neighbor – a woman who made her feel welcome and who offered to help look after us occasionally to give my mother some brief respite.

My mother insisted that her children were too hard to handle, but Betty our lovely neighbor said that she had raised children of her own and would certainly be able to look after us. The difference was that when we stayed at her place, we would never play up or cause her any trouble – even Rod was happy! My mother's children were just not being themselves when they went next door and this fact more than intrigued my mother.

It was something that gnawed daily at her conscience and it begged an answer to the question of why we did not behave at home. My mother put up with this for a while but eventually she asked her neighbor, "Why do my children not play up when they are at your house?" God bless her heart, Betty replied: "Children can't play up in my house because Jesus lives here!" This was a truly amazing statement for my mother to comprehend.

Mom did not know much about Jesus Christ or Christianity for that matter. All she knew was that Jesus died on a cross two-thousand years ago. It was therefore somewhat baffling to her that someone would speak of Jesus as being still alive and living in her home, and managing to control her children. Mom could not let these thoughts go away. It was impossible to store them away in a safe place in her mind where she did not have to think about it. My mother was seriously intrigued by this whole situation.

Betty started to invite my mother to monthly Church Ladies meetings – a gathering of Christian women where they had a guest speaker and supper afterwards. Mom said she was really out of her comfort zone but nevertheless she enjoyed listening to the private conversations as she busied herself in the kitchen. She never ceased to be awed by the fact that the other ladies spoke about Jesus as though He were still alive and part of their everyday life. This talk constantly puzzled and intrigued mom. She said that she did not remember any of the words of any of the guest speakers. She did not understand the message of Christianity, but she liked the company. She liked mixing with these Christian women, eating, washing dishes, and spending time in general fellowship with them.

It is important for us to know in the beginning of this work on my life, that we need to provide a sense of community for people. We need to create a place where they can be loved and accepted for who they are. People might not always understand our message – a message of salvation, of Jesus Christ and His grace for all people today. No, they might not always understand our message, but they do understand love.

People understand acceptance, and they appreciate being treated as if they belong. Mpm continued to go to these monthly gatherings not only because it was an evening out for her, but more so because she was feeling accepted and was lovingly welcomed at these events.

However, things were not so easy in my mother's mind. The Holy Spirit – the power of God – was challenging her. He was starting to challenge her because she needed to decide on what she believed about the entire 'Jesus-living-today' thing that the women at the meetings and more importantly, her lovely neighbor believed in.

It more than intrigued my mother's mind, but it was something on which she had to make a decision – what she was to think about Jesus living next door and her children not playing up when they went there – this perplexed her and she was seriously interested in discovering why all these women talked about Jesus being alive. One day it came up in a conversation with our neighbor and my mother was surprised when confronted with the reply.

My mother had said: "How does this Jesus live? How is He alive to you?" Betty simply replied: "Ask Jesus to do something special for you - something that will show that He loves you in a special way, in a way that you can't misinterpret as a coincidence. I believe that He will do that for you and show you that He is alive, and that He loves you."

My mother went home and began to pray. She felt awkward about her prayer, saying, "Hi Jesus. If you really exist, can you do something to show that you love me?" When she had finished praying, her prayer had an amazing effect. The next day, my unruly brother suddenly began to behave as perfectly as he would behave at Betty's house. My mother knew right away that this was an answer to her prayer and that Jesus had proved that He really is alive and is genuinely concerned with her life.

God had met mom at her deepest need – through her five year old son. His improved behavior was no coincidence! Mom concluded that Jesus Christ did exist! She realized He did not exist way out in the universe as a being interested with human affairs, but He was so interested that He came right down with the Holy Spirit to our family and made my mother's life more bearable in a very personal and meaningful way just for her.

My mother quickly went to visit Betty to tell her what had happened. I am not sure how, but she committed her life to Jesus Christ and accepted Him as her personal Savior. She was water baptized two months later. She had hesitantly phoned her own mother to invite her to her baptism but was told in no uncertain ways that if she continued with Christianity then she would be no longer her daughter. This totally devastated my mother but Betty said that she was in a spiritual war. Satan was the enemy, not her mother! The devil was simply using her mother because it would really hurt her.

For a season, perhaps – a year, my Grandma stopped talking to her and dissociated herself completely. This made my mother feel rejected, hurt, and broken that her own mother would make such a serious decision. However, she continued growing in her Christian faith with friends and with God. Eventually, her mother realized that this was not just some fad her daughter was into – this Christian business was obviously very serious and it was not worth losing her daughter over religion of all things!

Eventually the two women reintroduced themselves to each other, patched things up, decided to remain cordial and remain in loving contact with each other. My grandma gave my mother express instructions not to share her faith with her husband - my mother's stepfather, who was Jewish by birth but not in practice. This is how they continued from then on.

Dad was a church going Christian when he first met mom. After they married and began a family, Sundays became just another working day. He had stopped going to church because mom thought it was just stupid nonsense. Dad was not living a typical Christian life at that time, although he became extremely concerned when their first baby was still-born and Grandma invited mum to go to a Clairvoyant Meeting to find out about her dead baby in heaven. Amazingly, dad took a firm stand saying the Bible does not allow such things, so he would not be attending any such meeting!

Although someone might not be going to church and his or her faith might not be strong, it is still possible to have Christian principles from which you will not back down. In hindsight, I am proud that my father responded that way to my mother. Even though dad had not been faithful to God's command to regularly worship with other believers, God had remained faithful to dad's prior commitment and wanted to protect him from evil. Also, dad's response to my mother had made an impression on her that something was wrong in her life. So God had used the whole situation to fulfill His purposes for both my parents.

Yes, God was working in the Payne family! A few months after my mother's conversion, my father re-committed his life to Jesus Christ. We started to go to church as a family when I was about four years old. I recall that my younger brother, Tony was only little.

I can still remember some things from my life as a child. I remember winning a sack race – well not actually winning, as I think I got a bronze medal for third place – but I remember going on the stage to be presented with that medal, and I remember seeing a picture of me that mom had taken on that special day. I was so young with a medal around my neck and I was so proud of that medal. I also remember that at school we had certain annual events. Once we had a Billy cart race and if I remember correctly, my older brother, Rodney, had raced and he did extremely well. I was very proud that day too!

My brother and I, and his friends used to play marbles. I was not exceptionally good at the game but occasionally I would win a game, but not very often – these infrequent victories were enough, however, to maintain my interest.

My older brother Rodney loved to play marbles and I loved doing things with my brother as any child does. A child loves to play with his siblings and this was no different for me. Rodney was good at marbles and he was competitive against his school friends. He used to collect various sorts of marbles – I think one them was called Snake Eyes – and he had a good collection so he could barter and trade for better marbles all the time.

When he was a child, Rodney was also a terrific fighter. In the lower grades, before he entered high school, he was the best fighter in our school – which meant he had a few fights, and won. My brother never really enjoyed class bullies, so anyone who used to pick on others was quickly sorted out by *my brother!*

I was proud that my brother could fight well but he gained much of his experience in fighting and hitting others by hitting me! Fortunately, these things have been forgiven now.

Chapter 2

My Salvation

When I grew up as a boy, I became used to going to church every Sunday with my parents and my siblings. Life in our family changed from having Sunday mornings off to do what we pleased, playing in the streets, or whatever we did on Sunday mornings before – now, we would wake on a Sunday morning, have breakfast, get ready, and go to church.

Essentially, the difference between many Christians and non-Christians is that non-Christians have Sunday mornings to themselves. In fact, one study in the United States found that the only difference was that Christians went to church on a Sunday morning, and others did not.

However, with all the various buying habits, movie-watching habits, and all the available research data, the researcher found that the only discernible difference with the Christian church was that it provided something to do on a Sunday morning.

As a Christian, you learn to go to church on a Sunday morning, and somewhere in the Bible, it says you should train a child in the way they should go, so that in their later years, they will not depart from it. Therefore, it is a good idea to provide a solid foundation for your children, by encouraging them to go to church in their early years.

I have to say that church must not have made much sense to me, merely because I find some children are rather smart before the age of eight. At that age, I had not received the Christian message and did not take the Christian message personally, so you could not have called me a Christian.

My life was similar to that of my mother. She went to so many of those meetings, but she said she could not remember what the speakers had said in the meetings. She did not understand what they were talking about, but she liked the sense of community, and this sense of community at church was something to which I became accustomed. My mother, when she first became a Christian, was asked to teach Sunday school at church. For those reading this, who are not Christian, Sunday school is a special time for children to spend with a teacher at church, learning the stories of the Bible and learning about having faith in Jesus Christ.

Someone recruited my mother – most probably the neighbor who led her to the Lord – but someone smart recruited my mother and said, "We want you to teach the children about the Bible." For her to teach the children about the Bible, she had to read the next appointed lesson herself, understand what was said, understand the message in the story, and the points and questions to be asked of the children, before she presented the lesson each week.

Therefore, my mom grew fast in her understanding of the Bible, and understanding of the character of God, through teaching these children, and through her own research in preparation to teach the message. She learned much of Jesus Christ and God of the Bible in teaching Sunday school. I remember my mother had a board – much like a 3 x 2 footboard – with all kinds of stick-on characters and pictures.

I am not sure whether she cut all these things out and painted them herself, or she bought them specifically for each project. She would get all these stick figures out, display them on this board, and she would tell the stories about them. I really loved that thing, you know, and I really loved looking at those characters, and...I do not know whether mom would ever have allowed us to play with it and make stories... but I really liked it.

One thing I remember clearly from my early childhood is this board with all the characters.

As I have already mentioned, when I was a child I felt rejected by my father, particularly, because he was away from home for 14 hours a day, I was getting some sibling rivalry from my brother, and I was on the receiving end of some physical abuse from my brother. I can categorically say that as a child, I was more than slightly upset.

I remember going to my room and keeping our cat in the room with me – I talked to my cat and cried. Those of you with pets will know that animals are funny creatures – they seem to understand the tears that you cry. They seem emotionally tuned in to their owners and can comfort their owners in a special way.

They tend to understand, spiritually and emotionally, what their owners are going through and can bring comfort – my cat was no different. My cat was my friend, and I used to take my cat to my bedroom, and cry, talk to my cat while I stroked him. My cat would purr when I talked to him – he was my friend and my comforter. Sadly, one day, my cat died, leaving tragic implications for me.

For a child, losing a pet can be a traumatic experience, but I know my younger brother's children have lost their grandfather, and they do not seem too distressed about it. I am not sure if they have lost a pet before, but they seem to handle their grandfather's death really well. However, I took the death of my cat badly. I still remember crying many tears over the loss of my cat, and I did not get over it as fast as other children seem to do.

I held onto the image of my cat, and it made me very sad. My parents did not replace the cat straightaway – I do not know why, but perhaps they wanted me to resolve my pain fully.

One day, a children's evangelist came to our church. For those watching this video, or reading the book, who are not Christians, an evangelist is someone with a special knack or ability to present the message of Jesus Christ, and what it means to be a Christian, for people who do not understand what that means. Some things I say or do are like an evangelist, as I am conscious of people who do not understand the Christian faith, or are not Christian, so I try to present Jesus in the right light. This children's evangelist, gifted in communicating the message of Jesus, had been specifically trained to present this message to children. I had been going to church for a few years, but I still had not grasped the meaning of Jesus and why He came to Earth to die for our sins, and I was touched.

The evangelist spoke about how we, God's children, could have a special friend come into our life, and that friend would talk to us, would listen to us, and, most important, would never leave us. While I was still becoming accustomed to the death of my cat, the idea of a new friend coming into my life was not only exciting news, but also the most exciting news a boy could ever hear. The icing on the cake came when he went on to say that this new friend would never go away.

Years later in my life, I was to spend a long time living in the fear that, when I died as a Christian, I would still go to hell because of sin in my life. I struggled with fear, thinking that I was committing too much sin to warrant me going to heaven.

We will speak about this again in chapters to come, but essentially, that idea of living life as a Christian for the rest of your life, and then going to hell, seemed to contradict what this evangelist said about Jesus never leaving or forsaking you. I am a lot more comfortable these days in my beliefs, and I understand there is nothing we can do to stop Jesus from loving us, and there is nothing we can do to make Jesus go away. This young evangelist had said that so clearly to us children: we would have a friend that would never leave us.

He asked the children to come to the front and invite Jesus to come into, and be a part of, their lives. However, Jesus cannot come into a person's heart. Jesus sits on a throne in heaven, walks around heaven, performs things in heaven, but sometimes visits people on Earth – much to the surprise of many people. Jesus is a real entity, and he does not physically enter a person when they give their life to Him and become a Christian, but there is a dimension to God called a spirit – the Holy Spirit.

That Spirit can enter inside a person, start to live in that person, and start to direct the actions and thoughts of that person. So on that day, as simple children, we invited Jesus to come and live in our heart, not fully understanding that He would not physically be going to live in our hearts. That is how we said it, and that is how we understood it, but essentially, we were inviting the Holy Spirit to come and take up residence in our own spirits. On that day, I invited Jesus to come into my heart.

I am not sure whether this young evangelist shared with us that we were all sinners, and that we needed to be forgiven for all the bad things we had done in our lives. Essentially, the Christian message says that the wrong that you do in your life will add up, and you will have to pay the consequences for that, if you do not accept Jesus as your personal savior, because those consequences will continue with you through eternity, in a place of suffering called hell.

The essential message is that Jesus Christ came to Earth not only as a teacher and as a prophet, but He also came to die a sacrificial death to pay for the sins that you and I have committed. He came and lived a perfect life, without any wrongdoing, and then died. When He was put to death, He took all our sins on to his body and died for them in our place. Romans 3:23 says, ***"For all have sinned and fall short of the glory of God,*** " and Romans 6:23 says, "***For the wages of sin is death, but the gift of God is eternal life in Christ Jesus our Lord.***"

Whether you are a Christian or not, essentially one day, you are going to heaven after you die, or you are going to hell. The Christian message is that you need to accept that Jesus died for your sins, confess to Him that you are sinner, and invite Him to be part of your life, and start to rule your life. The Christian church believes that if you do not make that decision to follow Jesus, and commit your ways to Him for the rest of your life, then when you die, you will not go to heaven but to a place of eternal judgment.

I am not sure whether this young evangelist talked about sin, heaven, and hell, when he was sharing with us as children. All I remember is he said we could have a special friend, and that is what I am here to share with you – Jesus can be your special friend. I accepted Jesus and asked Him to come and live in my life. I was positive that it happened, because peace came into my life. There was a real difference in me. I was no longer deceived that I believed in something that did not exist.

Suddenly, I had a friend, and I had a real sense of knowing that my new friend was listening to me; instead of going home to my bed to talk to my cat at night, I went to bed at night talking to Jesus. My faithful mother taught me how to pray to Jesus, and how to talk to Jesus, and since that day, I have never been into some of the dark places that my life took me, without feeling that Jesus was listening to me and was there for me. I began to have a wonderful feeling of peace in my spirit, because I had a new friend who loved me, and He was the Son of God.

My mother would have us remember scriptures out of the Bible every week. She would Scotch tape a Bible verse each week on the bathroom mirror, so we would read the verse as we brushed our teeth and showered every morning. Each week, we had to remember the verse and where it came from – Romans 8:28 says, “***And we know that all things work together for good to those who love God, to those who are the called according to His purpose.***” That verse tells us that if you are a Christian and love God, then everything will turn out right.

Part of the Christian life is understanding the precious truthful promises in the Bible. My mother would select verses that she knew would improve our emotional and spiritual condition. She used to select those verses and stick them on the mirror each week. At the end of the week, when it came time for us to receive our weekly allowance (pocket money sounds so old-fashioned) from mom, we had to quote the Bible verse and say where it came from in the Bible. I know many scriptures personally, but I cannot quote where they came from in the Bible – I just know the scripture. I always told my mom the reason for this was that I was not good with numbers – and she would give me a knowing look, when she handed over my allowance. When this book is fully prepared, where I have quoted scriptures, there will be a scripture reference, where you can look up the verse in the Bible and find it written there, to show that it really exists. I know that you can do this through a book called a Concordance, which allows you to look up certain words in a verse and discover where that verse is in the Bible. Nevertheless, my mother wanted us to know where verses were, so she made us remember the scripture references. One reference special to the Christian faith, that most Christians understand and know, is John 3:16, where it says, "***For God so loved the world that He gave His only begotten Son, that whoever believes in Him should not perish but have everlasting life.***"

Essentially, this is the Christian message. If you accept Jesus was a sacrifice for you – if you accept Him and follow Him, you will have eternal life – you will have a life when you die, which will continue in happiness and peace and not end in suffering. John 3:17 says, "***For God did not send His Son into the world to condemn the world, but that the world through Him might be saved.***" Jesus came to Earth not for people to feel judged by Him or feel guilty by Him.

He came to Earth, so that people might come to know Him, and be saved by Him from eternal wrath and eternal punishment in hell. God is not here to judge you, because you are not a Christian, or because you are reading this book. God is not here to tell you that you are bad, and you are a no-good-for-nothing. He wants you to know that you are precious, and you are loved, but you need to accept His message to continue life in the best possible way.

Therefore, as a child, I accepted Jesus into my life and memorized Bible verses each week of my life. My mother showed wisdom by putting these memory verses on the bathroom mirror, but she was unaware of how big a foundation she was laying for my future. My mother had no idea of how the results of having so many scriptures in my memory would serve me in my coming years.

Chapter 3

Surfing and Golf Balls

Interesting title, isn't it? By the time I was eight, we had moved to Coffs Harbour, a small country town where I was to spend the next 10 formative years of my life. At the age of 40, my father had moved from Sydney, the largest city in Australia, to a country town with a mere 15,000 people inhabitants. Even today, Coffs Harbour, and the surrounding district, has about 30,000 people compared to Sydney, where four or five-million people live. You can imagine there was a big difference between living in a big city and living in a country town. One of the differences you notice straightaway is that when you walk down the street in a country town, people look at each other in the eyes, motion to each other, and acknowledge each other with a smile. That does not happen much in a big city!

After working 12-hour days for many years, my father sold his house in Sydney, moved to Coffs Harbour, and had a house built specifically for us and according to his design – and my dad paid for it with cash. At 40, he was completely out of debt. At 40, he had four children, and he was out of debt. Just for comparison purposes, his four offspring are now all 40-something and will be making sizable contributions to that great money drain (called mortgage or rent) for many years to come.

Almost everybody in their 40s seems to have a mortgage on their house – but at 40, my father had a house with no mortgage. I think that was a terrific achievement for my father, and something about which I have to be proud. My mother's sister and her husband had started a local business fixing brakes for cars, and my dad asked my uncle if he ever had a job position open that a simple man could do, and then could he have that job.

My uncle devised a plan to put brake shoes in an oven to recast them, and then re-bond them and fix them up. I do not really understand what that process was, but it turned secondhand brake shoes into as-new brake shoes and cost a lot less when replacing the brakes shoes in your car when they run out (something like brand-new secondhand?). Therefore, my dad got a job reconditioning brake shoes for cars and trucks.

My dad had been a supervisor in his previous job and had been receiving a particularly good salary. By moving to Coffs Harbour, he took a hefty drop in pay with the new job, but he did not require any training, and he did not have to work four hours overtime every day. It was another sacrifice he took on board, but he did not regret it. He moved to Coffs Harbour to bring his children up in a country town with better values and morals, and a better quality of life than in a big city.

I respect and love him for the time I spent in the country. As we now lived in a country town with beautiful beaches, he bought surfboards for me and my older brother, Rodney. We would load up with the surfboards, and he would take us to a part of the harbor with a safe beach, and allow us the time to learn to surf. I am not sure, but in the early days, I think we would all ride our bikes down to the beach and then surf.

On weekends, he would drive us down to the beach in the car. All I know is my dad must have put in some serious time on the shore, waiting for his sons to learn how to surf.

When you surf, you use a leg rope – a rope or a length of rubber – running between the surfboard and your foot, so if you fall off a wave when you are surfing, your surfboard will stay attached to you. You can swim back to your surfboard, climb on again, and paddle out for some more fun.

This is important. When you go out in particularly heavy seas, you need the buoyancy of the surfboard to keep you afloat and alive. If you lose your surfboard in a heavy sea, you could be in danger without a surfboard to hold on to, in an ocean full of rough, breaking waves. My dad insisted the surfboards he bought us just had to have leg ropes, and with that, off we went to the beach. This particular beach had a break that just went straight down into what we called dumpers. The surf did not really break along the break – it just… went down.

It was difficult to learn on this beach, but another part of the beach, further along the surf, used to break along the beach without becoming too big. Although it was difficult to ride these waves, we learned to get up on our surfboards and ride the waves. I am not sure how long it took my brother, but it took me almost a year to learn how to ride a wave.

Until we could master that, dad was not allowing us to go to another beach, because he loved us, and he did not want to see us hurt or broken in any way. He did not allow us to go to another beach to progress in our surfing abilities, until we had conquered that first beach. I am not sure how much time my father invested in taking us to the beach – but he took us to the beach a lot.

In summer, when there was daylight saving time, he would take us down to the beach in the late afternoon.

We would knock off from school at about 3:30, and by 5:30, my dad was home from work. He used to ride a pushbike to work to save gas, but by a quarter to six, we were all in the car, and as the sun would stay up until about 8, we could get in a couple of hours of good surfing. Often my mother would come, and she would cook us a barbecue dinner down at the beach – wonderful and happy times.

After a year, I could happily ride along a wave, and I was excited to move on to other beaches. I have to admit here that several times (twice that I can remember clearly and vividly), I almost drowned on a beach. Once, I was out in a heavy...rather large surf, and the surf was breaking along a rock wall. I got cramps in both my arms and my legs, so I could not paddle along the wave or stand on the board. If I had been hit against that rock wall, it would have probably knocked me out, and I would have drowned. Another time, I was in particularly big surf, I fell off my board, and I was continually swamped by waves breaking on me, one after the other.

When a wave breaks on you, and you go under, the foam of the wave is traumatic. Unless you go deep, where it is peaceful, it can really stir you up, and you could lose breath. It is turbulent, and it takes the breath out of you, while you are trying to hold your breath. After six waves, I had enough and was almost at the point of giving up and saying, "I'm dead." I just got this one last thought to try to pull myself up by my leg rope on my surfboard.

Instead of giving up, I pulled up, reached my surfboard, and was okay. The waves seemed to relent, and I could paddle out and remain safe. Safe, in that I could sit on the beach, puffing and panting for a long time, getting over the ordeal and the experience, but I will never forgot that it was a time when my life was in the balance.

As a surfer, I was not particularly competitive. There is an unwritten rule that says when you are paddling for a wave, and getting in to a specific position, it is your wave, and everybody else has to leave the wave alone and let you ride it.

However, it depends on your physical strength and your stamina, and it depends on how forceful you are in your personality to get into that position where others will respect you and let you have the wave. Some people are weaker in their emotional makeup, and weaker in their physical strength, and cannot consistently paddle for waves to move into that position where the wave is theirs. So, as a person who did not have a whole lot of self-esteem and physical strength, I did not have the physical prowess to consistently paddle for waves and get into that position to rightfully own a wave. I did not seem to catch many waves – the only waves I seemed to catch were those in which nobody else was interested – the smaller waves. Otherwise, I would wait until the others at the break had caught a wave and were busy paddling their way back out again, and catch an incoming wave, because there was no one else to compete with.

I was a surfer who went out into surf hundreds of times with my brother, but I did not enjoy the surfing experience as much as my brother did. Rather than competing with all the other surfers on the most popular breaks, I would paddle down the beach a little way to where there might only be one or two people, and I would catch the smaller waves.

Of course, by paddling away from where my brother used to surf, I had a more lonely surfing experience. I did not get to spend time with my brother, talking between waves and chatting with other friends. It was a lonely experience, but I enjoyed my surfing experience more, because I could catch more waves and enjoy myself. However, I did catch a few waves that I remember, where I had a good experience.

Once, I caught a big wave and was riding it, when the wave broke over me. I was traveling inside the wave, as it was breaking over me. This “tube” was particularly large, as I was able to stand fully erect on my feet. All this happened just as my brother was paddling out in the surf, and he saw me riding in this tube.

When I finished with the wave, I paddled back out, and my brother said it was a super tube, and he was happy with the wave I had caught – I had done a good job. My brother did not often comment on my surfing, but I remember that wave, and it often brings a smile to my face. Another wave I caught in those days, I managed to get three tubes from a single wave. As the wave opened up, I was riding the wave; then, it broke over me again, and I was back in the tube – this happened three times with one wave.

It was the best wave I had ever ridden in my life. I rode it for at least a hundred meters long, and I will always remember that wave. I paddled back out and told my brother about it, but he just dismissed it. My brother was very much about himself, and the waves he was catching. He did not seem to appreciate when I had caught a good wave.

It was all about him and everything he was doing. He was more than happy to share stories of the good waves he caught and what he had done, and I was happy to listen to them, but my brother did not seem too interested in hearing about the good waves I had caught. I remember that years later, when I was about 16 years, walking down to the beach with one of the best surfers in town – a Christian surfer.

We were walking down to the beach, and Rodney was mocking me about my surfing style, when the Christian surfer stood up for me and said, "Why are you poking fun at your brother?" My brother replied, "Because he deserves to have fun poked at him. He has got a hopeless surfing style and he is not a good surfer."

The Christian surfer replied to my brother, "I have seen your brother ride a wave with three tubes – the best wave I have ever seen ridden in Coffs Harbour. Don't you ever talk about your brother like that again in my presence."

I was so happy he had stood up for me, and many times in my life, when I have almost reached the point of being suicidal, I have remembered with tears that guy saying it was the best wave he'd ever seen ridden in Coffs Harbour – and it still makes me emotional, even today. He was a regular winner of surfing competitions in our area, so for him to say that was a precious moment for me.

Once when I was surfing, some dolphins came into the surf and started surfing the waves with us. A common enough occurrence for surfers but this occasion was a special experience – about 20 minutes after the dolphins arrived, a nursery of baby dolphins arrived, surrounded and protected by a group of mothers. As I was paddling out, one dolphin started to lead me toward the nursery – those protecting the nursery were obviously nervous, but after some paternal and maternal "dolphin talk", they led me to within 10 feet of the babies – a mystical and spiritual experience, and one I will never forget.

As a youth, I had a lot of enjoyment in my surfing life. When we were not in the surf, we spent a lot of time at the lakes in our golf courses, diving in to the mud at the bottom and searching for golf balls with our hands. It was in the late 70s and early 80s, and we would collect up to a hundred golf balls at a time, wash them, and then sell them for about $30 – a large sum of money for a boy to have then, all those years ago.

It took us on average about an hour to collect a hundred golf balls, and it would take us another hour, in front of the TV, washing and removing the mud, to make the golf balls clean and ready for sale. We did not count the time in front of the TV that it took us to wash the golf balls. We only counted the time it took us to find them, so we were making about $30 an hour – a serious sum of money for a person to be making in those years.

I do not think my dad was earning much more than $10 an hour in those days, so we were earning huge money. Our father tried to talk us into saving half the money we were making on the golf balls, by putting it into a bank or savings account. However, like so many things your father tells you to do, we never did it. My mother often laughed, as we went from being cashed-up and rich to broke and without a penny in the world. We had a life of surfing and collecting golf balls.

One day, my brother and his friend went to a lake on a golf course, where no one had ever gone before to collect golf balls – there was a rumor the lake had big eels or glass or something – a rumor that kept all the other boys away from the lake.

My brother, being somewhat more confident than most, finally overcame his fear (or should be lack of fear) of these stories, and he and his friend went into the lake to collect golf balls. I remember he retrieved literally thousands of golf balls from this lake. They went back to the lake time and time again. In those days, surfboards were between $200 and $300, and I remember they both bought surfboards with cash within a couple of weeks of going into that lake for the first time.

To own a new custom design surfboard was a real treasure for a boy. Many surfers had secondhand surfboards, as they could never afford a new one. I remember my brother going to a surfboard maker with specific ideas of how he wanted for his surfboard, and he had it custom-made for him – and he paid cash. I have never owned a new surfboard in my life.

Of course, you can buy a surfboard off the rack – they usually have 20 or 30 new surfboards available at any time – but it is a completely different ballgame to have one custom-made to your own specifications. My brother achieved that through diving for golf balls – going into a place where no one else had gone. That rather says something about my brother, who is now in business going to places where others are not going, because they do not have the courage.

We would collect golf balls all year-round. Even in the middle of winter, we would put on our wetsuits and dive into freezing lakes. Putting our head under the water, and diving in the freezing water to retrieve golf balls, was not the easiest of jobs. A professional at the golf course used to sell secondhand golf balls to all the golfers, who could not afford to play golf with brand-new $2.50 golf balls.

Two of our local 18-hole courses had several lakes dotted around, and other courses nearby had one or two lakes next to each hole, so there were plenty of balls going into these lakes from the "occasional" less than perfect golf shot. This golf professional would buy them from us at an average of $30 a hundred, and he would resell them for maybe $60 per hundred to the golfers. There were plenty of virtually new, good golf balls to be found hidden in the lakes.

He would pay us a dollar for the good ones, and maybe 15 cents for the not-so-good ones, but the average worked out at around $30 per 100, or 30 cents per ball. Sometimes, we found balls for which the professional would pay us a couple of dollars each; then we would go to buy a hamburger and a Coke to eat at the golf course and look after ourselves. What a life – having a shower, handing in the balls we had found and getting paid some cash, and then buying ourselves hamburgers to eat.

The professional had several rules that we had to honor – we were not allowed to sell our golf balls anywhere else but at his store – we were not allowed to sell our golf balls to players while they actually played the course – we had to show respect to certain golfers. He had a whole bunch of rules, and it seemed that Rodney and I broke every one of his rules – and on more than one occasion – and he came to realize that he could do better and found others who would obey his rules.

Therefore, we were not very happy, when he told us that we could not collect golf balls at that golf course anymore. As it was our major source of income, we did not take this lightly. We would sneak into the golf course in the middle of the night to collect golf balls. Sometimes we were caught doing that, but they were not quick enough to call the police and have us arrested. Then, we would sell the golf balls on the black market or to pawnbrokers, who bought and sold golf balls for us.

So, that is what we used to do as boys. I also had a paper route, where I delivered papers to shops in town, which would take me about two hours, once a week, and I would get $15. However, I found I had been spoiled by the $30 an hour collecting golf balls, so I was not very diligent in my approach to delivering the papers – but it was regular money, so I did it. I had been so spoiled by the income from the golf balls, and I have to say that ever since, I have never been able to earn $30 an hour.

The best I have ever achieved was when I took an hour to do a prophecy for a pastor, and I asked him if he could come to help us prophesy with our team of prophets. He wrote to me and apologized that he did not have the time to help our prophecy team, but he could send me some money to help, and he sent me a hundred dollars – the only time I have ever earned more than $30 for an hour's work

I operated a prophecy site for many years, and fewer than 10 people ever offered money to me. Therefore, that hundred dollars I received from that pastor holds a special memory for me. However, the point of that story is to let you know that $30 an hour was a rate of income that I have never achieved as an adult since.

Chapter 4

My Promises to God

When I was about 14 years of age, my pastor at Coffs Harbour Baptist church, where I used to attend, was an interesting and excellent pastor and a good teacher of the Word of God. I remember some promises I made to God were a direct result of his teaching.

As a person who teaches the Word of God myself, and who has preached often, the number-one thing you want to happen, when you are preaching, is for people to listen to your message, go home and reflect on your message, and make a decision in their life to act better or do something differently. I would be happy if that pastor ever got a copy of this book that I am writing today on my life, because several of his sermons had a major effect on the outcome of my life.

When I was 14, my pastor was going through a series of Bible teachings on particular people in the Bible, and drawing a message and conclusion from these people. His sermons would usually last for about half an hour, so I am not going to spend as much time on each of these people, as I remember the sermons from his preaching. However, I will spend some time sharing what he had to say about each of these people, because it forms a strong foundation for my life and what it has become today.

Once he preached on the life of David – a man referred to by God in Acts 13:22 as "***A MAN AFTER MY OWN HEART, WHO WILL DO ALL MY WILL.***" David was responsible for writing most of the Psalms we can read in the Bible. Later in my life, when I was going through a sad and depressing time, these Psalms were to have a profound effect on my life, but I digress.

David was to be a king, but before he became a king, Samuel, a prophet, anointed him by pouring oil over his head and declaring that God had chosen him as the next king. In those days, a prophet of God appointed the king. David had been duly anointed to be king, but the current king reigning became jealous of David, of his abilities, and of the favor God was showing to David.

People loved David, as he was an exceptionally good fighter in the army, and people used to brag about how many people David had killed, and how many people the king had killed – in comparison the king did not look too good in the people's eyes. King Saul was jealous of David, and for about 15 years, he pursued David trying to kill him. David was an exceptional man, because despite his suffering and being on the run for 15 years or so, he still praised God.

He still lifted his voice and his attitude toward God in a sense of praise and worship, and adoration, to God. Many of those praises and adorations to God are written in the Psalms, and we can see the words David used to praise God. Many worship leaders and songwriters today use lyrics taken from the words of David, when writing songs for Christians to worship God.

David has had a remarkable effect on the modern church, and especially on the worship that goes out from churches worldwide. David had to fight many conflicts and battles, both before he was king and while he was King. He wanted to build God a temple. He noticed that all of the people had lovely houses to live in, and he had a fine palace, but God Himself did not have a house in which He could dwell.

David decided that he wanted to build a temple for God, as the other religions in surrounding countries had temples in which they could worship their God – and currently the Ark of the Covenant was found in a tent. The only place of worship for God was in a tent, so he wanted to build Him a spectacular temple. David told the prophet Nathan about his intention, and Nathan gave his approval.

However, when Nathan spoke to God about it, God said that Nathan had been hasty in his words to David, and he was to go back to David and tell him he could not build a temple for God, because he had too much blood on his own hands. In other words, God was saying, "David, you've fought too many wars and killed too many people, and you've got blood on your hands, and I won't allow you to build a temple." Well, David was distraught about that decision. He was king of the land, and God had just told him he could not build a temple for God.

He had all the power and authority of the nation of Israel in one of its finest hours in history; yet with all the power, authority, and wealth available to Israel at the time, God instructed David that he could not build the temple. It must have been a real blow to David, because David was a person of worship and amazing love for God. However, God went on to say that his family's throne would endure forever. He made a promise that David's house, and the memory of David's time on the throne, would be remembered forever.

Jesus fulfilled that promise as a descendant of David, through Mary and through Joseph. The lineage of Jesus comes through the bloodline of David the king, and we remember Jesus as the king of the heavens and the Earth. Jesus' natural lineage as a human being was descended from David, so David's throne is remembered in heaven and will be remembered for the rest of eternity. During his life, David collected many things needed to build the temple, which he had built by his son, Solomon.

David was a king, and God was highly pleased with him. So much so, that there are many mentions in the Bible where God forgave a particular king, because of His memory and His love for David. God was continually boasting about David in many passages in the Bible, and because he ruled in Israel, David's throne continues today through the lineage of David.

What many people consider David's biggest sin was seeing Bathsheba showering one day, and then sending a special envoy to request Bathsheba come to him. When Bathsheba came to the

King's house, David took her to bed and had sex with her. Bathsheba was already married to another man, so David had officially committed adultery with her. That would have been fine, and David would have gotten away with it, except Bathsheba fell pregnant to David.

That was going to be a cause of trouble for David, because at the point of her conception, her husband was away at a war. Bathsheba's natural husband could not have been responsible for the baby, so Bathsheba becoming pregnant proved that Bathsheba had committed adultery against her husband – a very serious offense in Israel in those days. When David found out about Bathsheba, I imagine from one of Bathsheba's servants, that she was pregnant, David told the commander of the army to allow Bathsheba's husband to be killed in war.

That happened as the army was advancing on the enemy, and the husband was sent to the frontline of the battle. The army then withdrew and left him out there, fighting the battle alone, against hundreds of people – and he had no help, and he was killed. Not only did David commit adultery but then also allowed the husband to be killed. Many people, when they think of David, think of that sin, and Christians are quick to say that David was an adulterer and a killer.

God said the son conceived by Bathsheba and David would die, and when it happened, both Bathsheba and David were extremely upset. Later, Bathsheba conceived another son called Solomon and, before Jesus, Solomon was said to be the wisest man that ever lived on the face of the Earth. So wise was Solomon, that the Queen of Sheba came to visit him, because she had heard of his wisdom and his wealth, and she came to him and gave him many gifts, money, and precious items.

She marveled at how wise Solomon was, and she recorded that he was even more a surprise to her than she thought he would be. Solomon was a magnificent blessing to Israel, and he built the first temple of God for Israel. Solomon is remembered mostly through the Book of Proverbs, most of which he wrote – full of wisdom – and he wrote the Book of Ecclesiastes, which seems a rather sad book.

David was called 'a man after God's own heart', and the reason for this, in my understanding of things, so far in Christian life, is twofold. My first understanding is that David was a man desperately seeking to please God in everything he said and did. David was insistent on living a life pleasing to God. My second understanding is that David wanted to possess a heart, the same heart of God, when it came to loving his people and judging his people.

David essentially wanted God's heart and God's perspective on things, for him to rule people with wisdom and clarity in his position. Later, we read in the Bible that God offered Solomon whatever he requested, and He promised that He would fulfill that promise in Solomon's lifetime. Solomon searched his mind and finally said he wanted wisdom to correctly administer the people of God on God's behalf. God said, "You will not only have wisdom, but because of your non-selfish answer, you will have the riches and everything else also."

Solomon was a man after God's own heart in that decision. He was requesting the heart of God and the wisdom of God. Solomon, I believe, got that 'heart' issue, and the desire to have God's heart and God's wisdom, from his father, David. I believe that David was wise, too. So, when I originally heard this sermon (which went on for another 30 minutes longer that I have spent here), I was highly inspired by the life of David.

I went home as a young Christian boy and knelt beside my bed, and asked Jesus that if one day people could say that I was a man after God's own heart, and that I was like David. I am jumping ahead in the book, but I can confirm that many people have spoken in prophecy over my life on behalf of God, and they have said that I certainly am a man after God's own heart. God has spoken that through His people.

That was the first promise I made to God – that I wanted to be like David, and I was prepared to be like David. It is one thing to make a promise, but then comes the life, and David became such a beautiful person not only from the good things God did in his life, but also from the suffering that he went through. For God to perfect me and make me into a person like David, I had to experience a lot of suffering.

The second person we are going to look at is Abraham. First, you need to understand that Abraham was not a Jew, nor was he an Israelite. The Israelites were still in Abraham's loins – the Israelites were descendants of Abraham, although he was not an Israelite himself. He was just a man, who came from another culture and another religion, but what made him different from many other people was that he could actually hear from God.

God told Abraham to leave his father's house, to leave his family, to leave the country, and to travel to another land – God would not tell him beforehand where he was going, but He would let him know when he got there. Sounds to me as if that was not a particularly easy thing to do for Abraham! Many people today leave Australia or America to go and become missionaries in other countries, but for years beforehand, they know to which country they are going.

They start to learn some of the language and something about the country and its people, before they become a missionary and move off to another part of the world. However, it is another thing to be sent by God to a place about which you know absolutely nothing. It took a lot of faith on the part of Abraham to leave his farm, family, possessions –everything – just because God told him. He left as a nomad with his wife, totally in faith leaving everything to do so.

He believed God would look after him. God told him that he would have a son, and through that son, he would have many descendants. He believed God, although Sarah was barren and had not been able to bear children. They married when they were young, and Sarah was now about 80 years of age, well beyond childbearing age, even if she could conceive a son, but God told Abraham and Sarah that they would have a son, and Abraham believed Him.

Abraham went on for many years believing that he would have this son. God told Abraham several times about the extent of his descendants, and what they would be. God told Abraham to look at the stars, and when Abraham did, He said, "As many as the stars you can count, so too are the number of your descendants. Your descendants are going to be more than the stars in the sky – more than the grains of sand on a beach."

Abraham believed that this would happen, and every time he looked at the stars, he would be reminded of God's promise to him.

God called Abraham his friend. Now, we would like to call ourselves friends of God, but it does not happen very often in the Bible that God calls someone His friend.

About 15 years after God had promised they would have a son, Sarah became frustrated and fed up with waiting. She said to Abraham, "Perhaps God meant that you would have a son through my maid? Perhaps, I'll give you my maid, my bondservant and she can bear you a son?" Abraham would have probably rejected the idea at first, but he finally relented because of Sarah's sheer persistence.

He had sex with Hagar, the maid, several times, until she fell pregnant with a son. The son was born and the son's name was Ishmael. It was Abraham's firstborn son, but God told Abraham that Ishmael was not the son He had promised Abraham, and was not the son who would be the father of all his descendants.

Years later, Sarah eventually fell pregnant and bore a son, and they called him Isaac. When Isaac was born, Sarah became jealous of Hagar and Ishmael, and vowed that they were not going to share in the wealth of Abraham and the promise of Abraham. She kicked them out, and they went off into the desert. Hagar decided to keep her son far away from her, so she could not hear her son crying, because he was starving to death from lack of food.

This was breaking her heart, and she resolved to die. An angel, I think it was Gabriel, came to them, fed them both, and said that he would look after them. He promised Hagar that her son, Ishmael, would bear a nation, and that nation would go on forever. That nation – the descendants of Ishmael – was to become what we know today as the Arabs, and it seems that since then, the descendants of Ishmael have remained consistently jealous of the descendants of Isaac, resulting in many subsequent conflicts between Arab and Jew.

Sarah's son, Isaac, bore children, and his descendants become known as the Israelites. After several skirmishes, and several countries taking over Israel, the twelve tribes of Israel broke up and were dispersed – only two of these tribes are remembered and can trace their ancestry back to Isaac. Of those two tribes, the tribe of Judah became known as the Jews, and it seems that the other ten tribes of Israel became lost in history.

When Isaac was a youth, God told Abraham to go and sacrifice him. At that time, the idea of sacrificing a son to the gods was not a new or barbaric idea.

Abraham came from a religion and culture, which had a god that required fathers to sacrifice their children, cut their flesh, and all sorts of other things, to show that their love for their god was authentic and real. When God asked for Isaac's life, it was not a strange request for Abraham. However, he must have been bewildered and perplexed about how God was going to fulfill the promise of his son becoming the father of nations, when he was going to kill his son.

It must have been confusing for Abraham, to say the least, but even so, he was a man after God's own heart and a friend of God's.

He did what God required of him. He took his son to the top of a mountain, and on the way up, Isaac asked him, "Where's the sacrifice that we're going to sacrifice?" Abraham must have had a broken heart when he replied, "God's going to provide for us." It was almost a lie, because he intended to kill his son. To cut a long story short, Abraham built an altar with wood to burn, and then took his son, and put him on the altar. He was about to run a knife through Isaac and kill him, when God said, "Now, stop. You've proved to me that you love me."

They found a ram stuck in a thicket, and they sacrificed the animal instead. Abraham's faith must have been tremendous. To not only to wait for a son for so long, but also be prepared to sacrifice his son in obedience to God, and this is the reason God called him a friend. Many years later, God the Father had His own Son whom He sacrificed – He sent Jesus to Earth to be a sacrifice for the sins of the world.

God did not ask Abraham to do something that He was not prepared to do Himself – He gave His son to die as a sacrifice for all of us. As any father or parent knows, losing a son is extremely emotional – I know, because I have lost my own son – he is still alive, but I have not seen him for 14 years – but believe me when I say I am extremely emotional about it.

The idea of Abraham losing his first son, and then being prepared to sacrifice his second son, made God proud. God was always in love with Abraham, but God called him righteous because of his faith in Him. Because of Abraham's faith in God, he was called God's friend. I listened to that sermon and again, I was impressed, and I went home, and I asked Jesus if one day people could say on my gravestone that I was a friend of God's.

I was unaware of what I was asking at the time, and unaware of the heartache that would continue to be part of my life because of that request – but I prayed it, nevertheless. I wanted to be committed to a life that would make me become a friend of God – that was my promise to God – I wanted to become His friend.

The third thing that happened in my life was when, one Sunday night, someone who looked more like a biker than a churchgoer visited our church.

My father was at home, looking after the other children, so my mother and I were picked up by friends to go to church and listen to the biker. He had tattoos up both his arms, and he looked…real rough. I have often seen people like that on the streets, but rarely have I ever seen them in church.

I certainly had not seen someone with tattoos on their arm in the pulpit before.

He had been invited by our pastor to give his testimony about his life, and how he met Jesus Christ in his life. The guy started by saying that he had been addicted to heroin and had spent an immense amount of time and money getting the heroin and injecting it into his veins. He had been heavily addicted to the drug.

He went on to say that, at the same time, he was addicted to sleeping with prostitutes - sensitive sort of information for my ears. I had never heard anyone talk so explicitly about sex before, and especially not from a pulpit. He said he also did crime, and he ended by spending time in jail. I had seen TV shows about people in jail and knew it was a …rather unpleasant place. Listening to his story, I was amazed. I was shocked! I had never seen such a bad person in a pulpit before. There were places for bad people and, in my young understanding, a pulpit did not seem to be one of them. People who led clean-living lives, had grown up well, and had not done too many sins – they seemed to be the most likely preachers.

People who lived bad lives did not seem the people who would make a career out of preaching the Word of God and being in a pulpit. However, this fellow was in a pulpit, and his story was amazing. I was riveted to my chair. After he shared these things, he went on to say, in prison, he discovered the message of Jesus, and he became a Christian. He went on to share what he had learned about Jesus, about what Jesus had said to him, what Jesus had shared with him, and his knowledge of the Bible.

He shared the experiences he had with Jesus, and what Jesus had done for him and accomplished through him. I had known Jesus for about six years by this time, and I thought I knew Jesus well, and Jesus was a close friend of mine. Yet, this guy knew Jesus so well. He had seen Jesus in visions. He had talked to Jesus. He seemed to have been to heaven. He seemed as if he had this total supernatural life, and he knew Jesus so much deeper and better than me.

He was so in love with Jesus that He was just shining from him, and it was just so amazing! I was absolutely fascinated and remained riveted to my chair, as he was talking about his relationship with Jesus – I do not remember meeting a person so in love with Jesus, and someone who had experienced how much Jesus loved him.

He astounded me, and as you can tell from this book or this video that I am sharing, I was extremely impressed by this guy. He had an immense impact on my life. I went home from this testimony, and I said to Jesus that I had sat in church listening to Christians share their testimonies repeatedly on a Sunday night – good stories of them growing up in church, how good God had been to them, and how much they love God, but to me, they just seemed all the same.

I had never heard a bad person, someone who had come from a bad lifestyle, become so radically changed into someone who loves God and had been immensely changed and affected by God. I had never heard someone, who had come from such a desperate and despicable past, become such a beautiful and loving person who God obviously loves and is so full of the glory of God.

I was just so blown away by this guy that I said to Jesus that, when I grow up, I want a story like his. I want a story that is compelling and interesting, and a story from bad to good. I did not want a normal Christian story. I was unaware as a young guy at 14 of the implications of the prayer I was praying, and I am not here to say

Jesus allowed harmful things to happen in my life or the terrible suffering I have been through.

I am not saying that Jesus was particularly happy about the suffering and what has happened in my life that caused me to be who I am. However, I do know this: the prayer has been answered, and as you read the pages of this book, you will realize that I am somewhat like the biker I listened to long ago.

In these stories about David, I said to God that I wanted to be a man after God's own heart like David. I made a promise that I would commit my life to becoming a man like David.

In the story of Abraham, I learned of the massive faith that Abraham had, and I said to God that I wanted to be a friend of God's. I wanted people to know me to be a friend of God's, and I was prepared to live the life required of me to become that friend of God's, and third, I wanted a powerful testimony, sufficiently realistic or unbelievable that, when I talked about Jesus, people would be convinced that I knew He was powerful, because He had a remarkable effect on my life.

I wanted a story like that biker.

These are the three promises I made to Jesus, and the commitment I made to Jesus, and as you read this book, you will realize that God has profoundly answered those prayers.

Chapter 5

Hearing Jesus Speak

It is somewhat rare for many Christians to hear Jesus speak. If you ask the typical Christian whether he can hear Jesus, often they will reply He speaks to them in the Bible, or God speaks to them through pastors, but rarely will they say that they hear Jesus speaking to them.

You have to be somewhat mentally ill to admit readily that Jesus is speaking to you, but Jesus said in the scriptures that His sheep hear His voice, and they follow Him, and He orders them out. John 10:4 says, ***"And when he brings out his own sheep, he goes before them; and the sheep follow him, for they know his voice."*** So, it is clear, in the parable of the good shepherd, Jesus was saying He can actually talk to His sheep, and they listen to Him – meaning, by extension, a sheep would not read something written in a book. Sheep would hear the voice of the Master and follow the voice of the Master.

Therefore, you cannot say that when Jesus speaks, He speaks through the Bible, the written Word. Of course, He speaks through the Bible, but you can hear Jesus speaking directly to you. When I was a child, the first word I heard Jesus speak to me was in scriptures. As I mentioned in an earlier chapter, my mother used to put memory verses up on the bathroom mirror, and each week, we had to remember the verse, and quote where the verse was from in the Bible to get our weekly pocket money. Therefore, Jesus began to speak to me in verses, but how did He do that? I would be walking down the street, and I would be worried about how my brother was picking on me or doing something to me, and suddenly I would hear a verse in my mind.

It would come as a thought, saying, ***"I can do all things through Christ who strengthens me."*** There I was wondering how I was going to cope with my problem, and with that verse (Philippians 4:13), Jesus’ Holy Spirit told me I could cope with everything, because Jesus will strengthen me.

This was the first way Jesus began to speak to me.

Another way I heard Jesus speak to me in my life was when we used to sing songs in the Baptist church that were taken from a book called Scripture and Song – a book full of choruses and songs we sang to God and Jesus, and they were taken largely from scripture. They were large portions of scripture, rewritten in a way to form a song with music – you were essentially singing a psalm, or a passage out of the Bible. Therefore, they are very powerful songs, because they contain all the truth of the Word of God – and because they are in song, it is easy to remember them. Often, when I was worried, or going through a difficult time, Jesus would put a thought in my mind – it would be one of these songs, and as the song came to mind, I would immediately tear up and become happy.

Some of you might be going through something similar. Think to yourself, while I am sharing this, what a coincidence – sometimes you are going through the day, having a difficult time, when a specific Christian song comes to mind; you find yourself singing the song and suddenly start to feel happier.

Whether through a verse, a scripture, or a song, I knew very clearly, as a boy, it was actually Jesus speaking to me – having a two-way conversation with me. I might be walking down the street, or I might be in my bedroom talking to Jesus, and He would talk back in a scripture or in a song. I knew these things. Years later, now that I have progressed in the gift of prophecy, often a scripture will come up in a prophecy that I am delivering – but it will only be a scripture that I already know by memory. Rarely would Jesus use a scripture in a prophecy that was not already known by the person who is doing the prophecy.

I loved talking to Jesus, and I loved to feel His presence. I loved the peace that Jesus brought to me, and He was a living and real entity.

I knew from the way He communicated with me that He loved me. Another way that Jesus communicated with me was through the love of my pastor, Don Kemsley. He was the pastor of the Baptist church in Coffs Harbour, when I was young, and he had a tremendous love for me.

When he was speaking to you, he spoke directly to you. Someone else could come up and try to interrupt the conversation, but he would tell them to wait for just a moment, and he continued to talk to you. He made you feel the center of his attention when he was talking to you, and he made you feel loved and appreciated by him. He took the time to seek you out, to spend time with you, and share with you the deep things of God. He was a tremendous pastor – one of the favorite pastors in my life.

He was amazing. He was partially deaf – I am not sure if they had hearing aids back in those days – but he used to lip read. He took the time to teach me how to lip read as well. This was a great help with movies and music, where the sound quality was deficient and "challenging"; I could tell what people were saying.

He used to share a children's story at the beginning of church, after the songs – he would call all the children to the front of the church, and he would tell them a story. It was always a good story with many good moral points. He did not borrow any of the stories he told from a book, but he made them up himself. Even as a youth, I found that my favorite part of the service was when Don Kemsley was sharing his children's stories.

I can still remember a few of his stories 35 years later. He made me love stories, and he gave me the ability and a love for sharing stories. It is often said that Jesus speaks to us through people, and Jesus used to speak to me through my pastor. My pastor just had a way of talking to you and sometimes you just knew that it was not him, but Jesus, speaking.

I remember a long time ago, when my mother was worried about her own mother, because she was going to mediums and clairvoyants.

She was worried whether her mother was ever going to be saved, and Don Kemsley said, "One day, when your mother is older, and she's in her nursing home, she's going to come to the Lord." Don Kemsley had spoken a word of prophecy – he had spoken a direct message from God, through himself, to my mother. We shall learn more about the gift of prophecy, as we progress through this book, but essentially, Don Kemsley was speaking on behalf of God, something he did very often.

Often, I would go to a Christian rehabilitation center, not for my own problems, but because I just loved the people who ran the center. I would go there sometimes at weekends or for a week or two during school holidays. I was friends with the people who ran the rehabilitation center and looked after the children who stayed there. At the center, they would have a Bible study every morning, followed by a time of prayer. The seekers, as they called the people in rehabilitation, would always send up little prayers to God, and it always amazed me how many of these prayers were answered. It was if I could hear Jesus speak when the seekers were speaking.

Something the Holy Spirit told me many years ago was that is often the Holy Spirit, speaking through you, when you are speaking the truth from your heart. I would see the seekers share their hearts, and I would be hearing Jesus speak. I was introduced to the miracle of prayer through that rehab center. The prayers in the morning used to have dramatic effect before the end of the afternoon. It really built my faith to see prayers answered. One day, the generator broke, and despite prayers, they still needed to fix the generator continually. However, John Pierre, who ran the center, prayed specifically for a new generator – before the end of the afternoon, someone had come out to the center in a truck with a generator on it and said to John that they just felt that they should give him their old generator, which John accepted gratefully. I was there that day, and I was amazed to see how the prayers were answered.

Often, the center needed extra money, in addition to what they were receiving from Social Security for the seekers, and people would come with money and gifts to give to John Pierre and the center.

Seekers' lives were being changed through prayer. I would hear prayers for relationships and the restoration of relationships with parents and loved ones, and I would see the answers to those prayers daily. Jesus was constantly speaking to me through these situations.

Once, John Pierre was shopping, and while he was waiting in the shopping queue, as his groceries trundled past the checkout girl and her voracious till, he turned to my mother and said, with a smile, that he did not have the money in his wallet to pay for the groceries he was buying. My mother asked, "What are you going to do about it?" John replied, "If it's God's will, it's God's bill," and he smiled. Then a woman from our church came, said hello to John, and gave him an envelope containing some money – enough to pay for the groceries.

On many occasions, I saw Jesus speaking out of John Pierre's farm – seeing Him move and prove Himself real to me. I learned, at a very young age, that simply talking to Jesus was comforting and allowed God to be present. His presence would come, and I would feel a peace and a love when I was talking to Jesus and to God.

One day, Jesus would increase the ways He spoke to me, but that was later in my life and is for a later chapter. I hope that you have enjoyed this chapter. May God Bless You!

Chapter 6

My Sexual Awakening

As I mentioned earlier, I love to surf, and one day I managed to find a beach with a good break but with fewer surfers than on other beaches.

I was not a competitive surfer, and I was not very fit, so I did not like to compete for waves. I found the waves at this beach were not as large as waves at other beaches, but they were certainly satisfactory to surf, so I often frequented this beach, especially when I was surfing by myself and not with my older brother, Rodney.

One day, as I was surfing at this beach, I was surfing a wave right to the end of the beach, passed some rocks, and came across yet another beach. As I rode the wave into the beach, I found myself gazing at groups of naked men and women in the water, sitting on the beach, or just walking up and down the beach. I was surprised, as I had never seen a naked woman before.

I could imagine what they looked like, of course, but now I was seeing them in all their beauty on this beach. I was interested – it sounds like an understatement – but I was…interested. I got out of the surf, went up to a group, and started talking to them. A somewhat friendly woman explained they were nudists, and this was how they came to the beach, so they could have a suntan all over their bodies, as they liked to be natural. They just gathered on the beach, enjoyed themselves, and sunbathed in the nude. She said no one would think any less of me, if I took off my board shorts and joined them for a talk. Being somewhat encouraged by her, I took off my clothes, sat, and talked with them for a while. The following week, I returned to the beach where I met them again, and we spent more time together.

The group of three women and three men were all married, but I really enjoyed sitting and talking to a female who was naked – no arguments, as a young man, I really enjoyed that –and I really enjoyed that they had no problems with me looking at them. It was an amazing experience – in my heart, I knew that it was sinful, but part of me was saying that this is how Adam and Eve lived, and it was perfectly natural.

In the second week, one of the women said that her niece would be visiting her from the city during the following week. The niece was more my age, and she was a nudist too, and she thought it would be good idea for me to meet and spend some time with her niece. You can imagine the following week at school – my thoughts were not concentrated on schoolwork, but more on the weekend and meeting this girl. I have always had a fascination for girls, but I was not very good at opening up to them. I was not very good at communicating with them, but this time, I knew her aunt, and her aunt seemed to accept me. I seemed to get on well with adults, but I seemed uncomfortable with, or was not very good at, mixing with people of the same age as myself. However, when the next Saturday arrived, I was disappointed to find it overcast and threatening to rain. Despite that, I went down to the beach to surf and to check things out.

Around midday, after surfing, I went to the place on the beach, but I found that the couple was not there yet. I still held out hope that the woman would come with her niece, even though it was overcast and not very warm. I had hopes in my heart that things would change for the better – to what I believed would be better for me.

There was a guy sitting naked on the beach, so I sat naked next to him and started talking to him. He asked me whether I had come to the beach before, as he had not seen me there before. I said I had, and that I was waiting for a friend, but in the meantime, I could chat to him – and he seemed happy with that. After a while, he asked me if I wanted to go for a swim, and I did not have a problem with that. We were talking and swimming in the waves when, suddenly, I felt his hand on my penis – and I reacted. My penis was aroused by his touch, and he fondled it for a while. I was a little uncomfortable with this, but I was excited. Then I decided it was all too much, so I ran for my clothes, left the beach and began to cycle home.

As I cycled home, I said to Jesus that He had to get me a girlfriend – I threatened Him and said if He did not get me a girlfriend then I would go back to the beach. In the United States of America or Australia, they do not respond to terrorist threats, and the same is true of Jesus. If you threaten Jesus, He is not necessarily going to answer your prayer. Jesus' answer to me was complete silence. I was half hoping that I would meet a girl on the way home, and I held out right until I got home – then I turned my bike around. Frustrated and angry, I rode all the way back to the beach, where I found the man having a sexual experience with another man – I watched until the other man packed up and left.

Then I approached the man who had fondled me and said that I was here to meet him again. He was quite surprised, as he had thought I had left. He asked me whether I had gone home, and why I had returned. Nervously, I said I was interested to see what he was doing. He went to business and showed me some things that he could do – I found that through that experience, I had my first orgasm. It is an amazing thing for a child to experience their first orgasm. It opens the person to his or her sexuality, and starts them on a course that will lead them in good or bad ways.

I had found what people would later refer to as sexual abuse, and it was my fault. I was a willing participant – after all, I was the one who had put myself on that beach. I was the one who put myself naked on that beach and had returned to that beach. I was the one who ran away, but after threatening Jesus, I had returned on my own free will to the beach to experience a sexual experience with this guy. Maybe loneliness could have been the cause of this.

I often felt lonely – I did not feel loved much by my father – I felt uncomfortable around my brother, Rodney, because he picked on me and called me names – and sometimes I even felt uncomfortable around my younger brother, Tony.

I have noticed in nature, when a lion is looking at a herd of wildebeest, he is watching the young or the weak among them, because they are slower than, and not as fast as, the remainder of the herd. The lion will measure things up, look for a while, single out a weak one, then pounce and take it. The same is true of pedophiles and pedophilia. They can look across a room, full of children, and find the weaker and more vulnerable ones. Spiritually, they can sense who is a spiritually and emotionally vulnerable child, and they will target that child with their gifts and approaches.

I was vulnerable to this sort of attention – and this is exactly what I received. In this book I am talking candidly, and all my life, I have been honest and open about this – and I have to admit that what I did by going back to see that guy was no one else's fault except mine. It was not my father's fault or my brother's fault – it was no one else's fault but my own. I did it willingly. Somehow, during the whole process, he gave me his attentions, and I felt good. That is the thing about sin – it feels good. This makes us such sinners sometimes, because we actually enjoy the sin in which we become involved. No one is to blame for this, but my sexual awakening on that beach led to a life and lifestyle that caused me much distress and hardship.

Chapter 7

Sin life Begins

I have always been honest with people, and I have even grown to become honest with strangers that I meet – some people would call me 'transparent.' I am very open and honest in all my dealings with people, and it is something that I pride myself on – the honesty that I have. I love to tell the truth as often as I can, so it was something new for me to have a part of my life that was dishonest – hidden from my mother and hidden from my family.

It intrigued me that my penis could be aroused, and this led to an addiction. It led me to start to masturbate. Now, I know that many boys masturbate and then come across pornography, but not all boys had their first sexual encounter on the beach with...a sexual predator – a homosexual who took advantage of the curiosity of a boy.

Soon I was going down to the shops to buy pornography magazines. It was always embarrassing to bring such magazines to the counter, especially when there was a woman serving on the counter – especially when it was the younger girls serving on the counter. Maybe this is one of the reasons that I believe pornography has flourished prolifically, since its introduction on the Web. Now you can view online pictures and videos of people having sex, and all types of pornography, on the Web.

Formerly, you would have to go to a newsagent to buy a sexually pornographic magazine and become embarrassed when you purchase it, making you feel like a dirty old man going into one of those shops. Now, it is readily available on the Internet and is primarily targeted at males. I heard one statistic that about 50% of Christian males are viewing pornography regularly.

I began to masturbate and view pornography at a young age – around about 14.

I also began to reject the offers of my brother, Rodney, to go surfing, instead choosing to go to my own special beach and enjoy my own special fantasies. I would go surfing at Diggers Beach (my beach), and then, I would find a man who wanted to show me his pleasures and spend time with me. It did not stop me talking to the women or spending time with the nudists on the beach. I had the fantasy life of any young male, but when I was having sexual encounters, I was not having them with women – but with men.

Having these lewd sexual encounters with men on the beach had a dramatic effect on my faith and my personal Christian life. I found that I could no longer sing the worship songs or the choruses in the songs of adoration to Jesus and God in church. I still went to church, but instead of singing when the songs came, I would just stand there and listen. My mother once remarked, when a chef's wife told me that I had a good voice, and I told my mother about what she said, my mother said that she had never heard me sing – and that was true.

In the years between 14 and 17, I stopped singing. Because I am an honest person, I needed to be real with Jesus, and I found it difficult to be passionate about Him and sing to Him in love and adoration, when on weekends, I was having sexual encounters with men on the beach. Every week or two, I would meet a different man, and I started to become extremely selfish with these sexual encounters. I always insisted on my own sexual gratification needs being met, before I started to fulfill their sexual gratification.

I was not entirely happy about the selfishness that was increasing within me. Although I lacked inside me what I needed to be happy about myself, I liked to think that I was an essentially good person. However, in these sexual encounters, I was beginning to see a need and a desire for me to get my own way, and it was not very comforting. I remember once going to the bushes with a group of men, when one man tried to have anal sex with me. It was tremendously painful, when he started, so I pushed him away and told him that he was not going to have his way with me that way, in any form. Never, in any of my sexual encounters in years to come, did I ever have anal sex with a man.

I found it repulsive, extremely painful, and it was not something that turned me on. It was not something that I approved of, and I certainly think that it is an unnecessary form of sex in a sexual relationship between a man and a woman. Although, during the course of this memoir, you may find me talking about sins, you will also find that I do not readily judge others, because I am a person who has committed a lot of sin in my life.

They say that the pain of anal sex eventually diminishes, and the act becomes enjoyable to the person receiving it – this may be true for them – it may be true for homosexuals to enjoy receiving anal sex – but it was certainly not something that was enjoyable to me, or something that I wanted to participate in, and it's not something that I fully participated in either.

Keeping secrets about your personal life does damage to your soul. Sometimes, Satan would have you believe that it has done irreparable damage to your soul – but God is not limited.

That is just a little insight into the sexual sin that began in my life. I used to continue to go down to the beach, and try to continue my Christian life – although it was a struggle to have a close relationship with Jesus, while I was involved in sexual sin. I was sinning and I felt guilty, shameful, and dirty for what I was doing. If you have a homosexual tendency, I can understand that you might disagree with what I have to say. You may disagree with my attitude, but I want you to know that what I have said about the homosexual lifestyle, and the stuff I was participating in on the beaches, is in no way a slight on you – I am in no way judging you and saying that you are essentially a bad person. I am just saying that I do not feel that men were created for men, and I was living contrary to a genuine Christian life.

Chapter 8

Misunderstandings

I was different from most boys at my school, and my secret life began to affect me deeper than I realized. I was a funny individual who, on the surface seemed quite normal – an average sort of student in the higher classes at school – but underneath, in my secret life, I was having sex with men on the beaches.

I had friends at school, and I am glad that I was not a loner at least. Plenty of people at school are loners and spend time by themselves without friends. That was certainly not my experience. I had friends that I believe cared about me, laughed with me, and joked with me. I lived a normal life with friends, although I was confused and found it difficult to concentrate at school and to work, as hard as I used to.

Since my encounters on the beach, I was distracted at school. I found it difficult to study, and my concentration became affected – my whole life at school was affected by what I was doing on the weekends. Keeping a secret has real effects on you. Keeping a secret really affects you deeply – it is almost as if you are living a life of hypocrisy – on the one hand, living a life where your friends know you as a genuine little Christian boy, going to church every week, and on the other hand, you were at the beach sleeping with men on the weekend.

It had a serious effect on me, and my grades started to drop. Around this time, a couple bullies started to pick on me. One of them hit me, so I told my principal about it – the guy was expelled from school on my say-so, which made me feel condemned and guilty.

Afterward, I used to see him around with his friends from the other school, and I always felt bad that it had ended that way. I certainly did not go to the principal to have him expelled – I just went to the principal to make sure he would stop picking on me. There was another guy, who picked on me somewhat, and even in my dreams today, he still seems to be having fights with me – strange because he eventually became a friend. Later, he died in a house fire, but not before he had given his life to Jesus. I am pleased that he is now in heaven – so, why does he come into my dreams still picking on me? Maybe it is just something Satan is doing in my life. I was trying to be happy-go-lucky. I was trying to be the happy, encouraging, beautiful person I am, but I was having a real struggle.

My personal sin life was having a taxing effect on me, and it was having an effect on my ability to relate to boys and girls of my own age. My two brothers used to tease me about my surfing style. They called me a “Hunchback of Notre Dame,” because when I was going down a wave, I would hunch over – they thought it was particularly funny the way that I used to surf.

When I was around 16 (or in year nine), I decided to quit school and took up an apprenticeship as a chef, which had always been one of my dreams. When I was growing up, my mother used to cater for people and prepare group meals in a church catering team. She was a very good cook and, for all those years, was cooking en masse for these people. I had a real love for cooking, and a real desire to become a chef when I grew up. I took that opportunity, seeing that I was struggling at school – I was sick of school, I was not getting on well with people, and my grades were not going well either.

I later found out that the chef I was working with had a heroin habit, which was one of the reasons he was always impatient. I have always had a tremor in my hands, and this was not good for me in the kitchen, where, especially as a chef, you have to use a knife a lot of the time. You have to be good with a knife to be fast and efficient – but my shaking hands slowed me down, and as I was not efficient with a knife, jobs took a lot longer.

I spent hours of my life washing up, and as I became an “expert” at this art, I could add a “dash of speed” to the process, but washing dishes is certainly not an exciting career for anyone – a career change is often a more suitable alternative.

I remember once I had to cut a whole lot of pineapples in two – remove the insides, for whatever they use pineapple pulp, and then fill the two halves of the pineapple with fruit salad – the visual results were much more pleasant than the work itself, especially as the pineapple needles were doing some major surgery on my hands.

Straight after this, I was given the task of peeling and cutting a whole sack of …onions. The moisture from the onions, running into the cuts on my hands, was not conducive to job satisfaction – it was so painful that it caused me to burst into tears. Another chef noticed and offered to take over the job of cutting up onions, and I went back to … washing up.

Working in a kitchen was always difficult. Occasionally, I had to clean out the cool room; sometimes, I would find pieces of corn beef or lamb to eat – once, I found some of those expensive cherries they use, which are soaked in liqueur, and they were too tempting to leave just lying around.

I was always hungry in that kitchen, because the head chef was never hungry himself (because of his heroin habit), and he neglected to feed me as much as he should have. Therefore, cleaning the cool room became a task that I would look forward to, as it enabled me to stave off the pangs of hunger for a while longer. Then one day, the chef took my mother aside and said, "It's not working out with, Matthew. He's slow." I am not sure that was the real reason, but my apprenticeship was discontinued.

As I lived in a home of discipline, my mother said either I had to have a job, or I had to go to school. I decided to go back to school, which was difficult because I had missed two to three months' worth of schoolwork – with Mathematics and English, you learn things in progression, and I had lost three months' worth of learning. I was sad and disappointed, because I was put in lower classes for Math and English the next year.

At this time, I was going to an Anglican youth group at church – there were not enough children at our Baptist church, so instead, we went to a Church of England, or Anglican, youth group.

It was a good youth group, and I enjoyed it – I was able to maintain some sort of relationship with Jesus, although I still had my contradictory weekend lifestyle. I met a girl there called Narrelle (I could never remember her last name), who was a couple of years younger than I was. I really enjoyed her company, and although many would say it was just a crush, I think I fell in love with Narrelle.

At the youth group, we had a session where we would pray together in a circle holding hands – I made sure that I was always sitting next to Narrelle, so when it came prayer time, I could hold her hand. Holding her hand was especially precious to me for those times at least. Once, I asked her to be my girlfriend, but she declined – she said that she had gone out with a couple of boys before, but whenever she broke up with them, she could no longer be their friend. There was bad blood between her and her ex-boyfriends, and she said that she appreciated me as a friend so much, that she would never want that to happen between us. She always wanted us to be friends, "So, could we please just be friends?" That made me sad, but I was happy in a way, because I felt as if she had told me the truth about our life, and I started to feel comfortable around her – something that I did not feel with other girls.

Although I would like to call her my first love, I did have a nasty habit of picking on her and saying that she was fat. Her elder sister took me aside once and said, "Could you stop telling Narrelle that she's fat. She thinks she's fat, and we are all telling her she's not fat, and she says 'well, Matthew says I'm fat.' And, now she's convinced that she's fat, but she's a beautiful girl, so please stop telling her that she's fat." I told her sister that I liked her, and it was a way of protecting myself from being rejected, and her sister said, "Well, it's not a very nice way of protecting yourself, and please don't do it anymore." Even today, as I write this, I feel guilty for doing that to her in her life.

A while later, the school started surfing as a recognized sport. They figured that when the surf was up, and there were good waves about, half the surfers in this high school would skip their sporting lessons and go surfing anyway. The school decided that to keep these surfers inside, and keep them attending class, they would get a few teachers to teach surfing for sport – we went to classrooms for about a month to learn all their safety rules, and to learn about surfing, as though we did not know what surfing was. Then they took us to the beach, where we would use a buddy system – for half of the allotted time, one would watch over another, as they surfed, in case of any problems, and then reverse the roles for the remainder of the time.

One of the surfers was a girl who was a couple of years younger than I was. She was blond, had beautiful brown eyes and a brown-olive skin that in summer turned almost to the color of chocolate. She was one of the most attractive girls I had ever seen – and she was a fairly good surfer as well.

One day, I was paddling back out across the waves, when she came down, riding the wave – I was in the way, and she crashed into me. As I resurfaced, she was screaming, and I went over to her, picking her up by the arm. She screamed even more, so I grabbed her other arm, put her on my surfboard, and paddled her back to shore. It turned out that when she had hit my surfboard, she had broken her arm. She went to the hospital, where they put a cast on her arm; then, it was decided that she would come back as a buddy to two people, so she would just sit on the beach and watch others surf. Through this interaction, we became friends.

I found out that she liked to go to Digger's Beach, so sometimes, I would meet her, when I went to my beach for my weekly or fortnightly "forays", and we became special friends. We liked to surf together, and once, when she was on the beach sunbathing, I worked out a way to make her watch me surf – borrow her surfboard, as she would always be watching her surfboard (now with me on it, of course). I asked her whether I could borrow her surfboard and take it for a ride. It was a new surfboard, so her eyes were glued on it (and me) – every time I looked up, she was watching me. I rode a few waves, and even if I say so myself, I rose to the occasion and put on an impressive display.

Halfway through, she swam out and held onto the end of the surfboard – it was so beautiful that it reminded me of the movie, The Blue Lagoon. I asked her if she had ever learned to duck dive – a way of pushing your surfboard under a breaking wave, and up the other side, to save coming against the friction of the whitewash. She had never learned, so I was able to teach her how, until she became proficient. I forget her name now, although I think her last name was Spagnolo – but like Narrelle, she was a platonic friend, because I never had the courage to ask her out, to be my girlfriend – but she still brings a smile to my face, because of the special friendship that I had with her.

When I reached year 11 at school, my elder brother, Rodney, left home and moved to Newcastle, a city about four hours away by car. In spite of everything that had gone before, I began to miss my older brother. My younger brother was still growing up, and I got angry with him a few times and hit him. My father said that if I ever hit my brother again, he would smash me himself – and I began to feel slighted again.

It was wrong of me to hit my younger brother, but I felt slighted for the number of times that my older brother had hit me, and my father had never smashed him. Satan would still be keeping me in this bondage, if I were not a person who forgave and understood that my father just did not want my younger brother being picked on.

Chapter 9

Moving to Sydney

It was always going to be a big move from Coffs Harbour, a coastal town with 30,000 people in the hinterland, to a city of four-million people. I used to live in the city of Sydney when I was younger, before I moved to Coffs Harbour, as I mentioned earlier in my testimony.

Although moving back was quite a big move, as it meant moving away from my brothers and sisters, and my mother and father – away from my family – it was essential, because I was moving to get a job. As a country boy, I found it strange to travel on trains and buses – mainly because I had not traveled on them in Coffs Harbour – I went everywhere in the car or cycled on my bike. I also found it strange to meet people and not see them smile or say hello, as they do in the country.

I found that people in the city were quieter, more reserved, and more afraid of others. They say that you can take the boy out of the country, but you cannot take the country out of the boy – and that was true of me. This is still true, even after 25 years of being down here – I am still greeting people. I am still smiling at people, and I am still engaging people. Maybe they think it is strange to have someone talk to them, but for most of the time, they are happy to talk.

I moved down to my aunt's place in the northern suburbs of Sydney, about 45 minutes by train into the city center. My aunt was married to a rather quiet Italian man, and I liked to watch him eat the Italian dishes she would cook for him. He only ate Italian meals, so my aunt would cook a different meal for the rest of us, including her two boys.

I started to apply for jobs, and soon, I was offered a job in the mail sorting room of a major Australian bank. I have to admit that I never got the hang of sorting mail – trying to work out where a specific letter was headed, when the only details I had were a person's name and the address of our bank – not easy, as I was working in a ten-story building, and I had yet to learn everyone's name. I just did not seem able to do it. That spoke to my self-esteem and made me feel hopeless, because others had started in the sorting room, and had progressed to other jobs, yet I seemed stuck there.

However, one part of the job that I especially liked was that, twice a day, I had to go to other floors, collect checks from specific desks, and bring them back to the mail sorting room for further processing. All these years later, I am not sure what we did with those checks, but it was exciting to pick up the checks and see millions of dollars being written from one company to another. I think the highest check I picked up was for about $37 million dollars – it was amazing how much money was carried in those checks from upstairs down to the mail sorting room.

One day, I collected a check addressed to my favorite rock band, Midnight Oil. They were a fascinating band and exciting to see live – I often used to play their music in the car on the tape deck – yup, back in the days when a tape deck was considered technological wizardry. When the surf was up, we would play their music to get our adrenaline pumping and give us the courage to surf in the huge breaks. It was exciting to see a check written to Midnight Oil. Even more, I loved the idea of being paid each week, and I enjoyed spending the money.

I had to enroll in a technical college as part of the job in the bank. I had to get an accounting qualification to continue working at the bank. During the course, I met a girl, who would become close to me – but that is getting ahead of the story – more of that later.

The new income allowed me to have cash that I had earned – I liked that, even though it was only $200 a week – it was a lot more than the money I got collecting golf balls in my youth.

The bank moved me at one stage, and I had to go to a new bank. The manager at the head office bank told me that I was not working to their standards, and I was not progressing as they wished. I was put on probation and sent to a regular branch. The supervisor told me that the new bank would not be informed that I was on probation and would only be asked whether I was working out in the future.

I liked the new branch, and I seemed to be getting the hang of things. I began to learn how to be a teller – I was pleased with the job, and I even began to enjoy the traveling to the job. One week, the branch manager called me in to his office and said that he was very pleased with my progress – he asked me whether I was enjoying myself, and we had a good conversation. A week later, he called me in to the office again and told me I had to resign – it was not working out, and the bank was not happy with me.

I am not completely sure of the reason that he changed his mind within a week. It just seemed rather underhanded, and it took me many years to forgive the bank for telling me that I had to resign, or they would sack me. I know we are meant to forgive, but I still have bad thoughts about that Australian bank.

When you lose a job – when you cannot do a job successfully, and you are essentially sacked – it does take a toll on your self-esteem. However, before I lost my job, I had managed to visit Kings Cross for my first time – the infamous red-light district of Sydney and the subject of my next chapter.

Chapter 10

My Sexual Addiction Begins

While I was staying with my aunt, one of my cousins, Mark, took me to his work at the naval shipyards in Sydney Harbour. We had to get off the train at Kings Cross, and as we got off, he told me about Kings Cross, the infamous red-light district of Sydney, where you could see and meet street-walking prostitutes. For a person who had grown up with pornographic magazines and the TV news, it was not breaking news to me that prostitutes hung out in Kings Cross. However, as a hot-blooded male, I was certainly interested in viewing the scenery. Leaving the station, we had not even gone halfway down the street, before I saw what appeared to be a prostitute – I could tell what she was just from the cross between the miniskirt and a belt, which, for the occasion, covered her to a certain extent.

As we passed her, she asked me, "Would you like a lady for a short time?" This flabbergasted me, to say the least – that she had been so bold and just asked me that question. I said, "No thanks," and without trying to give anything away to my cousin, Mark, I continued walking down the street towards his naval base – but inside, my heart was racing. My mind was running on overdrive, thinking how I could get back to see this woman, or one of the others who hung around Kings Cross as prostitutes. I was wondering to myself how much these women would charge to hire their services. Unaware of my internal thoughts, my cousin showed me his naval base, and he went in to collect something, while I waited outside. When he came back, we set off again through Kings Cross, where I saw another couple of prostitutes – and became excited again.

We left and caught a train, but my mind was running wild.

The next day after work, I caught a train to Kings Cross, with a hundred dollars in my pocket. I was taken by surprise, when I walked up to one of the “ladies”, and she asked me, “Would you like to see a girl?” I was even more surprised, when she told me it would cost $20. This would have been in 1985, and $20 dollars was not a great deal of money – and I had come prepared to spend $100. With the $100 in my pocket, I could get to see five. I could not believe that with the money in my pocket, I could actually have sex with the woman standing in front of me. I went inside with the woman, and after I had settled the financial arrangements with a couple of heavy looking dudes, she asked for a key, and then we went upstairs to her room.

Inside her room, there was a bed, but not much else in the way of furnishings. She asked me to undress, which if you have read my earlier adventures on the nudist beach, I was not afraid to do. I was quite happy to see her undressing in front of me as well, and she seemed to have no inhibitions and was not afraid to take off her clothes off. Soon enough, I was on the bed with this woman, wondering what I should do next.

I think the woman was aware that it was my first time, and that I was nervous – the natural tremor in my hands combined with my nervousness, I must have been shaking more than usual. Within a few minutes of being on the bed, I was being shown how to have sex, for the first time in my life – and I was enjoying myself.

I quickly learned that kissing was not permitted, as it was not included in the prostitute’s charge. I was rather disappointed about this, because it did not seem intimate – and, because I had never kissed a girl before, which made me sad. I want to make it clear here that I have decided to hold nothing back in my testimony – I feel that the more honest truth I share with you, the greater the message will be at the end. The greater the message, and the greater the understanding you will have of my life – where I have been with all the hurts, with all the hard times, and with all the sins that I have committed.

God does not approve of sex outside of marriage. He makes that very clear in the Bible. Whether that is homosexual sex, as I had earlier in my life, or whether that is sex between a man and a woman, who are not married, God does not condone sex outside of marriage. God performed a wonderful job with designing men and women, and in doing such a good job, God left it open for us to have a free will and to make our own choices – to choose whether we are going to have sex before marriage.

The good thing about God – and the sad thing about our condition – is that God created us with a free will. He did not create us to be robots, to be ordered around or pulled on strings. We have a free will – to choose to do what is best for others, or to do what is best for God, or to do whatever we feel like.

Many people ask, "Where is God with all the suffering in the world? Where is God? Surely, if there was a God there would be an end to suffering." How do you propose God stops the suffering in the world? The suffering in the world mostly comes from people doing the wrong thing – people with a free will, and the ability to choose between right and wrong. What would God have to do to stop the suffering? He could just come back and impose martial law? – not going to happen! One day, Jesus is going to return and rule the Earth, but until then, people still have a free will.

Although many people would not care to admit it, the act of having sex is a spiritual act. When you have sex with a partner, there is a spiritual residue left over between you and your partner. As an example, I was watching a movie where a guy went into a city to spy, and went behind closed doors, into the palace, the command post of the government in the city – while he was there, he slept with one of the women. Next day, he returned with the army and attacked the palace, running through each room, shooting everybody in each room. When he came to the room with the woman he had slept with, he hesitated and did not shoot her. Another man came through the door, saw his hesitation, and shot the woman.

After watching the movie – the pause button had not been invented yet – my dad asked me, "Why did the guy hesitate when he saw the woman?" I said, "Because he'd slept with her, I reckon." My dad said, "No, it's more than that. It's because he was spiritually bonded to that woman." It is true – when we have sex with a person, we become spiritually connected to that person. Maybe that is why many people feel so guilty about seeing the person the next day and feeling the pressure of having started a relationship. Therefore, many people have casual encounters and casual sex – one-night stands, where both parties agree that it is only going to be for one night, and to have sex just for the sake of having sex. That is all well and fine – God allows that to happen, because He has given us a free will – but He does not wish that on anyone, because it leads to heartache, hurt, disease, and much more.

God is not a killjoy, but He does know what is best for us. The more we have sex, the more we lose our identity to the people with whom we've had sex. I had sex with so many people, so many girls, and so many men, that I truly lost myself. Prostitutes would call me a 'punter', and they make a living out of guys with addictions such as I had. Prostitutes talk to each other, and joke about the punters, and about the things they tell people like me with addictions.

Prostitutes look down on people like me and think we are easy bait or an easy mark. We are victims, just as they are, but I had no idea that I was. When I visited the first girl, I had no idea that it was going to start an addiction in my life that was going to cost me a great deal of money. I had no idea that this addiction was going to put me through so much heartache and pain, and keep me broke for much of my life.

I had no idea what I was getting into – but God knew exactly. It is amazing that God stuck by me all the time, although I was not going to church, and I was not even talking to Him. He was there. Jesus was there. My two brothers and my sister own their own homes, but I do not own my own home today, because of this addiction. Like me, you might say sex is a gift to us and it should be enjoyed.

You, as an adult, should be able to choose what you do with your own body, right? Right? Yes, you are right. Yes, you are allowed to choose. God created you for you to choose – but in the Bible, He makes it clear what is right and what is wrong. Is God ashamed of prostitutes? Does He despise them? No – a thousand times – No. In fact, Jesus was descended from a prostitute. Through the bloodline of Mary, Jesus was descended from a prostitute.

In the book of Joshua, there is the story of Rahab, similar to the story I mentioned a short while ago about the man storming the palace. Joshua had sent out spies, into the city of Jericho, to determine how they were going to attack the city. While they were in the city, they were protected by Rahab, a prostitute (or for the more semantic scholars – a keeper of a house of entertainment), who was overawed with the deeds of the God of Israel. In return for her protection, and for her help to escape their arrest, she pleaded with the spies, "Please, don't kill me, when you come to attack my city, but take me with you. I want to serve your God."

Rahab and her family survived the attack on the city, and she later married an Israelite and started a family tree, which eventually led to the birth of Jesus.

Many years before Joshua, there was another woman called Tamar in Genesis 38. At that time, there was a Jewish custom (actually a rule): in the event of the death of a husband, the wife would be married to the next oldest brother – and so on down the line – as a way of keeping the family name alive. With Tamar, her husband died, and then, after she married the next brother, he died also. However, the next brother in line refused to marry Tamar, as he might not want to be with a woman, who had been with two of his brothers. She thought it was unfair to break the Jewish Law, and she pleaded with her stepfather, who decided to side with his son and chose to break the Jewish law.

Feeling slighted at this, Tamar decided to disguise herself and dressed up as a prostitute. On the day that she was ovulating, the best day for her to fall pregnant, she approached her stepfather and offered her sexual services to him. The stepfather agreed, and although he did not have any money, he offered his staff as security, for the money with which he would pay her later. He had sex with her, and she fell pregnant. Later, when she was no longer disguised, the stepfather found out she was pregnant and was going to stone her for being an unfaithful woman. She produced the staff he had given her as security and said, "The son I'm having is your son. This is your staff." Obviously, the stepfather had gone back to pay her, but could not find her because she had disappeared.

If God was a prude, or He was embarrassed about sexuality, or by the fact of a woman being a prostitute, He would have never sent a Son into the world with a genealogy that included a prostitute and a girl sleeping with her stepfather – they are part of the story to show that, in God's sight, everybody is valuable.

However, my one encounter with the prostitute did not stop me from going again. It only inflamed a passion and desire in me that was to continue for many years.

My trips to Kings Cross soon began to make me late coming home from work, so I had to make up excuses and lies for my aunt and cousins. I did not like to lie, but it was a case of excusing me for coming home late. That is the problem with sin – often, you have to do something that is not right to cover up for something else you are not doing right, and so the cycle expands. However, I soon moved out of my cousin's place, so I did not have to lie about my whereabouts anymore, because I was staying in a boarding house where no one seemed to care.

I quickly learned that the older prostitutes frequented Kings Cross during the day, but in the evenings, especially on Friday and Saturday nights, the younger girls came out into Kings Cross. Being young myself – 18 years of age – I certainly preferred sleeping with girls who were 20 or 21, or at least closer to my age. I also quickly learned that the four strip clubs in Kings Cross had between 15 and 20 girls working inside as prostitutes. Quite logical I suppose – the strippers were paid to get the men aroused, then the prostitutes would come around and offer their services to alleviate their frustrations – the traffic up and down the stairs was virtually continual.

I also learned that if I did not like one of the available girls, when I first arrived in the club, I did not have to wait long, before other girls arrived after being with other clients. I did not have to go with the first girl who approached me, but I could say, "No, no, no, no, no" to all their requests and wait for one who was pretty and attractive and desirable to me, in my mind's eye. After all, beauty is in the eye of the beholder, and I preferred someone who was very beholding.

I had no idea that the prostitutes in this club were heroin addicts. I had no way of telling whether someone was high. I had no concept of the fact that these girls were addicted to the drug, and every cent I was giving them was going up their arm with their addiction. In addition, I had no real concept that I was abusing these girls – that I was virtually raping them. I thought that they performed sex willingly to earn money, and I was providing the service – essentially, I thought I was a nice guy and a nice client. I did not mistreat them, abuse them, hurt them, or become violent with them – I thought it was a fair trade of money for their services. I was deceived. I was abusing them. I was to find out later in life that the truth was that I was just like their father – abusing them. I was a sick individual, but as is often the case when you are sick, I was not aware of how sick I was.

I wondered whether to include all this in the book, but I decided that if I am going to tell the truth then I might as well tell the whole truth. It is difficult to write this, as my mother is going to be one of the editors, but I made this decision for the sake of the readers and for the sake of people who have lived a depraved life such as mine.

One night in a strip club, I saw one of the strippers grab a man from the audience, take him on stage, and have sex with him. It blew me away. It was a total surprise – it would be for anyone – to see a couple having sex, live, in front of their eyes, not 20 feet away from them.

With further investigation, I found this was a regular part of the entertainment. I asked one of the bouncers whether it would be possible to put my name forward as a guy who would be willing to go and have sex onstage. I figured that paying $10 to get into the club, and have free sex, had to be a better deal than paying $50 dollars for a half an hour of sex upstairs with one of the girls. With my earlier trips to the nudist beach, I was used to being naked in front of others, so I had no inhibitions about going onstage and having sex with a girl – and that is exactly what I did.

The following week, a bouncer arranged for a girl to ask me. In the middle of her strip routine, she sat on my lap and whispered in my ear, "Are you the one who's coming forward to have sex?" When I replied, "Yes," she got off my lap, removed most of her clothes during the next couple of songs, then came back, grabbed me and pulled me onto stage. I had sex onstage for the first time, and I thought I was in my element, because I was getting the sex free. I began to understand how actors feel when performing on a stage in a play or performing in a movie – there is a feeling of being a star, and I found that enjoyable. It became a regular pit stop for me on a Friday or Saturday night, when I went into the city. I found that having sex onstage put me in a better frame of mind, when I went out to nightclubs and bars later. I was no longer desperate to have sex, because I had already had sex, so I was calmer and more relaxed, when it came to picking up girls or going out with my friends to clubs.

As you can see from my story, I had become a depraved individual – certainly not the behavior of the young Christian boy that I used to be – certainly a surprise for my mother, and the rest of my family, to read what I got up to. People who read this book, or have watched the video on the Internet, might be quite shocked by that last story. It would not be difficult for you to guess that my church days were over. It will come as no surprise to learn that, since I moved to Sydney, I had stopped going to church. There was so much guilt in my life that I did not want to walk into a church – and I certainly did not want to sing songs and pretend that I was in love with God, or pretend that I was passionate about Jesus, when I was involved in so much sin.

To a Christian, that is essentially one of the reasons your non-Christian friends or other non-Christians do not go to church. Often, they are living a life where they know they are doing wrong things. They feel too honest about themselves, and they do not want to appear hypocritical – they do not want to give up their lifestyle, so they just do not go to church.

If the typical non-Christian only knew that they could go to a church and meet God, be in His presence, be around loving people in church, and no one would threaten them, pressure them to become a Christian, or judge them for the life they are living; then, many more people would go to church. Currently, I go to a church where there are gays, lesbians, transsexuals that come to church. My pastors do not judge them, because everyone is loved in my church.

I was about six months into my addiction, when I met the girl in my accounting course, and we would meet for dinner in between classes. At one of these dinners in a cafeteria, I asked her how many valentine cards she had received, and she said she had not received even one. I blushed a little, and then I stepped up the courage, and asked her out on a date. I was happy when she accepted.

I thought I loved this girl. I cannot even remember her name anymore, which shows how much I loved her. Anyway, I thought I loved her, but essentially, I was just being selfish. I liked kissing her, holding her hand, being in her company, and having sex with her. She was a virgin when I met her, but as many other guys, I played the whole guilt trip on her – "If you really love me, you'll have sex with me." – she consented and gave away her virginity to me.

I was not a nice person, and I did not treat her like a gentleman. I eventually lost my job at the bank and started to work cooking hamburgers at a McDonalds – soon after that, she broke up with me. I had dropped out of the accounting course, and we were no longer meeting up once a week at the classes. She had begged me to find a better job than cooking hamburgers – that was no job for a person who passed out of high school with reasonably good marks. However, I did not do what she begged me to try – to get some self-esteem. Although I was never sure of the real reason, she broke up with me. Perhaps she realized that she could do better in life and find someone with a higher standing. If I was not willing to take up the challenge of finding a well-paid job and a successful career, maybe she was not going to hang around waiting for me to find my self-esteem or find the job, of which she knew I was capable. I was unhappy. It broke my heart that she broke up with me and left – and sadly, I returned to the arms of the prostitutes.

Chapter 11

Working at McDonalds

I applied for a job at McDonalds when the bank had sacked me. I essentially was applying for all sorts of jobs when I was out of work, because unemployment benefits were not as exciting as getting the bank wage and certainly did not help me with my addiction of prostitutes. Having a low income did not help me.

I applied to several jobs, and I got a job at McDonalds, working as a crew member – essentially working at the back of McDonalds, cooking the hamburgers. It took me a while to learn how to do everything in the back area, but once I had learned, I was soon promoted to being in charge of the back area. Although I was not the manager, I was in charge of the duties of the back area and in charge of the staff, and I enjoyed being in charge and the responsibility.

I used to open the shop. I used to go to the back area and heat the oil and put it through a filter. I would remove all the crumbs from the cooking oils so it would last longer, because the crumbs would not burn in the fat, making it lose its quality. So I used to filter the oil. I used to restock all the meat needed, and all the buns needed, and all the salad needed, for the hamburgers. I used to turn on the grills, and heat them for half an hour, before the store opened.

I did various things, including doing the stock take, and the responsibility of opening up the shop on Monday to Friday. I enjoyed McDonalds, because there were clear training videos on how to do things, and there was a systematic guide for every job. You not only had a step-by-step guide to do the job, but when you started the job, you had someone doing it in front of you and showing you systematically how to do it, and then standing there watching you, and correcting you as you did the job.

I so loved that job, because I could become perfect at doing my job. I could become proficient, perfect, and fast at doing my job. That gave me self-esteem. It made me feel like I was a bit of a winner, although I felt I was a failure. At school, I did not get good grades – I was a failure in relationships, as all my girlfriends left me – I was a failure when it came to the bank, as I had been sacked (or at least told to resign) – but here at McDonalds, I was beginning to feel like a winner.

Before she broke up with me, my girlfriend at the time was begging me to get a better job, but the McDonalds system was so encouraging – the managers were so positive and happy. It was a good environment; I worked with some good people, and I started to enjoy myself. Working out back with me was an older woman (sorry, a more mature woman). She was beautiful herself, but she introduced me to her daughter, and I went out with her daughter on a date.

Her daughter and I did not click, but another guy in the shop went out with her daughter on a date and they clicked, and he became her boyfriend. For a while, I treated him badly as a manager, because he succeeded in making her daughter his girlfriend. I always felt that I was a loser, when it came to attracting women to becoming my girlfriend, and that was the main reason for sleeping with prostitutes.

I was not aware of what was wrong with me, but essentially, McDonalds was making me feel like a hero. I was soon promoted to where I became a crew trainer myself. Regulars staffed the day shift from eight in the morning until four in the afternoon, so there was not much change of staff, whereas young casual workers usually staffed the night shift from four in the afternoon until eleven at night.

Often, I was asked to stay on and do a double shift, when one of the workers failed to turn up or rang in sick, and because on the night shift, there would always be a new worker, I would be asked to train the new recruit on how to do the job. I enjoyed training people, showing them how to do their job, watching them, and helping them until they were proficient. I enjoyed this work, and I became a good crew trainer.

Eventually, I came to the notice of the training manager of the store, who had the responsibility of training everyone in the store. Although this was only one store in the whole McDonald’s chain, it had between 120 and 200 people working in the store, with between five and ten new people starting every week – staff was continuously changing so training was also a continuous task.

McDonalds were big on having a correct way of doing every one of their jobs – even the lowly French fries were subjected to a complete set of procedures – it might not sound very appetizing to a customer, as he chomps on his chips, but there is a correct way to shake the fries, before they are placed into the box – brings a whole new meaning when the waitress asks, “Do you want fries with that?” Whatever task you had at McDonalds, no matter how small, you went through a series of three tests to ensure that you were proficient at that task. First, they would test you openly during a quiet period, and then they would up the pace and openly test you again during a busy period. Finally, they would test you during a busy time, without letting you know.

It was important to everyone to pass as many tests as possible, because there was plenty of competition – as you became more successful, you were scheduled for more hours, which meant you earned more money.

As a crew trainer, I was responsible for carrying out all these tests on the staff, but once I came to the attention of the training manager, he started to get me involved in other types of training, and I became an important (and very busy) person. One area I became involved in was the weekly unloading of the truck delivering goods to McDonalds. In Australia, the wholesaler for McDonalds was called FJ Walkers – I am not sure if they were confined to just Australia – but they would collect all of McDonalds’ requirements, warehouse them, and then distribute to the individual stores on a weekly basis to replenish their stock.

Once, all the truck drivers went on strike, and all the McDonalds' stores suffered. So it was decided to stock each store with two weeks' worth of stock, at any one time, just in case the truckers went on strike again. McDonalds is the biggest food franchise in the world, and it did not get there by selling five Big Macs per day, so there was an enormous amount of food delivered regularly.

While I was busy supervising and helping with the unloading of the boxes into the cool room, I became friends with one of the regular tuckers and began to chat with him. One day he was sharing with me that he had fought in Vietnam, and he became emotional about having to shoot a Vietnamese soldier three times – "If he had just laid still, I wouldn't have shot him, but he kept on trying to get his gun, and I had to protect myself, and so I had to shoot him again."

He said that incident just replayed repeatedly in his dreams at night. It caused him a great deal of trouble, and because of this, he had struggled with heroin addiction for many years.

When I was setting up the store in the mornings, often Jim, the store owner, would be around, and he liked to talk to me. By that time, I had become proficient at setting up the store, so it only took me about an hour to get everything ready, so he would call me into his office to have a chat. On the wall of his office, he had large photographs of various racing horses. He pointed out the horses that he owned, and which had won major races.

One of his horses had come third in the Golden Slipper, a feature race for two-year-old fillies and mares, and the richest race on the Australian calendar for young horses. He later sold the horse for a few million dollars, and it went on to become a stud breeding horse. His fascination for his horses soon became a fascination to me, and shortly I was visiting legal gambling places to gamble on horse races – and that addiction with gambling was to stay with me for many years.

While I was at McDonalds, we had an annual award ceremony, and we would all go out to dinner. The store would run with skeleton staff, because most of the crew and the managers went to the awards. One year, my mother came down for the awards, and it touched my heart that my mother would travel six-hundred kilometers, and come to stay in Sydney for a couple of days, just to attend the awards ceremony.

At the awards ceremony, I received the award for being the best person to set up the McDonalds store in the morning. As I was responsible for setting up on Monday to Friday, while several other crew were looking after Saturdays and Sundays, this was extremely encouraging, because I was up against maybe twenty or thirty other boys. As I mentioned before, McDonalds were hot on testing and rating peoples' abilities, so this recognition made me feel good.

This was to stand me in good stead, when, years later, I applied for a job at McDonalds to become a manager. I put Jim as one of my references and, when the interviewer rang him, Jim said, "Don't let him out of your presence, until you've offered him the job. He was one of my best crew I've ever had. He never had the self-esteem to apply to be a manager, and if he's in there applying to be a manager, you've got one of the best people I've ever met in your store." The guy hung up the phone and said, "You're hired," and I said, "Why? Why haven't you interviewed everyone?" He told me what Jim had said about me, so I was especially good.

Why were things so hard for me at the bank? Maybe my personality needed clear directions on how to do something. If I am told how to do something, and I can understand the directions, then I will ensure that I become good at what I do. The McDonalds' system made me shine, and that made me very happy.

I reached a stage at McDonalds where I was intending to become a manager, but no manager jobs were available. I decided to look for other jobs, and I took a public service examination. If I could achieve good grades in the examination, I would be accepted in the government public service – I passed, and I was accepted to become part of the public service.

When I left McDonalds, Jim offered me another job with higher pay, as he wanted to keep me – but I turned the offer down, saying I was going to work in the government – but he was sad to see me go. In my career, I have worked with three McDonalds' owners – each of them was a multimillionaire, yet they all treated me like a son. They had a special relationship with me that went beyond my being a worker – they loved me.

When I left McDonalds, I was sad but very inspired. Today, many people are ready to bad mouth McDonalds, because of their junk food image, but I will always be quick to offer a counter argument – at McDonalds, I learned how to manage staff, to train staff and to do a job with excellence. Since my time there, I have rarely found a job since, where it has been so enjoyable to work, and with a standard of success and excellence that can be measured against others. The McDonalds experience gave me plenty of experience when it came to training and managing staff in the future.

Chapter 12

Visiting Brothels in Sydney

So, why is a Christian guy like me talking about visiting brothels? Well, it is all part of my story; this addiction in my story does form a large part of my life. What I thought was an unbreakable addiction lasted for many years, so the prostitute part of my story played a large part in my life and features in many more chapters of this book.

I do not share these details to encourage people to visit prostitutes or to lead that sinful lifestyle, but I share this for those who actually suffer from this addiction, so you can be encouraged to overcome that addiction. I share my story with women, so they can understand what sort of man sleeps with a prostitute and to give encouragement that this addiction is not terminal – there is light at the end of the tunnel. Of course, you can skip on to other chapters, but I encourage you to bear with me.

I soon learned that the prostitutes in Kings Cross were not the only prostitutes in Sydney. One day, I discovered advertisements in the popular newspapers, mostly from brothels, offering the services of prostitutes. The strip club in Kings Cross was also a brothel, but nearly all the girls in Kings Cross were addicted to heroin and were not of the highest quality. I do not use the word "quality" in a derogatory sense, and I am not trying to suggest or offend any prostitute by saying that they are of a lower-grade, because they are addicted to heroin. I am getting myself into trouble here – a classic case of "foot-in-the-mouth syndrome – the taste of my own shoe leather is not very palatable. Let me explain by saying that when a guy is looking for the girl-next-door type to make his wife, or to have a serious relationship with, he looks for the best qualities in a girl – and one of them is not being addicted to drugs. When I discovered the advertisements in the paper, I went to check the one closest to my workplace. The first thing I noticed was that the prices were substantially higher than those in the brothels and strip clubs in Kings Cross.

I also found that when you first arrived, you were asked to sit in a waiting room, where all the available girls would come and present themselves to you. You had to remember the name of the girl you liked, and then you would tell the woman in charge that you wanted to go with that girl. To understand the mind of a sex addict, which I was for many years, I can tell you that a particular adrenaline fired up within me, whenever I approached a brothel – brought on by the idea that between ten and twenty girls were going to parade before me – all dressed, manicured and made up to look and smell their best. I was going to be in a room with a parade of beautiful women right before my eyes.

Of course a disgusting thing about this was that no matter how sweet they smelled, and how pretty they looked, many of them had been with another man just before you came in. It takes a pretty sick individual to have sex with a woman who has just come out of a shower, and changed from seeing another client, just before she sees you.

And no matter how pretty the girls are, you can never come to grips with the fact that "normal" guys have girlfriends that they have sexual relations with, and only losers, like you, have to pay for sex

Particular brothels specialize in Asian women, while others concentrate only on Australian women. Some might specialize by having a mixture of girls from several races, and others by having a selection of younger girls. Brothels come in all shapes, sizes, and specialties. However, as a rule of thumb, during the daytime, the women are slightly older than the women during the nighttime – no statistical evidence or reasons, that is just the way it is.

One other thing I discovered was that you had to book one of the girls for half an hour and no less. If you have never visited a prostitute, I am not saying this to encourage you – although there is no way of saying it without encouraging somebody – I am trying to impress upon you the pain that this addiction caused in my life – but I have to say that many prostitutes that I have met have been very easy to talk to, very warm and understanding. They are girls, with whom you would have no trouble going out for coffee, and not get bored by someone who cannot hold a conversation. Prostitutes are very versed, and well trained to bring a man out of himself, to make a man feel at ease, and make him feel accepted. Something like 50% of prostitutes have clients that are married men or are already in a relationship.

For this to happen, not only is that man a bit of a sex addict, but also there is often something lacking in that man's relationships. The statistics will tell you that many men visiting prostitutes are already in a relationship. For the wives and girlfriends, it is highly possible that even your partner is visiting a prostitute – I am not saying this to scare you in any way – it surprised me more than it might surprise you.

These girls are well versed in talking, and I was to discover later what happened to me on the beach earlier in my life was called sexual abuse, and I was not responsible (or entirely responsible) for what happened.

Although I felt guilty, ashamed, and that it was my fault, essentially it was not my fault. I was too young to be responsible for what happened, and the person who performed sexual favors with me on the beach was essentially breaking the law with a minor, and was taking advantage of my situation and me. I also discovered, later in life, statistics show that 92% of prostitutes have been sexually molested abused by a father, a stepfather, or some man in their life when they were young.

I think we are talking here of some form of chemical reaction. There was chemistry with many of these prostitutes, and I enjoyed sex with them – I do not want to glorify it, but there was a total rush of adrenaline when I picked a stunning girl and took her to bed. People often wonder why I am not so desperate to have a woman in my life, and I often wondered why I did not want to remarry. It is just that when it comes to sex, I was oversexed.

I had slept with so many pretty girls that prettiness was not the deciding factor, when I was looking for a girl. Girls were marvelous to talk to and, added to that the fact we had both been abused when we were younger, created chemistry – we had something in common with each other. I would like to have sex with a girl, and then to just lay on the bed and talk to the girl. I would ask her all sorts of questions. I would ask girls why they had become prostitutes, and many of them said it was because they enjoyed sex – and I believed them.

My problem has always been that I have been an honest person – if you have been watching the video series or reading the book, you will have realized there is nothing I have held back when sharing. I am honest, and because of that, I believe others when they say they are telling the truth.

I am very gullible and innocent when it comes to believing others; I am like a child – I just believe what I am told. For many years, I believed that many prostitutes just enjoyed having sex, and that is why they did it. Another plausible answer that they often gave me was that they enjoyed the money they were earning from prostitution. An amazing statement, but certainly plausible – today, a high-class brothel in Australia costs $230 for half an hour.

I receive $500 every two weeks on my pension, so even on my government pension, I could still afford to sleep with one of those girls, once a month, if I wanted. The girl receives half – $125 for half an hour – a good rate of pay, if you work half an hour, every hour. It is certainly believable that many of them do it for money. There are even higher-class prostitutes, who earn more than that, but we will get into that another time.

Many prostitutes, who do not have a heroin addiction, or buy thousands of dollars' worth of clothes every week, can pay off houses and real estate with this job. I am a funny guy, because I just believe anything – yup, I am gullible. When I asked them what they did for fun, many of them replied honestly that they liked to go shopping.

Some of them said they enjoyed particular sports, while others liked going to the movies or reading books. I especially liked the ones who went to the movies or read books, because I was a reader, and I liked to go to the movies every week. Then, I would ask them about their favorite actors, and their favorite movies – and before long, the half an hour was finished.

I would ask the girls all sorts of questions. I really loved how comfortable they were with their nakedness. In years to come, I would go with other girls, who were not prostitutes, and I found many of them were uncomfortable walking around the house naked and covered themselves up – but prostitutes mainly are comfortable with their sexuality, comfortable with their bodies.

However, I noticed sometimes when you paid for half an hour in a brothel, a girl would be rushing you into the shower after fifteen minutes and pushing you out the door in twenty minutes.

I did not like that. I had paid for half an hour, and because I was a selfish person, I considered it rude to be dismissed ten minutes short of my half an hour. If that happened to me more than once in a particular brothel, I would just move on to another brothel.

I could visit a new brothel in Sydney every week, and it would have taken me a long time before I would have exhausted all the brothels in Sydney – but even then, you could always go back, and meet the girls again. However, if a brothel or the girls were pushing me out of the door within fifteen or twenty minutes, I would move on to another brothel where they respected my half an hour. For many years, I never saw the same girl twice.

I have never had much opportunity to talk to men who were addicted to prostitutes, or spend a lot of time with prostitutes to confirm or deny whether I am different from others. However, I liked my variety, and I liked the adrenaline rush of sleeping with a new girl every time.

I never tired of sex, and it seemed as though I had an inexhaustible sex drive, and I continued to go from brothel to brothel meeting different girls, talking to different girls, and sleeping with different girls. I went on to discover there were prostitutes who were even more expensive than those found in brothels – escorts – but this discovery only resulted in my expenditure on prostitution doubling.

I have mentioned it before – and I will no doubt mention it again (maybe you can call it an official disclaimer) – in this book, and the associated video series, I am in no way attempting to glorify my addiction to prostitutes by saying it is a good thing. Any man who visits a prostitute is sexually abusing that prostitute as a person. He is not loving her or respecting her as a person, but is merely being a jerk to her, to himself, and, above all, to God.

It was not until I realized that that I could free myself from my addiction to prostitutes – although that freedom would take many years to come – and my life could be filled with true joy. Stay with the videos, or read to the end of this book, and you will see how I achieved that breaking away from the addiction, and how the power of God was used in my life.

Chapter 13

My Government Job

In an earlier chapter, I mentioned that while working at McDonalds, I took and passed a government's service examination – not an easy examination, but I had answered the questions to the best of my ability.

Within a month of passing, I was called for an interview, and I was offered a job at Telecom, a government-owned enterprise in charge of telecommunications. Back in the 80s, all the phones in the Australia were installed by Telecom – they had the monopoly on phone services, so if you did not like Telecom's prices, you had to go without a phone. In spite of rampant inflation, it is now much cheaper to make an overseas call than it was thirty years ago – one small step for competition, but a giant stride for humanity.

I went on a training and orientation course with Telecom, and I began to notice that in our small group of ten trainees, I was the one who seemed to talk the most. When the instructor asked questions, I was always the first to try to answer the question – I was also the first to ask questions, and I seemed to have plenty of those. Between the two – answering and asking questions – I was speaking a tremendous amount.

Part of the introduction to the course was a round-robin session, where we introduced ourselves and spoke a little about ourselves. One guy said he was unique, because he came from a family with eleven children, which I thought was amusing. When he had finished, I said I only knew of one family that had 11 children, and it belonged to an awful doctor out west in Toongabie – I stopped going to see him because he had a terrible bedside manner. I asked him, "Where do you live?" and he replied, "Toongabie." I asked him, "Is your father a doctor?" and he replied, "Yes, you're talking about my father." That was so embarrassing – my normal rosy hue changed to that of a ripe beetroot, before I could blink my eyes. It was not the first time (or the last time) in my life, where my talking before thinking was going to get me in trouble. The age-old principle of "engaging brain before opening mouth" was appropriate, and much of the Book of Proverbs is highly relevant in this regard.

I was transferred to the payroll section of the local networking engineering department of Telecom – and if anyone knows the Telecom, we were responsible for paying the guys who were digging up roads, laying the communications lines, and filling the holes in the road (occasionally).

My boss was a woman, who always looked out for me, joked with me, and was very patient and kind to me. My workplace had about five staff, who were all friendly to me. Up until this time, I had grown up with a speech difficulty (or maybe it was just laziness), but I had a habit of saying my name as "Maffew" and counting as in "one, two, free" – I had a problem with the letters "t" and "h", especially when they were close together. I became friendly with another boss, in a nearby office, who encouraged me by saying, "You can change it. You just need to concentrate and try to change it each time you use those words." Her encouragement made me believe that I could do it, and I managed to change –now I say my name properly, and nobody thinks that I am simple anymore.

Soon I was promoted – with an increase in pay – to a vacant post in the office, where I was responsible for calculating the amount of overtime to be paid, and completing the necessary forms accurately, so they could be keyed in by the computer operators. My work was always checked, of course, and I always managed to keep the checkers busy with my mistakes. In the three years I worked for Telecom, I never managed to overcome the problem of making mistakes. Although I did not feel that I was particularly good at the job, because of all the mistakes, and I was transferred to various departments as a payroll clerk, I was never laid off or sacked. I have heard that it is almost impossible to be sacked from a government job – apparently, it was true.

The guys working in our section often had to go on workers' compensation, because they had hurt their backs or legs while working – out of a thousand staff in the section, we had about seventy or eighty active workers' compensation claims. Telecom did not use an insurance company to pay insurance or workers' compensation to people – they were their own insurance agency, and they paid their own compensation.

I became somewhat of an expert on workers' compensation, although there was a large number of forms that needed to be completed – doctors' certificates, accident reports, supervisors' reports, and so on – and they were all necessary, before anyone could be paid by Telecom. This was frustrating for the men who still had to pay their doctors' bills, while they were still waiting for their workers' compensation claims to be processed.

I managed to find a way of streamlining the complete process, and I finished by going out to the workforce to teach the supervisors about the necessary documentation and how to complete them. Unless the complete batch of documents was submitted at the same time, there was going to be a delay in processing the workers' compensation – at the time I started, the average time before a doctor was paid was about six months after the person had been to the doctor. After training the supervisors, and explaining the process to the workers, this payment delay was reduced to twenty-one days – not bad, even if I say so myself.

I started to move all over Sydney with this job, and eventually moved out west to a place called Penrith, where I moved in with an old friend of the family from Coffs Harbour, who I had grown up with. I also managed to find a second job working part-time at McDonalds at nights over the weekends. Unlike my two previous jobs at McDonalds, where I worked in the back area as a cook and a crew trainer, here at Penrith, I was given the opportunity to go out front and serve customers in the drive-through area.

It was not until I started to serve customers that I fully realized how important the back area was to ensure there was enough food to serve all the customers. There is plenty of pressure on the people serving, especially when the food is not ready for the customers. Nowadays, the system has changed slightly, and McDonalds has become extremely efficient.

Penrith had a water-ski park with a square lake, where skiers were pulled around by a machine running on lines for about a kilometer around the water. In the summer, the park was open until 10 in the evening, so I spent a lot of time (and money) on the water and became proficient at water-skiing, especially on one ski, which I preferred to two skis. I remember once carrying out a very tight turn close to a line of people waiting to ski – it was so tight, and I had to lean over so much, that my ear was almost scraping the water – the spray from the ski was so huge that it covered the people waiting in line, and a few others, whose original intention was to remain dry for the whole evening. It is remarkable, when you are going through difficult times, how you hold on to small memories such as these.

My flat-mate at the time, Terry, was the DJ at an "over 25s" disco at the Penrith Leagues Club, and I would go there to keep him company and to dance with the girls. I was only about 20, and they did not seem to mind dancing with a younger guy, although everyone else that came to the club had to be 25 or over and had to show identification. I was fit in those days, so I used to dance a lot with the girls, and over time, I managed to build up a group of "regulars" with whom I danced a lot – I could have danced all night (where have I heard that before?).

There was a side room at the club, and from time to time, I would take some of the girls there for a kiss, and maybe later, I might take them home. Once I had a relationship for about three months with a woman there, who had a couple of children. It was a purely selfish relationship, as it was based on sex and my needs, and I do not think I was being entirely responsible. I think she was looking for someone who would make a good partner for her, and I do not think I was prepared to become a ready-made father. My mother also assumed that I was not just kissing this girl as a friend, but I was actually having sex with her. My mother said that a woman with children only wants one thing – she has needs and desires, and she certainly knows what sex is, so sex would obviously be part of the relationship. My mother was on my case, and I began to feel slightly guilty about having sex outside marriage, but as I had an addiction to prostitutes, I managed to keep my conscience from condemning me… too much.

With my job at Telecom, and my part-time job at McDonalds, I was earning about $27,000 a year, and I began to start thinking of saving money. It is reprehensible that you can reach a stage where you try to use extraneous excuses to continue an addiction, when your conscience has become immune to how wrong the addiction is. Around this time, I started visiting places in Penrith where I could receive a "dirty massage" – a massage with a sexual act at the end. This suited my budget better, as it only cost half the price of going to a prostitute. I was still able to talk to the girls, and although less than half of them knew anything about giving a massage, I began to enjoy receiving a massage. When I eventually became married in the future, I would enjoy receiving a massage from my wife, and I certainly enjoyed giving massages to my wife as well.

Whilst I was in Penrith, I enrolled for one night a week in a cooking class specializing in several cuisines, and the first semester started with Chinese and Asian food. I tried cooking some of the dishes at home, and I must have been good at it, as my flat mate always seemed to enjoy them. At the classes, I met an attractive girl, and we seemed to hit it off well. I was certainly attracted to her, and eventually I gathered up enough courage to ask her out, to be my girlfriend. She turned me down, saying she was not an exclusive girl and just did not go out with one man. However, she surprised me when she said she had three guys in her life, with whom she slept, and she would be willing for me to become one of the guys, but she would not be exclusive for any of us. I was used to having sex with prostitutes, so I did not have an issue with her having other men in her life – I was not jealous. Of course, I wanted to be part of that situation. Any red-blooded guys, regardless of their faith level, wants a relationship to lead to sex, and in that regard, I was no different from anyone else. We often used to travel on the train together to work.

Once, she came to my workplace to visit me, but I was on a training course in the city for a week. The guys at work said that I had gone – they did not say I was on a training course; they just said, “Matthew isn’t here. He’s gone.” She must have got the impression that I was not working there anymore, and she never came back. I never saw her again. After that, I felt rejected, sad, and I felt let down – and like many others, when we get let down, we blame God. I felt God had let me down, because she was a pleasant girl and could have been my girlfriend – at least I could have been part of the group. This drove me back to a local brothel.

Around that time, I had managed to save $2500. With the extra cash from the second job, I could now start to save money, and I began to consider buying a house – all I needed was a $50,000 loan with maybe a deposit of $9,000. I asked my father for a bridging loan of the $6,000 for the bridging loan, which I would pay back to my father, while at the same time repaying the loan to the bank for my house. My father refused me, saying that I had not proved to him that I was a regular saver, and he could not take the risk that I might not pay him back. This caused me to be angry and upset with my father for many years, as I felt that he had been kinder to the other children, and he had let me down.

In hindsight, I have forgiven him, and I have come to terms with not having a house like my brothers and sisters, but at the time, it really upset me, because I thought I had missed a wonderful opportunity. Satan has a way of reminding you of lost opportunities, and he likes you to focus the blame somewhere. While I was being overly concerned with borrowing $50,000 and going into debt, the owner of McDonalds, one day, took my breath away, when he showed me his bank statement reflecting that he had more than a million dollars’ worth of debt. He said, “You just got to learn to manage debt. You can’t really achieve any big success in life, unless you borrow money from others.”

My flat mate and I liked to go to movies once a week, taking turns to pay for the drinks and popcorn. It was a form of escapism to a place where I could feel better about myself, and it developed into a habit, where even today, I still enjoy a weekly visit to the movies. Then, my favorite movies were true-life dramas, fictional dramas, thrillers, action movies, and comedy. This has not changed much over the years, although I have now elevated "chick flicks" to third spot, after true and fictional dramas. Everyone loves "chick flicks", especially the girls, and even today good friends accompany me to the movies.

I had my 21st birthday in Penrith as well, and all my family turned up – we all went water-skiing in the night – it was a beautiful night, and we had an exciting time, and it was to be one of the good memories in my life.

As I mentioned before, even when you are suffering, you always remember the good times, and they keep you happy. My flat mate had been offered a job with a radio station in the city, and he asked me whether I would like to move with him to the northern beaches of Sydney and live in an apartment there. The northern beaches of Sydney were almost two hours away from Penrith, and it would mean I would have to give up my job at McDonalds there. However, I decided to move with him, and start a new chapter in my life.

Chapter 14

My Experience with Sydney Escorts

We moved to the northern beaches of Sydney, to a very picturesque suburb called Dee Why. Although I had grown up surfing on the beach in Coffs Harbour, I only managed to go surfing twice in Dee Why. With the move, my second income from McDonalds had stopped, so I was taking a big drop in money, as I was only earning an income from Telecom now. While I was living in Dee Why, I glanced through the Yellow Pages and found an escort agency that operated nearby. I rang them up and inquired about the girls.

First, I inquired about the price to hire a girl and found out that you cannot book a girl for half an hour, only for an hour, which automatically doubled the price that I was used to paying for prostitutes – but the quality of the girls, and the quality of the escort agency, demanded that it was more than double what a brothel would charge. It was going to be expensive – I do not remember how much I paid for a prostitute in those days, but I discovered it was more than half my weekly income to hire an escort.

It was not a major problem, as I had food in the fridge, I had already paid for my weekly bus ticket, and the rent and bills had been settled. I had money in the bank, so I could afford it, but it caused me to swallow hard. I asked the woman about the girls, and first, she asked me what sort of girl I was looking for, did I have a preference in hair color, what age would I prefer? I told her that I preferred brunettes of about 18 to 20 years old. She went through the list of girls who were available for that night, and I finally picked one. I would have to wait about 40 minutes for the girl to arrive, so I decided to spend that time cleaning up my room and making it presentable.

A prostitute had never visited my house before – I had always visited a brothel before. One needs to be presentable and have a clean house, unless you want to be embarrassed and show how messy you are. I was nervous and had a knot in my stomach, but the adrenaline was pumping, and there was a sense of excitement about going into the unknown. The price for the girl was substantial; I was going to meet her unseen – something I had never done before – and it made me nervous.

She soon arrived, and we chatted for about five minutes over a fruit juice; then, she asked me to lead her to the bedroom. Although she had everything timed to the second, it was different for me to have a girl in bed for an hour, rather than half an hour, and I found it extremely enjoyable. Within a day of my next payday, I was on the phone again to the escort agency. This grew into a habit for me to ring escorts regularly – and it was to become an expensive habit for me.

Although this habit seemed enjoyable to me, I have to tell you that this lifestyle was in fact a life from Satan. It was not the answer to my inner loneliness – nor was it a quick fix for my broken state. It was a life from Satan, and it was a trap from Satan. The girls acted as though they were enjoying themselves and were fun to talk to, but, in fact, I was sexually abusing them. I was abusing them spiritually, emotionally, and sexually.

I thought I was treating them right. I thought I was a fun customer. I really thought that I was doing them no harm. That is what I thought – that is how you justify things when you are doing something wrong. These girls were someone's precious daughter, and they were born for better things than having strange, ugly men on top of them and having sex with them. No girl chooses to be a prostitute, when she is young.

When two girls have their little pretend tea parties when children, they do not talk about their future and their desire to become a prostitute. No girl decides to be a prostitute or an escort, just on a whim. A lot of thought goes into this decision, and sometimes, desperate situations drive a girl into prostitution.

Most girls who work in prostitution have, at one time or another, been sexually abused. One statistic states that 92% of prostitutes have been raped or sexually molested in their past. I am not sure whether this figure was based on streetwalkers in United States, or if it included escorts, but I do know that many prostitutes have been interfered with when they were young. Many of them also suffer from drug addiction or are in desperate situations where they need money.

Through the escort agency, over the next year, I was to meet many girls studying at a university, who were using prostitution to pay their way through university – to pay their university fees, rent, food, and a way to survive. It was impossible to tell, from their looks, that these girls were not the typical girl next door. In fact, many of them could, if they had the choice or opportunity, have been models. Modeling is very overrated, as it is a difficult, time consuming and somewhat boring occupation. I think that people overrate models. Modeling is a very hard job, and very time consuming, and somewhat boring doing the same thing all the time. However, the escort agency I used was able to send remarkably attractive girls to my place. Many girls just did it for the money, and I do not want you to get the opinion that women have to be sexually molested before they become a prostitute.

Women today have more control over their sexuality and over themselves – they have more liberty and freedom within themselves to make choices, and they are a lot stronger and have more willpower. Therefore, there can be many reasons that girls choose to go into the escort business these days. The girls were always attractive, and I never managed to have the same girl twice. I liked my variety – and "variety is the spice of life" – but this spoke to something much deeper.

I enjoyed meeting people – I am a people person. I love meeting strangers, talking with them about their lives and interests, and drawing people out of themselves. Later in life, I was to become a taxi driver, which turned out to be an ideal job for me, as it allowed me to meet and talk to strangers continually. However, one day I was at home, when I received a phone call from the escort agency. They had never rung before, so it was a shock to hear them on the phone. They asked me whether it was convenient for me to talk. It was convenient, but I was wondering what I had done wrong. She told me that I was a good client, and that I had consistently received good feedback from each of the girls over the last few months that I had been using their services.

She went on to say that, although they have a large number of girls working for them, there is a need for the agency to continually provide new girls, who had never been in the business before, had come to their doors, were being interviewed, and accepted. The agency had found that the new girls were nervous about going out on their first escort job, so they were looking for new men – responsible men and clients – who would be the first man the prostitutes were sent to. She asked me whether I would consider being one of the men she used essentially to "break in" these prostitutes to give them their first experience of prostitution.

My heart was racing, and I was very excited. From my time in Kings Cross, I knew that the bouncers and their friends (and even members of law enforcement agencies) were used to "break in" the girls. My heart was racing that this woman would even consider me to sleep with a girl that had never slept with a client before. I said it would be fine, and I would be pleased to do that for her. She asked if I wanted a girl tonight, explaining that she had two new girls starting tonight, and only one guy who was happy to see either girl, and could I possibly act as a stand-in tonight. I was somewhat taken back, but I asked her to describe the two girls. She said they were both blondes – would that be a problem? I said that would not be a problem, made my choice, and waited for the girl to arrive.

Forty minutes later, the girl arrived. I was nervous. After welcoming her with a drink of fruit juice, we went into the bedroom, where the girl was wondering what to do. I was essentially there to put her at ease, show her what to do, and what I liked and enjoyed as a client – and she did exactly as I explained to her. It was an experience, which was to become addictive for me.

I began to spend a lot more money on the services of the escort agency. It is difficult to explain that I was no longer sleeping with prostitutes – I was sleeping with girls to give them their first-time experience of sex with a client. Many men might consider this to be a privileged position and wish they could get into such a position with an escort agency or brothel for themselves.

I want to tell you the truth about it. Satan had me in an ultimate noose. He had me eating breakfast cereal for over a week, or closer to two weeks at a time. Sometimes I would order a girl almost weekly, and this would leave me with no money for food. I had to take my food money to pay for the services – I just ate cereal and the cheapest form I could find – in Australia, it is called Weet-Bix and it is … cheap. The most expensive part is the milk – and if you mix that with water, you can live very cheaply. It is not good for your system, and it is not good for your health.

Satan had me in a real bind, spending all my money. A strong sense of shame came on me. As a Christian, I knew I was doing the wrong thing, and I was always feeling bad, but I continued without stopping.

There seemed to be no repentance in me, because I did not feel as though I wanted to stop anytime soon. I would feel bad, but then Satan would switch tactics and convince me that I was a good client, I was being kind to the girls, and it was good that girls were being sent to me, rather than some jerk, for their first client. According to Satan, I was doing good, compared with all the others – and sometimes we listen to his lies. In truth, I was just as bad as the guys in Kings Cross, who used their privileged positions to abuse the girls and lead them into a life of prostitution. I was conspiring with the agency, and I was sexually exploiting these girls.

Years later, when I stopped visiting prostitutes, I realized that the decisions we make in life could be very harmful to others. The world today is becoming dark and out of control, because we are moving further and further away from the things of the Bible. Many people might be angry with me, because of what I have disclosed.

Many people will see that I was despicable in my actions, and they would not be wrong in their judgment of me. The difference between many people and me is that I have hidden nothing in this. At one stage, I even considered watering down the details of my experiences with sex workers, as I did not want to encourage men to go ahead along similar lines.

In no way do I want people to become encouraged and see prostitution as a great way of living. I know some men might be tempted to do that, but that is up to them, and it is their free choice to do so. However, like the Bible, my account is honest about the good things and the bad things I have done in my life. I am not writing to brag about my sins – I am trying to be as brutally honest as I can.

I was enjoying myself with these girls, but I was abusing them at the same time. I was having sex with hundreds of girls, but I could only afford to eat breakfast cereal – I could not even afford to make sandwiches for lunch. I lived an immense lie in my life. I was terribly dishonest. For a person who is honest, it is hard to live a lie. I was not even aware that my mother knew I had an addiction – she had worked out that if it was not gambling, then I must have had an addiction to sex.

Yet, through all my shameful life and all my sin, Jesus has always been with me. Many Christians would believe that if I could continue to sin so blatantly with my life, then I was never a Christian to start with. Maybe you are even thinking, "No, Matthew was not saved and he was destined for hell." I choose to believe that Jesus was telling the truth when He said, "I'll never leave you or forsake you," – that no matter what you got up to, He would never leave you. Although I was not going to church out of guilt and shame, I could still feel Jesus there at my side. Whenever I talked to Jesus at night, sometimes He would talk to me and show me His presence.

I was essentially living in a pigpen feeding the pigs, just as in the parable of the prodigal son. God was allowing me to earn all this money, which I wasted selfishly and stupidly. I was a typical addict.

I had all sorts of ideas that I was a good person, and I was not hurting anyone. After all, the girls had not been sex trafficked, and they were doing it freely by choice.

I justified myself by saying I was paying for it, and I was a nice client – even the escort agency agreed that I had excellent feedback. However, the truth was that I was a broken shell of a man, who simply could not get a girlfriend or a responsible hold on my desperate loneliness.

I was abusing girls and introducing them to a life of prostitution, which may keep them in chains for many years, until they are too old to practice the life anymore. Each client of a prostitute is hard for her to forget. I have discussed this with many prostitutes over the years to come, and they find each client is … just another nail in the coffin – they just become hardened to men. The problem with us humans is that we are all so good at justifying our sins.

Many people might consider that they do not even sin, and they are essentially good people – we are so good at making excuses for ourselves. Satan, on one hand, makes us feel ashamed, and worthless as a Christian, for what we do in our life, and then on the other hand, he then shows us others apparently worse than ourselves, so we think more of ourselves than we should.

The truth is that we are all lost, and all of us need to discover the truth, and need to be set free of the chains that bind us. All of us need a glimpse of the potential God has given us and need to die to the desires of the enemy and sinful flesh.

In the Bible, Joseph had a dream that his brothers and his father would bow down to him. However, when his brothers heard this, they decided to kill him – fortunately one of the brothers managed to change their minds, and they sold him into slavery instead. Joseph was bought as a slave by Potiphar.

Potiphar promoted him to become head of his household and to manage his affairs. Later, Potiphar's wife found Joseph attractive, tried to seduce him, and asked him to have sex with her. He refused, so she ripped his cloak and told the other workers that Joseph had tried to rape her. Joseph was sent to prison, and he was to spend many years in that prison suffering.

Often, we are in a similar prison – we are in chains, and we need to be set free. God has a plan for all our lives, and He wants us free to exercise His plans. It is never God's plan for us to suffer, although He will use it sometimes to teach us a lesson and to make us more effective for His service in the future. Many people in this world are simply doing the best they can with the pain and the brokenness in their life.

> Some people use drugs, some use alcohol, some use stimulants – some even become addicted to Facebook. All of these are cop-outs – to make us feel good and cover up the pain. However, God does not want you to put a Band-Aid on a gaping wound. He does not want you to use stopgap measures to ease your pain. He wants you to heal your heart. He wants to heal your heart. He wants to break the chains that bind you. He wants to forgive you and take away your secret lie, so you can be a living testimony to the power of God's grace. If you are not a Christian, He wants you to give your life to Him to control, so He can bless you with godly desires to give to mankind, rather than just taking from mankind.

My story is a sad story – it is dark at the moment, but as it is a long story, it may get even darker before we see the light at the end of the tunnel and begin to realize the final destiny.

Chapter 15

Multilevel Marketing

A former housemate contacted me, saying he had a business proposition to share with me. At the time, I wondered what sort of business anyone would possibly want to show me. I was a little suspicious, but I went and saw the business plan – I must admit that I was quite impressed, and I felt sure I could make some money out of this business.

I will not mention the name of the business, but it is a very popular multilevel marketing business, where you own your own business, and have others join you to sell products, and systematically build the business for you. It was an interesting concept, because it showed that you could earn an immediate income, and build it into a business where you could earn a passive income, or royalty income, in the future. What I found interesting was the way the growth of the business depended on introducing others to the business. It was not a "pyramid scheme" in the strict sense, as it concentrated less on direct product selling, and more on the introduction of other people. I showed it to my friends and family, but none of them took me up on my challenge. Typically, I suppose, they were not interested in joining the business. Maybe, they found the name of the business to be off-putting, or the idea of recruiting of others did not seem to be attractive. Jesus spoke of this when He said that a prophet is not accepted in his own hometown and among His own family. It seems that people who know you, judge the idea without seeing it, and they judge it in accordance with how they see you.

They cannot see you doing anything successfully, so they do not even bother to look at the business. However, I soon found a friend, who was a McDonald's manager and was already involved in the business. His name was Darren, and he was remarkably successful in the business, so we managed to build up the business to where he became a direct distributor, and we achieved sales of $16,000 in just one month. Because I did not have many people in the business with me, Darren was doing quite well, and I was learning how to talk to strangers, how to create prospects, and how to convert prospects into viable business plans.

Part of the portfolio of the business was that they had a book of the month program, where one of the leaders would suggest a motivational book to read – one per month. Because of this, I began to pick up a passion for reading and started to read regularly – many people stop reading once they leave school, but I was starting to generate a love for reading.

It is often said that "leaders are readers", and good leaders are always reading about various subjects and growing by learning from others' experiences. I found this to be true, and I wanted to become a leader with what they called a diamond direct distributorship, with six people each bringing in monthly sales of $15,000. This would have meant a passive income of around $150,000 every year, which back in the late 80s was a substantial amount – and this was my goal.

At the larger conferences, I noticed many of the distributors held a chapel service, where they could share their relationship with Jesus with the others. I wanted to build this business, so that I became respected as a diamond distributor, where I would be able to travel around the world and lead people to Jesus. I had found something that I really wanted to do. I took Darren to one of the services, when we were at a conference, even though he was a typical New-Age believer. When we left the service, he said that he could feel a lot of good energy in there – more than likely, he was feeling the presence of the Holy Spirit in the meeting.

While I was doing this business, I never really had much money, as I was still seeing escorts. Although the business was giving me good ideas on how to be successful, and was helping improve my self-esteem, it also proved that no matter what you are doing, you have to heal the inner hurts and wounds in your life, before you can move on. It does not matter how successful you are; there are always wounds, and I was still trying to address those wounds through my continued addiction to prostitutes. However, the business was starting to give me a bad attitude when it came to work, and I found myself getting discouraged with my government job, so eventually, I resigned from Telecom. My father was to say that this was one of the worst decisions of my life, and he was always saddened that I left a government job. He thought it was immature of me to be leaving such a good job. One of the benefits of the multilevel marketing business was that it allowed me to meet a girl who showed that she was interested in me – that is the subject of our next chapter, so let's not jump ahead too quickly.

My involvement in the business lasted for a couple of years, when Jesus told me that He wanted me to quit the business eventually – and this time I listened to Him. So, the next time I was due to sign up for another year in the business, I just let my membership lapse. Many of us think we have to do it our way for Jesus – if we only win the lotto, then we would have the money to go into ministry for ourselves. The truth is that if Jesus wants to raise you in ministry, He will arrange for you to get a good name among people, He will give you the platform, and He will open the doors for you to minister. The business had lasted for a couple years, before Jesus told me it was time to move on. I did not leave the business, because I was not successful, but I discovered later that my successful people had left as well. The person who had sponsored me had left the business, and the person who had sponsored him had left as well. That is not to say that people cannot become successful in a multilevel marketing business – there were months when we had turnovers that seemed successful, but in the end where it matters, we were not successful enough.

Looking back, I am glad that I obeyed Jesus. Now with my articles, videos and books, I am reaching an audience, and I am happy with where I am, and God is happy that I obeyed Him back then

Chapter 16

New Love

When I was part of a multilevel marketing business, it was part of my "duties" to meet the people in my downline (the members you have recruited, or who have joined the program after you did, and whose sales or referrals generate income for you). One day, at one of our meetings, I was introducing myself to the new members of my business, when a pretty girl came up to me and introduced herself as Sharryn. She asked me a few questions about the business, and then she asked whether she could meet me to talk with me privately. I was somewhat shocked by her being so forward, and I reminded her that there were people above her in the business, who were better qualified to explain the business. She insisted, asked for my phone number, and we arranged to meet her following Saturday.

The following Saturday was one of the few occasions I went surfing in the morning, while I was in Sydney. I had gone surfing that morning and had worn myself out, so I went home and climbed into bed. While I was sleeping, I received a phone call from Sharryn. She said, "Where are you? You were meant to be at my place." Suddenly remembering about the meeting, I quickly dressed and went to see her, spending some time with her at her place. I warned her that Jesus had told me that I was going to leave the business, so I was not really the person she should be asking about the business, as I was not feeling positive about it. Anyway, she talked to me and asked me things about the business, and we had a good afternoon together. About a week later, we met again at a nighttime meeting. I had to leave early, as I had a date. As I was about to leave, she said to me, "Are you trying to make me jealous?" and smiled. I was somewhat shocked that she was so forward – shocked, but quietly excited.

I went out on the date that night, but the only thing I had in my mind was this girl, Sharryn. She was about 17, and she was pretty – I was not the only one who thought she was either – but she was a very driven girl. She had what people would call "spunk" about her. She had this 'never say die' attitude, and when she set her mind on something, she would normally achieve it. Obviously, she had set her mind on getting me, and she was going to make sure she got what she wanted. I rang her after the date and went around to her place – we had our first kiss, and it was not long after that I was in the bedroom with her.

I have to say that you need to separate love and lust. Men usually only want one thing, and I do not think I was any different with Sharryn. I think that I was more interested in the sex, than I was in chatting and getting to know her. Although I was a Christian guy, I was not living according to the Christian faith, I was not being faithful to God, and I certainly was not behaving the way a Christian guy should behave. At this stage, many people would have called me a backslidden Christian – a term people like to use about Christians doing things the "world's" way rather than God's way. I do not like the term "backsliding", but according to their definition, I certainly was a backsliding Christian. I think that God has a way for every person, and God gets His way often with certain people.

My mother was praying for me, and many others from my family were praying for me. I think God respects the prayers of the righteous for their loved ones. Over the next month, I only slept at my place about five times, as most of the time, I was at Sharryn's place. I jokingly told her it would be better if we moved in together, as it made no sense to pay for a room in an apartment that I was not using. She turned around and said something that shocked me. She said that she would only move in with me, if I agreed to marry her – and this took me by surprise. There was no precious night out with dinner – no ring – no romance involved – just a blunt statement that I could not move in with her, unless I agreed to be married. I said, "Of course, I'll marry you," and at the time I suppose I meant it, but I thought that it would be a subject that we would have addressed later.

We moved into an apartment with another couple. They seemed okay when we moved in, but shortly afterward, they began to fight each other … a lot. They told us not to worry, as they would have makeup sex which they enjoyed; however, I did not like the couple, and I felt like moving out – we did not live there for long, and within a couple of months, we had moved out. The house where Sharryn's mother was living had caught fire, and Sharryn took off on a plane to help her mother with the house. She came back for a week, then left again, and said that she needed to help her mother again. This time, she took several weeks – maybe six weeks – and I was ringing her often to ask her when she was coming back. It reached a stage where I rang her to say, "Are you coming back? Like, are you going to come back? Don't you care about me?"

It seemed that Sharryn's mother was more important – and that disturbed me, as I was starting to wonder whether Sharryn really cared about me. During one of our conversations in those weeks, Sharryn informed me that her breasts had grown a cup size. Even now, I still do not understand what a cup size means, but she told me they had grown. I said it was exciting news for me, but I was wondered what was going on – whether she was putting on weight.

It took quite a while, but I eventually concluded that we had broken up – it was a painful time for me, as I was frustrated and sad – I even remember asking my father for his opinion on what I should do. At the time, I was in telesales – selling insurance over the phone – and I remember asking one customer for a date, and she agreed. She seemed interested in going on a date, but I rang her back and said, "I'm not sure of whether I still love Sharryn, and it would not fair on you for us to go on a date while I still have feelings for her." I suppose that shows that I do have a good personality – I cared about other people.

I had broken up with Sharryn, but I was not pursuing another girl, although part of me still wishes that I had gone out on that date. The girl seemed to have liked me, and maybe something may have happened. However, I will never know, because I made that phone call, and I was apologetic and honest with her. I was up front with her and told her I had feelings for another girl, and until I was sure about that, I could not continue.

A few weeks after we had broken up, Sharryn rang me to say that she was pregnant, she was going to return to Sydney, and we were going to marry – real breaking news! When she arrived back, I was going through my first depression – the first clinical depression I ever had. I was sure there were demons involved in my depression, because it seemed so dark. We traveled up to Coffs Harbour, four-hundred miles away from Sydney, to see John Pierre at the drug rehabilitation farm I used to visit when younger. John Pierre was gifted in the deliverance ministry and was gifted in casting demons out of people. I wanted to have those demons dealt with, because I believed they were causing my depression. Regardless of where they had come from, I wanted those demons fixed. Sharryn was upset with my decision to go to Coffs Harbour, saying that I thought we both had demons. She was not happy with the decision, but she knew that I would not marry, unless I had been through the process, so she came with us. When we arrived there, John Pierre was not available, so my mother secured another pastor to come around to our place.

Unfortunately, the other pastor did not believe a Christian could have a demon, so essentially he just counseled us and said the best thing for Sharryn would be to become a Christian, and he explained the Gospel to her. She was already a Catholic, but she still gave her life to Jesus. I remember that night at dinner in my parent's house, Sharryn said to my father that she had become a Christian. My father was happy with that, but he was not too happy about the girl who was planning to marry his son, so he just smiled. Later, we visited a Christian couple, Keith and Liz Francis, who advised me not to go ahead with the marriage. When we arrived back in Sydney, after meeting my parents and Keith and Liz Francis, my mother phoned me. She said that I should keep Sharryn as a girlfriend, until after the child was born, and I should maintain a moral bond with her to see whether our relationship grew stronger. My parents were extremely worried, because Sharryn had essentially broken up with me, and then decided to marry, because she was pregnant. My parents said that plenty of girls have a child outside wedlock, and it was a big decision for me to commit myself to something I was not too sure of – it would be best to wait.

My parents essentially said that I should continue to live in sin. My mother would have been the last person to recommend that, but they were scared and were worried about me, and they did not want their son committing to marriage. On the other hand, Sharryn's mother was all for the marriage and was putting pressure on Sharryn to get on with it and get me to agree.

One day, I remember we were sitting on the back porch steps of our apartment, when I told Sharryn that I would not be able to marry her. I told her I had decided to wait until our child was born and see in which direction our relationship was heading – if the relationship was still fine, healthy, and growing, then I would marry her. I was taking the advice of my mother, but Sharryn broke down with some convincing tears and asked how she could ever trust me to marry her if she waited. She turned around and said that if I do not marry her straight away, she would leave, and I would never see her or my child again. I was shocked, and tried to talk her around, but she stood her ground and repeated that I would not see her or the child again, if I wanted to back out of the marriage. I asked her whether she loved me, because I was not convinced that I loved her myself. With tears rolling down her cheeks, she nodded her head and said that she did love me.

Therefore, I said to myself, "Well, that will have to be enough". I am sharing all this, because it is the truth as I see it, and it is the truth as I remember it. I did not think there would be much chance... I have not talked to Sharryn for more than 14 years, and I am not sure there would be much chance of her being interested in reading a book about my life. I have an inclination that my son might want to read a book about my life, but I am writing this book as though he might not ... we have been estranged for 14 years, and I have only talked to him on Facebook a few times. I have decided to include things in this book that he might not necessarily be happy with, but for the sake of honesty, I am not leaving parts out, and I will tell my full story.

One word of caution for the others reading this book – whenever sex between couples is involved, pregnancies can happen. I was not sure how Sharryn became pregnant. I know it had something to do with our sexual relationship, but I was sure then that Sharryn was on birth control. I do not know why the birth control did not work, but I do not think I would have been foolish enough to have sex with her if she was not on birth control. Many men and boys, who have made women pregnant, shake their head, wondering how their partners became pregnant. All I have to say is that if you want to enter down the sexual road with your partner outside marriage, be prepared to face the consequences – and the consequences of my actions was to enter a marriage of which I was not sure.

Chapter 17

The Marriage

When we decided to marry, I was not earning much of an income – I am not sure whether Sharryn had a job then in Sydney – so essentially, we had no money. We were both receiving government unemployment benefits, and when you are on those benefits, there is only enough money to pay your rent and buy food. I had no money for an engagement ring or a wedding ring; in fact, we had just enough money for a wedding ring for myself. Therefore, Sharryn used her mother's engagement ring and her mother's wedding band. Although I was not overly worried about superstition, in hindsight, I do not think it was a good idea to use a wedding band from a mother, who had been divorced in her first marriage – anyway, I did not have much of a choice. Should I ever decide to marry in the future, I will make sure I have a job and some way of buying a wedding ring and an engagement ring. I do not think I want to go through the same sort of wedding again. It was a rush affair – Sharryn wanted the wedding before she began to show her pregnancy, so we only had a couple of months to get it organized.

In Australia, we call this sort of wedding a "shotgun" wedding (although I understand it is a universal term) – a wedding you have, because the woman is already pregnant. These days, we are better equipped with choices for women – many women in these circumstances just have an abortion and get rid of the baby. I personally would not have chosen abortion, though. However, Sharryn did not want to make this choice – part of her wanted to become a mother to make up for the lack of love she had received from her own mother. Her mother was a "do it my way or take the highway" person, and if you did not conform, you would not receive any love – her mother's love was a conditional love. Sharryn had run away from home at some stage before I met her, so I think Sharryn was eager to have a child of her own and to experience love.

Not all my friends and family had a good opinion about my marriage. It must have been difficult for them to come along to a wedding, where most of them could see the relationship was not going to work out. I am pleased that many of them did not express their concerns, but came along and wore happy faces on the day. I was taking a tremendous risk in doing what I was doing, but I felt that I was honoring Sharryn, and I certainly did not want to face the choice of never seeing her again and never seeing my son – a choice I did not want to make, and I was later to discover that Sharryn was not making an idle threat, and she was more than capable of carrying it out.

Sharryn's mother must have paid for the wedding dress. I do not think Sharryn ever owned the wedding dress, because after the wedding, I never saw the dress again. Maybe you think I should know about these things – whether she hired a wedding dress or borrowed it from her mother. However, I do not remember seeing that wedding dress ever again – perhaps that was an omen, too. My friends and family turned out for the wedding held in the back garden of my aunt's place, where I had stayed when I first moved down from Coffs Harbour to Sydney. All the food was made and prepared by my aunt and my mother, who also paid for the wedding. I discovered years later that my mother also paid for the marriage celebrant. She said it was particularly difficult to pay a marriage celebrant to marry her son into a wedding of which she did not approve, but she did it out of love for me. I remember, on that day, Sharryn looked beautiful and attractive in her wedding dress. I was hoping this was going to be a fairy-tale marriage, and everything would work out fine. However, the first thing my mother-in-law did on that day, when she greeted me, was to pat my stomach saying, "This will have to go." I cannot remember her making any other endearing comments, and this was to be the first volley, of many comments that she would make to me, that did not go down too well.

Maybe I looked handsome in those days – I was 23, in a suit, and with a smart new haircut. I never considered myself handsome, although Sharryn said that I was handsome – that was her opinion. I just did not accept it. In life, you do not really accept how good you are sometimes. Many of us have a low opinion of ourselves, and it does not matter how many people tell us that we are an attractive, handsome, or nice person. Unless we accept it ourselves, and we can see it in ourselves, we are not sure, and we live with this sense of low self-esteem. Back then, I was certainly a broken person. I had slept with too many men, and too many prostitutes, to have a positive self-image of myself. I assumed that for me to receive any form of companionship, or sexual involvement, meant that I had to pay for it. To my surprise, I had a woman in my life who wanted a sexual relationship with me, without me having to pay.

I was happy to see my family at the wedding. At speech time, I turned the microphone on and said that anyone could say anything they wanted. I remember Terry, who I lived with at Penrith, got up and shared some funny things about living with me. One of the things he shared was, “Matthew seemed to have an aversion to taking out the trash, and once, I really wanted to test it and saw weeks of trash build up without me budging an inch – eventually, I could stand it no more, and had to take it out myself – Matthew got his way.” He said a few other home truths about me, and had the audience laughing (including myself). Although I was not sure whether everything was going to work out, I did not mind my friend having a few laughs at my expense.

Within a few hours, Sharryn and I left the wedding and went to the Sydney Hilton Hotel, where a friend of Sharryn’s mom had reserved a room for us. We went there with Darren, and a friend of mine, who chatted with us in the hotel room, until they left us around midnight to begin our married life. When you have had sex before marriage, there is not a lot to look forward to, especially when your partner is already pregnant. We did not have a formal honeymoon, and life was just going to be what came of it. We had to face it – in about six months’ time, we were going to have a baby, and we had to prepare ourselves for that child.

Chapter 18

Move to Brisbane

In one way, I was now happy, because I was being consulted, and my opinions were taken into account – at least by Sharryn. As I did not have a job in Sydney, we decided to move to Brisbane, about six hundred miles north of Sydney, in the State of Queensland, to be closer to where Sharryn's mother lived. Looking back with hindsight, it was somewhat of a bad decision, because there was more work in Sydney. As Sharryn's mother was a forceful woman, I think the final decision was taken out of our hands. She seemed to get what she wanted out of Sharryn, and I think Sharryn's mother wanted her grandchild to grow up somewhere she could keep a close eye on him – maybe that was the reason that we moved to Brisbane – anyway, we moved there.

As I mentioned before, Sharryn's mother was a forceful woman, and she gave the impression from early on that it was "her way or the highway." In other words, she got her way most of the time, and she made it very clear to Sharryn and myself (and to anyone she dealt with) that if you did not agree with her way of doing things, you were going to have an argument (and not a little argument either, but a massive argument).

In addition, I found when I got to Brisbane that it was difficult to get work. It was like a country town. In the papers in Sydney, there were plenty of jobs advertised, and there was a reasonable chance of getting a job. In the Brisbane's papers there were hardly any jobs advertised, and I found it a real struggle to get a job. After staying a couple of months at her mother's place, we decided to move out. I am not sure whose decision it was to move out, but I think the time had come to move out from under the feet of her mother – it is never a good thing for a married couple to live with the in-laws. It was most probably a mutual decision, and we moved to an inner city suburb of Brisbane called West End, where we were about a 25-minute walk from the CBD, and I really liked our new place – a small apartment that did not cost too much – we could afford to live on the unemployment benefits.

Sharryn soon got a job serving in a cafe in West End, and although I remained unemployed for a while, I eventually secured a job as a driver for Domino's Pizza. As Sharryn had a car, it was a relatively easy job, because they do not mind you putting miles on your own car. They paid an hourly rate and an allowance for each pizza delivery you made with your car. I was soon promoted to the job of a trainee manager – it meant working more hours, but it meant more pay, and I was happy. The manager at Domino's and I worked well together, and we became friends.

It was good for me to get out of the house and do some work to bring in an income. I cannot remember on what Sharryn and I spent our money, but as we both had an income, we became very good at spending our money. We both had an income, but we never seemed to save any money – it just seemed to disappear. I know that some of the money was going toward Sharryn's packet-a-day smoking habit, but that did not account for all the money. On my nights off from work, I would go to a legal gambling house and place bets on horses – a habit I had picked up when living in Sydney – but I usually managed to double my money (go in with $20 and come out with $40). Sharryn and I would go to the movies or for a meal somewhere regularly – I was enjoying these times, and I even began to enjoy living in Brisbane. I enjoyed the time with my wife, before our child arrived, and I was happy. There was one point when Sharryn did not seem too interested in sex – I am not sure whether it was when she was still pregnant, or after she had the baby, but for about a year, Sharryn struggled with the idea of sex, which was frustrating for me to say the least. However, the baby was soon to arrive, and that is the subject for our next chapter.

Chapter 19

Brandyn Arrives

Sharryn was having difficulty with a buildup of fluid in her legs, so she went to the hospital for a checkup – they told her that they were going to perform an emergency caesarean section to remove the baby, as my wife's life was at risk. I got a phone call at work from Sharryn saying that she could not leave the hospital, and could I bring some clothes for her – she was going to have my child the next day – six weeks premature. I arrived at the hospital just as Sharryn went in for the operation, and when I went in to see Sharryn, the first thing that struck me was how small my son was. He was only about 5 inches long and weighed fewer than 5 pounds. He was so small that they did not allow the baby to come home for over a week, although they allowed Sharryn to come home almost immediately.

He was so small that I remember, when we first started to put him in diapers, the smallest diapers we could find covered three-quarters of his body and would have probably drowned him. That was how small he was, but I was so proud to have him, although he used to cry a lot. At first, I was happy, and I was happy for Sharryn – she seemed a happy mother. However, – this is difficult for me to share, but it is a part of my life that you should hear – within a year of his birth, the dynamics in the household had changed, and it seemed that Sharryn was giving our son all the attention, and I was not receiving much attention at all. I became so jealous of my son to the point of actually hitting him – not because he was naughty, but because he was just being a baby, and I was frustrated with him. One day, Sharryn noticed a bruise on Brandyn and immediately rang my sister to ask what she should do. My sister told her to take the child away from me and for her to move away from me. I remember, for many years, I did not forgive my sister for that advice, and I blamed my sister for the first breakup between my wife and me.

In retrospect, it was a dangerous situation for my son to be in – a defenseless child with a jealous father – but men are funny creatures and can get themselves into some strange situations. I make no excuses, because it is certainly something that I definitely was not proud of – something Satan loves to accuse you of, and tries to make you feel guilty for, but everything in my life has been forgiven by God. I am not suggesting for one moment that it was not a bad thing, but it was the correct decision for Sharryn to take my child away from me and move out herself. I was devastated when she moved. I think, around this time, we may have been having sexual difficulties at home, and I think this may have added or exacerbated the problem I was having with my child.

When we separated, my parents came up to visit Sharryn, and I was extremely sad. They brought a couple of Christians from a local Brethren church to see me and talk to me. They seemed to accept me, despite what I had done. My parents and the two Christians advised Sharryn that I could get through this, and it would be a good thing to move back in with me.

Although Sharryn and I were separated, I remember that we had a couple of dates together, especially one where we went for a picnic in the park and she kissed me. Although it is more than 20 years ago, I remember that kiss, and that she showed me that she loved me, even though she had every reason not to come back to me. As a mother, she had to be careful with her child – she was a good mother in that sense. She did not have to come back to me, but she chose to come back and to trust me. I never abused my child again. I had learned my lesson.

When a woman lives with an alcoholic husband, who beats her up and abuses her, I think it is a good thing for a woman to move away from her husband. I certainly learned a precious lesson when Sharryn moved out on me – my behavior was just not acceptable. It is a real wake-up call when someone moves out, and something you are enjoying is taken away from you. It was a shameful part of my life, probably one of the most shameful parts. I just know that the victory that is found in Jesus Christ and the ability to confess that this situation happened in my life, but to have the freedom to share it with you in my biography that I really was a mess.

Marriage is not always the answer to a broken individual. The answer to a broken individual is to get prayer and counseling, and to mend the wounds in that person. Sadly, Sharryn and I lived a co-dependent marriage. We lived a marriage where we were two broken people who came together, but we just seemed to inflame the problems that we both had. It is an issue happening to many couples – men become jealous of their children, because the wives might spend too much time with their children.

If you have been through this, or are going through it, I challenge you to address your own hurts and issues in your life, rather than taking it out on your children, or, for that matter, taking it out on your wife. I cannot say that I excuse Sharryn for her behavior, by spending so much time with my son. I cannot say she was entirely blameless, but my son certainly was not to blame, and he certainly did not deserve my behavior. Sharryn moving back in with me, and the time around then, proved to me that Sharryn, at one stage in my marriage, did in fact love me.

Chapter 20

Taxi Driving

While I was working at Domino's pizza store, ownership of the chain changed hands, and because our store was not profitable enough, they decided to close its doors. I was out of a job again – I happened to see an advertisement in the local paper for taxi drivers, so I decided to inquire about the job. They gave me a few details and told me the next taxi driving training course would be held shortly. I went on a training course for about a week with the taxi company, and then I had to study for a written test – the government had four tests they used for taxi drivers – but that was not too difficult, as they provided all the questions (with the answers). Then I had to go for a driving test, but the instructor was more interested in telling me about her daughter's wedding plans than in watching the road or watching what I was doing – however, I was glad when the test ended, when she passed me and said that I was okay to get a taxi driver's license. Last, there was a Police checkup, and as I had a good record then (I may have been a sinner but I definitely was not a criminal), I was issued with my first taxi license.

I started driving for the company using one of more than a hundred of the company cars they kept at the taxi base – they did not seem to mind taking on people who did not have experience. The cars were not the best of cars, and they were definitely not in showroom condition, I was to discover, and the cars were serviced irregularly – I think they just waited until the car had a problem, before they did any work on the car. I also learned for future reference that I should only drive for this company when I was in a crisis. Driving for a private owner of a taxi was a lot more enjoyable, and the cars were far better maintained.

On my first shift as a taxi driver, I did not make much money. I had parked on a taxi rank close to my house, and from four until six in the morning, there were a few jobs on the taxi rank, until everyone had returned home from the clubs. The system was to wait at the taxi rank, until I was called on the radio, but while I was there, I did not receive any calls. Taxis were pulling up behind me, staying there for a while, and then leaving. I thought they were leaving, because they got sick of waiting. I was not aware that I was on the wrong radio channel to hear the jobs – jobs were being called, but I was not hearing them. I eventually went and inquired from the driver of the car behind what was happening – why were cars leaving – and he told me what radio channel I needed to be using. I went back to my car, changed the channel, and within 20 minutes, I had a job – I was earning money at last.

The operators, who called the jobs on the radio, were very knowledgeable about the city. They seemed to know where every street was in the city, and Brisbane was a big city – about 60 miles by 60 miles. When it was busy, you could always drive around the city, and people would hail your taxi, but most people in Brisbane were conditioned to go to ranks and wait. The first call from the dispatchers at the taxi operator would be to a specific suburb's rank – if you are the first car at that rank, you would call in for the job, and they would dispatch the job to you. Second, if there were no car at the specific rank, the operator would call the suburbs block, and if you were within the limits of that suburb, you would call in and make a bid on the job. The taxi operator would decide which of the cars that came in on the block call was closest. Last, there was an open call, meaning that there were no taxis in that suburb, but there may be in adjoining suburbs, so the taxi operator would ascertain the closest car from the bids that came in.

Once the operator had found a suitable car, he would read the pick-up address and any special instructions, such as, "Ring the bell and ask for Mike." You needed to understand the address and to write it – have you ever tried to write while you are driving? – it is the same as trying to write what I am saying while watching the video – not easy. During the day, this was not too difficult; things were mostly honest, and the other taxi drivers did not seem to steal your jobs. However, at nighttime, if you showed any hesitation in receiving the job, or there was any indication in your voice that you did not understand where the job was, often your job had disappeared by the time you reached the place – another taxi has cruised past and taken the job. Sometimes, it was an innocent thing – someone just hailed a taxi, and the taxi picking it up had no idea that the person had rung for a cab, and they just picked up your job. However, I often felt there was intent behind it, and some taxi drivers were just out to earn a quick buck and were not too worried that their next job might just be your job.

However, I loved driving taxis – it was an enjoyable job, and as I grew in experience, the money started to increase. The hours were long and taxing – 4 a.m. to 4 p.m. or 4 p.m. to 4 a.m. – twelve hours at a stretch. I remember as a child, I missed my father because he was away from home for 12 hours a day, and it seemed as though the same thing had started to repeat itself in my life when it came to my son.

I loved meeting new people and having conversations with them. I found most people were honest with taxi drivers with what they had to say. Maybe some people felt comfortable and opened up to share some intimate things about their life. However, I think that people sometimes used the opportunity of a taxi driver just to "dump" stuff on them. Sometimes, people are feeling upset, or in a bad way, and they need someone with whom they can discuss things. As a taxi driver, you are a handy person on whom you can dump things. Often, people would share information that was not very wholesome, but that goes with territory of being a taxi driver – however, I grew to love people, and I grew in my ability to draw people out of themselves.

I did not often pick up the same person, so maybe they felt more willing to share, with a stranger, some things happening in their life, than they were willing to share with their friends. The passengers were of all different types – people with a whole lot of bags on their way to the airport or with a small briefcase on their way to work. Sometimes, they had come straight from the shower in the morning, smelling nice with deodorant or perfume – I always enjoyed picking up those passengers, as it always put a good smell in the car. Then there were people coming home from work, and they were just plain tuckered out, while others came smelling of cigarettes and alcohol after a busy evening at a nightclub in town. All different, and each with a different set of things to "dump".

Although I became used to driving on the day shift or the night shift, I must say that to drive a taxi on the night shift does require a particular personality. Many people, who catch a taxi at night, are not always on their best behavior, and they do not treat taxi drivers with too much respect. Some of them were drunk wanting to pick a fight with anyone they could, and a good person to annoy was the taxi driver on the way home. I found that, as I grew in my self-confidence self-esteem, I was less able to pick up people at night, because their behavior used to annoy me. I had to have a personality that just allows insults to go over your head and not react to them. However, I had a few memorable trips over the years driving taxis, and a few of them include these.

Once, a couple of girls coming out of a nightclub climbed into my taxi. They said they had passed all the other taxis in front of me and had decided to catch my cab. On the way home, the two girls were chatting amicably, and they seemed happy talking with each other. We dropped one of the girls at her house, and we then continued on to the other girl's house. As we drove, the Lord influenced me and gave me a thought that I should speak to the girl. I said, "On the way home, there with your friend, you were all happy and excited, and that was a total sham. In fact, you're going home right now to take a whole lot of sleeping tablets and commit suicide." The girl opened her mouth in shock and asked me how I knew about this. I told her that Jesus had laid it on my heart to speak to her, and I asked her what was going on, and why was she in such a condition.

She said that her boyfriend had broken up with her, did not want to be a friend anymore, and did not even want to talk to her. It had broken her heart, and she felt as though life was not worth living anymore. I spent an hour outside her house (with the meter off), until I was sure that she was okay to go inside, and she was not going ahead with the suicide.

So many times in the taxi, I had an influence on people, and each of them was a divine appointment. Once, a lawyer jumped into my taxi, and while we were on the way to his destination, I asked him about his business and what he had planned for the day. He said that he was on his way to resolve a dispute between two heirs of a manufacturing business – two men had started the manufacturing business – one of the men had one son, and the other had two sons. Now that the sons were operating the business, the family with two sons was taking the other family to court, saying they should get two-thirds of the money of the business, because there were two sons, whereas the other family only had one son in the business. Without much thought, I said that the best start to settle the dispute was not to focus on splitting the company two-thirds, one-third – rather, to look at the current profits of the company, and with today's current profits, it should be split 50/50. However, any profits that increase from today onward could be shared two-thirds, one-third. The lawyer was "gobsmacked" with my answer. He said I was wasted driving a taxi, as I had a lot more potential in life. He was so happy that I had given him an idea that he could take to his clients, as it made a lot of sense, and he was grateful to me for doing his job for him.

I remember another time, when I picked up a senior partner of a law firm in the city, about one in the morning. When I asked him how things were going, he became sad and said that his law firm was having many problems financially. I asked him why that was, and he said the cash flow was not good, as many of the firm's lawyers were not asking for prepayments or partial payments for the law cases. They just believed that the firm had deep pockets and could handle any financial situation. Although he had instructed the lawyers to take partial payments, they had not done so, and now the company was struggling financially.

I told him that they should hire a company that performs time-and-motion studies, makes recommendations, hires and fires people, and changes the internal structure of the company. "You could pay them a couple of thousand dollars an hour to do this study. Then you can tell your lawyers that one of the recommendations is that every lawyer working a case has to take partial payments – it is no longer a suggestion; it is something that has to be done, or that lawyer will lose his job." I went on to say, "Your problem is that you are too friendly (along with some of the other partners), and people are taking advantage of your good personalities and your friendliness. They are not taking you seriously, but if you let it be known that you are going to hire one of these companies, and there is a possibility that people might lose their jobs, then people are going to pay attention. Have this company make the recommendations you want made, and then people will pay attention, because they think their jobs are on the line." When I was finished, the partner was in tears and thanking me profusely for my advice.

When I look back on these three situations, I believe that they involved the gift of prophecy. I believe that God was working through me with words of advice directly from heaven – often in the taxi, God was intervening and giving me messages to give to people. As you can see from my stories, my job as a taxi driver was more than just picking a person up, and taking them from one place to another.

Just a little insight into a job that was to become one of my favorite jobs – driving a taxi.

Chapter 21

Separation

Sharryn and I were always having arguments, but one day we had an argument, and she told me she wanted me to leave. It was a warm summer evening, and she was out in the courtyard drinking my home-brewed beer with the next-door neighbors. I had brewed a batch – a rather good batch, even if I say so myself – and I had put half the batch away, as I was keeping it for a few extra months to improve the quality. I had told her not to drink any of it, but when I went to the cupboard that night, I found my special collection was gone – she was drinking all that beer with her friends. I went outside and said to her that I had asked her not to drink that beer. She just replied that I should pack up and leave – I was so shocked.

I later learned in court counseling that often the person who decides to leave a marriage knows for months before, and they do their suffering and grieving before the breakup, so when they break up, they do not seem as distressed as the other partner, who has just discovered they are breaking up. I had no idea that my marriage was about to break up. I thought everything was going on quite well with my marriage. I tried to reason with Sharryn that our marriage was okay, but she would hear none of it. She had made her decision and was quite forceful about wanting me to leave. I asked her if I could sleep in our bed that night, or did I need to sleep on the couch, and she said I could sleep in the bed. The next morning I went in and silently said good-bye to my son. I caught a bus into the city, rang my parents, and got on an early train at 7:30 in the morning to go to Coffs Harbour, about a 300-mile trip.

On the train journey to my parents place, I remember just shaking my head all the way, and for about half the trip, I was crying. My mother and father met me at the station, and my eyes filled with tears when I saw them. My mother hugged me, and my parents told me they knew from the beginning that the marriage was going to break down, and that there was no use trying to fight for my marriage, because it was not going to go anywhere with Sharryn.

It had been decided that it was over, and that was it – but I had a hard time believing that. I knew Sharryn could be forceful on the day, and for a while, I tried to talk Sharryn around – but to no good end. While I was at my parent's place in Coffs Harbour, my sister came to visit. She had just completed a study on the effects of sexual abuse on a person's personality. She had a list of 25 personality characteristics that someone who has been sexually abused might manifest. On the study course, they had told her that if someone manifested six of these personality characteristics, there was a good chance that they had been or were being were being sexually abused – and if they manifested more than 10, then it was definitely not a coincidence, but a fact, that they had been abused, and you could approach them as such. My sister told me that she already knew that Sharryn had been sexually abused by her stepfather. She asked me to go through the list and see how many personality characteristics, I could find, that might be applicable to Sharryn. I counted 15 of them – but as I was going through the list, I was alarmed, because the list contained many characteristics that were true in my life. When I had finished the list, my sister said that she had found only 11 that applied to Sharryn, and that I had done well to find 15 – then she turned to me and said, "If Sharryn has 15, then you must have more than that."

To my surprise, she bluntly asked me, but in a concerned tone, "Who abused you?" I was in such a state, having lost my wife, my child and most of my reason for living, that I could confess what had happened to my life. I started to cry and told her about my sexual awakening with the man on the beach. Surprisingly, my sister and my parents did exactly the opposite of what I thought they would do when they heard this information. Instead of being sick and disgusted with me, they told me about my addiction to men and that my addiction to prostitutes was a natural progression from what had happened. They actually came over and hugged me – and many tears were shed – the complete opposite of what I thought for many years would happen, if I ever opened up. I was deathly ashamed of my life

– it was secret, and it was something that I did not share with anyone. However, they were treating me differently.

One of the main things about being sexually abused is the feeling of shame that somehow you were responsible for what happened. The guilt of sexual abuse lingers for many years and manifests itself in many of the personality characteristics of its victims, continuing until they are addressed. Thanks to Jesus Christ, I have been forgiven for the part I played in my sexual abuse. I remember, I shared with them that I had willingly gone back to the man, and willingly taken part in what happened. However, my sister and my mom said that even that man was taking advantage of me. Self-forgiveness is a difficult thing to do. We often forgive others for the wrongs they have committed against us, but self-forgiveness is the most difficult thing to do. Satan will use all his power to keep your secret from coming out, and if it had not been for my sister taking that study, my secret may have never come out, and I would still be suffering.

Whenever something like that happens in your life, and you keep it secret, Satan has power over you in that area of your life, and it affects every other area of your life. When I figured that I had lost my wife and child, and I had nothing left to hide, I could openly share what had happened to me. Having the term sexual abuse used to explain what happened to me on the beach was very helpful when it came to my time of healing – and the healing of my life.

Perhaps someone has interfered with you or touched you sexually as a child. Now is the time to seek a counselor to help you work through the experience. I hope my story has opened some people up. I hope by sharing my story of abuse, and the life I lived, will help people open up and let people know clearly that it happens to many others. I pray that God would open you up, and if you have been affected somehow, that you would seek counseling and share that little secret you feel is dirty.

Chapter 22

Suicidal Thoughts

I was at my parent's place for about two weeks after the separation from my wife, and it was around this time that I started to give up all hope of living. During the time since my wife had told me to leave, my feelings had become worse – and they were not getting any better – they seemed to get worse as the time since the separation increased. Remembering the good times (and not the bad times) that I had with my wife, and missing those good times, was making me extremely sad. It was difficult trying to come to grips with not being with my wife again. The idea that I was not going to live with my wife anymore, and I would become a part-time father, tugged at my heartstrings and was heartbreaking.

I can fully understand why some men in custody fights with a former spouse take a gun and kill their family and then themselves. I can understand the idea of wanting to end it for the person you loved and for yourself. One day, I was having a shower, and while I was in the shower and thinking about my life, I just decided unexpectedly that I was going to kill myself. I did not know what or how I was going to do it, at that stage – all I knew was that I had decided I was going to kill myself, and suddenly, this amazing sense of personal relief swept over my body. I do not know if there is such a thing as demonic peace, but now more than 20 years later, I remember that feeling in the shower of this weight being lifted from my shoulders – and I felt at peace with my decision.

While this had been going on, my mother had a feeling in her spirit that there was something wrong with me, and that she should send my brother Tony in to see me. I was getting out of the shower, when Tony came into the bathroom. I quickly struggled to cover myself from being nude, and then Tony asked me what the matter was. I told him that I had enough of everything. He turned to me and said, "At this stage I can understand you want to give up, and I can understand why you want to kill yourself." I did not understand how he managed the jump from my saying, "I have had enough" to "I want to kill myself", but at that stage, I was not aware my mother had sent him. He said it must be a big thing to lose a wife and a child, and he understood my grief.

My brother was working as a counselor and rehab worker at the drug rehabilitation center on John Pierre's farm I used to visit when I was young. He told me he had lost a couple of men he worked with to suicide, so he understood what was involved with depression and suicide. He said if I killed myself, he would tell my parents, and my family, I had just succumbed to depression and suicide, and although this was a terrible position to be in, it was just a natural progression from really deep depression, and they were not to blame themselves, as I was in a position that could not be reached. He assured me that if I were to kill myself, he would make sure the family was okay with my decision. I thought that was tremendously considerate of him, and in a way, it lifted something from me. I felt accepted and not judged.

He talked about the guys he worked with at the drug rehabilitation farm, and he said that when he tries to talk to them about life and their issues, they say to him, "How would you understand, you've never been there?" He went on to say that most men he dealt with had been sexually abused, and they were right, as he had not been sexually abused. He was always left speechless, when they leveled that at him, because he knew they were telling the truth. Then he said to me, "But you know the truth, and you've lived the life of being sexually abused, and you've had an attraction to men, and you've been addicted to prostitutes. You've suffered from loneliness. You've lost your wife. You've lost your child. You've gone through a bad relationship with brothers picking on you."

Then, he became emotional and said that he is sorry that he had picked on me, and he said he could understand me wanting to give up. He said that it was his job to make sure that I had a reason for living, and so he continued, "This is it. I can understand you don't want to live because you've lost your wife and child, and I can understand that you don't feel you're loved enough from your family, but think about all those who've been sexually abused. Think about all those who've been in sexual relationships with men, and all those who have been sexually addicted to prostitutes – all the men and women, who've had a break down in their marriage, lost their children, and lost their relationships – so many thousands of people you can speak to. If you could only get up from here, and if you could only get up and heal your life – thousands of people who would benefit from your story, if you could just heal yourself and get on top of things – thousands of people who would be touched just by hearing your story and hearing how you did it. They would be happy to hear that you made it. If you can't get up for your friends and your family, at least get up for them."

A fresh burst of hope revived in my heart, and on that day, I decided I wanted to live. A part of me died to self and died forever. A new part of me wanted to get up and do God's will – to believe in the promises that God had told me that one day I would be in ministry. I chose to get up that day to share my story with others, who have been broken and abused. Part of the reason for this book is that most of the healing has been done in my life, and now I have a story to share that will inspire people.

Chapter 23

Start Cooking Course

My mother wanted me to keep busy, while I was separated from my wife and living in Coffs Harbour, so I started working at a local Meals on Wheels, where they cook meals for elderly and disabled people. I worked with the chef in the kitchen, helping prepare the meals and serving the meals, when they had been made. When I mentioned I was going apply to a technical college in Brisbane, the chef wrote a reference for me – a good reference, which I believe influenced my interview, when I applied for the professional cookery course at The College of Tourism and Hospitality (or COTAH). I was told that more than 300 people had applied for the course, so I was surprised and happy when I got one of the 20 available positions. I believed that God was shining on me, and I began to enjoy the course with all the studying. I drove taxis to supplement my income on the weekends, and I could get have my boy, Brandyn, around every second weekend – I was starting to enjoy my son. I made friends at the college course, and one of the friends, Sara, enjoyed spending time with my son and me.

It was fun making various types of food and cooking with professional equipment – on the course we were taught several methods of cooking, such as braising, roasting, frying, and deep-frying. The course was giving me a real love again for living. I felt I wanted to continue to train as a chef, and I had hopes that, one day, I could get a job as a chef. I did not give up my hopes, although I had failed with my first apprenticeship out of high school as a child. My new friend, Sara, loved me, but as she already had a boyfriend on the course, our relationship was purely platonic. I learned that platonic friendships are enjoyable and good fun, and you can become close friends, even when the girl is in a relationship, as long as her boyfriend is happy with you being friends.

The course was not easy. It was difficult, as you had to have an 80% pass mark for all written tests. Sometimes, I had to take the written tests more than once to achieve the necessary pass mark. It was not just a matter of remembering the questions, and finding out the answers before the retake of the test, because a computer randomly generated the questions each time, from a bank of several hundreds of questions – to pass, you had to know your stuff! However, I enjoyed learning, and I did not give up my desire of becoming a chef. Once a week, during the course, we had to cook for a proper restaurant – the college had a restaurant where people came and paid $20 for a three-course meal (yes, it was that long ago. Today $20 would not even pay for the starter). The restaurant was licensed, so they could order a bottle of wine with their meal and have it all served by a professional waiter, also training at the college. It was enjoyable to receive feedback from proper customers on our food. I really enjoyed the training at the college as a chef – I was not the best in our class, but I definitely was not the worst. I remember those times with fondness, as I was distracted from the sadness of the breakup with my wife. By applying myself to the training and the cooking, I could take my mind away from all the feelings of sadness.

Chapter 24

Going Back to Church

When I started training for the chef's certificate at COTAH, I had to move out of the accommodation where I was living. I decided that it was time to share accommodations with a Christian, so I looked in the paper for a Christian shared accommodation, where people were advertising for a roommate. I found a Christian (let's call him Phil) advertising a place in the southern suburbs of Brisbane called Slacks Creek. I rang Phil, made an appointment, and I moved into his place.

Phil went to a Pentecostal church every Sunday, so I decided to go to church with him. I had never been to a Pentecostal church before. As a youth, I had been raised as a Baptist, and apart from an occasional visit to a Brethren church, I had only been into Baptist churches in my life. I had never experienced a Pentecostal church before. When I walked into this church, WOW was I shocked! Not only did the number of cars outside shock me, but also, when I walked into the actual building, I was amazed at the music the band was playing, and by the number of people in the church. There must have been more than 200 people standing and singing songs in the church. A professional hot rock band played the music – I had never seen anything like this – three electric guitars and a (loud) drummer – an amazing amount of music coming from the speakers on the front stage. I had been to rock concerts, and seen bands performing in clubs and entertainment centers in Sydney, so I knew about entertainment – and what was being played in this church was without doubt entertainment.

I was amazed at the number of people inside the church, because I was accustomed to seeing a church with about 80 people – not 200 plus. The church was popular, and in my opinion, the music was good. Many in the church had their hands raised – I had seen that on TV reports, but I had never seen it in person before. Never, in a Baptist church, have I seen people with their hands in the air and singing loudly – and they all seemed to be enjoying themselves. I had never seen anything like this church before, but it seemed an exciting place to be. Soon, I was introduced to the pastor and others in the church. I remember they were all friendly and made me feel welcome.

I think it is so important for people in a church to make strangers feel welcome. Nowadays, I make sure I introduce myself to new visitors to the church, to make them feel welcome, and make them feel as if they know someone at church. This was the way I felt when I visited this church: I was made to feel welcome, and it seemed that more people than just my flat mate were interested in getting to know me.

The messages in the church were engaging, contemporary, and above all, interesting. I was excited that it was not just dry doctrines being taught in the church with a boring voice – the pastors were excited about what they were preaching. It was exciting to listen to, and the subject matter was interesting. There was nothing derogatory I could say about the church that I remember or even noticed. As you may have noticed in the book so far, I am not afraid to say outright when something is not right, but I could not find anything in that church I did not like – a good experience for a Pentecostal church, especially since I had heard plenty of bad reports about Pentecostal churches. Perhaps, you attend a contemporary church but do not necessarily attend a charismatic Pentecostal church – take it from me that it was exciting and enjoyable to go. Maybe you need to open yourself up and not always listen to what others say.

Within a few months of being there, I was invited to go on a men’s camp – about 20 to 25 men went for a weekend where we had a head pastor from an Assemblies of God Church as a speaker. He told us about his church, which had about 400 people – double the size of our church. My good friend, Sarah, says that I am always into numbers, and I often quote numbers throughout this book, but 400 was impressive to me, because it was four times the size of any Baptist church that I had ever attended. I paid attention to this senior pastor, because I believed what he had to say must have been relevant, as he was running a big church. At the end of the weekend, the pastor said he was going to pray for, and prophesy over, each of us. He then explained what the gift of prophecy was – God speaking a personal message to you through another person. He said that when he prays, he will say, "Thus saith the Lord" when God is speaking through him to you.

He went down the line praying for people and prophesying, and when he came to me, he prayed for a little while, and then said, "Thus saith the Lord – at the moment, you're in a very dark place. It seems you're in a dark tunnel, and you can't see any light at the end of the tunnel. You have even given up, thinking that there is no light at the end of the tunnel, but I can promise you there is light at the end of the tunnel, and one day you're going to see that light, and walk in that light. Then God is going to use His gifts and heal you and heal your emotions, and heal you spiritually, and then He's going to raise you into ministry." That was a remarkable prophecy.

On another occasion in the church, a man preached on the spiritual gifts – the gifts of the Holy Spirit – 1 Corinthians 12:7-11 "But the manifestation of the Spirit is given to each one for the profit of all: for to one is given the word of wisdom through the Spirit, to another the word of knowledge through the same Spirit, to another faith by the same Spirit, to another gifts of healings by the same Spirit, to another the working of miracles, to another prophecy, to another discerning of spirits, to another different kinds of tongues, to another the interpretation of tongues. But one and the same Spirit works all these things, distributing to each one individually as He wills."

At one of his training sessions, he spoke on the gift of Word of Knowledge – supernatural information you say to a person about their life in the present, past, or future, specifically in their present or their past, that you could not possibly have known normally. It is information similar to that given by Jesus to the woman at the well, when she had five husbands, but the one she was living with currently was not her husband (John 4:16-18) – supernatural knowledge that God has supplied.

When he had finished teaching, he asked us each to choose a person in the church we did not know and to pray for that person. We were to give a Word of Knowledge to that person, so in our prayers, we were to pray for something we would not normally know, and we would supernaturally receive information we could pray about together. I was nervous, and I was wondering what sort of general prayer I could pray for a person and touch something in their life that I did not know. I started to pray, and when I finished, the person was in tears and said I had spoken a Word of Knowledge about their life that I could not have possibly known. I was so surprised – then, he prayed for me and prayed for healing in the relationship with my son and that the relationship would become closer. How could he know about the estrangement from my son, and that I only saw him once every two weeks? That genuinely touched me. I knew a Word of Knowledge existed, and later in life, I would come to share it more. I have already mentioned that I shared a Word of Knowledge with the girl in the taxi, who was planning to commit suicide – I was operating in the gifts of the Holy Spirit.

One day, Jesus said to me that I needed to be baptized. I was watching several people on the stage giving their testimonies and being baptized. For years, I had not been baptized, although I grew up in a Baptist church, because we had to give our testimony. We had to give a five-minute talk about why we wanted to be baptized, and I was too nervous to pick up a microphone and speak on stage. I could never see myself doing it, but Jesus showed me a vision – I saw up into heaven, and I felt this real peace – and He said, "I want you to get baptized, and then I want you to baptize people in my name."

Within a month, I was baptized, and I shared my testimony, although I was somewhat scared. One day, I was at home praying for my wife, Sharryn, and I was having a difficult time praying for her, because she was already living with another man – I was trying to pray for a breakup, and for her to come back to me, although sincerely I wanted to really bless her. Suddenly, a prayer started coming from my mouth that I was not thinking about –it just came out my mouth. It was a beautiful prayer, and I had tears welling up in my eyes, as I heard myself praying. At the end of it, I asked Jesus what was going on, and He told me what had just happened was in tongues – I had prayed in tongues, although it was in English. He said that the gift of tongues was available to me, whenever I had the courage to use it. This was awesome, and I have prayed this way many times since –in English but led by the Holy Spirit.

I lived in Slacks Creek for about a year, and then I decided to move closer to college, and so I moved away from that church.

Chapter 25

My Divorce

I have taken a six-week break from writing this book and from making the videos that form the basis for this book. The subject of my divorce to wife came up on the agenda, and I entered a stage of hurt and pain – I just could not face talking about my divorce. I had been told, and I have realized because of this short delay, that I have a lot of unsolved pain regarding my divorce. A few days ago, I received a prophecy from a prophet who said the Lord wants me to come in a vision to His throne room and cry out my pain and suffering to Him, and let Him finally heal me of all the pain. He promised, in the prophecy, He will remove the last vestiges of pain, so I would not have to deal with the pain of my past ever again. That was encouraging to me.

Anyway, back to the divorce. We had been separated for some time. My wife was living with her boyfriend and was now engaged to him. How she could be engaged, while she was still married, remains a mystery to me. The divorce papers were served on me, and the court date was set. My wife was quite surprised that I was not going to contest the case. The case came up on a day when I was busy with my cooking course, and I was in the middle of cutting and preparing ingredients for a dish the chef had instructed us to make. I suddenly realized that this was the day of my divorce, and my wife would be in a courtroom divorcing me. I had already told my wife that I would not go to court to attend the divorce. I put down my knife, left the room without saying anything, and I went out into the hallway. I was just going to get my bag, but I was in a bad way. I was in tears, and I was contemplating suicide. I was thinking about ending my life, because the situation with my wife divorcing me was just too much.

While I was in the hallway, I got a tap on the shoulder, and when I turned around, it was my friend Sara. She asked me, "What's the matter?" and I replied that my wife was divorcing me that day, and I was going to kill myself. It was not a cry for help – often many people mistakenly say those contemplating suicide are just trying to get help or trying to make a statement. I was not saying I was going to kill myself to be talked out of it. I was just stating how I felt, to someone who had grown quite close to me over the past year we had been doing courses together.

It was six weeks before the end of my second six-month course of cookery was to be finished. If I finished the second course, I would have been two-thirds of the way to be qualified as a chef. All I would have to do is get an apprenticeship, and go to college once more, and I would receive my official chef qualification. Her eyes filled with tears when she saw me crying. She said she had met my son, Brandyn, and I should not kill myself, because he would think it was his fault, and he would never understand. He would miss his dad, and he would have a terrible life, so I must stay alive to bring up my son and give him hope. I was not convinced that was sufficient reason to stay alive. I had lost all hope, and I was in a terrible position and crying. Not many people say they are going to kill themselves for fun, and as I mentioned earlier, some people say it just to get attention or to make people feel sorry for them. However, I know, without any doubt, that I was in the position where I wanted to kill myself.

It was not the first time that I had decided to end my life in suicide, but this time I was serious about it. I said I would think about it, left her there, got my clothes and my bag, and went home. I did not have the strength in me to return to the course. My whole reason for living had been taken away from me. The joy in my life had disappeared. I had been hoping for a long time that God would restore my marriage. I had been praying and hoping that the Lord would do a work in Sharryn's heart and return her to me. I did not know whether that was possible, but I had always kept a glimmer of hope that she would reconsider and come back to me, and I believed that God might do that for me.

However, here she was in court divorcing me, and the court's decision was going to make it final and make it impossible for me to have my wife back in my arms. I can understand why many men, who become divorced from their loved one, return with a gun to kill their wife and children, and then turn the gun on themselves. I think that if you researched this, you would find that many separated and divorced men have killed themselves for this reason – they have given up all hope. They lose the love of their life, and have nothing to live for, and I was no different from these men. I have a lot of compassion in my heart for men I see on TV, who have killed their wife and children – I know exactly where they are coming from. I had no desire to kill my wife and her boyfriend, but I certainly was sad, and I was in a bad way on that day.

You may wonder why I did not attend the divorce case, and all I can say is that I simply did not want a memory in my mind of standing opposite of my wife, whom I loved, in a courtroom and watch her divorce me. That was the one memory I did not ever want in my mind. In my opinion, I had no say in her divorcing me. There was no help by the government to restore my marriage. It seemed the law in our country says that if a couple lives apart for a year, then the wife can say that there were irrevocable differences between us. That is not strictly true, because she did not attempt to talk things through, and the differences were not so large that we could not have worked through them, but according to her, our marriage was in such a state that it could not be fixed. I have to say that I was not a particularly nice person back then, as I had a lot of hurt in my life.

While I am writing this, I still feel I have some pain that has not been dealt with, as I mentioned before. I was not the best person to whom she could have been married. The beginning of mental illness was starting to manifest in my life, and I might have become difficult to live with. My jobs were not the best jobs, and they certainly were not high paying jobs. I was not the most fantastic husband…and I was overweight – plenty of reasons that my wife could have had for giving up on me and choosing to be with someone else. When we separated, she never did give me a reason for the break up with me, except to say that she had fallen out of love with me – a line out of a movie called "The Bodyguard" we had watched six weeks earlier. Therefore, I was upset and it had thrust me into suicidal thoughts.

Chapter 26

Writes First Book

So, here we are – I was divorced, and I was having suicidal thoughts. I seemed to be over them, when I started to live for my son's sake, and the visits with my son became even more important to me. At the time, I had a job driving taxis, and I quite enjoyed my time driving taxis.

After my wife had left me, I was abusive to her at one stage, and I had slapped her in a confrontation, as I was extremely angry with her. I am not sure whether I have mentioned this before, but I was charged and had a restraining order against me. It was official, although she did not charge me with assault – but what I had done went down on record. At the time, I decided to write her a poem to say sorry for what I had done and to share my feelings with her. About a year later, I noticed a piece of paper in her purse, and I asked her what it was. She said it was the poem I had written her – it seemed it had lasted a long time, and it was important to her, although she had left me to live with another man. Although I was not going to come back, the poem had an effect on her. What I got from this was that I was reasonably good at poetry, so I began to write a series of poems.

I wrote a poem about a homosexual surfer, an alcoholic (although I had never been a fully fledged alcoholic, I could certainly put myself into the mindset of an alcoholic), a street kid in Kings Cross, a heroin-addicted prostitute in Kings Cross, a beautiful Christian – I wrote many poems. I think, in one season, I wrote between one hundred and two hundred poems. At this stage, I thought about becoming a writer, and I decided to write my first novel, something that my English teacher at high school had always encouraged me to do. I bought a book on how to write a novel, and I read the first chapter while waiting at the main taxi rank in Brisbane for a person to get in my cab. The book was by a man, who lectured at university on how to write a novel.

His first words in the book were, "I'll begin the introduction in this book the same way I introduce my first lesson at the university for people who want to write a book, and I'll introduce it this way. If you're serious about writing a book, if you're serious about writing a novel, nothing's going to stop you from writing that novel. You're committed to it, and you're going to do it despite the setbacks, despite anything. You're going to sit down and write yourself a novel.... Stand! I want all of those who are serious about writing a novel to stand. Nothing is going to stand in the way. You're simply coming to this course to get some pointers on what to do."

In the book, he said that many people in the audience would stand to their feet, and then he would then tell all those committed to writing a book to leave the university lecture room. "Don't procrastinate and listen to me on how to write a book but leave the room right now and go and write your book. When you're finished writing your book, come back to my next year's lectures on how to write a book and learn the fundamentals of book writing. You can edit your novel and fix your novel up. But if you're truly serious about writing a book, go out there and write the book. If you're reading this book right now, and you're going to write a book, well, shut the book right now and go and write your book." That is exactly what I did! I shut the book right there and started to write my novel. In the taxi, I had plenty of time to write – I bought an A4 exercise pad, and I started to write my novel.

I picked about eight of the characters I had written poetry about – the heroin-addicted prostitute, the alcoholic, the gay surfer, the street kid – and started to write about the characteristics of each – their favorite foods, their past, how they grew up, their age, their height, and what they looked like – then I started to flesh out a few other characters I thought I would bring into the story – and then I started to write my novel.

I was six weeks into it, and I had written between 150 and 200 A4 pages in my exercise pad. I decided I wanted to get some instruction on how to write the book best. At that time, I bought a computer and bought another book on how to write a novel, as I had forgotten the name of the earlier book. I read the book – by an Australian author – and then I started to edit and rewrite what I had written, to bring more conflict and suspense into my novel. I am not sure how long it took me, but it was about another 30 days, working at a chapter a day, and I managed to expand the book to about 400 double-spaced A4 pages. It was a good book, and I was very pleased with it.

I called the book *The Fallen Ones,* with a basic storyline revolving around an ex-gay. A gay surfer abandons his homosexual lifestyle and becomes a Christian. He meets a heroin-addicted prostitute in Kings Cross and starts a heterosexual relationship with her. At the end of the novel, she kicks the heroin habit and starts to rehabilitate herself, and eventually they marry and live "happily thereafter"…. It was not a fairy story, as the ending might suggest, as it was full of tension, street kids, pedophiles…and a serial killer – actually, it was a somewhat dark novel. Several people who talked to me about the book said that it was a cathartic novel, as it enabled me to get a lot of my pain and issues onto paper – I could express myself about how I felt.

When I had finished typing, and the book was ready, I contacted several prostitutes in Brisbane and asked them whether they would read my novel and give me feedback on anything I needed to change to make the novel ring true. Most of the feedback returned saying, "You don't have to change anything." I asked them how many characters could they see themselves as – most said between four and eight, with a few saying as high as ten. One prostitute said she never wanted me to ring or contact her again, and she would post the manuscript back to me, because the serial killer scared her. She said that I was a dangerous person, if I could think up such a story and include such a killer in the book.

I found that was one of the best feedback reviews I received, because I had always wanted to write a convincing killer novel – I had seen movies, such as *Seven* with Brad Pitt, and some of the Anthony Hopkins movies where he played a serial killer – apparently my serial killer was impressive enough to frighten a girl away from me forever. I was proud of my first novel, and I entered it in for a fiction award – I did not win the award, but I was still proud of it. Over the next 10 years, I often revisited my novel – sharpening, editing, perfecting, and polishing every paragraph and sentence – until I felt it was ready for publication. I still have fond memories of that book, but I had reached the stage in my life where Jesus told me that He wanted me to discard the book – it was too dark, and He did not want that book to be around. He had His own reasons – with which I will never argue – but my mother was very happy when I told her that Jesus had told me to throw out the book. She was in tears on the phone, saying that she had been praying for this to happen, and this was an answer to prayer for her. My first book was no longer around – but I realized that I could write a book.

Chapter 27

Custody Battle

Not too long after my divorce, my (ex) wife served me with papers saying she was going to ask for sole custody of my child, Brandyn. In the affidavit that accompanied the custody papers, I noticed she told 17 flagrant lies to support her argument that she should have sole custody. Apparently, in these affidavits you say a whole bunch of derogatory things about your former partner, by building a case that your partner has anger issues or drug problems and cannot be trusted with a child. You go to the extreme of convincing a judge that your former partner is not to be trusted and does not have the character to bring up a child in a full-time capacity. When I read the affidavit she had written, I was shocked, angered, and upset. I was upset, because all the lies were going on public record. Some of the derogatory things she said about me had some vestige of truth, but were taken out of context that they did not give – however, 17 of the points were outright flagrant lies. I talked with her good friend and told her the affidavit was the last straw – I was not going to fight for my name, and I would rather just lie down and die.

However, I left it for a month or so, until about a week before the court case, when I decided that now I was going to stand for my name. I caught a train to my parents' place at Coffs Harbour and spent some time writing. I went to see a magistrate and asked him how I prepare a defense in a custody case – and he said I should write my own affidavit, with my own claims against my wife. In the affidavit, I was to address the issues she had brought up and reveal the truth or an argument against each point, and to defend myself. It took me a week to prepare the affidavit and have it signed, and then I took everything back with me to Brisbane.

I presented my affidavit to the family law court, and I asked if there was a possibility of a government lawyer who could defend me. They said that I had left it late, but they would see what was possible. The next day I received a phone call from some lawyers who lived near to me, and they said they could meet me later in the day. I went in to meet them, and two days later, we went to court to launch my affidavit. My lawyer talked to the opposing lawyer, who said the case was going to be adjourned. They were going to put the case off and in the meantime, I was to wait until the case came to court again.

Later, while I was driving my taxi, I met a trial lawyer and asked her what would happen with the case when I had witnesses who could testify in court that my wife had lied in at least eight of the incidents. The trial lawyer told me that in a court case, when the first witness could prove that my wife had lied, the court case would be stopped – the court case would be adjourned to a criminal court, where my wife would be charged with perjury and could possibly go to jail, because it was a serious offense to lie under oath. I started to have second thoughts about my defense and the affidavit I had written.

One day, I went to the university to pick a passenger in my taxi. I asked him how he was and he said, "Great." While I was driving, I asked him what was he doing at the university, and he said he had been there to meet someone, and he was now on his way to the airport. Then he said, "But we're not going to talk about me this time. I can see that you're very friendly and talkative to people. We're going to talk about you." He went on to ask me about my life, and what was I up to – eventually we got around to my custody fight with my ex-wife, and I was busy with a court case on the matter. I mentioned that if I presented my affidavit in the court case without making any changes, my ex-wife would probably go to jail.

Then he asked me, "What did Jesus say about that? Don't take your brother to court before the pagans, before the non-believers. It's not a good witness." I said, "So what are you saying?" He replied, "Jesus is saying for you not to fight, but just let your wife have her way." He went on to say several things that were very encouraging and gave me a few scripture verses. It was only a 45-minute trip, but it was the most encouraging trip. It turned me around from feeling sad and down to being happy and encouraged. He got out of the taxi, took his bags, and said, "Good-bye, Matthew." I pulled away from the curb, but within a couple of seconds, I pulled back into the curb saying, "That's got to be an angel." I rushed in to the airport and thoroughly searched everywhere, but he had simply disappeared.

Years later, I asked Jesus, "Was that an angel?" to which He answered, "You know it was an angel." I asked Jesus who the angel was, and He replied that I had met Michael the Archangel in the flesh. I have often wondered why I had met such an important angel, but I was happy to have met an angel. Anyway, I did not seem to listen fully to Michael that day, as I should have done – even when God speaks clearly to us, often we do not listen or do what we are supposed to do. I continued in my battle to gain shared custody of my son. I changed my affidavit, and took out the defense that Sharryn was lying, removing the chances of her going to prison. I rewrote the affidavit, so that it said some nice things about myself and refuted some things she had said. We went to a Government body for a mediation process saying that we would come to an arrangement with which both parties would be happy.

First, the lawyer needed me to sign an interim agreement, which would indicate what would happen between the start of negotiations and the time the court made its final decision. I agreed that, "I will see my son one weekend in two weeks as is suggested, the normal access that fathers have in Australia." I agreed to the interim agreement, but I did not realize that it would take another 18 months before the case went to court and the final decision was made. Another thing I did not realize was that it was not a binding agreement – by law, my wife did not have to stick to the agreement we had reached during mediation, and after just six weeks, my wife abruptly changed the details, and there was nothing I could do about it.

This really shocked my son and he did not seem to understand what was going on and put him through some personal trauma. He was only four, and he could not understand why he was not seeing his daddy so often, and he felt somewhat guilty. The custody battle started to take its toll on me – I was emotional throughout, and my patience was pushed to its limits, causing me a great deal of concern. I will never suggest that anyone should just lie down and accept the terms of their partner, and not try to negotiate better access to their children when the marriage breaks down. However, I certainly do not recommend going through a long and drawn out process of fighting over your children. If I were going to change one thing, I probably would have just accepted seeing my son once every two weeks, and if I had my time again, I do not think I would have gone through all the hassles it caused me.

Chapter 28

Child Abduction

How do you abduct your own child? Not difficult – what you do is put some plans into place, and then you get your child legally on your day of access, and you take off with them – not difficult at all. What lead up to this was I had my name in a single's magazine, a woman contacted me and we began to have a form of a relationship. At first, she wanted to be in a relationship with me, and then she changed her mind. She told me to move in with her, and I moved into her house, but not into her room. When I moved into her house, she was keeping me up long hours by talking to me, and I talked a lot, as I was a lonely person, and I was going through the issues with my son.

Every time I tried to go to sleep, the phone would ring, and I told her to take the phone off the hook, so I could get some rest. She said that it was probably a spiritual battle started by my wife – "she's attacking you, and by taking the phone off the hook, you're saying to her that she has won, and that you're a loser." I said, "I don't care if she's won; I just want some sleep." However, she was a very controlling woman, so she had her way and the phone remained on the hook. A few days after I had moved in, she asked me if I were a manic depressive. Today, they call it bipolar, but at that time I had never heard of the term manic depressive, and I asked her what it meant. She told me it was a person who had highs and lows, and she then took me to a doctor for a blood test to see if it would confirm her diagnosis of me. I think she had started to get involved in psychology in a course she studied and knew a little about mental illness at the time.

If I were manic depressive, then she did everything that she should not have done to a manic depressive. She turned to Revelation, chapter 11 in the Bible, which talks about two prophets who came just before the return of Jesus to send plagues to the Earth, to give judgment to the Earth, to prophesy over the Earth and cause destruction. She said to me that she believed that she and I were these two prophets. I was in a state of mania – I was in state of sleep deprivation – and I was going crazy.

The prophecy reads:

The Two Witnesses
Rev 11:1-6
Then I was given a reed like a measuring rod. And the angel stood, saying, "Rise and measure the temple of God, the altar, and those who worship there. But leave out the court which is outside the temple, and do not measure it, for it has been given to the Gentiles. And they will tread the holy city underfoot for forty-two months. And I will give power to my two witnesses, and they will prophesy one thousand two hundred and sixty days, clothed in sackcloth." These are the two olive trees and the two lampstands standing before the God of the earth. And if anyone wants to harm them, fire proceeds from their mouth and devours their enemies. And if anyone wants to harm them, he must be killed in this manner. These have power to shut heaven, so that no rain falls in the days of their prophecy; and they have power over waters to turn them to blood, and to strike the earth with all plagues, as often as they desire.

The Witnesses Killed
Rev 11:7-10
When they finish their testimony, the beast that ascends out of the bottomless pit will make war against them, overcome them, and kill them. And their dead bodies will lie in the street of the great city which spiritually is called Sodom and Egypt, where also our Lord was crucified.

Then those from the peoples, tribes, tongues, and nations will see their dead bodies three-and-a-half days, and not allow their dead bodies to be put into graves. And those who dwell on the earth will rejoice over them, make merry, and send gifts to one another, because these two prophets tormented those who dwell on the earth.

The Witnesses Resurrected
Rev 11:11-12
Now after the three-and-a-half days the breath of life from God entered them, and they stood on their feet, and great fear fell on those who saw them. And they heard a loud voice from heaven saying to them, "Come up here." And they ascended to heaven in a cloud, and their enemies saw them.

When she told me that, and I read the scripture, I jumped onto that and said, "Yeah, that's true. I always thought I was destined for big things, and I'd had a prophecy over my life that said I'd be very popular in ministry one day." Everything lined up with that prophecy, and lined up with the story of the two witnesses, so I agreed and started to believe in that. However, I got to a stage, where I just could not get any sleep. I was so high on mania and delusional that she took me to a doctor, and he was worried about me. The doctor gave her some pills for me called diazepam – a mild sedative and a sleeping tablet. I begin to take the sleeping tablets to get to sleep – as you may know, sleeping tablets can become addictive to where you cannot get to sleep without taking a couple of the tablets. You have to take more and more tablets.

I was taking the sleeping tablets, and then one day, I went to discipline Brandyn. I went to hit him, but he ran to a corner of the room and curled up in a ball. He ran to a corner of the room and curled up in a ball with his hands over his head. The controlling woman I was living with said that my son had been beaten, and that was a typical response from a child who had been severely beaten. I said, "Who would be doing that?" and she replied, "It must be your former wife, Sharryn."

Once in the middle of the night, I woke at three in the morning with a terrible feeling that some form of witchcraft was about to happen. I woke the woman, and she came to my bedroom. As we looked out the door, a bloodcurdling animal scream came from downstairs. It happened a few times, and the woman became extremely scared – I knew it must have been a demon, and it did not cause me a great deal of worry. I let it annoy her for a while, then I told the noise to be "quiet in Jesus' name" and it stopped.

The next morning I got a phone call at 7 o'clock, and it was Brandyn. He rang me and asked me, "Dad, are you going to come and pick me up today?" I had mentioned to the woman that I was going to abduct and run away with my child. He had rung me on Tuesday morning, and I was planning to run away with him the next Friday, when I had access with him. I said, "Yeah, I'm going to pick you up today."

I was sure my wife had orchestrated the attack the night before, and I was sure my wife was somewhere down the road in her car when the attack took place. I had prayed for the car to stall and not to come close to the house, and I think that is why a demon came outside the house, because it could not get any closer. The attack had happened a mere four hours before the phone call in the morning, so spiritually, I was wide awake when my son rung me, and I was reading between the lines.

My son asked me whether I was going to pick him up today and I said, "Yes, I'm going to come and pick you up from the day care and take you out for the day." Taking him out for the day was something I did every second Tuesday. Then he said, "When are you going to come and pick me up, Daddy?" and this was something that he never asked me. I used to turn up when I could, and he was used to me just turning up sometime during the day.

There was never a set time, so alarm bells went off when he asked me what time I was coming in. The Holy Spirit told me how to answer, and I said, "I'll come in whenever I like, Brandyn, just as normal. I'll come in anytime." Then he said, "Daddy, can I bring my playing cards today?" I replied, "Yes. Yeah, yeah, of course you can play your cards," and he said, "Mommy says I can only bring my cards today, if I bring them back. Can I bring the cards back today?" I said, "Of course, you can bring your cards back today" – but the underlying message was, "Is Brandyn going to be abducted today?"

I think the woman I was living with was talking with my wife, Sharryn. To this day, I believe they were in cahoots together, and she had told Sharryn that I was becoming antsy, and I was going to try to abduct my child. When my son asked me whether he could bring back the cards (whether I was abducting my child that day), my reply, "Of course, you can bring back your cards" was sending the message, "Yes, Brandyn is going to return today. We're not abducting him today."

My son then asked me, "Daddy, Mom wants to know who won?" Actually, he said, "I can only bring my cards, if you told Mommy who won," and I discerned from the Holy Spirit that Sharryn was asking who had won the night before with the demonic attack. Led by the Holy Spirit I said, "Ah, Brandyn, whenever we play snap together sometimes you win, sometimes I win. When you play Mommy, Mommy wins. Depends on what game we are playing, but in the end, Brandyn wins." I overheard my son say to his mother, "Daddy says Brandyn wins." My wife snapped at him and told him to hang up the phone.

Earlier in the conversation, my son had asked me whether we could meet with his mother and go swimming together at South Bank, a recreational center in the city with a couple of swimming pools. My wife knew that I liked to see her in a swimming costume, as it made me feel particularly romantic. When Brandyn asked me if I could meet my wife around lunchtime with him and go for a swim at South Bank, I told my son, "We'll decide whether we're going to do that, when I pick you up. I can't tell you if we're going to do that now." I had a feeling that my wife was listening to every word, or was going to grill him later for all the answers. I knew that Sharryn was trying to pinpoint me to have a meeting with me. I had a feeling that if I agreed to the time I was going to pick him up, or I agreed to a meeting with her at South Bank, then someone else was going to turn up and do me some bodily harm.

Alternatively, someone was going to spiritually come and try some satanic stuff on me – whatever it was, I did not want a confrontation for which I was not ready. Later, when we picked up my son and took him for a drive, as we were going over the bridge where we could see South Bank Park, I said to him sitting in the back, "We're not going to South Bank today. We're going to ride the motorbikes in the city and play games." My son replied as clear as day, "You're the winner, Daddy!" I have told this story to many people, and it does not seem to have made sense to most of them, but my son with that short statement was saying, "I fully understand that you and Mom were having a spiritual battle last night, and Mom wanted to know that you're the loser, or she was the winner. And, I fully understand what's going on, Dad and I want you to know, by not going to South Bank, you've shown you're the winner, and you're the better man."

I was so surprised that my four-year-old son was so smart and understood what was going on in this spiritual battle. We went into the city to go for a ride on one of the full-sized toy motorbikes at the entertainment center. As he was riding, I noticed a bruise on his arm, and I asked him how did he get the bruise? He went white as a ghost and told me he had fallen off his bike. I looked at the woman with us, and we both shook our heads. The bruise was proof he was being abused, and the white face of shock was proof he was covering up.

I said, "Aw, that's pretty bad. You'll have to be more careful on your bike. Did it hurt? Aw well, it'll get better soon." The woman and I looked at each other, and I said, "You're right, he's being beaten." However, we spent the rest of the day having a great time together, but when I took my son back to drop him off at the day care, for the first time, my son did not want to go back inside. I told him that I loved him, and I put my arms out to show how much I loved him. He put his arms out as if he were hanging on a cross and said, "I love you this much daddy." He had a tear in his eye, and he pointed up to the sky and said, "I love you as big as the sky, Daddy." It was a very emotional moment, and I felt sure he was scared, and he wanted me to take him away that day. When he said he loved me as big as the sky, I felt the way God the Father must feel about all His children.

I felt that my son was being sacrificed on the cross, and he was going into a dark place for the next three days, until I could take him away. Therefore, when Friday eventually came around, we went ahead and did it. We picked him up, but for some reason, the woman wanted to go for a picnic. We went for the picnic, and then we went home and packed everything we needed to take, and started to drive out of our suburb. As we were packing, I suddenly had a feeling of urgency from the Holy Spirit that Sharryn was on her way, and she was almost there. I got the feeling that we had only five minutes to leave, and I shouted at the woman that if she did not leave within five minutes, I would drive the car myself. The suburb where we were living had two exits – one toward the city center and the other away from the city – and we took the exit we would not ordinarily use away from the city.

On the way out of the suburb, the woman's phone rang, and she started to explain to the caller where we were and where we were heading. I asked her who was on the phone, and she said that it was my ex-wife Sharryn. All day I had the feeling that the woman had been delaying and messing around to give Sharryn time to finish work, and to come and confront us, as we tried to escape. I think Sharryn wanted a confrontation to make me give up finally and totally back out of my son's life – I think she had something planned for me that was so scary or harmful, it would make me back off for the rest of my life. I grabbed the phone from the woman girl and said, "No more answering the phone until we've reached where we we're going – we're going to drive 2,000 kilometers and settle in a new town and not tell Sharryn where we are." By the time Sharryn discovered where we were, through the government unemployment agency, it would mean the only way Sharryn could get me back was to move there and fight for custody up there. By the time it came to court, my son would be going to a good school, he would be happy with me, and she would not be able to get custody.

That was the way I had decided to fight, so we took off, and within a couple of days, we were a thousand kilometers away. We were staying at a motel, relaxing by the pool, when the woman said she wanted to go to the beach. I said, "We seem happy enough here; we don't need to go to the beach" – but she insisted, and she had a way of arguing that just made you give in. We packed up everything into the car and started driving to the beach. When we were about halfway there, we pulled into a service station, as she said she had to fill the car with gas. When she came back from paying for the gas, she said could not drive the car, as she had lost the keys.

I asked, "What's going on? You could not have lost your keys. They must be on the counter in the shop." I went into the shop and I asked, "Where are the keys? My friend lost her keys," and they said, "They're in the safe." Again, the Holy Spirit was giving me notice that things were going down, and things were out of kilter.

As I went outside, a police car pulled into the service station. I walked up to the police car, and as the police got out, I asked, "Are you looking for me?" They asked, "What's your name?" and I replied, "Matthew Payne." They said, "Yes, we are looking for you. We've had a report that you're sick, and we want to take you to the hospital. Will you come with us?" I said, "Sure. Can my friend come? We've come in my friend's car." They said, "No, we prefer you to come in our car, and your friend can follow us."

My son was wondering what was going on, so I gave him a big hug, climbed into the police car, and was escorted to the hospital.

Chapter 29

First Breakdown

After the police picked me up from the service station, they drove me into a hospital in Rockhampton, about a thousand kilometers from Brisbane. They took me into a room with a doctor and asked me what was going on. I told the doctor that I was one of two prophets in the Bible, that witchcraft was happening, I was in the middle of a custody fight, and I was abducting my son, because my wife was a witch, and I was meant to save and judge the world. You can imagine how that sounded to a doctor – it certainly gave him enough evidence to prove I was having delusions, and I was out of my mind. I told him about God telling me that I was a prophet and that my wife was using witchcraft. However, some doctors do not believe in the spiritual world or in curses and witchcraft. I must have come across to him as a definite loony. Yes, I certainly came across loony. I had not slept well for almost three weeks, and I was in a bad way – I think he did ask if I was having trouble sleeping, and whether I was taking sleeping pills.

He asked, "Would it be all right if you came into the hospital? We want to keep you overnight to monitor you and see how you are." I said it would be fine, and we went up the elevator into the hospital, "That was fine." The doctor and I went in the elevator to go up to the hospital with a psychiatrist and the police. The psychiatrist asked me, "Does the TV ever give you special messages?"

I had never experienced that myself, although I had experienced TV shows where something said resonated well with me and brought me to tears, because I felt the Holy Spirit was speaking to me through the characters. Jesus was singing a love song to me through the music. The psychiatrist was looking for signs of schizophrenic behavior, when he asked whether I got any special messages from the TV. I said to him, "Yeah, I get messages from the TV. I get a message." Then I told him about the advertisement for the Lotto on Australian TV. I said, "Yeah, TV gives me a special message that if

I play the Lotto, I can buy a Ferrari one day with a briefcase of cash, and it motivates me to buy lotto tickets."

One of the police officers smiled and tried to suppress a laugh. Then I told the psychiatrist about another advertisement of TV – for a shampoo called Decore that makes you smell good and improves your chances with women. I said, "The TV also gives me the message that if I use Decore shampoo, I could reckon on striking it lucky with the women." One of the police officers doubled up with laughter and could not help himself. I had no idea about schizophrenia, or what the question was trying to pinpoint, but the police officer was laughing his head off – I was laughing a little myself – and the psychiatrist had a strange look on his face. Anyway, they took me into the hospital and locked the doors. About an hour later, my son was allowed into the hospital to visit me, and he gave me his teddy bear, saying it was for me. He had been told that I was sick, and he had decided that I needed his teddy bear to get better. I was emotional, and I may have even cried, because my son was going to be outside, and I could not be with him.

In the hospital, they had rules about the timing of when to go to bed. When the time came to go to bed, they gave me something to go to sleep, but it was not as powerful as my usual diazepam, and after about half an hour trying to get to sleep in my room, I went back out to the nurses and told them I could not sleep. They said, "We've already given you something for sleep so just go back for another half an hour and try again to go to sleep." I tried again for about 45 minutes, and then I went back out again and told the nurses, "I need something to get to sleep."

My mind was starting to feel like it had a thousand cords attached to it, all pulling at once in different directions. It was starting to feel bad, so they sent me back to the room and said they would be in shortly. My mind was pulling itself apart in a thousand different ways with these imaginary cords, and my patience was wearing thin. I lifted the sheet off the bed and I started to repeatedly fold and unfold the sheet; then, I started to look for something I could unscrew from the bed and take out and hit one of the nurses. It was as if I was undergoing tremendous torture, but I realized that if I became them violent, they would jab me with a needle to knock me out and lock me in one of the padded cells I had seen down the corridor.

I later discovered I was suffering from severe sleep deprivation, and because I could not get a strong enough pill to sleep, I was going out of my mind. I knew my mind was reaching a stage where I was having scary visions and hallucinations – a point of no return – and if it continued for another hour or two longer, I would be out of my mind for the rest of my life. I knew my mind was in real trouble, and I was scared. Finally, a woman came in, as I was folding the sheet again and talking to myself, and spoke to me. I did not respond, and she had to shake me several times before I gave any sign of recognition. She said, "Matthew. We've rung the doctor, and he's approved some medication. Here, take this and swallow it and you'll be able to go to sleep." I took the pill, swallowed it, and went to sleep. Finally!

I was diagnosed with manic depression – they call it bipolar today – and it was something completely new to me. I was told that I had a mental illness, and that my idea of being a prophet was a delusion of mine – it was not true that I had been called to be a prophet, and I should give up on that idea. When I had entered the hospital, I had been run down physically and was suffering badly – an inner ear infection requiring antibiotics and painkillers to stop the throbbing – a sinus infection requiring Sinutab to remove the pain and throbbing – an asthma spray to prevent asthma attacks – and they had taken all these medications away from me. Within a couple of days, I was suffering physically, as they allowed people to smoke in the ward, so every time someone smoked, my sinus would flare up, and I had a painful headache.

On one night when I was tired, feeling sick, and they would not give me my medications, an Aboriginal girl came to me and said, "I heard you're a Christian. I can't get to sleep. I haven't been able to sleep for many nights. Can you pray for me to get some sleep?" I was sick, annoyed, tired, and I was locked up in a place I could not get out of, but I laid my hand on her and prayed for her to get some sleep. The next day at breakfast, she was shouting that she was happy, because she had the first full night of restful sleep, since before she had entered the hospital. She was so happy that she gave me a hug and told everyone that 'if you need prayer for anything, see Matthew.'

I got into such a bad physical state in the hospital that my mother came to visit me in the hospital. She flew up from Coffs Harbour, and I could visit with her in the park and have lunch with her – the hospital staff felt it was safe, as I was with visitors, who would bring me back to the hospital. My mother was distressed, but I was pleased that my father allowed her to fly up, so she could stay for a few days. She was distressed, because I thought I was one of the two witnesses, and she was distressed, because this woman was in my life.

Apparently, the woman had phoned Sharryn to let her know the motel where she was staying, and she had been there when Sharryn and her mother came to pick up Brandyn and take him back. Anyway, I was allowed release from the hospital, even when there were no visitors. One day, I was allowed to go out for a break, and I decided I would go down to that part of the hospital where there was a free pharmacy to get medication for my sinus, my asthma, and my inner ear infection. Although I had asked several times in the ward, they had refused to give me my medication. They kept on telling me that I had to get permission from the psychiatrist to take so many medications. The psychiatrist never seemed to approve (or maybe he was never asked), but they did not seem to care, so I went down to the casualty pharmacy in the hospital.

When they came to my name, they asked me where I was living, and I said I was staying in the psychiatric ward upstairs, and I needed this medication. The next thing I knew, guards came down, picked me up, and I was locked back in the psychiatric ward without the medication. I was told I was not allowed to go out anymore, which upset me even more. The woman I was with talked to a social worker and demanded to see my files. We decided to start a legal action against the hospital for malpractice, because they were not giving me my medication when I needed them. The hospital must have got wind of the action, because my medication appeared almost immediately.

On the 10th day, a doctor came in and said, "I'll release you today with the medication you'll need to take for your mental illness and your medications that you came here for. You can pack your bags and leave today, if you tell me that you're not hearing from the Holy Spirit anymore." When he said that, Jesus spoke into my mind and quoted a Bible verse by saying "He that denies me before man, so shall I deny before the Father." That was a clear warning from Jesus that He wanted me to respond and not to deny His name or deny that the Holy Spirit was still speaking to me.

With the inspiration of the Holy Spirit, I said to the doctor, "Have you heard of the Aboriginal girl that couldn't sleep? I prayed for her so she could sleep. I've decided that most of the problems you call mental illness in this hospital are largely spiritual problems. I believe that with prayer and encouragement from me, many people here can begin to feel better. I think I can do a lot of good work by talking to the patients here and praying for them. For as long as I'm getting free board and accommodation, my Social Security is stacking up in the bank. I'll stay as long as you want me to stay, and I will continue to pray for people."

He became upset and shouted at me, "You pack your bags now! You're leaving now." I was happy and overjoyed. I packed my bags, and I left the hospital with my mental illness and my medication. In the car, on the way back to Brisbane, I read the scripture verse that spoke about being locked away for ten days in prison, and I was glad it applied to me. It reads:

Revelation 2:8-11

The Persecuted Church

"And to the angel of the church in Smyrna write, 'These things says the First and the Last, who was dead, and came to life: "I know your works, tribulation, and poverty (but you are rich); and I know the blasphemy of those who say they are Jews and are not, but are a synagogue of Satan. Do not fear any of those things which you are about to suffer. Indeed, the devil is about to throw some of you into prison, that you may be tested, and you will have tribulation ten days. Be faithful until death, and I will give you the crown of life. "He who has an ear, let him hear what the Spirit says to the churches. He who overcomes shall not be hurt by the second death." '

When I read that about that church, I became emotional because that is exactly what happened to me – I was locked away for ten days exactly, not eleven, or nine. It was as if God was saying, “I'm very happy with you, and I even predicted this in the Bible that you'd be tested for ten days.”

The psychiatrist had told me when I got back to Brisbane, I should check in with a psychiatrist and continue to receive outpatient psychiatric help, and I agreed with him that I would do that. I left the hospital, and I travelled back with the woman I was with to Brisbane.

Halfway back, I had a fallout with my lady friend, and she dumped me in a gas station on the side of the road with no wallet and no clothes – it was in the afternoon in the middle of winter. As she drove off, I went across to another person at a service station, told him what had happened and could he please take me into the nearest town. He laughed and said, “Yeah, women!”

He took me to the nearest town, where I went to the police station and told them that a crazy woman had dumped me there and I needed to get back to Brisbane, but I had no wallet, and I had no clothes. The police officer said, “Yeah, we heard about that. The gas station rang us and said there had been an incident there. You must be him.” I said, “Yeah, well I'm him. I have a mental illness, and I've got my medication, and I'm not dangerous. She's one of those women, who will fight with you, if you don't agree with her. That's what happened, and I don't want to be cold in the middle of winter, and I need to get back to Brisbane, but I haven't got any money, and I haven't got my wallet. Is there anything you do to help me?”

They said, "We've got an organization in town that does charity work, and they're here for situations like this. Go down to the butcher and ask for Bob, and he will probably help you out." I thought that was a good sign because my dad's name was Bob (Robert) and my middle name was Robert (Bob). I felt that this charity in town was there for good things – it seemed as if the phone call from the gas station to the police had set this up, and the police officer seemed happy in the way I had presented myself to him. I went down to the butcher and told Bob my situation, and he took me up to the travel agent in the town, where he bought me a bus ticket. He said, "Here's $10. Go over and buy yourself a meal and wait at the bar for the bus, and see you later." I took the $10, went over to the bar, and bought a hamburger and some fries. While I was eating at the bar, a couple of guys said, "You're new to town? What are you doing here?"

I told them about everything that had happened, and that I was now waiting for the bus to take me back to Brisbane. One of the guys said, "Do you want a beer?" I said, "It's times like this when I certainly could do with a beer, but I haven't got any money left, so I can't shout you a beer back." He said, "Ah, we're going to be here for a couple of hours; we'll shout you a few beers. This has got to be one of the funniest stories we've ever heard." I was glad that it was funny for them, and I think I had three or four beers and a great conversation. Then I went to the bus for a four-hour trip back to Brisbane.

To this day, I am grateful for the provision God had provided in that town for me. Little things such as that – well it was not such a little thing for me – serve to encourage your faith. Although I was not in a great position with God, I believed that God had certainly stepped up to the mark, looked after me, and provided for me in that situation. I hope this small part of the story is an encouragement for you.

When I reached Brisbane, I moved into a friend's place for about a week, and then moved into a shared accommodation with a stranger. On the second night, the harassing phone calls started again. I felt that the woman who had dumped me had gone to Townsville for my phone number and was making harassing phone calls to make sure that I had moved out. I asked my friend whether he had given out the number of where I had moved. He said, "Some woman rang after you, I thought it was okay." I said, "Yeah, well, that was the bitch that dropped me off, I'm sure," and he did not have the name of who had called. I moved out the shared accommodation, but this time I did not give a forwarding phone number.

It would take me a couple of years to get over the fear of a phone ringing. It used to lock me up with fear for a while, every time I received a phone call late at night, but God could heal me of that fear and fix that up. I went and checked myself in to see a local psychiatrist. They were happy that I had checked in with them and started to make appointments for me to visit them regularly, so they could check me out.

Chapter 30

Miss My Son for a Year

After suffering my breakdown in the Rockhampton hospital, I had returned to Brisbane. What I had done was to break the law by abducting my son for longer than a weekend, and the government was not happy with that. My ex-wife Sharryn was certainly not happy with that, and she did not allow me access to my son for at least a year, and because the courts were not involved, it was just her own personal decision.

I had to initiate the matter in court to gain access to my child, and she made it obvious that she did not want to give me access to my son. She would not return my phone calls – she would not let me come to see him – she removed any opportunity to see him at day care. I was left in a position where I could not see him again, until the courts made their decision and said it was okay. It was a deeply distressing time for me, especially as I mentioned earlier that my friend Sara had told me I should carry on living for the sake of my son because my son would not understand why I chose to end my life through suicide. She had told me to carry on living so I could see my son and have an effect on his life, and consequently, he became the reason I was living. With the removal of my son from my life, I found not much purpose in life – very little reason to continue living. It was a sad and depressing time for me, as I had to spend a whole year without him.

At the beginning of the year, I was not aware how long it would take to process the matter through the court to force my ex-wife to let me see my son. I had thought it would be a simple process, taking just a month or two. However, it took a year – if I had known that at the start, I might have been a little more relaxed and exercised more patience. As the months went by without progress, it became upsetting for me as a father of a young son. When I had abducted him, I had a tremendous relationship with him.

It was obvious that his mother had abused him, and I feared for him. It distressed me that the last image he had of me was in the hospital when he gave me his teddy bear – after that, he did not see his father again for over a year. All through the whole abduction fiasco, my sole motivation had been to remove my son from the environment of his abusive mother, so I could protect and look after him. Not everything in my life has been motivated by selfishness, self-gain or by feelings of self-importance – from an attitude of wanting everything for myself and wanting things my way. Although my testimony so far might not reflect me as a pleasant person toward others, I had been doing my best to get through life and cope with events – many of my earlier decisions came from the pain and the consequences of sexual abuse in my life.

I was operating out of weakness and deep emotional pain, and this had an effect on how I lived and on the choices I made. I did not see my son for about a year, and then the courts ordered Sharryn to let me see my son again. I was happy when they finally reached that decision – it had been a long drawn-out process, and I have empathy for all those fathers who cannot see their children. It seemed that not seeing my son for a year, and not being able to cope with my life, were the main reasons for my life being out of kilter, and was God's way of preparing me for my life, my son's life, and my relationship with my son. It was like a pre-test for me to focus on having a genuine reason to live, and not being dependent on my love for my son.

Chapter 31

Life of a Cab Driver

Twenty years ago, my job – and my life – was driving taxis. I did this on and off for about six years, and most of this time I spent driving at nighttime between 4 p.m. to 4 a.m. I would normally only drive on Wednesday through Sunday nights, although on Wednesday, Thursday, and Sunday night, I would only drive while I could earn $20 an hour with the taxi – I received half the money raised ($10 an hour) – so, on those nights, I only drove until about 12, because the hourly rate dropped sharply when people were in bed asleep, because they did not have to go to work the following day. It was only Friday and Saturday night people stayed up late, so it was busy all through the 12-hour shift. I became an experienced driver, and I was able to earn plenty of money in the time allotted to me.

Around this time, I lived on top of a hill in a suburb called Spring Hill – a ten-minute walk from the Brisbane CBD and only a three-minute walk from the major high-rise buildings in the northern part of the city. In addition, right there in Spring Hill – only one block from my house – was the city's finest and best striptease establishment called *Players*. The owner of the establishment allowed taxi drivers free entry (as opposed to the normal $10 entry fee) into his club, and to have free brewed coffee and sodas.

Taxi drivers were encouraged to spend their downtime in the strip club, and to get to know the strippers and the wait staff, and to enjoy themselves. The club had plenty of naked girls running around. It had a stage where the girls would strip every 10 minutes, and a back area where the girls would take off all their clothes and lap dance with the men. Although it was against the law, the men could touch the girls, but the law turned a blind eye to what was happening. It was a sort of illegal club, but it was never closed, although the owner of the club was serving alcohol without a license, which was definitely against the law.

Although he did not have a liquor license, he stocked a full bar and charged normal bar prices for the alcohol – it was a big money spinner for him – and this was on top of the 50% he received from the strippers of the money they raised with the striptease and the lap dances. He would also charge an entrance fee of $10 from each person who came into the club. If a person was prepared to cough up the $10 entry fee, they could go for a night's drinking in the strip club, surrounded by naked and scantily dressed women – I suppose it could be classified as an enjoyable place to hang out.

The place was always full, and it proved a handy place to drop off passengers, park the taxi outside, have a cup of coffee, and spend your downtime with the chance of plenty of passengers coming out of the club looking for a trip home. I was never sure of how long the trip was going to be, but it was a profitable choice for me to spend time there. On slow nights with the taxi – usually Wednesday, Thursday, and Sunday – I would return my taxi by midnight and then stop off at the club for a few drinks. I had that physique which gave me the capacity to consume alcohol without too many problems or aftereffects. I became friendly with a few of the strippers at the club, but I did not book any of the girls for lap dances.

When any of the new girls approached me, and asked if I wanted a lap dance, I would reply, "No, I just visit the club and I'm a friend of the strippers." If they wanted a lift home with me on a Friday and Saturday night, I could take them home without them worrying about me knowing where they lived. The girls used to talk among themselves about me, and the other strippers would confirm that, "Yeah, Matthew isn't a sleaze. He respects us, and he is a good fellow to talk to, and yes, you can get a lift home with him without hassles."

Often on a day-off from work, I would bump into one of the girls when I was in the city center, and we would stop for a chat, and if they were off duty, they would pitch in, and we would go for a cup of coffee or go to a movie. A couple of times I was invited to their place for dinner, and once I was dropping a girl at home, when I was invited in for a drink and to smoke some marijuana with her (I know people usually refer to it as "pot" or "grass" but the American euphemism for it somehow escapes me at the moment!). I did not use marijuana very often, because with my mental illness, it used to make me feel extremely funny. I once smoked some marijuana with this girl, when I was 30 kilometers south of the city, and when I got in my taxi to drive back, I was decidedly under the weather (and under the influence), and it certainly made for an interesting trip home. I learned my lesson quickly.

I was pleased that I managed to return the taxi in one piece, but I never participated in smoking marijuana when I had to drive a car again – definitely not a mixture that I would recommend. Driving under the influence of anything is a definite "no-no." I remember, once after a drinking session, that my driving ability (or lack of it) was so bad that I parked the car, called a taxi home and went back to pick the car up the following day.

In the strip club, because I was in taxi uniform, people would often approach me and ask who the best stripper in the place was, or whether I could recommend a stripper. I had a standard reply, "Do you prefer a brunette? Do you prefer a blond? Or do you want the one who I believe is the best?" The girls were always happy with the recommendations I gave for them, and often during their breaks, they would sit with me and shout drinks for me while we talked. I told them that it was not necessary to shout drinks, as I was happy to buy my own, but they said they felt somewhat indebted, because they were earning money from my recommendations. Other men would ask me where they could find street-walking prostitutes, who hung around outside the strip club, and I would recommend the best girls who I was friendly with, although it was never someone who I had used for sexual services.

My addiction to prostitutes continued from my earlier years, and on a Friday night, about 8:30, when it got quiet, I would visit a prostitute for half an hour of sex, and then continue working. On a Friday night, the prostitute would cost about $120 for half an hour, so I would have to continue working afterward on a Friday night, because it took not only the money I had already earned, but also the money I would have owed the taxi owner. I developed a work style, where on slow nights I would take a 20-minute coffee break around 8 p.m., and then knock off around midnight and drink until the early morning. On Friday and Saturday night I would stop the taxi around eight for a break, or sometimes go out for a meal with another taxi driver, and then about midnight, I would stop for a ten-minute coffee break. Then I would knock off about four in the morning, go to the club, and drink until six.

Many people talk about their non-Christian life, as though it was a difficult and unenjoyable life, and how their life was transformed with Jesus Christ and has been better ever since. Well, I was a backslidden Christian, and I was not attending any church. My life was driving taxis with strippers as friends, and I was sleeping with a prostitute once a week – it was an enjoyable life, and I was happy driving taxis. I enjoyed meeting and having conversations with strangers. I certainly did witness for Jesus in the taxi sometimes and share what Jesus was like to people. Some of you may see that as hypocritical, but even in my sinful lifestyle, I could still lead people to Jesus. I will talk more about the taxies another time, but at the time, this was my life.

Chapter 32

Meet Chloe

As I have mentioned many times before, I had an addiction to the services of prostitutes. I spent plenty of my time securing the services of, and then spending copious amounts of my money on, prostitutes. One day I was at home in Spring Hill, a couple of blocks from the strip club I mentioned in the last chapter, and I was looking through a "*Picture*" magazine for local prostitutes, when I discovered an advertisement for a prostitute in Spring Hill. It was the first time I had seen an advertisement for a prostitute in Spring Hill, and her name was printed there. Her name, Chloe, was not her real name, but her working name. I rang the number on the advertisement, and Chloe answered the phone. I asked her the typical questions about herself, what she looked like and did she kiss? I was surprised when she said that, unlike many prostitutes, she did kiss – and what surprised me even more was that she lived in Spring Hill, in an apartment block I had walked past many times. In the past, I had even commented to a roommate that I would love to live in one of those apartments.

I went round to the apartment block and pressed the security intercom downstairs. From the intercom, she said, "Is that Matthew?" I said, "Yeah, it is." She opened the gate and told me directions on how to reach her unit. I opened the gate, went up, pressed the buzzer on her door, and Chloe came to the door. There was nothing outstanding about Chloe in the looks department. She was certainly attractive, but I had seen so many attractive girls that I was maybe becoming immune to natural beauty. However, when I walked into the apartment, I noticed her lounge was tastefully decorated with painted American Indian carvings, totem poles, and ceramics. Her bedroom had the same decorations, carvings that looked like ceramics.

After we had sex, I asked her whether she made the decorations herself, and she said that she did. I asked her how long it took her to make them, and she replied, "It depends, but usually between two and five hours. I asked her whether she ever made them for her clients, and she said, "Not really. It is a lot of time to invest". I have always been able to feel a spiritual presence when I had found it before, and I could feel a spiritual presence coming from the carvings and the totem poles. I asked her a little about her spirituality, and she said that she connected most with American Indian folklore. She considered herself one, which I found to be interesting and intriguing.

As I mentioned before, I used to go from one prostitute to the next and only see a prostitute once. However, before I walked out the door with Chloe's card in my hand, I was already contemplating seeing her again. I did see her a second time, and it was just as enjoyable as the first time, as well as I had more time to talk to her about her spiritual beliefs and the carvings. I still had my manuscript, *The Fallen Ones,* which I had written about prostitutes, and I asked her whether she would be interested in reading my manuscript about a couple of Kings Cross prostitutes. She said she was not really a reader, and that she did not read often, but she said she would read my manuscript. Every few hours I would ring her up and ask her how much she had read, and she eventually she told me to stop ringing her, as I was interrupting her reading, and she would ring me when she had finished the manuscript.

As a taxi driver, I would often be asked by men coming out of *Players* to find a prostitute for them, and I would normally take them a place called Fortitude Valley, where prostitutes walked the streets just as in Kings Cross in Sydney. However, after I had met Chloe and spent some time with her – and found out she was a fabulous person, easy to talk to, funny and pretty – when I came across guys who seemed respectable, I used to tell them that I knew a working girl just up the road. If they were prepared to wait a tick before I turned the meter on, I would give Chloe a ring to see if she was available.

Most of the time when I rang her, she said it was okay for the man to pop up and see her there. Then Chloe would ring me back on my phone so I could pick up the guy and take him back to his home. It worked both ways, as we were both getting business, but after a few weeks, I got tired of hearing what the guys thought of Chloe and hearing their feedback on the girl that I had recommended to them. I started to feel a little jealous, and I was saddened sometimes by the disrespectful comments they made about her. I reached a point where I would simply drop the guy off at Chloe’s place and then go and look for other business instead of coming back to pick him up and take him home – I did not want to hear what he had to say about the girl with whom I was beginning to fall in love.

It was not hard for me to fall in love in those days – the girl just had to show me some attention. Although Chloe was a prostitute, and the attention she was showing me was paid for, I still was heavily attracted to her and became very much in love with her. I told her one day that I would continue seeing her, when I dropped off clients, or when she rang me to invite me for a cup of coffee – but as for seeing her as a client, I could not see her anymore, and she was shocked. She asked me why that was so, and I said that I had fallen in love with her, and I could not see her anymore. I could not use her body in that way anymore, because I loved her.

Yeah, it sounds strange, but I had never faced this situation with a prostitute before – it was a new thing for me to be in love with a prostitute. She was shocked and tried to talk me around by saying, “Well, instead of just having sex with me, each time you see me, you can make love to me. And, I’ll kiss you back, and it’ll be just as if you are making love to me. You said that you love me and wouldn’t it be enjoyable for you to come and be with me in that way?” I said, “No, I can’t. My mind would be too involved.” I continued to drop clients off at her place to see her, but the only way I would see her is when I went to have a cup of coffee with her. This went on for a few months, and on Friday and Saturday nights, I would drop a few clients off at her place. Sometimes, she would make between $500 and $1000 with the clients that I would drop off each week. It was easy for me, as I was in a place where the guys were asking for a prostitute – in a way, I was happy, as I was helping her out and making her job easier. We continued in this way for a while, and I think I only had coffee with her twice in the whole of the next three months.

One morning, about five, when most of the Brisbane prostitutes had finished work and gone to bed, I felt I wanted to use the services of a prostitute, and I had money for it. I rang Chloe and asked her if I could break my rule and see her just once. She laughed at me and said, "You're kidding me. This is a joke." I said, "No, it's not a joke. If you're available, if you're still working I'd love to come and see you." She said, "And, pay? You're going to come and pay me and book me for half an hour? You love me, and you're breaking your own rule, and you're going to come in and see me?" I said, "Yeah, if that's okay?" She replied, "That's okay; ring me from the bell when you get there."

I reached her place about 20 minutes later. I rang the bell downstairs, and she said, "Is this Matthew?" I said, "Yeah," and she said, "You are making me all excited, Matthew." That sounded promising, but I did not fully understand what she was saying. As soon as she opened the door, she embraced me and started kissing me. It was like a scene from the movies where the couple shut the door, start kissing, and clothes are taken off (or thrown off) all the way to the bedroom. It was one of those scenes I had seen happening in the movies – but this was really happening – and just as in the movies, we went to bed and made love.

I was to discover later that she had come to love me. After reading the book, she had fallen in love with the author of *The Fallen Ones*. She had gone through a stage where she believed I was too naïve and not street-smart enough to have written the book, so she had phoned a longtime friend of mine, who assured her that it was my book. She told me that she had fallen in love with me because of the book, and because I was her first client to say he was in love with her and had actually left. She admired my courage to leave, and in one way, it had broken her heart, but she was happy with my inner strength that it took for me to stop seeing her.

The half-hour booking extended through to breakfast, after which we made love again, and then talked, had coffee, and then went out for lunch. Eventually, I spent the whole day with her until the evening, and from that point onward, we started to date each other as boyfriend and girlfriend. When this happened, she already had a boyfriend, but she broke it off with him. We started to go out together, and sometimes when I was not working, I might go round to her place to visit, and when a client came to see her, she would just put me out on the veranda and close the screen. I would read a book until she had finished with the client. She would see the client out, and then we would start chatting for a while until the next client came, when she would close the screen, and I would carry on reading a book.

I remember the first time it happened; she told me not to peek through the window, as she did not want me to watch her when she was busy with a client. It was not something that I was particularly into, and the thought would not have crossed my mind to look at her having sex with a client. I am told this does not happen often, because prostitutes do not normally date a former client. It may sound like a strange situation, but all I can say is this is all true, including the part where Chloe fell in love with me because of a book. We moved from just dating to where we became engaged, when I asked Chloe to marry me.

My parents came up to visit me in Brisbane, and I told them I was dating a prostitute, I loved her, and I wanted to marry her. Mom had always known me as a bit of a strange guy, who had been hurt by his first marriage, and had wondered whether I was going to find love again. I was so happy when my parents sat together with Chloe over coffee and cake. My mother actually paid for the bill, and when Chloe went to give her some money, my mother said, "No, you pay the bill next time." I thought it was funny to see the exchange between the two women – it was if there was a subtitle, "I want to see you next time, and I want you to still be with my son next time." There was this feeling that my mother had no shame of her son dating a prostitute. It was a healing to me to see that – it was similar to the story of the prodigal son. I replay that memory sometimes –

the depth of my mother's love for me was such that she would accept a girl she knew would later that day sleep with men for money, but her son loved this woman. She showed her no judgment in her eyes. It is not every mother's wish that her son should become engaged to a prostitute, but my mother was happy, and that day was special.

We became engaged, and Chloe was talking about how she wanted the wedding. Chloe lived with her foster mother, and there was enough space at her property for her to keep a horse. She planned to marry on an island – to ride up on the horse on the beach, jump off the horse, marry, and then go riding into the sunset with me on the horse – she was planning an idyllic wedding. About the same time, I decided to stop with my medication, as I figured I was beginning to feel well again…and I was putting on weight. My roommate's friend said, "The medication is slowing you right down. You have a glazed look in your eyes!" Therefore, I went off my medication, which is not something I would recommend to people with psychiatric problems; however, I have to say that Chloe was a truly beautiful woman, I loved her very much, and I was feeling in excellent shape.

Chapter 33

Lose Taxi Job

I worked on and off driving taxis for about four to five years, but there was a period where I lost my taxi license for three years, because the law requires you to have a clean driving license – with its full points – for you to drive a taxi. If you lose your driving license, then you need to wait three years, before you can get another taxi license. I waited the three years, and then I drove a taxi for another couple of years, during which time I collected enough demerit points for me to lose my driver's license again, which meant I automatically lost my taxi license. That was a bit of a blow.

Chloe had worked out that I needed to earn a couple of thousand dollars a week to marry her. I had devised a plan to lease about four taxis – driving one taxi myself and managing the other three taxis – to earn the $2,000 a week I would need, so Chloe could retire from working as a prostitute and become my wife. After plenty of research, I calculated that $800 a week of the necessary $2,000 would have come from driving a taxi myself. Therefore losing my job was a major disappointment, as I enjoyed driving a taxi. Losing my taxi license meant that I would just have to wait for three years, then I could get a new taxi license and drive taxis again.

Although I had been through the license-losing scenario before, I found it difficult to handle, because I really enjoyed driving taxis. It was so much fun to pick up a stranger and to travel from one place to another just talking to a stranger. As you might have realized, I enjoy talking, and I enjoy conversation. For me, it was an exciting time in the taxi, earning money just by talking. I enjoyed the driving as well. I enjoyed driving all over Brisbane. I enjoyed driving back into the city with the radio playing the music loud. I enjoyed driving along the highway, at two in the morning, with hardly another car on it. I have always enjoyed driving; therefore, it was a real blow for me to have to wait for three years before I could drive a taxi again – it was disheartening and discouraging – and I was extremely sad.

Chapter 34

Break Up with Chloe

Before I say anything else, I have to say that Chloe was a major light in my life. She was a beautiful person. She was funny. She was attractive to me. She was spontaneous. She danced just as I did. She loved to laugh. She was a thinker. She used to think on her feet. She used to reason out situations. She would read between the lines. She would read the story behind the story. She was smart. I could carry on with this list forever and a day. I loved her so much. When I lost my taxi license, she said that I would not be able to earn the $2,000 a week we would need, and we would have to break off the engagement. I was so sad that it broke my heart – I think it broke her heart, too. She told me the job situation was not the only cause of the breakup, but she said she had heard from Jesus. She knew I was a Christian, and she had heard from Jesus, "Matthew's going to marry another woman in the future, and you're not her, and if he marries you, this will prevent him from marrying the woman I've chosen for him."

She said the news saddened her, but she had to obey Jesus. In all my time, with so many prostitutes, I had never told one of the girls that I was a practicing Christian – a Christian at least, maybe not so much practicing. I had never shared with them that I was a Christian, as I did not want to dishonor the name of Jesus before those girls. I was not the type of Christian, who had sex with a prostitute and then told her she needed to be saved. I am sure many prostitutes have heard that story before, and it does not wash well knowing that the person having sex with them wants to convert them, when he is actually seeing them for a need in his own life. I have never told any working girl that I was a Christian, but I got so close to Chloe that I told her that I was a Christian – I was not going to church, but I knew Jesus and had a good relationship with Him.

Chloe told me once that she did not have a problem with Jesus, as she rather liked Him. However, she did have a problem with

Christians, because she had been raped and sexually abused by Christians in a foster home – by her foster father and foster brothers, who had called themselves Christians. Once, when Chloe and I were making love, I asked her why she never made a noise, and she told me she had learned to remain silent when she was raped in her foster home – she had to be quiet, because others might hear what was happening, and they would have caused problems for her if they found out.

When she told me Jesus had said she should break up with me, because He had another wife lined up for me in the future, I told her I did not want anyone else – I wanted her – but she was insistent that she was not going to cross Jesus. I could sense that she was a little hurt that there might be a better woman than her, but she believed Jesus and was prepared to let me go. On the first day of our relationship, Chloe had asked me what we were going to do with the money I had paid her for the half-hour session (the session that had lasted for the rest of the day and led to many wonderful things afterward). I had suggested that we might go to a forthcoming Australian musician's concert with the pop singer, John Farnham, and the opera singer, Anthony Warlow. After we had broken off the engagement, we still remained friends and saw each other from time to time, and I went with her to the concert.

While we were watching the concert, a small girl went up to the stage with a rose and gave it to John Farnham – Chloe was noticeably affected by this. I asked her, "What's going on?" She told me she was remembering a time as a young girl when she had given John Farnham a rose, and this was a special moment for her to be with me at this time.

A few days later, I met with her again, and she told me that she could no longer be my friend. Full of tears, I asked her why she was saying that, and she said that Jesus had talked to her, saying I needed to get some emotional and spiritual healing. Her friendship with me was just a crutch for me, as it was not allowing me to face my demons. I needed to work through my issues and receive healing, so I would be better for a future wife and better able to serve God. Breaking up the engagement with her was a big loss, but losing her as a friend was heartbreaking. That was what I missed most with my wife Sharryn – I did not mind so much breaking up as her husband, but I really missed being a friend. Here Chloe was saying the same words, when she said she could not be my friend, and that really upset me.

However, she asked me to promise her something and I asked, "What?" She said, "No, just promise me that you'll do something for me," and I replied, "I need to know what it is, before I promise." She said, "No, just promise whatever I want, you will do it." I replied, "Okay, I promise." Then she said, "I want you to promise to publish the book, *The Fallen Ones*, about the prostitutes." I said, "Why?" She said, "How can people ever love me, if they don't understand me? How will they ever understand me, unless they read this book?" I asked her, "Is it good enough?" She said, "Yeah. Promise me you'll publish it, and when I see it on the bookshelves, I'll contact you, and we can be friends again." I was in tears, but I was happy there was a way I could be with her and see her as a friend again – I would publish *The Fallen Ones.*

I was really sad to lose her as a friend – I was brokenhearted. Not many people in my life knew of Chloe – it is not normal to say that you had a fiancée who was a prostitute, as it could have been embarrassing. My older brother, Rodney, knew about her, as did my mother and father. My ex-wife, Sharryn, met her and knew about her – but not many other people knew about her. She was a special person for me – someone I dearly loved – someone I wish I had married – and someone special enough to cause me to publish books such as this. This is a tell-all book, and I am not sure how many women would be interested in what I have to say. I enjoyed Chloe, and I love her. She is a darling, and I hope to meet her again in the future, if God can arrange it.

Chapter 35

Writes Second Book

After I had sadly broken up with Chloe, I was somewhat depressed. I needed to know whether I could write another book. I wondered if the book *The Fallen Ones* was the only book that I could have written.

I wanted to know whether I was a writer, and I could produce another book – develop characters and develop a plot line in another one. I did not want to be a "one-hit wonder." I wanted to develop a second book, and I decided I wanted to write one as a prophecy over my life. I wanted to write something that would project and lay down a basis for the future life I wanted to live. I wanted to dream about my future and to put that down through a fictional character, so one day, I might achieve my musings. I chose the title for my second book as *The Chosen Ones*.

My first novel had been about the prostitutes in Kings Cross and was called *The Fallen Ones,* so the choice of *The Chosen Ones* seemed close enough to be a logical sequel. I decided the main character in the novel was to be a writer who had been locked in a psychiatric ward (which I had), and who had met an Aboriginal girl while there (which I had). Both wanted to become famous, and through the Aboriginal girl, he met an actress who was still at school at the time, but was taking part in a play written by her teacher. He became acquainted with the teacher, who said he could co-write and co-direct the play with the student to whom he had been introduced.

The writer, who was only twenty in the book, became the co-director of the play, then took over the leading role when the girl's leading man fell off a horse and broke his leg. As the new lead in the play, he has his first kiss with the girl. Things develop, and as the girl becomes an accomplished actress, he becomes first her director, then her fiancé and finally her husband.

Then my developing writer character wrote a film, based on his first novel, with his new wife as the star. Although the film was made in Sydney, it became an International film and went on to win twelve Oscars. The characters went on to use their stardom and higher profiles to preach the good news of Jesus, and how, in those changing times, Jesus wanted to restore and rebuild His church. They preached about warnings and judgments of things to come. I set my two characters up to be spokespersons and preachers, similar to the two witnesses – the last two prophets mentioned in the Chapter 11 of the Book of Revelation.

The book was feeding into what I assumed was my delusion – at the time, I did not think it was a delusion – that I would be one of the two witnesses. I still had the opinion then that I possibly was one of the two witnesses, so I was writing a book, *The Chosen Ones*, possibly projecting how I was going to become popular in the world.

My brother made a website for *The Chosen Ones* and uploaded it to a free website, where you could get free space if they could put banner advertisements on your website. I put it on free space. I totally lost that web address, and now I cannot find the book. Somehow I lost the manuscript of *The Chosen Ones*. I had no digital copy or printed copy of the manuscript, and I lost the website address of *The Chosen Ones* – I was totally lost. At one stage, God had told me to throw out *The Fallen Ones,* but I had not done so, instead, I had "thrown out" *The Chosen Ones*.

I wrote a good novel – an exciting novel to read, and far less sexually graphic than *The Fallen Ones* I had written previously. It was tame in comparison, but I was happy with the book, as it was a good story and something of a page-turner.

Chapter 36

Boarding House Life

When I lost my taxi license because of too many demerit points, I lost my ability to drive taxis. I had to go on Unemployment Benefits, and my income plummeted from $600-$700 a week down to about $200 a week – a dramatic (and drastic) decrease in money. Certainly, a decrease that made it difficult to live in a house, to pay for food, and for my extra activities. I had to move out from sharing an apartment in Spring Hill to a boarding house.

The first boarding house I moved into had about twenty people living there. They supplied breakfast cereal, toast, and orange juice in the morning, and a cooked meal in the evening. I had a good room and a TV, but it was boring, as I did not have much money to go out and do things. I did not belong to a library at the time, so I could not borrow books to read. Sleeping, then watching TV in the afternoon soon became a bit old really fast. In the boarding house, I met a guy who suffered from post-traumatic stress syndrome, and when he went through the characteristics, it sounded much like the characteristics of bipolar, which I had.

I remember I had a few other friends in the boarding house – one had a car, and he took my son and me out in the car once to the beach. He had a job, and when he came home after work, he used to enjoy my friendship. A few people in the boarding house did not like me, joked about me and made fun of me – not too interesting.

Around that time, when I took my son to the beach, I remember him telling me that his name was no longer Brandyn Payne, but had changed. His mother had changed his last name to that of her fiancé. I found it sad and depressing, as I did not think you could change a child's last name without the father's permission – but obviously, they did it. My son still has this last name, but for the sake of his privacy, I will not say his last name – even if I could spell it – but it upset me. It was as if my son was not my son anymore. Brandyn was only about seven at the time, but he knew that it affected me. He knew that the name change had affected me, and he saw how emotional I was about it.

Later, I moved into another boarding house, but I did not stay there too long, so I moved to another boarding house that supplied breakfast and dinner. While at this boarding house, I became friendly with a guy who had a concreting business and was in charge of many workers. He was a hard worker, but he loved to go to a Brisbane casino and gamble on roulette. He would make several bets on particular numbers, and the bets would amount to between $500 and $700 each time – the first time we went out, he won about $5,000 and he shouted me a meal

We had a few drinks and had a good meal. He loved my company. At the time, I busy editing and polishing *The Fallen Ones*, because I was going to self-publish it one day. My brother had said that if I went to Coffs Harbour, and helped him in his business for a while, he would self-publish my book for me, but at the time, I thought it was going to cost $6,000 for a thousand copies of the book. I did not know any other way of self-publishing then, and my friend from the boarding house said, "If you go to Coffs Harbour with your brother, and your brother does not publish your book for you, I will give you the money." I thought that was remarkable.

The second time we went out gambling, we were in the middle of making the bets, when he said he had to go to the toilet and would I continue betting. That was extremely stressful for me, as I placed three bets while he was away – I placed $2,100 worth of bets while he was in the toilet. Thankfully, I won on two out of three of the spins of the wheel and actually increased our winnings before he came back. I remember that it gave me a wonderful sense of pride that he trusted me enough to gamble on his behalf and spend his money. It also impressed me that he offered to publish my book, but I said to him that my brother would pay for that, so there would be no need.

While I was at this boarding house, one of the guys there had a visit from his younger sister. I think I was about thirty at the time, and his sister was about twenty, so she was young compared with me, but she was attractive. My heart leapt at how attractive and how sweet she was. I started talking to her once, and then, on another occasion, I met her and I filled myself with the courage to ask her out on a date. She said, "Yes," she would love to go out with me. I found out soon enough in the first date that she was a witch, when I overheard a question her brother asked her, "Did the spell work?" I was curious about what that meant, and I asked her and her brother what was going on. It turned out that she had put a spell on me, when she had first met me – some form of love spell so I would become extremely attracted to her.

The spell certainly worked because I was extremely attracted to her, and we went out on a few dates together, and I began to like her. I remember once we were walking through South Bank Park, and I was about to say, "You need to know Jesus. You need to give your life to Jesus", and before I could utter the words, she said, "Don't say that." When I asked her what she meant, she said, "Don't say what you're going to say." I asked, "How do you know what I was going to say?" She said, "I can read your mind." I became upset with her, because she did not want to accept Jesus, and she did not want me to make that statement. We had a little argument and walked away from each other in a huff, but we came back to each other and patched things up.

I remember another time, when I was lying in bed with her, I was about to say, "Gee, your perfume smells beautiful," when she said, "It does, doesn't it?" I said, "What?" to which she replied, "You were about to say my perfume smells beautiful," and I said, "Yeah, it does smell beautiful, and again, you read my mind." She said, "Yeah, it's a skill I have."

Some people in the Christian world maintain that neither Satan nor people can read your thoughts. I found that Christians hold onto many things they believe are the truth but are not so. For instance, some say that Christians cannot be possessed by a demon – many

Christians firmly believe that a Christian cannot have a demon. However, in my experience, I have had demons in my life as a Christian and have seen the complete change in myself when the demon has left. My whole behavior had changed when the demon was cast out. So again here was an issue I have seen firsthand, when I was about to say something and this girl reading my mind twice.

So, I firmly believe that Satan can read minds – some would say that the only way Satan can read a mind is when he places a thought in your mind, then tells you what your thought is. I do not believe that either, because she would not have put a thought in my mind. The idea of giving her life to Jesus was opposite to what she wanted, so we had a mini argument over that, when we were walking in the park. Certainly it was not a thought she placed in my mind to try to convince me she was reading minds. Years later, I met a Christian guy who had been involved in witchcraft for a while, and he said that one of the lower levels of witchcraft is the ability to read minds. He said it was one of the simpler things witches do, and he went on to tell me about astral travel – something we might call going to heaven in a vision, or moving or travelling in the spirit.

They could be in their house in Australia, then travel (astral travel) to America, walk into a room, and see, hear and experience things in America. Then they could return and be able to tell you exactly what was happening in that room.

Despite this, she was exciting – we talked about marriage and looked at wedding dresses. I liked her, because she was pretty, but more so, because she was spiritual. I was deeply attracted to the spiritual element in her life, and it helped that she liked me as well.

As a Christian reading this, you might be shaking your head saying, how foolish can one man be? Surely Matthew knows that he should, as a Christian, marry a Christian. In one instance he wanted to marry an American Indian believing prostitute, and now here he wanted to marry what many would say is an enemy of the Christian faith, a self-confessed, practicing witch. All I can say, in my defense, was that I was a very lonely and sad individual. I liked pretty women that loved me, and I enjoyed sharing a spirituality with the women I loved, whether that was what I believed or not.

In boarding houses, either you have people you like, or you have people you do not like. In every boarding house, there are always people with whom you will not get on. However, if you are fortunate, there will be a person who you do get on with, which makes your stay enjoyable. That is the extent of my experiences there.

Chapter 37

Talks to Jesus

While I was at the boarding house where I met the witch, I found a book at a Christian bookstore called *Experiencing the Inner Depths of Jesus Christ* by Madame Guyon – a book about how to communicate, and how to have a personal relationship, with Jesus Christ. In the book, it explained how to start maintain a two-way conversation with Jesus. It was exciting to read and easy to apply, so I started speaking sentences with Jesus.

Recently, I heard from my brother, Rodney, that a childhood friend called Stuart is talking to Jesus back and forth now. Apparently he had borrowed the book from Rodney and taught himself how to talk to Jesus. It is a good book, and I suggest you buy it begin applying it to your life. One day at the boarding house, I went for a walk, so I could put the book to the test. I had a talk with Jesus, and He said to me that He wants me to stop fighting for my son. My wife had said that I could not see my son anymore, and at the time, I had legal forms ready to fight her in court, so I could enforce my right to have access to my son. The message from Jesus here, you will notice, was the same as the angel I took to the airport, saying not to fight in the courts with my former wife

Jesus told me in that conversation I was not to fight over my son, as though he were a piece of furniture. He told me I should leave my son to my wife, and her new fiancée, and walk away. Jesus also told me to move away, as my son was the only reason I was still staying in Brisbane.

I did not have a job, but there was more of a chance of a job in Sydney. Jesus said, "I want you to move to Sydney. I want you to stop fighting for access to your son."

There was a pause in what he was saying, and then I heard it said I was not to stop thinking I was one of the two witnesses. I had reached the point in my life where I thought I might be one of the two prophets who were coming to warn and judge the world (ie The two witnesses).

I want to stress here that Satan always seems to know when you are speaking to God, and sadly, sometimes he speaks to us, who are close to God, with a spirit that masquerades as the voice of Jesus.

I had heard correctly from Jesus, when he told me to stop fighting for access to my son, and to pack up and leave from Sydney. I had then been deceived by an antichrist spirit, which told me not to give up on my belief that I was one of the two last prophets to judge the world.

At the time that this lie was said to me, I had no idea that an antichrist spirit was talking to me. I thought that was also the authentic voice of Jesus. The whole idea that I was this future coming to the world, powerful prophet really messed with my head and had helped land my in hospital, and yet as a sincere believer in Jesus, and His voice, I had to consider everything I heard him (supposedly) say.

Many might read this and run away and think, "I am happy with the Bible. I don't want a false spirit speaking to me, and I don't want the risk of being deceived by a spirit when I think it is Jesus." And this reaction is valid, and this fear is one of the major reasons Christians don't enjoy a rich relationship with Jesus today.

The book by Madam Guyon was a life changing book for me. I have had thousands of hours of worthwhile and edifying conversations with Jesus, since that time, and thousands of people have been helped and blessed by my ability to pass on a personal message from Jesus to them (prophecy). This was all made possible, because I first read this book, and also because, even when I found out I had an antichrist spirit trying to trip me up from time to time, I persisted with my faith and communion with Jesus.

Chapter 38

Losing My Son Brandyn

I would like to talk about losing my son for a moment. Through learning to talk with Jesus, because of the book I had read, Jesus told me I was not to fight for custody of my son, but I was to leave my son and move to Sydney.

When I was going out with Chloe, one day we went out with our sons to a fireworks display after dinner. Later, we dropped my son off at his mother's place, and Sharryn came out to meet all of us. Chloe introduced herself as my fiancée, and Sharryn was cordial as she could be. Later, in the car on the way home, Chloe said to me that she did not think she would ever say this as a mother, but I needed to stop seeing my son, as my former wife was doing witchcraft on me.

Chloe had been watching me over the last year, and she had noticed that every time I saw my son, I would become depressed and despondent. She had thought it was because of seeing my son, but after meeting Sharryn, she realized that Sharryn was evil and was doing witchcraft on me – it was the witchcraft making me down and despondent every two weeks. I would start to recover my mood after two weeks, but then I would see Sharryn, and it would start to affect me again. Chloe said to me I was never going to recover and get things done in my life, if I did not get away from Sharryn and stop picking my child up every two weeks, I would never recover, because I would always be under the influence of witchcraft.

There exists a spirit of witchcraft that is very prevalent in Christians that can give them a quite controlling and demanding nature. You notice in this story of mine, I continually am coming up with women that I encountered that were domineering, "my way or the highway" sort of women. This controlling spirit is mentioned in the book of Revelation in the Bible, where Jesus warns His church about it and people with it. The spirit is named the Jezebel spirit, and it most often attacks people who are being used by God powerfully or are going to be used by God powerfully. I do not understand how Christian men and women who have this spirit actually do powerful witchcraft acts on people they don't like or are having conflict with, but the presence of this spirit and behavior in Sharryn was what Chloe was warning me about.

While I was at the third boarding house, before I had my talk to Jesus, I learned that Sharryn had remarried. Sharryn told me I could not see my son Brandyn anymore, to which I replied, "I'll see you in court." She laughed and said, "We both know what happened last time you had a custody battle." The last time I had a custody battle with her, I ended in a psychiatric ward with a breakdown. I was currently off the medication, so I was unprepared, and I did not want to go through a custody fight.

I did not have the papers at home, although I had completed the papers to lodge with the court, and I was working on my affidavit, when I had the conversation with Jesus – when He told me to move to Sydney and stop fighting over my son. I felt that Sydney was a dark and evil place, and I did not want to go there, but Jesus was saying He wanted me to go. It was a difficult thing to do, to walk away from my son. It was a difficult thing to obey.

I felt as if I were Abraham. I felt as if I were putting my son on an altar and sacrificing him. As I write this book, it has been 14 years since I last saw my son. I think it was 1998 that Jesus told me to move to Sydney. I rang my parents and told them what Jesus had told me to do. They said to bring my stuff and stop in at Coffs Harbour on the way to Sydney, so I could stay with them for a while. I could not say good-bye to my son, because Sharryn would not let me even talk to him on the phone, so I left Brisbane in tears, again. The train pulled out, and I went to my parents' house in Coffs Harbour.

Chapter 39

Going Back to Sydney

I left early in the morning, on a train from Brisbane, and arrived in Coffs Harbour around lunchtime to stay at my parents' house. After a few days, my mother persuaded me that I was not ready to get a job in Sydney, and that I should get some qualifications in a TAFE course. I chose a six-month course on call-centre work, so I would be able to answer phones in a call-centre. After I completed the course, my mother persuaded me to do another course on office work. I was not sure whether my mother wanted to get me ready to go back to Sydney or was trying to equip me to get a job.

I wanted to go back to Sydney, get a job, and have something to do with my life, rather than being bored just staying at boarding houses, sleeping all day, and watching TV at night – my regular lifestyle in boarding houses. Therefore, I stayed at my parent's home and completed two technical college courses – similar to a community college in America. I passed both the courses, although I did not do exceptionally well. Because of my nervousness and my shaky hands, I had a problem with my touch-typing speed, and even today, I need to look at the keyboard when typing.

In my stay in Coffs Harbour, I managed to spend time with my brother. He had a business, and I spent some time helping him in his business. Although he had promised earlier to help me with the publishing of my book, he made no further mention of it. It is funny in life; sometimes when you do not have remarkable self-esteem, you find it difficult to accept gifts. I think it was not so much that my brother would not give me money for the book. I just think that I did not ask him for it. My brother was smart and creative in business, and since 1999, he has been in business for himself, and he has gone through many hard yards because of it.

Back then, he was only starting, and he had an idea to make CD-ROMs of a whole conference with the audio synched with the screen

PowerPoints – it was as if you were actually at the conference, watching and hearing the person speak. It was good, and from that, he went on to do many other good things. At the time, we developed a good relationship and spent some good time together. Jesus had told me years before to keep in touch with what my brother was doing and to maintain the friendship that we had always. Even today, I phone my brother, Rodney, at least once a week, whereas I only phone my sister and younger brother only once a year. My brother is like my best friend, and we have a wonderful relationship that flourished in the year I spent in Coffs Harbour.

While I was there, one day, I went down to the beach, and I started to talk to Jesus. He told me to go to another beach and sit on the sand, but when I reached the other beach, it was dark, and I was nervous that someone might come up behind me. Jesus said, "I've got angels behind you, and no one can get you. You just sit there," and I sat there in the darkness and talked to Him for about half an hour. We had a wonderful conversation, and as I was crossing back to the main beach to walk home, I asked Him, "Where are you right now?" He replied, "I'm just beyond the breakers". At night, the breakers are a dangerous place to be, as the sharks wait there for the fish. However, as I took one step to go into the ocean and meet Him, all the water receded by 50 meters.

I asked Jesus, "What's going on?" He replied, "You're not going to meet me tonight, but you're going to meet me soon." I then said, "Hang on a second, Jesus. You said in the Book of Revelation that you were coming back soon, and that was 2,000 years ago, and you still haven't come back. So when you say to me that you're going to meet me soon, how long do you mean, because soon isn't a word I want to hear, because 2,000 years... I want to meet you now. I don't want to meet you soon, because soon means 2,000 years in the Book of Revelation." He said, "Matthew, you're going to meet me very very soon," – and the following week, I was on the train to Sydney.

Chapter 40

Meeting Jesus in the Flesh

I was back in Sydney for a few weeks, and I was staying at a backpacker's hostel. Late one night, I was at McDonalds with a friend having something to eat, when a man walked past, and I could feel he had plenty of spiritual energy on him. He asked me whether I had any money to give to him, but I was in my Christian judging mode, where you do not give money to strangers – you buy them food, but you do not give them money, because they can spend it on alcohol and drugs. I have subsequently changed that opinion, and I just give them money these days, but at that stage, I said to him, "I can buy you something to eat. Do you want something to eat? Have a seat." I sat him next to my friend while I went to buy him a quarter-pounder meal.

I got him a quarter-pounder, fries and a Coke, and when I returned with it, he said, "Where's my coffee?" I said, "A quarter-pounder meal doesn't come with a cup of coffee. How do you have your coffee?" He said, "Two sugars and milk." Two sugars and milk was how I used to have my coffee, and it just triggered within me, "Ah, he has his coffee the same as I."

I had to wait for another twenty minutes, before I could get his cup of coffee – waiting in line at McDonalds can be a real test of patience. When I came back, he was drinking the Coke, and he was eating his hamburger. My friend said he was going and left – I think he was surprised and disgusted that I would invite a homeless-looking man to eat with us. After he had left, I said to the homeless man, "Let's go further up in the restaurant where it is warmer," and he said, "Sure." We sat, and I noticed people were walking past me, looking at me with a questioning look in their eyes, as if to say, "What are you doing with that guy?" I was tired. I wanted to go home. I needed to go to the toilet, and on the way down to the toilet,

I was asking Jesus in my mind, “How long must I stay with this guy?” Straightaway the chorus of the song *It Ain’t Over Till It’s Over* started playing over the radio in McDonalds. The song had answered my question to Jesus.

I freshened myself up by splashing some water over my face, and I said to myself, “Maybe I’ll have to stay for an hour or two and talk to this guy.” I came back to him, and just as I sat, he spat on the ground and said, “You have to spit the evil out of you” – just as it says in Revelation 3:16 “*So then, because you are lukewarm, and neither cold nor hot, I will vomit you out of My mouth.*” He was saying you have to spit out the evil.

He seemed to have a cough, so I assumed he was spitting phlegm out of his mouth. Then he said in a clear voice, “It’s amazing isn’t it?” I said, “What’s amazing?” He said, “It’s amazing when you ask Jesus, and He answers you with the chorus of a song on the radio.” I was absolutely stunned! It was as if Jesus had said, “Spend time with this homeless man.” All the hairs on head stood on end, and the Holy Spirit’s presence came on me. I was enormously shocked by his statement. It was as if he knew exactly what had happened to me. He then asked me whether he could share with me some of his understandings of what Jesus was teaching, when He was on Earth, in the Gospels.

To understand this better, I had been reading the New Testament for some time, but the Books of Paul where difficult to understand and had frustrated me. At the time, Jesus had told me, “Just read the Gospels, and only read the Gospels, until I say to stop reading them, and as you read them try to work out what I was saying and what mood I was in, how was I feeling and why I said what I said. So, go through the Gospels and just try to work them out.”

Now this homeless man said, “Can I share with you some of my understandings of what Jesus meant in the Gospels?” and as it was my favorite subject, I said, “Sure, go ahead.” He spoke for about a minute, and my head was full of information. Every sentence that he said was rich and profound. After a whole minute, my whole head was so filled with information that I could not fit anymore, and I would not be able to remember.

I had a similar situation when I was at Coffs Harbour, listening to a guy speaking on the Internet for about an hour and twenty minutes. Around the hour mark, he had been talking about something totally new and foreign to me, and my head was filled – it was information overload. I had to stop the teaching to try to remember it, and I had to come back later to listen to the last twenty minutes. It had taken an hour to fill my head with a subject I did not know. However it had taken this homeless man just one minute to fill my head, and I thought, "I'll have to tell this man to be quiet and stop speaking, because I won't be able to remember what he's been saying." I looked at him; he had a smile on his face and he was talking enthusiastically. He was happy sharing what he had to share.

I thought, "He obviously knows so much more than any person I've ever heard in my life, and it would be so rude of me to tell him to shut up." I let him continue for another ten minutes and every minute was as profound as the first. It was utterly amazing! Then he said, "Can you buy me another cup of coffee?" and I replied, "You can go to the front and ask them to refill your coffee." He went up to the front, and while he was there, he spat on the ground again but he missed and spat on a girl's leg instead. She freaked out, and then her boyfriend freaked out and called the manager. Anyway, the manager did not kick the homeless man out, he got his cup of coffee, but he did not come back to my seat and went to sit by himself a little way from the girl and her boyfriend.

In my head, Jesus said to me, "Go and apologize to the couple that the homeless man has the flu, and he spat once before to get the phlegm out of his mouth. He was spitting on the floor. He wouldn't have meant to spit on your girlfriend." I got up, went to the couple and said, "The homeless man, I was with him before and he spat on the ground. I think he has the flu. I don't think he meant to spit on your girlfriend. I think he was just spitting on the floor. I know it's gross but I don't think he meant to do it to you."

The guy said, "Are you his keeper?" An unusual word to use, and it had a biblical ring to it for me. I said, "No, I'm not his keeper. I'm just looking out for him, and I bought him a hamburger earlier, and I just want to explain his side, so you're not too upset. He has just spent ten minutes explaining the Bible to me, and I've never heard anyone on Earth with the knowledge that he's got. Look at him." They looked, and I said, "Doesn't he look like the pictures of Jesus? He is dressed in an Arab robe just as if he has just come off the streets of Palestine. He's like the spitting image of the pictures of Jesus, and I think we're in the presence of Jesus, and if it is Jesus, he might have been just testing what sort of person you are." Anyway, I said, "Sorry for the thing. I'm just blown away by what he said to me, and I just want to apologize to you."

I went back to my table, and just as I was about to sit, the homeless man got up and walked straight to the couple, putting out his hand, and said "Have you got any money?" The couple had about $15 in notes with some change, and I think they gave him about $20. I think I had persuaded the couple that he was Jesus by what I had said. Then I saw the homeless man go from person to person in McDonalds, asking them if they had any money.

Later, I went to sit next to him, and he was counting through the money – he had about $45. In all the time I have been in Sydney since that night, I have never seen anybody come into McDonalds asking for spare change and receive more than two dollars, if they are fortunate. Never in my history in McDonalds has anyone ever received a ten-dollar note, or a five-dollar note, and certainly not $40. Certainly not the way he was asking, "Have you got any money?" in a rough voice

You could hear him all over McDonalds, as he went from person to person. It was a miracle that the manager did not kick him out, because they normally kick out the homeless, vagrants and heroin addicts asking for money. He had $45 with him, and he asked me, "Do you want to go and score some marijuana with me?"

I said to him, "I've got a mental illness, and marijuana plays with my mind. I wouldn't be participating, but if you want to score some marijuana, I'd be happy to go with you, and you could smoke it, but we could spend some time together." I was still not sure at the time whether this homeless man was Jesus, and had little understanding why, if it was Jesus, that he wanted to smoke pot, so I said, "You could get a night in a backpacker's – maybe a few nights – in a backpacker's with that money. You would not have to sleep rough, so it might be better to spend the money that way." He replied, "Yeah, you're right, but if you're not going to smoke with me, that takes out the fun."

Just then, the manager decided to kick him out. I went down to go out with him, and as I walked out the door, I looked across the road, for just a split second, to check whether my bus was there. When I turned back after a split second, he was gone. He had vanished into thin air. I ran up the street back and forth looking for him, but what had happened the way he had gone in a split second had no human reasonable explanation. It was divine.

Sometime later, when I had the courage, I asked Jesus whether I had met Him. He said to me, "I told you I'd meet you soon," and I broke down in tears, because He had been so humble to come and dress as a homeless man. He had certainly tested me in many ways that night. If a person you bought a meal for said in a rough voice, "Where is my coffee," you might have said to yourself he was altogether too much. If you were with a good friend, most people would not invite him to their table. When he spat on the floor, that might have been too much for you. When Jesus told you to apologize to another person, on the homeless man's behalf, how many of you would have done that? When he asked to go and score marijuana, how many of you would continue to think it was Jesus? And to many of you reading this, you still are not convinced I met Jesus in the flesh that day.

So many things confirmed I had met Jesus Christ. I was talking to Him once, and He said that if the ten minutes were transcribed into writing, it would take me ten years to understand what was said in that ten minutes. It was so profound, and I knew that it would take me ten years to understand it. That was in 1999, and in 2010-2011, I wrote a book called *The Parables of Jesus Made Simple*, and I describe 54 of the parables Jesus had told. After I had finished making the book ready for publication, Jesus reminded me that it would take ten years to understand what He had said. I had just produced the book, based on much of what He had taught when He was on Earth, and He said that I would come into the understanding of what He had shared that day. I encourage you that Jesus is real! I have met Him twice in the flesh. In chapters to come, I will talk about meeting Jesus in visions.

I have met Him an amazing number of times in visions. Whenever He comes to me in the flesh – and to another pastor friend, who has met Him in the flesh – He has not said, "Hello, I'm Jesus". The times I have met Him in the flesh, He had been a homeless man, and He looked different. Jesus told me that He has a kind of cloakroom in heaven, and He uses it to put on a body to wear to Earth, and He always looks different. It is up to the Holy Spirit in your heart to help you recognize when you have just met Jesus. It is the same with angels, as they do not announce they are angels, when you meet them in the flesh, but something inside you says that was an angel. I do not have to meet Jesus in the flesh anymore, because I meet Him so many times in visions, and I can have heart-to-heart conversations with Him in visions.

I do not have to meet Him in the flesh anymore, but it is just as much fun meeting Him in visions. I hope this has encouraged you to feel excited. I hope that one day on Earth, you can meet Jesus in the flesh yourself.

Chapter 41

Ministering to Prostitutes

Shortly after my visitation from Jesus in the flesh, I was living at a backpacker's hostel in Sydney, Australia on the northern beaches, and I was travelling into the city. God put it on my heart to spend some time in Kings Cross, seeing as my book, *The Fallen Ones* was set in Kings Cross. I was in Kings Cross one night, and I found some young women from an organization called Youth With a Mission or YWAM.

They were busy singing songs in a dangerous part of Kings Cross, the "red-light district" of Sydney – a particularly rough neighborhood. I waited for a break in their singing, went up to them, and asked them if I could pray for them. They agreed, and I prayed for them. Then, they asked whether they could pray for me, and before I had time to back off, the first started to pray…and the second. They were going around in a circle. When the third prayed, she said, "Thus saith the Lord," an indication that God is going to speak, and a prophecy is going to be said. Therefore, I listened to the prophecy, which went something like, "I'm God, and I've called you, and I'm going to send you where angels fear to tread. I want you to minister to the girls there and show them my love. Show them I care for them and do what you can to shed my light in their lives." She finished praying, and I thanked her for the prophecy, and the next girl prayed.

As I eventually said good-bye to them, I was thinking that the prophecy was about me going into one of the strip clubs in Kings Cross. Earlier in the book, I shared that I used to frequent one of the strip clubs to see prostitutes, and even to participate in sex onstage. The particular strip club I mentioned was still active – and still is even now. I felt a calling to go there and visit them, not as a regular addicted client, but to go in there and minister to the girls and show Jesus' love. The prophecy was saying that it was dark and evil where angels fear to tread. In other words, there is plenty of demonic activity in the place. God was saying, through this young YWAM girl, He wanted me to go into this place and minister His love.

I was still living in the backpackers, where I met a person at a nearby bus stop, and we became friends. We were travelling through part of Sydney, and we found a suburb where he said he knew of a church, and he had heard this church was good. We went to this church, and the minister told us both to stand in the middle of the service. He did a prophecy over my friend, and then told my friend to sit down. Then he did a prophecy over me and said the same to me as the YWAM girl had said, "I'm calling you to where angels fear to tread, and I want you to minister to the girls there and show them my love." – word for word the same.

Here were two complete strangers saying the same thing to me, and neither knew each other nor me. Both felt a compulsion to prophesy over me, and it just confirmed my feelings that God was with me, that He wanted me to go and minister to the girls. Now, I do not know how long I tossed the idea around. I know that I moved locations in that time. I had to move out of the backpackers, and I moved into a boarding house that supplied breakfast and dinner. I would serve a three course buffet dinner at the hostel, and then walk into Kings Cross, reaching the strip joint around eight in the evening, and stay there for most of the night. At first, I started to pay to go into the strip club, and then the bouncers just started letting me in free each night, although they wondered why I was going there.

I used to stay in one of the strip joints until about midnight, and then go on to another to relax, listen to the music, and watch the dancers. I would talk to the bartender and some of the girls. All of them knew I was not there for business, and the bartender often used to serve me free Cokes. I would go there about midnight, stay there for an hour, and then go back to the one where I was "working".

In my time there, I found that the prostitutes would spend all their money – between $200 and $500 – each day on cocaine and heroin for their habits. They would spend plenty of time with clients, earning the money, and then shoot all that money up their arm with drugs. I also found that a Mars chocolate bar was like giving a prostitute a hundred dollars cash. Normally, a hundred dollars cash would result in $50 for them and $50 for their bosses, but a Mars bar would be the same in gratitude from a prostitute than giving them a hundred dollars. I would buy chocolates for the prostitutes, and just sit and talk to them, when there was no business for them. I would sit around and talk to them. Jesus just wanted me to be real. Each of them found out that I was not in the strip club to hire them, and I was not particularly interested in watching girls undress.

They were particularly interested in me, because I stood out, and I was strange. I went to this strip club six nights a week, so over the months, all of them came to know me, and all of them realized that I was different. They would ask me outright from time to time, "Why are you here?" I would share that Jesus told me to come into the club, and because He could not be there Himself, He sent me in just to love them, tell them that they are loved, and that He accepts and loves them.

Sometimes, I would see the prostitutes break down in tears, as the message of love touched them. As I bought more and more cups of coffee and chocolates for the prostitutes, some would ask me whether they could not possibly pay me back, and could they take me upstairs and do something for me. They felt indebted to me, like any decent person in the world would, when you continue to do them a favor. They felt they owed me something, as I had given them so much. I spent my spare money on chocolates and cups of coffee and just loving them. It was the ideal job for me, because I had spent many years addicted to prostitutes, and talking to them in bed after I had sex with them. It was wonderful to sit down and just talk with the prostitutes. I knew a little about the lives of prostitutes, and how they separated their personal lives from their business lives. I had spent time with Chloe, and I understood prostitutes more than the typical punter would understand them.

I had written a book on prostitutes in Kings Cross and knew something about the situation. Although I still admit I was nothing more than a punter, I had never lived a life of a prostitute, and I certainly would not have the gumption to be practically raped ten or twenty times a night by guys. I certainly would not have the personal fortitude to handle having sex with so many guys, so I do not want to dismiss that it was not a life that I was living, and it was not a life that I fully understood.

Sometimes in this book, I might seem to demean or put down the role of prostitute, as though I was in some way better than they were, and they should have provided me with the service for which they were hired. I might have overstepped the boundaries sometimes in explaining my dealings with prostitutes. I want people to understand fully that through spending time with the girls that I came to love them for who they were and valued them as individuals.

I certainly learned to value them, as I spent money on them, just giving them things that had no real advantage for me, except that I was becoming a powerful witness in their life. I was showing the love of Jesus in their lives, and I think a few of them had never discovered it before. One of the prostitutes took about three or four months, before she sat with me and introduced herself to me. I knew all about her. I knew her name. I had seen her strip and I knew a fair amount about her. She already knew my name, before she started talking to me and said the other girls had said I was okay.

Then she started to break down in tears. She said, "I promised myself that I'd never do this. My mom was a heroin-addicted prostitute, and I swore I'd never become one myself. But here I am; I'm a heroin-addicted prostitute, exactly what I swore that I'd never do. Why is this?" I explained to her that it says in the Bible "What a man thinks upon, so shall he become." I explained that we sometimes focus so much on something we do not want that it just manifests in our life, because we have given it so much attention. It was just a simple law of psychology acting out in her life. She was sad. I was pleased that I got the chance to talk to her, hold her hand, and tell her she was loved.

Another girl once told me that she was a Christian, and she said that she was one of the 144,000 Christians who was going to be used in last days mentioned in the Book of Revelation. She believed that she was one of those 144,000, and she said she was not always going to be in the life of prostitution. One day she was going to be living as a witness for Christ and doing good work for Christ, but now she was addicted to drugs, and she just found herself there.

I found that many of these girls did not wake one day and choose to be a prostitute. There are many clichés about prostitutes, saying they are all sexually abused. I have mentioned that I have heard figures that up to 90% of prostitutes have been sexually abused but some choose prostitution for other reasons. Whatever the reason, they are in a dark place, and most prostitutes that I dealt with in that club were addicted to heroin and cocaine, and spent an immense sum on those substances in their life.

I was upset. This was happening around the year 1999, and I must have been about 32 then. I had spent since age 18 addicted to prostitutes. I had been addicted to prostitutes for 14 years by then, so I had slept with many prostitutes. Even while I used and ministered Jesus love to these prostitutes, I still had a sex addiction, and I was still seeing prostitutes. Outside Kings Cross, I was seeing them in other areas, and the girls I was talking to did not know I had an addiction to prostitutes. I could separate that.

Sometimes people look at Christians and wonder why they are being used. Many people would ask me – most probably as you are asking now – how could God be using you to minister to prostitutes and bring them love, acceptance, and His salvation message, when you were addicted to prostitutes, although you were not sleeping with them in Kings Cross? I have to say that if God had to choose all the “Holy” people and the perfect people to serve Him, then He would never have anyone serving Him. He would never have any people stepping up to the mark and doing the hard yards and actually serving Him. Sometimes He has to choose people who are available – not always the best, but people who are willing to step out and do things for Him.

I was soon to meet a woman from another church, and she invited me to move out of the boarding house and move in with her. Around this time, she told me that my time in Kings Cross had finished, and I should stop visiting the girls in Kings Cross. In the next chapter, we will talk about living with her.

Chapter 42

New Living Arrangements

I met a woman – I forget her name as I forget many names – in a church who seemed full on and passionate about Jesus, and she was somewhat attracted to me. One day we were talking, and she said, "Why don't you move in with me and my daughters?" She lived in a two-bedroom apartment, a smart apartment. She and the girls moved into one room and gave me one room. We were living there for a while. She began to know the prostitutes in Kings Cross I was ministering with, and she went to visit them, and bought presents for them one day. She was the one who told me that I needed to stop visiting them, my life in Kings Cross had finished, and that God had told her to tell me that He had closed the door in that area.

I lived with her in an apartment building where they had a pool. I used to take her three girls down to the pool, and we would swim in the pool. I had one favorite – the middle child who was about eight – I know we are not meant to have favorites, but I had a favorite. I used to put her on my shoulders and throw her off into the pool. The younger daughter also used to enjoy that. The oldest daughter was too big for me to do that, but we used to have a fun time in the pool. I enjoyed living with the woman. At the time, she had a boyfriend, so there was no physical relationship between the woman and me, but she was an interesting woman. She had some way-out ideas, and with my being bipolar, it was strange to discover someone with way-out ideas. Normally, I was the one with the way-out ideas, and others seemed sane around me. I shared with her that I thought I was one of the two witnesses – she thought it a little way-out for her, and she did not agree – although she thought she was a prophet herself.

She did not agree that she was one of the other witnesses, and she did not believe that she was a prophet sent to judge the world, although she did have strong ideas about judgment, speaking judgment in a church, and prophesying judgment. She went through a stage of taking me from church to church, going into strange churches and blasting out judgments over the church. We went from church to church doing that, and after a while, we started to get a reputation.

Although the police were called to one of the incidents where we made a scene, we continued from church to church blasting them. Many prophets early in their ministry think that is their goal – the reason they are on Earth is to rebuke the church and tell the church that they are wrong. Before I received the grace message, or fully understood the message of grace, and the new covenant message of Jesus Christ, I believed that I was like an Old Testament prophet. I did not understand the role of a New Testament prophet. I thought it was my role to go in and blast churches with God-fearing condemnation, and to speak the wrath of God over churches. She was cool and turned on to doing that. Most Sundays we found ourselves going from church to church blasting them, and that seemed something she enjoyed.

It was alarming to walk into a strange church and blast them. It certainly took you out of your comfort zone, but you believed you were doing God a service in warning these churches. I believed it was a necessary part of being a prophet. I knew the prophets in the Old Testament were hated, rejected, and maligned. However, I believed I was right within the role of a prophet. I was right in the middle of what I was meant to be doing, because she was convinced we were to be doing that.

I was convinced it was the right way to go, and that was the relationship we had. She was a controlling woman. She liked to make the rules and liked to say that it was her way or the highway. She was not open sometimes to negotiation – it was like a battle of wills. I suppose you could call me a weaker individual, a person who certainly did not enjoy confrontations and did not enjoy arguments. So most times, when I believed I was not going to get my way, I would just back off and do it their way. I discovered, many years later in a teaching on anger, that for many years, I had just suppressed my anger and apparently, suppressed anger leads to depression, and I suffered much with depression. I understand it comes from not dealing with my anger effectively.

Here was someone in my life, who was strong-headed and strong-minded, and she liked to get her way. I succumbed to that and did mostly what she decided. She got in trouble financially. I was giving her my whole pension that I was getting and keeping $20 every two weeks for myself. She was certainly getting money from me every two weeks, and I expected that she was paying the bills, but she shared with me she had not paid the rent, and we had to move out.

She decided she would lease a trailer and live in a trailer park. We leased a trailer, sold all her furniture and moved out to a trailer park. Once we were coming home from church, when we stopped to get some milk and bread. I gave her a five-dollar note, she went into the shop, but the shop refused to take the money because it was ripped.

Her children came back to the car and said, can they have the ten-dollar note and I said, "No, the shop has to take the money and give it to the bank and the bank will give it the five-dollar note. That's how you take notes like that out of circulation. Just tell your mom the shop has to accept it." The children were not happy with my answer, so the mother came back, and got in my face, saying, "Give me the ten-dollar note." I gave her the ten-dollar note, and she went in and got the stuff.

She came back into the car and told me I was wrong to argue with her in front of the children. I said, "I wasn't wrong" and she said, "Yes, you were wrong." Then, I refused to back down. This was one incident where I was not wrong, and I was not going to back down on the incident. I was told before we got home to the trailer park that I was to pack my bags and leave. She was kicking me out.

I had her pension card, and I had been using it sometimes to travel around the city. The pension card allowed you to travel for a dollar and ten cents for the day, because you were on a pension, and we got cheap train and bus travel. She asked for her pension card back, so I could not use that for the trains. The train fare now was going to be about $3.50.

The Lord Jesus told me to leave, so I took my bag, and I started walking. It was a few miles to the train station. I was walking with this heavy bag and three times, I stopped and asked Jesus, "Could I go back to the house?" He said, "No, this is for you to trust me in faith. I want you to leave." Three times, I picked up the bag again and went towards the station. As I approached the station, on the ground outside the station, was a pension card in someone else's name. At the time I was not on a disability pension, only on unemployment benefits, so the pension pass on the ground would mean the train fare was only going to cost a dollar and ten cents. The woman had given me the ripped five-dollar note, and that was my only money. I took it to the stationmaster and told him that if he handed it into a bank, they would give him five dollars. He understood and gave me the ticket and … I was officially homeless.

Chapter 43

Becoming Homeless

When the woman I was living with kicked me out of the trailer park, I had five dollars to my name, so before I left for the station, I rang my auntie's place to see if they were home, and if they could take me in, but I could not reach them.

I did not have a mobile number for them to use to ring me back, so I caught the train into the city. I knew of one place where I could get a meal in the city, so I went there and had a disgusting meal I was not happy with, but it was free, and I ate it. I was talking to a few homeless guys there, and they told me of another place where I could get a meal. I decided that I would spend each night in Kings Cross and go to the strip joint and stay up all night, and then sleep in the park in the morning. I was not going to sleep alone in a park at night.

It was a frightening situation becoming homeless. You walk past many homeless people during the day, and you might not much feel pity for them. However, it is another thing to be alone in the city, with no money or help, and find yourself homeless. I went up to Kings Cross, and I went to the strip club where I used to minister. I went in there with my bag, and they wondered what was going on. The strippers asked me, "What was with the bag?" I told them I was homeless, and one of the strippers said she would ask her roommate whether I could stay with her. She came back to me, and she said her roommate did not know me and was not comfortable, as I had not been in the strip joint for six months. She said she would ask another prostitute. Another prostitute approached me and said, "Matthew, are you homeless?" I said, "Yeah" and she said, "You can stay in my room."

I said, "Have you got a couch?" She said, "No, you can sleep in my bed with me. I trust you." I said, "I snore" and she said, "I've slept with snorers before; that's fine." I was happy. When the strip club closed, I went with her in the morning and went up to her room and slept in a bed. The next day, when I got up, she said, "Can you clean up my room?" I said, "Fine." She got her wallet and gave me $50, and she said, "Here's some money for you. Use it as you will. There's a homeless shelter called the Matthew Talbot, and it's down the street. Go and check if you can move in with them."

I went down to the homeless shelter that day and was told that I could come back the following day, and they would look at admitting me. I went back that night to the strip joint at night, and one of the bouncers got angry with me. He was normally friendly, and we had a good relationship. He got angry with me, so I went to see the manager, and I said to him, "Can you call your dogs off?" meaning, "Can you get the bouncer off my case?" I did not realize that the word "dog" in a criminal setting, especially in Australia, usually refers to a person who reports on other prisoners, or if you are beaten up by another prisoner, you reveal his name to a guard – you are the worst of the worst criminals.

All the criminals in the prison look down on you, if you get a reputation as a dog. It is a reverse justice system, where if you stand for justice in the criminal system, you are called a dog. What I had said about his bouncer, in criminal language, was that he was the worst of the worst. I had no idea that I had said that.

I went back to the club, and the bouncer was still angry, so I went up to the other club, where I used to relax. I was in the club for a few hours, and then the bouncer came up to find me and said, "Let's go for a walk." He said, "No harm done. I'm sorry for getting angry. I'm not going to hit you or hurt you. Let's go for a walk." I went for a walk with him, and we went around one corner and around another corner, and then he met with two or three other guys. They started talking, and he said, "Let's just start walking." We went around to a dark alley, which turned out to be behind the club. He said, "I'm just going to ring my manager and see what you called me, because I think you called me a dog. I'm going to see if that's what you said."

When he opened his phone to dial the number, the three guys with him started to hit me. They surrounded me and started to hit me.

Soon, I was on the ground, and they were kicking me. I was in a serious position. I was on the ground, and I was saying to the guy on the phone, "I'm sorry! I'm sorry! I'm sorry I offended you! Please forgive me!"

I was saying sorry for about 30 seconds, when Jesus said to me as clear as day, "Are you finished saying sorry to him?" I said, "Yeah, Jesus." Jesus said, "They've got a baseball bat there, and when they've kicked you unconscious, they're going to beat you with the baseball bat and kill you, and then dispose of you. So are you finished saying sorry?" I said, "Yeah." He said, "Well, get up and run to the police station." Although I was surrounded by three guys, I do not understand how I managed to escape from them and run to the police station. I think that three angels came up behind the guys and put their arms in a locked position, so they could not reach me. I am not sure what happened, but that day I was meant to be killed, and it did not happen. I went to the police station, and I told the Kings Cross police what had happened.

They said, "You're a regular down at that club," and I said, "Yeah." They said, "Can you tell us about that club? Do you think they're dealing drugs?" I said, "Do you think I'm a fool?" They said, "Why?" I said, "You already know that 50% of the men, who book the girls, come there to try drugs for the first time. They only book the prostitute, so she can supply them with heroin or cocaine and help them shoot up with the drugs. The women supply the drugs and are booked for the twenty or thirty minutes it takes to shoot up the drugs. All the girls are prostitutes, and they have expensive habits of between two and four hundred dollars a day. All the clients and the girls are getting their drugs from within the club, because the girls never leave the club all night. So, I estimate between $20,000 and $30,000 worth of drugs is done in that club every night."

The police said, "That's serious drug consumption happening in that club."

I said, "Don't tell me you don't know about it. Of course, you know about it. It is happening in your own backyard. So why are you even asking me about it?" The police went with me to the strip club and got my bag for me. They told me that it is not healthy for me to stay in Kings Cross anymore, and that I should leave.

I went down to the Matthew Talbot hostel the next day, booked in, and started to stay there.

Chapter 44

Move into Homeless Hostel

After the incident with the bouncers in Kings Cross, and my explanation to the police, they collected my bag from the strip joint and who drove me to the Matthew Talbot hostel for the homeless.

It had to be seen to be believed – they had about 150 men staying in the homeless hostel. I first saw a caseworker, and he took all my details and my identification. They said they would give me ten days credit, until my next unemployment benefit money came into my bank, and then it would be my decision whether I wanted to move out, and not owe them any money, or whether I wanted to pay the $160 rent for food and accommodation for the next two weeks.

I was happy that I had a roof over my head for ten days. They gave me instructions on what to do. They told me where to put my bag. First, I was taken up to a dormitory with fifty men in each section on our floor. A man took my bag and put it in a locker, where no one could take it, and said, "Just put some items in a cabinet next to your bed, but do not put any precious items there."

It was difficult for me to sleep with people snoring in the room. I need almost complete silence to get to sleep. The toilets in the hostel were terrible. You had to hold your nose to go to the toilet. They absolutely stunk. Even ten minutes or half an hour after the cleaners had been into the toilets to clean, they still stunk. With hundreds of men using these toilets, it was a terrible smell.

You could get free clothes at the hostel, but because I was overweight, there were never any clothes to fit me. Many men got free clothes at the hostel and used to throw their clothes out into a laundry bag every night in the hostel, so they could continuously have showers and be in fresh clothes each day. That worked for some. It did not work for me, because I was overweight, and anyway, I had enough clothes in my bag. I found that the breakfast was pleasant. They had scrambled eggs or baked beans in the morning plus cereal. I found I enjoyed the breakfast. I found lunch was not so enjoyable.

I found a church just up the road in Kings Cross that served fresh meat rolls, so six days a week, I would go out for lunch to the church and have a good time there. I stayed in the hostel the ten days, then asked Jesus, "Could I move out to a backpackers?" and He said, "No, stay at the hostel." I stayed there for another two weeks and started to get to know people in the hostel. The hostel was full of people who either had mental illnesses or were straight out of prison – there were some heavy dudes in the place.

It was a men's hostel, and no women were allowed inside the hostel. Although they were heavy guys, I was not afraid of them, because we were all in the same boat. People seemed friendly and ready to accept one another. I got to know one guy. I had watched him, and many people were talking to him. He had a real aura about him. It just seemed as though plenty of love was coming from him. The guys seemed to buzz around him and always wanted to talk to him. I said to myself, "I want to know that guy."

His name was Michael, and I did get to know him. He was a lovely guy. I found out later that around the hostel, inside and outside, he was the person who handled all the marijuana deals. His supplier allowed the guys to have credit. The guys could book a hundred dollars' worth of credit and get a hundred dollars' worth of marijuana on credit until payday, and then they would have to pay the hundred dollars off. The guys were always in debt to Michael, and always coming to him for marijuana. He smoked marijuana himself. He used to make money on every deal, so he was always cashed up. I found that he had a Christian faith, and although he had some strange beliefs in his Christian faith, he was essentially a Christian. Many people would query that, and many people reading this book would query me being friends with a drug dealer. I think that if Jesus was on Earth today, He would also be friends with prostitutes and drug dealers and gay people, and people that we would call "bad sinners".

Michael was a good person, and he was enjoyable to know. I stayed for another two weeks, and at the end of the two weeks, I asked Jesus, "Could I go to a backpackers?" and Jesus said, "No, stay at the hostel." Two weeks after that, when I got paid, I asked Jesus if I could leave, and Jesus got angry ...well, raised His voice at me, and said to me that, "I want you to stay at the hostel, until I tell you to leave. How are you ever going to understand the homeless and have compassion for them, unless you're one yourself? I don't want you asking me when it's time to leave. I'll tell you when it's time to leave, and until then, you stay at the homeless hostel."

That solved it for me, and I settled into the life of living in a homeless hostel. About a hundred and fifty residents stayed inside the hostel, although up to five-hundred people would come for breakfast, lunch and dinner. Breakfast was free, but dinner cost a dollar; however, after a particular time, the meals were free, so if you were prepared to be served last, you could still get a free meal. Hundreds of guys lived outside the hostel, because they refused to pay the $160 every two weeks to stay inside the hostel. Yet they stayed within the block of the hostel and used to come into the hostel for three meals a day, and leave their bags in the hostel. They used the hostel for showers, to wash their clothes, and for services such as doctors. They used the hostel to get their mail.

In Australia, you have to have a mailing address, when you are homeless, to receive unemployment benefits or the pension. If you do not have a mailing address, you get no income from our Social Security system. Many people who are homeless, if they are not linked to such a hostel, have no income. Therefore, when you see them on the side of the streets asking for money, you do not know whether they are getting any money, because our system is so screwed up. If you do not have an actual address to live in, you are not paid. Many people used the hostel as a mailing address and would go to check if they had mail each day. You could get a cup of coffee for fifty cents, and they had snacks available in a shop in the hostel, where they also sold smokes.

I do not understand how the guys could live out in the weather. Several lived under a railroad bridge in Woolamaloo in Sydney, near a police station, and they used to sleep under the bridge, so even in the rain, it was not wet there. Plenty of guys slept around the hostel. I do not understand how they coped with being homeless. At least I had a bed in the hostel, although I had to put up with the snoring and the cold in winter – I had a roof over my head and a comfortable bed in which to sleep.

So, I did experience homelessness, but I did not experience it as much as I could have experienced it. It could have been a rougher life, but it certainly did achieve God's goal in my life – to build in me a deep and profound love for the homeless. If you listen to my teachings, or if you read my book on the parables of Jesus Christ, you will discover that I have a deep compassion for the homeless. I feel that people seem to overlook them and disregard them, and do not see them as the person who was beaten up on the side of the road, in the parable of the Good Samaritan.

They do not even consider the homeless as a next-door neighbor – a neighbor you are supposed to love and show compassion to. That was changed forever in my life, and I certainly learned to love and appreciate the homeless from that experience.

Chapter 45

Life in Kings Cross

Living in a homeless hostel was difficult. Living among a hundred and fifty men snoring and sleeping, and making all sorts of noise during the night, was difficult. As I have said, it was difficult to go to the toilets. Often in the morning, I would get up, have breakfast, then go to the toilets at a McDonalds somewhere, so I did not have to put up with the stench in the hostel toilets.

As I mentioned before, I used to visit a church during the day, six days a week, where we would have fresh rolls. It was good to have fresh bread and fresh rolls with meat and salad. In the Matthew Talbot itself, the bread was day-old or two-day old bread, and you could taste the bread was somewhat stale. They had watered-down tea, and it was not so exciting to have lunch there – so we seldom had lunch there.

At the Matthew Talbot, I met a Maori guy called Tama, who I had originally met in Coffs Harbour. I had shared my testimony at a Baptist church, and he was there that day and was affected by it. When I was in the homeless hostel, Tama came up to me one day, said he remembered me from Coffs Harbour, and asked was I the person who gave his testimony at Coffs Harbour? I said I was, and we became friends, Tama and me. We found some Christians who used to do an outreach in Kings Cross, and they used to preach and sing songs to people who visited Kings Cross and the locals. Tama and I got involved with their church and started to travel by train on a Saturday night to the church. The person who ran the church was Gary Payne – no relation, just the same surname – and he moved in the gift of healing. His touch and his prayers for others healed many people. Once he prayed for me, and he knocked me over. In Pentecostal churches, you often see people being knocked over, when hands are placed on their foreheads.

Someone putting his hand on my forehead had never knocked me over in a Pentecostal church, but when I went forward for prayer with Gary once, I was knocked over. I noticed once that when Tama was knocked over, he fell forward instead of falling backward. I had been told that only a prophet falls forward, and I was still under the delusion that I was one of the two witnesses of Revelation, chapter 11 – that I was going to judge the world, and God was going to use me and another person to judge the world.

When Tama fell forward, I concluded that he was to be the other prophet. I do not think Tama was too motivated about thinking that he was the other prophet. He just wanted to be a friend and hear about God. I abused his friendship, by thinking that he was the other prophet, and Tama and I hung around together for much of the time. As I have mentioned before, I had a friend called Michael, and he and I spent some time together. We used to go to the church in Kings Cross to get rolls and eat there. He was a good friend and a spiritual friend, and we discussed many spiritual things with him.

Michael had a good turnover of clients dealing with marijuana, and he was always cashed up. I do not think he often spent money on me – mainly because I never asked him for money, although he would have willingly shared. He was an interesting person to know, and in years to come, I have still bumped into Michael, and he is a tremendous person.

Another person I became friendly with in Kings Cross was John, who used to deal marijuana up on a street opposite Hungry Jack's in Kings Cross. He dealt marijuana on a street notorious for marijuana dealers, and street children often got marijuana and dealt marijuana on this street. John really liked me, because I spent time with him and his girlfriend. We would sit a table and order cups of coffee. He would buy me a cup of coffee, and we would buy a paper, and I would be there talking to him for half the day. We would just be having cups of coffee, and people would come past us, and he would ask them if they wanted to score any marijuana.

In the six months I was there, the detectives never brought him in or busted him for dealing marijuana, because he just looked as if he were having a daily cup of coffee there. He did not look like someone just hanging around the street dealing marijuana, so he was very thankful for me. He was open to the Christian faith and to me sharing about Jesus. I was going to church then, and I was feeling good with my faith.

I had Tama, John and Michael as friends. I had plenty of other friends in the homeless hostel. I gave money to many people at the hostel. I shared in an earlier chapter about three guys from the strip joint in Kings Cross, who kicked me and beat me up. I thought at the time that angels had probably grabbed their arms and stopped them from catching me, as I ran to the police station, but I found out later, when I asked Jesus, that two angels had laid either side of me and took the blows of their kicks. None of the kicks really damaged me, although I suffered with a few bruised ribs, but I should have been unconscious with the number of kicks aimed at me. This must have perplexed them. I was in Kings Cross for another six months, even after I had moved out of the hostel there.

The manager of the strip joint had said to me that it was a dangerous place for a 'dog' to hang out, so I said, "I'll let Jesus look after me, like He looked after me the night you tried to kill me. He'll look after me again." I was a little afraid of the club still. One night, Jesus asked me to go back inside the club, where they had tried to kill me – I went inside the club and hung around there for twenty minutes, and then came out. A couple months later, He told me to return to the club again. Jesus was essentially saying to the owners of the club, "This man is mine, and he's not afraid of you. No matter if you tried to kill him, he's going to do what I tell him to do, and there's nothing you can do about this guy." I was happy that I could obey Jesus and do what Jesus told me to do. I had a good time in Kings Cross. I developed many friends. Food was easy to get. I used to share my money with the other homeless in Kings Cross.

Within two days of receiving my unemployment benefits, I had given out all my money to the homeless who asked for two dollars or five dollars or whatever. I would share all my money. I used to live on free food, after I had paid my rent. I knew many people there. I knew many guys who were happy to get money from me and became friends. In one situation there, I thought I was one of the two witnesses, and I thought I had to kill people with a curse. The Bible said fire would come out of the two witnesses' mouth, and this is how people were to be killed. Rather than literal fire, I thought that the fire that came out of my mouth would be a curse. Once, a guy made me annoyed, and I cursed him. I said, "Within a month you'll be dead." He walked towards me, and he said, "Today, you'll die." I was standing around with twelve guys. When he walked toward me to hit me, nine of them stood in the row behind each other, and they said to him that he would have to fight them first. I was surprised that so many of them stood together and would fight for me.

One of them told me the guy carries a shiv, an old-fashioned knife that a person carries to stab people. He told me that the guy carries a knife, and he is not afraid to use it, so if I could get out of Kings Cross, now would be the time to do so. That ended my time in the Cross, although Kings Cross was very much alive. As a local in Kings Cross, I discovered that I found out information within ten or fifteen minutes of it happening. A prostitute would die of an overdose in Kings Cross, and within fifteen minutes, I would hear about it.

People working in Kings Cross were either locals or visitors. I found that that the church I was with visited Kings Cross, but they certainly were not locals. The locals did not really respect them as much as they respected people who lived and breathed Kings Cross. I found that to be a message you could send to Christians: If they want to do outreach in red-light districts, or districts with street-walking prostitutes, they would be better off hanging around in the locations, buying the prostitutes cups of coffee and getting to know them one on one, rather than setting up camp and trying to witness to them all from the side of the street, and never getting to know the locals.

I found that many locals loved me. At the end of the year, they were having a New Year's celebration, and I was still commanded to be part of Kings Cross until that time. They were having a New Year's celebration. Everyone was kissing, and hugging each other, prostitutes were going up the street hugging everyone they knew and kissing them. The bouncer who ordered the hit on me came up to me, shook my hand, and gave me a hug. He said, "We're friends again," and I said, "I love you brother, always loved ya." He said, "I know." After I gave him the hug, Jesus said, "It's time for you to leave Kings Cross." God Bless!

Chapter 46

Normal Life Adjustment

After six months in Kings Cross, just after I had the altercation with the guy who said he wanted to kill me, the Matthew Talbot arranged for me to go and live in a share-house with two other men, who had been formerly living at the Matthew Talbot hostel. The rent at the place was $80 a week, and the market rent in Sydney at the time was about $130 a week for a normal room in a house. It was cheap, so I moved into the house, but I found I was accustomed to living with a free breakfast, free lunch and free dinner, but I was not used to preparing meals for myself. They did not teach you in the Matthew Talbot how to look after yourself and how to cook meals.

Because I had nervous breakdowns, I had lost my confidence, and I was used to the system. Some would say it's the same with prisoners who come out of prison, and they become institutionalized. They are used to having everything done for them, and the same was true of me. I found it very difficult to budget, buy food, and cook food at home. I did not buy much food from the shops.

What I found myself doing was leaving by eleven each day, having lunch at the church in Kings Cross, having dinner at the Talbot, and coming home at night. Although I was living away from Kings Cross, I was still a resident of Kings Cross. I was still in Kings Cross daily, and during the days, I spent time with John, when he was dealing marijuana, and I still spent time with Michael and Tama.

Michael was homeless at the time and came home to stay with me for a few weeks. He stayed in my bedroom at night, rather than living on the streets, and used to go back to Kings Cross each day to deal with the marijuana. The caseworker managing my case caught on to the fact that Michael was staying with us – it was against the rules to have a homeless person stay in my house, but that is the way I was. I was a rule-breaker, as you have probably realized from this testimony, and I have broken the rules on more than one occasion, but the compassion within me made me feel for my friend, Michael, and to have him stay in my place. Michael shared much of his money with others and gave people marijuana free, and looked after his friends. He never really had a place to live in. He lived out in the streets, and so I felt sorry for him.

When I got a place, I went to stay there. I had reached a stage where the caseworker was making life difficult, and although I did not pay rent, I found myself in the unfortunate position where I needed to move out – something a person who does not have complete control of their faculties would do. Just before I had moved out of the Talbot, I had applied for a disability pension in Kings Cross, and after a psychiatric review by a psychiatrist, I was given a disability pension, because I was clinically depressed. I was relieved that I did not have to fill out a form every two weeks, and report to Social Security to be paid, and since then, my money was automatically paid in to my bank account every two weeks. The pension was $100 more than the unemployment benefits.

Now I had more money. The next chapter is another chapter in my life, where I take off and have an adventure, where I believe I was doing God's will.

Chapter 47

Move to Tamworth

Earlier on in my book, I shared that I had met a Christian guy at a bus stop, and we went to a church, where a minister prophesied over me, saying that God was going to send me into a dark and lonely place, where angels fear to tread. Then I went in to the Kings Cross brothel and strip joint, and ministered to the prostitutes of Kings Cross for a year. They had assumed I was some sort of detective, but when they discovered I was homeless, they realized I was not a police officer, and they tried to kill me. Anyway, the guy I had met at the bus stop by the backpackers had a father who lived in Tamworth. He continually told me that I should meet his father, because much of what I had to say about the Book of Revelation, and the end of the world, were similar to what his father had to say.

He said his father was restoring a church in Tamworth, built to the specifications of the Israelite's temple in Jerusalem, and these churches were called Tabernacles. He encouraged me to go and visit his father. I had been to meet his father once, and this time I decided I needed to go on another pilgrimage to Tamworth. I took my Maori friend, Tama, with me, as I still believed he was the other prophet of the two witnesses.

We moved up to Tamworth. First, we moved into a trailer park and lived in a tent. I bought a single-bed mattress, and Tama slept on the ground, but I slept on a mattress. We were there for many months. I got the idea of visiting some churches, but first, we found one church that we were interested in, and we started going to that one church. I got it in my head that I needed to prophesy to all the churches and warn them of God's impending judgment. I believed in those days that God was a God of judgment, and He was an angry God, and He was going to pour His wrath out on the world. I believed that God was upset with humanity, and He was not happy with the goings-on with humanity, and because of that belief and mindset, I believed I was one of these two prophets, and I had to speak warnings to the church. Whether that is true, I felt I was told by God that Tamworth was a sinful city and was going to be judged by God.

One day, I went to a Social Security job placement place called Centrelink, and used their computers there free. I got a whole lot of Bible verses out of my head. Scripture references just appeared in my head. I got a whole lot of scripture references out of the Old Testament prophets and put together this document, which was warning the churches. I had a scripture reference, and I had half a page of text that I explained what that scripture reference was saying about the church and the town of Tamworth. Then, I would get another scripture reference, and then I would explain that, and so on, until I had about eight pages.

I took off one day and hand-delivered the warnings to the churches. I had done about eight churches, when my mobile phone rang. It was the police, and the police officer said I should stop handing out the warnings, because the churches were unhappy. I said, "How many churches have rung?" He said, "Seven," and I said, "Well, I've only handed out eight. I'll bring the rest of my copies to the police station, and if any more than eight churches call, you will know that it wasn't me that handed them out."

It was interesting that seven out of the eight churches had rung the police about messages saying that I thought I was one of the two witnesses. Seven out of the eight churches had called the police in a united effort to have me prosecuted and exposed. On my way in to the police station, I received a text message reading, "Well done, good and faithful servant." I had no idea where the text came from. I showed it to my friend, Tama, and his eyes filled with tears and he said, "It came from Jesus." Tama was a good sign. Whenever the Holy Spirit came upon him, he used to cry. I thought that Jesus had used someone's phone to type a text message to me.

Once before this, when I was in a cafe, a friend of mine saw a number of angels come and sit down with us. My phone was on the table, and a friend texted me and said, "Why did you send that message?" I rang her up and said, "What message?" She said, "You just sent me a prophecy that I gave to someone else yesterday, and it's word for word the same. Why did you send that?" I said, "Well, I didn't send it." She said, "Well, it came from your phone," and I said, "Well, I've been sitting here, and I didn't text you. Maybe an angel did it." I laughed. At the time, the angels were sitting with us and maybe one of them picked up my phone and typed in a text message to my friend.

Years later, when we got a text message from a strange phone saying, "Well done, good and faithful servants," I was quite open to the fact of it being Jesus sending us the text message. Maybe I was deceived into thinking I needed to hand out warnings to the churches – maybe I was deceived into thinking I was correct to act as an Old Testament prophet rather than as a New Testament prophet – maybe I was deceived into thinking I was one of the two witnesses. Aside from that, I felt that Jesus was happy I was obeying whatever spirit was directing me to do what I did.

Sometimes, I have followed the antichrist spirit that masqueraded as Jesus' voice that has directed me to do things. I believe I was directed then to hand out the warnings by something false, but Jesus was impressed. I went in to the police station, and I handed them the prophecy and the judgments. The police said, "So Tamworth's going to be judged is it?" I said, "Yeah, well that's what the prophecy says. If the churches don't repent, and the churches don't look as though they're going to approach me and repent. So, it looks like God's going to judge Tamworth." They said, "When is He going to judge it?" I said, "I don't know, but soon."

While we were in town, we made friends with a couple of homeless people. There was a homeless man who lived under a bridge. He used to be a former lawyer. One day we had some pizzas, and we asked him if he wanted some slices of pizza. He sat with us, had a drink, and had a couple slices of pizza. Halfway through eating the pizza, he went into a trance and started to speak. Immediately Tama started to cry, because here was Jesus speaking through this homeless guy in a trance. He said some lovely words to us, and Tama asked him questions and Jesus answered the questions, and it was remarkable.

Another time, before we came to that, the seven prophecies were in a church we were visiting. We were in the church watching the worship, although Jesus had told me that this was not the right church for us. As I was in the church, I felt a presence come in the room, and I looked around. I saw Jesus approaching, and He said to me, "I want you to really concentrate this time, Matthew."

I really concentrated on the vision, and Jesus stood where the present worship team was standing. I could see a crown of thorns on Him, and I saw His whole face red with blood. I saw on Him what were originally white garments, but they were now stained red. He put His arms out wide, like He was on the cross. He turned around, and at the back, His garment was ripped away, and His back was torn into shreds – shreds, as if you had been dicing some meat. His back was cut into strips, and you could see right through it into the organs, and it was terrible and disgusting. It was ten times worse than anything you saw in *The Passion of the Christ*.

He turned around to face me, and He said to me, "Is this what they're singing about, praising Me for dying on the cross?" I said, "Yeah." He said, "Well, why are you the only one who can sense I'm here? Who were they singing to?" I said, "They're singing to you," and He said, "Well, I'm here and they can't see me. Why haven't they stopped? Why isn't there someone in the church that can recognize that I'm here and they stop to welcome?" I said, "I don't know, Jesus" and he said, "If I appear to them right now, as I've appeared to you, would they stay singing, or would they run out the back screaming?" I said, "Most of them would run out screaming," and he says, "Well, you make sure when you worship me that you're always in the attitude to worship. If you're not in the attitude to worship me, well, you just sit still and listen to the songs." I said, "Okay, Jesus," and He left. He walked out, and that was the clearest I have ever seen a vision of Jesus, and it was amazing. It was like meeting Him in the flesh. He looks like He had jumped off the cross two-thousand years ago and appeared in His body to me.

Another time in the church, Jesus was saying that He did not want me to be a part of the church, and I said, "You can't be serious." He says, "Yeah, I am serious." I said, "I'm not going to believe you, unless I see you come in here, and I see you get kicked out." He said, "Is that what you want to see?" I said, "Yeah." Immediately, a homeless woman, who we had been talking to, and had invited to the church, appeared at the door, wheeled her shopping trolley full of clothes in, and started dancing around the church. The minister and a couple of the elders grabbed the woman and took her to the back. The woman lit up a smoke, and they took her outside and put her trolley outside. At that stage, my Maori friend, Tama, became very upset and started to scream. He was still screaming, when the police arrived, and they took us to jail and charged us with disturbing the peace.

Since then, we were not allowed to set foot in the church. It was after that, that I started delivering the warnings to Tamworth and the churches. The police already knew we had a history with the churches. A couple of days later, we met the homeless woman who had come into the church. As we were talking to her, she went into a trance and said, "Matthew, why didn't you believe me that that wasn't a church that I was part of?" I said, "Sorry, Lord." She said, "See all those stars in the sky?" We said, "Yeah." She said, "My Father made them. If my Father can make all of them, don't you think He knows what's best for your life?" We said, "Yes," and she reached into her trolley and got out a little angel wrapped in paper. She unwrapped the angel, gave it to Tama, and she said, "Your mother gave me this to give to you," and he filled up with tears. She came out of the trance and said, "Have we got any money for some smokes?" We gave her $20, and she bought some smokes.

Again, Jesus had spoken through a person to us. Tama was then to tell me that his true mother, not his stepmother, had died years ago; she was a Christian, and that the angel was special to him, because it came from his mother in heaven, that he had a gift from heaven, from the woman who was manifesting Jesus at the time. I have met Jesus in the flesh, as I have shared in a previous chapter, and I have met Him in the flesh a couple of times through homeless people. I have also met Jesus other times, when He has been in a body that He brought from heaven.

I have seen Him a couple of other times in the flesh and did not talk to Him, but I knew it was Him. Once, when we were at the Talbot, Jesus came down a couple of times. Michael and several other Christians at the Talbot recognized it was Jesus, and He would come to visit us. When I was at Tamworth, I went to a news radio station, gave them the prophecy, and asked whether they could read it out on the radio? They said they could not. Then, I went to a TV news station and said, "Can I give you a prophecy, and can you read it out on the news?"

The girl who attended me said, "Are you these two prophets who think they're judging the world?" I said, "Yeah, that's us," and she said, "Well, you leave right now! Get out of here, or I'll call the police!" I said to her, "It's pouring with rain outside. We're living in a tent. We haven't got umbrellas. If we go outside right now, we'll get soaked, and we'll probably get a cold. Can we just stay here, until it stops raining?" She said, "You get out now, or I'll call the police." I said, "But it's pouring; we'll get soaked. Surely, if you're a Christian, you can treat us as Christian brothers. You know, you can forgive us for believing who we think we are and just give us some grace. You know, give us some love. Don't kick us out in the rain." She said, "Get out now or I'll call the police," and she called to an assistant and told him to ring the police. We had already been in trouble with the police, so we left

We took two steps outside, which half-soaked our shirts, and then the rain stopped. I marched in to her and said in a loud voice, "The rain has stopped now! We're going to walk home, and when we get home, it's going to start to rain again, and it's not going to stop raining, until this town's been judged." We walked home and true to my word, the rain started.

We moved into a hotel, and then into a boarding house, and the rain continued while we were in the boarding house. Tamworth went under water. Major parts of Tamworth were flooded. It caused plenty of business destruction and business loss, and one-third of the State where I live went under water in flood. I remember clearly what I said to that newswoman, as if it was yesterday. The police were not smiling anymore when that happened.

Chapter 48

False Prophets

Shortly afterward, we moved back to Sydney, but before I left Tamworth, I was in a shopping centre where we used to go to daily. We were in the shopping centre one day, and I saw a girl who worked there. She had a hole in her stocking. I reached down to the hole in the stocking on her leg, on her calf muscle, and touched her, and said, “You’ve got a run in your stocking.”

As I touched her on the leg, she screamed at the top of her lungs, and I was very embarrassed. I left the shop, after buying what I had to buy. She used to serve customers in the shops, so she was one of the workers in the shop. The next day the police arrived, and they charged me, but her testimony said, ‘I put my hand up her dress,’ – I had not done that. I told the police that they would have witnesses to her scream and have witnesses with me pulling my hand away, but they would not have any witnesses that showed me with my hand up her dress.

The police said, “Why wouldn’t we have witnesses to say that?” I said, “Because I never had my hand up her dress, and you wouldn’t have any witnesses saying so, because they never saw that. All they saw was my hand coming away from touching her on the calf, and her screaming, but that’s all they would have seen.” They said, “Okay,” and I was charged to appear in court for an act of indecency.

Another thing that happened, when Tama and I moved back to Sydney, was a website suddenly appeared on the Internet proclaiming, “Matthew Robert Payne – False Prophet.” It was up for a while, and I achieved a little notoriety, but it was the first time people had displayed web pages calling me a false prophet. The web page said that Tama and I claimed to be the two witnesses, but we were not, we were out of our minds, and we were false prophets.

Not only did the people of Tamworth call me a false prophet, but also I was put up on false charges. I understand the police charge many people, and many of them declare their innocence. I have to agree that people can be charged with things that they did not do. I have freely admitted in this book to sleeping with prostitutes, driving a car under the influence of marijuana, and having sex with girls on stage in Kings Cross. I have transgressed the law in many ways, so I should be man enough to admit to putting my hand up this girl’s dress – but I did not. Later, I was admitted to a psychiatric ward and while I was there, the court case was held in my absence, and I was charged with The Act of Indecency. Sadly, because of this sexual assault charge, I was never allowed to drive a taxi again…

Chapter 49

Move Back to Sydney

After I had been threatened with violence by a guy in Tamworth, Tama and I left on the next train in the morning for Sydney. Leaving behind circulating rumors that we were false prophets, we moved in to cheap accommodation for backpackers in Sydney. There were five beds in the room, but we were fortunate that we were the only two people in our particular room. Tama and I spent our time at night, sleeping on the beds, and then during the daytime, we would go out to the homeless hostels to get some food. We had to pay rent there, of course, so every two weeks, I would pay the rent with my money, and every other week, Tama would pay with his money.

I remember one day in particular, and this was to become a happy memory for me. I was returning from a food van in the city, where they served restaurant quality meals at 8:30 in the night. I had a bread roll with me, and as I walked past a Chinese restaurant, I noticed a homeless man I knew from the Matthew Talbot, so I went inside to say hello to him. I refused his offer of some Chinese food, but when he saw the bread roll in my hand, he asked me if I wanted to have communion with him. When I gladly replied, "Yes, that would be great," he reached into the bag with all his possessions and pulled out a bottle of red wine. He motioned for the waiter to bring us a couple of glasses, and then we prayed, broke the bread and had some to eat, and afterward, we each had a glass of wine.

I have to say that it was one of the most memorable communions I have had in my life. We chatted while he finished his meal and the rest of the wine. When we went outside, he reached into his pocket and gave me $50. I pushed it back into his hands and said I could not take it from him, but he said, "Jesus told me to give it to you." What I have forgotten to tell you was that earlier I had asked Jesus, whether I could find $20 on the road. I wanted to go to All-You-Can-Eat Pizza Hut, and then go onto a movie, and I just wanted $20. I had a Christian friend, who was continually finding $5 and $10 notes on the road. I had just had enough faith to ask Jesus, "Could I find $20?" Now, here was this man who wanted to give me $50 – a man whom I had seen sleeping outside the Matthew Talbot in the pouring rain with a blanket over his head. When he thrust the $50 into my hands, and told me Jesus wanted me to have it, I asked him where he was going to sleep that night. He said, "The wind blows, and you don't know where it comes from, and you don't know where it goes. So it is with me. I go where the Holy Spirit leads me." It was typical of something Jesus would have said. I was amazed at him. This was a real person, not an angel, and it was exciting that my prayer was answered in such a unique way.

I left him, and went around the corner to McDonald's, where I bought a super-size Coke for $3.50. In McDonald's someone asked me for some money, and I gave him two dollars, and then, as I came out of McDonald's, another girl came up and asked me for two dollars. I felt a compulsion in me to ask her how much she needed to collect that night, and she said, "I need to collect another $20." I reached into my wallet, took out $20, and I gave it to her. I am well aware that some people collect money to support an addiction, but nevertheless, I gave her $20. She hugged me and started to cry – it was one of those hugs, where she held me tightly and just would not let go of me. When she did let go, she asked me what would possess me to give her $20. I said, "Jesus told me to give it to you, and He loves you dearly. I do not know what you need the money for, but Jesus wants you to know that He loves you." I have to admit it was a joyful time for me and still remains a fresh memory. I certainly would not have had the $20, if the homeless man had not have given me fifty. Jesus knew that by asking the homeless man to give me $50, He could provide $20 for the young woman. It was amazing.

The next day I went to Pizza Hut All-You-Can-Eat buffet and watched a new movie at the cinemas due to a gift from Jesus, a real answer to my prayer for $20. It's little things like this, when Jesus has seen fit to bless me, or answer a prayer of mine, and provide for me, that give me sweet memories and a strong love for Jesus.

One day, back at the backpackers hostel, I felt within my spirit that Michael the Archangel came into the room and told me to threaten Tama and question him, as I held a knife to his throat. If the answer was, "Yes," then I should take the knife away, but if the answer was, "No," then I should cut Tama's throat. I suppose only a mentally-ill person could do such a thing and be put to such a test.

I remember Tama had never been scared of me, but when Michael the Archangel came in to me, and I spoke to Tama, he rolled up into a ball and was really frightened. The authority was coming out of my voice, and I had never seen anyone become so frightened of my voice before. I was convinced that an entity had entered me; however, when I questioned Tama with a knife to his throat, he answered the correct way, and I removed the knife. He was later to tell my mother I threatened to kill him, and it had a dramatic effect on him. He left the hostel, which I can understand, as it shook me up, too. I was not in a good headspace. At about the same time, I remember writing an e-mail to my brother, saying that he needs to read my book, *The Fallen Ones*, or I would come up and kill him – not the sort of thing you do, if you are in your right mind.

I remember that the police arrived at the Backpackers the following day, and they gave me a choice of going to the police station or going to a psychiatric ward. I chose the police station, where I was charged with sending a threatening e-mail through the Internet, and they closed my e-mail address. Anyway, I moved out of the Backpackers because I could not afford it, as Tama had moved out.

I moved into a Salvation Army homeless hostel (Foster House), and I stayed there for about a month, while I continued to get my meals from other homeless hostels. The meals at Foster House were not very good, so I used to have breakfast there, go out for lunch and dinner elsewhere, and then come back at night. I remember being told to leave Foster House, because apparently, I had been witnessing to one of the staff, and the staff did not appreciate it.

Although I was living a life with sin in it, I was a very zealous Christian and used every opportunity to share Jesus with people. I just did not consider that someone working in Salvation Army was not saved. I was so surprised that this girl wasn't saved. Unfortunately, I was kicked out of Salvation Army, and although I currently attend a Salvation Army church (and have done for many years), it took me a while to get over being kicked out of this Salvation Army hostel.

Chapter 50

Second Breakdown

After I left the Foster House homeless hostel, I decided – I felt led by Jesus, who I assumed was the real Jesus (but turned out to be the antichrist spirit), to go to Brisbane and search for my former wife to see whether I could re-establish a relationship with her. I moved up to Brisbane, and I moved into a shared accommodation arrangement with a woman, who was advertising for someone to stay with her. Initially, she seemed sweet and happy-go-lucky. She also had an Asian boarder with her, so I boarded downstairs. I developed a sleep pattern where I slept nearly all day, woke in the afternoon, stayed up till late at night, and then went back to sleep. I had a little color TV that I could watch downstairs, and the meals were supplied, so it was full-board accommodation. During this time, I started to have strange visions. I started talking to what I believed were six Christian girls around the world – each of the girls had voices with a particular resonance, so I could recognize each of the girls speaking to me. They said that they wanted to be my wife and marry me, and all of them wanted to have my children.

They started to talk sexually with me, and I thought the talk was strange for Christian girls, even though we were speaking telepathically. I was not too bothered, until the girls became sexually and vulgar, and I realized I was talking to demons masquerading as real human beings. I asked them several times for their e-mail addresses, or their phone numbers, so I could phone them. They said there was no need for e-mails, as I could talk to them anytime – night time or daytime, or whatever time it was in America. I thought it strange they could talk to me anytime. Around then, I received the message that I needed to look for my ex-wife – I felt led by a Jesus speaking to me. At the time, I didn't realize that a fake Jesus (antichrist spirit) had started to talk to me. This fake Jesus told me to go and look for my former wife, Sharryn. I went for a walk, and after I walked about eight kilometres toward a hotel, a song started playing, through my head, that has a lyric that goes "And I would walk 500 miles..." I carried on walking to this hotel, where the fake Jesus had told me I was going to see Sharryn and have a reconnection. Apparently, she would have broken up with her boyfriend or her husband at that time. So I went to the hotel, and as I was waiting for her to arrive, I was asking Jesus when she was going to come.

I was waiting at the hotel, when the band started to play "I would walk 500 miles." I thought it uncanny that I was now listening to the song that had been playing in my mind – it resonated with me, especially as I had just walked eight kilometers. The Fake Jesus soon told me that Sharryn was not going to meet me at this hotel, but I would to walk another four kilometers into the city. I walked into the city and went to a bar, where I had been promised she was going to meet me – she did not meet me there either. I decided to walk the four kilometers back to the previous hotel. I was confused why He had lied to me, but when you are in that sort of situation, you make excuses and begin to wonder why you have been told a mistruth.

I went on to another pub in the Toowong suburb of Brisbane. I went in, and after a couple of beers, I started dancing with a girl – we were getting on fine, and she told me she liked me. I told her that I was looking for my wife, with whom I had broken up years ago, but I felt I was going to meet her tonight, but this was not the pub, so I had to go to the other pub. She was upset, so I said, "Well, see it from my perspective. You know, you get a chance to rekindle something. Wouldn't you jump at it?" She replied that she would, and she respected me. She wanted to give me her number, but I did not take it. I was too focused on meeting with my wife. I went to the other hotel, but it was closed, although I thought I saw a car outside. I could see the car in a vision, and I could also see another car driving straight through it. Jesus said that the car was starting and was going to show me where the house was. Earlier in the evening, I had received the name of a street, now I was following a car as it travelled left and right. Eventually it turned into a street, and it was the street with the same name that I had received earlier.

I went up and down the street, but there were no lights anywhere. It was 4:00 in the morning, and there were no lights to show that someone had just come home. I decided to walk back to the Gap, where I was staying – and then I realized that I did not have a key to the place – all those months I had been staying there, and I did not have a key to the place. I seldom went out, so when I arrived back home, I had to try and wake the landlady from her sleep. I did not have much success, so I decided to go for a walk and ended walking back into the city. I was becoming hungry, and I found a place to eat and stayed there. I had my film script of the *Fallen Ones* with me.

I do not remember when I had collected it from my belongings, but Jesus told me to throw the film script away. I asked Him why, and He replied, "It'll come back to you, if you're meant to make the film. So, throw it away." He also told me to throw my wallet and my mobile phone away. It was amazing, but I threw everything away. Keep in mind that it was a spirit of the antichrist masquerading as Jesus that was having me do all these weird things. I was hearing a combination of my real friend Jesus and the counterfeit one, and I could not tell the difference between them. I slept out in the city that night — it was cold that night, but I managed to have some sleep. While I was asleep, I heard voices speaking to me, and I imagined I heard my ex-fiancée Chloe talking to me — she was telling me to go to a particular address. As I was in the city, I went to that address and entered the house. The people inside were drinking, so I asked for Chloe or Michelle, but they said, "There's no Michelle here." I was confused, because it was the address Chloe had said in my mind.

I was confused about a lot of things, and my mind was playing tricks on me, and I thought I was going crazy. The next morning, I walked back to where I was staying, but I still could not get in. I started to walk back in to the city, and by about 11, it started to get hot. As I was walking past a house, Jesus (the false one) said to me, "Go for a swim in the pool in that house," and I said, "I haven't got any swimming trunks." He said, "Just go in anyway." But I said, "There might be someone home. I'd get caught if I go into the house." He replied, "Go in anyway, and there's nobody home. I want you to undress, and then I want you to do ten dive bombs into the pool. And if you do ten dive bombs, I'll take the homeless off the streets of Sydney for you." I said, "What if there's someone home? Doing dive bombs and being naked in someone's pool — if someone's home, there will be a lot of trouble for me."

Jesus said, "There is nobody home, and who do you trust? Do you trust me, or do you trust yourself? And again, who do you love? Do you love the homeless? Do you care for the homeless on the streets of Sydney? I promise I'll take all the homeless off the streets of Sydney, if you do these dive bombs." So I undressed, and I started to do dive bombs. I had done about four dive bombs, when this man came out onto the veranda and looked out at me naked in his pool. He shouted, "Get out of my pool!" I replied, "I've got to do six more dive bombs, before I am finished." He shouted again, "Get out of my pool! I'll phone the police." I replied, "I've got to do six more dive bombs." With that, I put on my tracksuit pants and carried on with six more dive bombs. Then, I grabbed my shirt and jumped the fence.

As I was walking up the street, in my soaking tracksuit pants and top, a police car pulled over, and they asked me, "Were you just in the pool over at that address?" I said, "Well, I'm soaking wet. What do you think?" The policeman said, "So, you admit to being in that person's pool?" When I said, "Yes, I was," he asked, "Is it okay if we take you to the police station?" I replied, "That would be okay, but you can't take me in that car. You've got cloth seats there, and I'm soaked to the skin. If I sit on those seats, I'll make the seats wet for the rest of your day, and you'll have to change your cloth seats. You need to get one of those paddy wagons, where it's a metal seat, and I'll sit in that. He asked, "Will you wait for the paddy wagon?" and I replied, "Yeah, I'll wait." While we were waiting, I asked whether we could go into a pub to get a Coke and something to eat. They said there was plenty to eat and drink at the police station, so they took me to the police station, where they interviewed me, and then put me in a cell wearing a pair of funny pajamas.

I was feeling vulnerable, as I did not have any underpants. That night I could not get to sleep, and I kept thinking that Sharryn was speaking to me. I believe I was having a vision of heaven, where I had let my father into heaven. Apparently at the time, I thought my father was evil, and he had followed into heaven behind me. Then he took over and destroyed heaven — then heaven fell into Satan's hands, and heaven was out of control. I sat there in silence, but in my mind Sharryn kept asking me, "What's the matter, Matthew?" Then I said, "Just be quiet." I was quiet for about an hour, frozen stiff, thinking that I had just destroyed heaven. Then Jesus — this time, I think it was the real Jesus — said, "Matthew, you remember the Book of Revelation? There I said that I created a new Heaven and a new Earth, and everything's in control?" Then He went on to say, "Nothing's destroyed here in Heaven. That didn't really happen. Your mind's just playing tricks on you. Everything's fine with us here in Heaven."

Life gets confusing, when you have a false Jesus speaking to you, lying to you, and a real Jesus too, and you cannot tell the difference.

About an hour later, they brought in breakfast and said that I was going to take a shower. As they led me to the shower, the real Jesus told me to take a shower, and then lie naked on the bench, and when they come in to get me, just say, "I'm the boss! I'm the boss! I'm the boss!" He told me someone will grab my arm, trying to take me out, but I was to pull it away forcefully, and just shout, "I'm the boss! I'm the boss!" I was scared of going to jail, and Jesus told me that if I did this, it would allow me to be taken to somewhere safe. When they came in to get me, it happened just as Jesus said it would happen. Half an hour later a stretcher came in, and one of the ambulance people looked like a bouncer, who I knew from Kings Cross. I asked him if he was from Kings Cross, and he said, "Do you think I am?" I said, "Yeah, I think so. What are you doing up here?" He said, "Just taking you to a safe place." I knew that Jesus was right, when He had said I was being taken to a safe place.

So I went with them to a Brisbane hospital, where I was admitted to a psychiatric ward. They interviewed me, and then give me some sleeping tablets, so I slept all that day and the next night, as well. In the time leading up to this breakdown, I had a false vision that my father had died. I had seen him walking along a rock wall in Coffs Harbour, when a wave had washed him away to be eaten by a shark. A few days after I was admitted to the hospital, I gave them my parent's phone number for my next of kin. My parents turned up, and I screamed at my father, saying that he should be dead. I had spirits or demons manifesting in my life. Apparently, I was really ugly and spiteful and hateful to both my mother and father. They were really shocked. My mother later told me they went back to the car in tears, and my mother kept saying, "We've lost him." My dad soothed her tears and said, "No, don't speak like that. We'll get him back." It must have been a very traumatic time for my parents to have their son totally out of control.

I have to say to you honestly – having your mind completely out of control is not fun, at all. Certainly having Jesus speak to you, and then having demons pretending to be Jesus, and not being able to tell the difference is terrible. If part of you knew what was going on, you could have just put a stop to the voices speaking to you, and tried to manage it that way, but at the time I did not know there was a false Jesus talking to me — I was unaware there was a demon pretending to be Jesus. I just could not understand things.

In the hospital, a Baptist worker used to come and visit people. She was a Baptist chaplain, and with her weekly visits, it was good to connect again with a Christian, but I made sure that I did not discuss anything Pentecostal with her. As Jesus shared in his parable of the sheep and goats, hospitals, like prisons, are lonely places, and a mental-health ward is just as bad, only more boring, with less happening. Eventually, a social worker arranged for me to be re-established with my former landlady to give me board and accommodation. Between breakdowns, I had been off my medications for years, but now after 10 weeks in hospital, I had recovered my right mind, so I moved in again with the landlady.

However, I think my anointing made my landlady become angry with me. I wouldn't toe the line and do everything, when she wanted me to do all the chores for her. Eventually, I moved to another boarding house, which supplied meals. It was a shoddy boarding house, where I had to share a room with another guy — and he seemed happy to become violent with me, if he got the chance, but he did not get the chance.

I moved out of there to another boarding house, where I had stayed before and had made a few friends. It took a short while, but I decided that I wanted to move back to Sydney. I had not achieved what I thought I was going to achieve — or what the false Jesus had led me to believe was going to happen. I was tired of being bored, so I decided that I wanted to move back to Sydney and get a job. But before I went to Sydney, I needed to go to Coffs Harbour to spend some time with my parents.

Chapter 51

Move to Coffs Harbour

Once again, I took a five-hour train trip from Brisbane to Coffs Harbour, but this time I did not cry all the way, as I had when my wife left me. I was originally planning to stay for two weeks, but when I reached my parents' place, my mom convinced me that I should stay longer to get my head together, and become more stable. I went to see a mental-health worker there, and I met a psychologist for the first time. Normally, I had spent time with psychiatrists, but this time I spend some time with this psychologist, as he interviewed me with my mom. He asked me what happened in my initial breakdown and asked me to explain my feelings about what had happened. It was the first time in 10 years of mental illness that someone actually sat with me and asked what went wrong, and how did I feel. Everyone else in psychiatric medicine had assumed that I was just hearing voices, and everything that had happened to me was just a hallucination — it was not real. The psychiatrists had assumed that these hallucinations were just things our mind made up, but I can assure you that whether they come from God as a vision, or they come from Satan, they are scary, and you really do experience them.

One weekend, I went to a Christian camp called "A Walk to Emmaus," where I was shown the love of God and the love of Christians. You are sponsored by a person, who arranges for you to go on the camp. The sponsor gets in contact with a whole group of your friends, and people that love you, to write you sincere letters from their heart about what they think of you. I remember reading my letters — letter after letter of people saying that they love me — it still brings tears to my eyes, and I become emotional even bringing up some of the things people said. One of my Christian friends said, when he looked at me, he saw a transparent Christian — a fair dinkum Christian to use his Aussie vernacular — a real Christian, who is real to his faith. My mother said she had been watching me, while I was at home, and I had demonstrated the fruits of the Spirit, and I was a pleasure to live with. These letters still mean a lot to me.

When I talked to the psychologist in Coffs Harbour, he said that I had spent too many years feeling unwell, and that it might take a few years for me to reach a point where I would feel normal again on medication. I have to say that those years have passed, and now I feel relatively normal. Even though mental illness still causes me to have depressions and changes in speed that make me feel as though I am living in a washing machine, I cope well. But my moods are more stable now that I am on medication, than when I was off my medication.

Chapter 52

Back to Sydney

Now I had developed a good relationship with my parents again, I caught the train down to Sydney and moved into a boarding house. I was going to arrange to live in a Baptist housing place, which would have been cheaper, but I could not get into the housing place, so I had to make do with a boarding house — unfortunately, I re-started my earlier addiction to prostitutes and massages, and I started to spend my money (when I had money) going to these places. It seems that, at every boarding house, you seem to meet at least one person whom you get on with, and with whom you spend your time. I made friends with an accountant who seemed normal.

Our boarding house supplied breakfast and dinner, but on weekends, they only supplied breakfast, so we spent some time at a Turkish restaurant in Ashfield and had our weekend meals there. At this place, I got to experience pizzas and pide, a kind of roll pizza, and kebabs. My accountant friend was a great guy, and I remember once, he was having troubles spiritually at his room — there was something demonic happening — so I went to pray in his room, and I remember that fixed the problem. Later, he also said he felt an evil presence outside his room, so he just asked Jesus to protect him, and the evil presence left. He said, "Go in the name of Jesus." — something I taught him, and it worked for him. I had planted a seed of faith in my friend.

I introduced myself to a mental-health unit on the same street as the boarding house. I just walked in off the street one day and said, "I'm from Coffs Harbour, and I take this medication, and I need a mental-health worker." They interviewed me and allocated a psychiatric nurse as my case manager. She had me phone my mother to say that I was there and said I could come in anytime to use their phone to talk to my mother. I started looking in the papers, and I went for an interview at the University of New South Wales for a job as a kitchen hand, essentially just washing up, and some food preparation.

Apparently, no one else went for the job, so I got the job and started to work. I was getting $16.50 an hour, a good wage compared with America, but the work was a bit depressing.

It was all right for a few months, but as things started to settle, depression started to kick in. Once I was at work, and I was singing, "I get knocked down, but I get up again, and nothing's going to keep me down," a popular song by the Mighty Bosstones, which was a kind of theme song for me. An older lady working with me said, "One day you're going to get knocked down and you're never going to get back up again." I said, "Okay. Well, I'm leaving," packed my stuff, and left for the day. The boss rang me on my mobile and asked me what was wrong. I said that she had insulted me, and I did not feel like working in such a workplace. He said he would discipline her and asked me to come back to work as soon as I can. I came back a few days later.

A few months later, I was working, and I had to be at my mental-health unit by 4:30 in the afternoon, so I worked hard to knock off about quarter past three, instead of working normally till about quarter to five. Next day, I came in to work and started back at my normal pace, when one of the younger female chefs said, "Why don't you work as fast as you worked yesterday afternoon?" I said, "I had to get to an appointment, so I was really rushing," and she said, "Well, I've never seen you work so fast. You should work that fast all the time." I said, "Well, try working as fast as this," and I took my apron off. I said, "I'm finished!" and I quit my job.

While I had been working full time at that job, I had stopped receiving my disability pension. However, all it took was to go back and make one phone call, and within two weeks, I started to receive my disability pension again. I started to do temping jobs for an agency called Troys that sent me out on dishwashing jobs — I started to enjoy the variety of the temping work. One of the ladies at the temping agency was looking after me mostly. I told her I would like to work two shifts a week, and I would work a shift for her, if she had an emergency and could not get anyone else. I liked to work on an emergency to help her out when I could, and it made me happy to have a good rapport with her and the people who ran Troys. One of the owners of Troys had a daughter, who had schizophrenia, so she could relate to me and my mental illness. They were happy with my work, and I was happy to work with them.

Chapter 53

Aftercare Housing

While I was working at the temping agency, I enjoyed working two days a week. However, my case worker approached me one day, at home, and said that a position had come up with an organization called Aftercare, who looked after and housed people who had mental illnesses, and who had come out of the hospital system. They provided temporary accommodation for between six and eighteen months to prepare people for the transition into government housing. Government housing allowed you to get a one-bedroom apartment for $80 a week, about half the market rent in any other place. I went for an interview and passed, so I moved into an Aftercare place. They teach life skills, such as how to clean your apartment, how to cook for yourself, and how to do grocery shopping. I did that, but I cheated somewhat, as I was working in a job – I paid my roommate some money to do the cleaning every second week — that is until an Aftercare counselor found out about it, and I got in trouble. She said, "You're to learn to do cleaning yourself, and you have to do it yourself. You can't pay your roommate to do it."

I remember once I stayed out for two days straight, and the Aftercare people found out that I had two days up without sleep. They alerted the mental-health people, who sent a crisis team around for two weeks, to make sure I was okay. Apparently, when you stay up for two nights in a row, it makes you high, and you become manic. I have done it hundreds of times since, when I want to experience some peace and enjoyment. A friend of mine says that the manic high is better than any drugs. I have to confess that it can become addictive, and it can become enjoyable. You can be become creative, when you are manic, and you can have an enjoyable time. Although I had lived with mental illness for almost 20 years, I could still be a person who did naughty things, and sometimes stay up for a couple of nights. The key to staying up is to keep your mind busy and occupied. Anyway, my roommate told on me and said I had not been home for two nights — it took two weeks' of visits, before they released me, but they did not put me in to a hospital.

So I continued with my temporary work, until I found a job at Sydney University as a salad hand — like an assistant chef or a chef's assistant — someone who does almost the same as the chef, but does not receive as much pay. I enjoyed my time, when I got to work with Hahns and Graham at Sydney University. I was third in line for the salad hand job, so I did not always get work every week, but I did have regular work with them. It was good to be working on functions. I had always wanted to be a chef, and it was good to be doing something other than washing dishes, such as preparing and serving meals, and doing all the jobs a chef would do. I was enjoying myself and having a great time working with them.

Once I was at the shopping centre to get some groceries, and I really needed some work to pay the bills. I started praying for God to get me some work. In the middle of my prayer, my mobile phone rang, and it was the lady from the temping agency, asking me if I could work for the next day, as she was desperate. Before I could even finish the prayer, it had been answered. There is a verse in the Bible that says, "I will answer you before you even call to me." It is an amazing scripture, but it is so true, and it worked in my life.

However, I could never save money — as fast as I earned money, I would spend it on sex workers. It is a sad thing — it is sad to live a life addicted to sex workers. Sometimes in this book, I might seem to give the impression that I had this tremendously exciting lifestyle of seeing nude girls every time I slept with them. But getting stuck in the clutches of an addicting lifestyle is something that really takes the spirit from you and causes so much sadness. However much I worked, and I enjoyed working at Sydney University, I certainly did not enjoy the fact that I was always without money. As fast as I earned money, I was spending it. The more I worked, the more I spent on sex, and it was as simple as that. What brings a person to a lifestyle of paying for sex to get something for their life? What sort of sad life do you have to live to be a person like I was?

Chapter 54

Telepathy with a Medium

Undoubtedly, an interesting subject to raise: why is a Christian speaking with a medium with telepathy?

If you have read my story so far, you will probably wonder what a Christian was doing in a brothel, having a dirty massage, or what a Christian was doing having sex with homosexuals? There is much in my book that is "different" from many Christians and the "normal" Christian life. This happened when I was living in my new unit provided with aftercare.

I was fast asleep and in the middle of a dream. In the dream, Jesus said to me, "Matthew, I want you to contact," and He mentioned the name of a popular medium in the United States – a name I knew because I had been watching a show he had on Australian TV.

The first edition of the video I made of it had become corrupted and the only reason I can work out why this happened was that I mentioned the medium's name. The next time, I did not mention his name so I will not receive a lawsuit. Anyway, I was contacted by Jesus in the middle of my dream and He said, "I want you to contact so and so." I asked Jesus, knowing it was Jesus' voice, "How do I do that?" Jesus said, "Just say his name."

I said the medium's name I knew from TV and he answered, "Hello, who is this and what is your message?" I said, "I'm Matthew Payne. I'm from Australia. I'm still living at the moment. I'm not someone who's dead, and I have a message from Jesus for you." He said, "What's your message?" And I said, "Jesus," and I showed him a picture of Jesus hanging on the cross, "has told me to tell you to stop doing your practice of bringing spirits back from the dead and speaking to departed souls. He said you need to stop practicing as a medium and find another way of earning an income. He says that He does not like what you are doing and according to the Bible, it is a forbidden practice and He wants you to stop right away." And he asked me, "Is there any further message?"

I said, "No, that's the message. See you later." but he did not say, "Bye." When that happened, I woke up. I must admit that when Jesus talks to me in my mind, we talk from mind-to-mind just as I had done with this medium, but when I talk to Jesus, it is just natural. When I talked to this medium, I had something like a shock wave come through my head and it was like two waves connecting.

I would certainly realize and recognize it if it ever happened to me again. It was a strange occurrence. I have heard that witches and people with the dark arts can communicate through telepathy. They can talk to each other from place to place without e-mails, a phone, or chat. As a Christian, I know it is possible because I have done what they call telepathy. I have talked mind-to-mind with a person.

I woke up after I had contacted this medium and I asked Jesus, "Did that happen?" Jesus said, "Yes, of course, it happened," and I asked Him, "Why did you use me?" He said, "I had to use someone to tell him and you are a good person." I said, "But why me, of all people? He is a popular medium. Why did you use me?" He said, "Because I knew that you would do it."

I was a little surprised because he is quite a popular person. He is certainly not an insignificant person as I was. Jesus continues to surprise me at the things He gets me to do and the things He allows me to do as a little person with hardly anyone knowing me. Jesus asked me to request something in prayer. He said that I do not often request things when I pray, but because of this occasion, I can request something in prayer. That is the subject of the next chapter.

Chapter 55

Visions and Dreams

After I had spoken to the medium, I was talking to Jesus and He told me to ask Him for something in prayer. He said, "Matthew, you never ask me for things. You are constantly just talking to me, but you never ask me for things so I want to give you something."

It was similar to God talking to Solomon and saying, "Ask me what you desire and I'll give to you." I remember Solomon asked for wisdom. God was pleased with that and gave him everything else as well. Many people ask me how do I have so many visions and how is it I see angels and Jesus, and go to heaven. I have so many visions and I can only trace it to this; when Jesus told me to ask Him for something, I asked, "What should I ask you?" He said, "Well, that's up to you."

I stopped for a moment and thought about it. The verse in Acts, which is a quote from Joel 2:28 says, "*And it shall come to pass afterward That I will pour out My Spirit on all flesh; Your sons and your daughters shall prophesy, Your old men shall dream dreams, Your young men shall see visions.*" I just got the idea of dreams and visions in my head and I asked Jesus, "Could I have visions and prophetic dreams?" I thought that if He were to give me something, could He give me the ability to have visions and to dream prophetic dreams?

Since then, Jesus has opened the floodgates to the visionary experience. I have read books by famous authors and not so famous ones about visions and the supernatural. Many times, when I read books about the supernatural, I have found that I have experienced many of their experiences as well.

That is a confirmation for me that I am seeing the truth. I am not being lied to and I am not seeing something faked by Satan. For instance, I have been to heaven and met children who were former abortions and I have met them in the park, communicated with them, and talked to them often. I love talking to the orphaned children.

A few other books I have read mentioned there are various places where children live in heaven. One of the books mentioned there was a place where abortions lived and played. It was a comfort to my heart to know that they exist. Someone else has been there and seen that place and I was not the only one who had experienced that thing.

Visions and dreams started to open for me. I do not have the prophetic gift of interpreting dreams so when I get a dream that I feel is prophetic in nature and is serving as a prophecy over my life, I will pass it on to people who do dream interpretations to interpret that dream. I have had many, many visions and I will say that I have seen Jesus a hundred times.

I will try not to say that I have seen Jesus too many times, just a hundred times although I have seen Him many times. About six weeks ago, I was walking out of my house and I saw Jesus' cloak blowing in the wind, which I normally do when I see Jesus. He said, "Hello" and I said, "Hello. I've been seeing you every second day now and it is amazing." He said, "I'm with you every day and I just choose to manifest myself every second day."

In my heart, I asked for a scripture verse to confirm that was true and He said, "Lo, I am with you always," and it was special. I shared it with my pastor Mitch and he confirmed that Jesus is always with us, and it can be taken quite literally that Jesus is always with us. It is handy to see visions and to meet Jesus face to face. To have Him sitting on your couch smiling at you and waving at you as you are doing a video.

I believe Jesus can be at all places at once, just as God the Father. I believe that He can be down here on my couch in a vision, smiling or waving at me, and at the same time be seated on the throne in heaven, interacting with people in heaven or walking through heaven. I believe that He can be at all places at once and can interact with us human beings on a human level.

He is God and He has the ability to be in several places at once. We will continue in the next Chapter.

Chapter 56

Visions in the Park

I hope that you enjoy what I have to say here. This was late at night when I was coming home, at about 11:30. It was on my birthday and I had been out with some people to celebrate. It was like a special day, being my birthday. It was only a few weeks after I had asked for visions and dreams, when I contacted the medium via telepathy with Jesus' instruction.

I was walking through a park that had bats in the trees which make this terrible sound just as if they were demons. It is a screeching sound and it is difficult to get used to. Jesus had taught me to walk through the park despite the screeches, to just go through the park at night.

I was walking through this park on my birthday and I was coming to an intersection where there is a grassed area you cannot approach, and you move to the left to leave the park. When I reached it, I believed there were several people from heaven standing there and I could see them in my mind's eye.

In the part of my mind where memories make movies, I could see a group of people standing there. I noticed Jesus and He said, "Hello" to me, and I was happy. He bid me "Happy Birthday." I saw another person and a name just came to my mind and it was Sidhu Sundar Singh.

He was a famous preacher, an apostle who walked through India and had died. He was in the park and I was so surprised and so happy to meet him. I had read his writings. I had read accounts of his life and his life influenced mine. I wished I could be like him and to be a measure of how good he was.

It was such a surprise to meet him on Earth and he was humble, and happy to meet me. He said a few words to me, which I cannot remember at the moment, but they were meaningful words. Then another name came to mind and it was Keith Green. About 25 years ago, he was a popular Christian artist who had died in an airplane crash with one of his children.

Keith Green's music had a big influence in my life. Again, I was absolutely surprised and shocked that Keith Green was in the park as well as Sidhu Sundar Singh and even Jesus. Although they used to live on Earth, they now live in heaven. They are saints who have come from heaven. Jesus is not a saint, but Sidhu Sundar Singh and Keith Green were former Christians who have come down from heaven to visit me.

At this stage, some might be wondering about the biblical precedent for this event. You remember that Elijah and Moses came down to visit Jesus at the Transfiguration on the Mount when He transfigured himself? So it is possible for someone the world considers "dead" to come forth out of that existence in another realm and come visit people on Earth.

It had happened to Jesus and now it was happening to me. I was happy to meet Keith. You feel honored when someone like Sidhu Sundar Singh, who was one of the most powerful men to have walked the Earth, actually goes to meet you who is just a normal person. It is simply amazing.

It blows my mind that I am able to meet someone like that. To meet Keith Green as if he were living now. I would probably never have the chance of meeting him, but because he has been to heaven and because he is living in Heaven's realm, Jesus can bring him down to Earth to visit me and say hello to me. It meant so much to me.

Someone told me that the test of proper visions is that they make you draw closer to Jesus, make you increase your faith and encourage you to walk closer to God. These visions certainly did back in 2000 and 2001, and I still have fond memories of meeting those two with Jesus on Earth.

My eyes were opened! They were officially opened. I could not only sense the presence of Jesus, Sidhu Sundar Singh, Keith Green, and the other angels in the park, but I could see them with my spiritual eyes and be able to converse back and forth. I was able to hear them and ask questions and to be able to receive answers to my questions.

It is almost like meeting the person face to face in the flesh. Because I have met Jesus in the flesh, many people wonder whether they could meet Jesus in the flesh as well. Meeting Jesus in a vision is almost as good as meeting Him in the flesh and conversing with Him face to face is something that is amazing!

After I had spoken to the medium in my dream, Jesus had asked me what I wanted and I had prayed for visions and dreams. Now, within a few weeks, I was experiencing visions of the Lord, which were amazing and changing my life, making me feel special and unique.

I felt like one of the happiest and luckiest people on the face of the Earth because I was meeting people who had such a big influence on my life. They were not just saints from heaven. They were not just people in the history of the church I knew about. Keith Green and Sidhu Sundar Singh had a tremendous influence in my life.

I could not have asked for better people to come and visit me, and it was a tremendous present for my birthday.

Chapter 57

Government Housing

I had a caseworker who was helping me with the accommodation where I was living and helped me fill out an application form to receive government housing.

Government housing is based on about 20-25% of your income, which makes it inexpensive for me. I think it is $80 a week now and I get about $350 a week. It is a good deal. The woman from the aftercare organization helped me fill out an application.

Before we filled it out, she made me save some money and buy a fridge, a washing machine, and a few other things needed in an apartment. They are supplied by the government housing organization so I saved up and bought those things. She had me fill out a form and I went for the interview. My first application to the government housing organization was rejected.

I was sad about that because I was depending on government housing to help me with a less expensive option of housing. The woman who helped me apply, my caseworker, said it was the first application she had ever done for one of the clients that had been rejected. She knew the people in the Department of Housing and there was a worker there to whom she was close.

She contacted her and explained that my application was rejected and I had not been accepted for a house. Another friend she talked to in the Department of Housing said I should appeal the decision. I should fill out a form for an appeal and go for an interview as an appeal and reapply.

My caseworker said to her that nothing in my situation had changed, none of my circumstances had changed, and none of my working conditions or anything else had changed. What was the sense in making an appeal? The government worker said most people give up when they are rejected, so they do not appeal. However, most appeals are upheld and people are accepted after they make an appeal.

Through the grace of God, we completed another application and made an appeal. I went into the interview asking God to be with me, and in the interview I broke down and cried. I shared how I needed this house, and how I could not figure out a way of paying $150 a week for rent especially as this low-income housing was just for myself. If nothing else, I think the tears convinced the person handling the appeal that I needed what I was asking for.

It could have just pushed the woman over the edge to decide in my favor. Within a week, we received news that my appeal had been successful and I was now on the list for government housing, and they will find me a house. I went on a trip to my parent's house. I was at my parent's house in Coffs Harbour when we received a phone call saying that they had found me a house in Croydon, in Sydney's inner-west, about a 20-minute train ride from the center of Sydney's central business district.

It was an apartment in a pleasant, leafy and quiet suburb. We came down and viewed the apartment and it was pleasant. My mom said, "It was the sort of place that she would stay in if she had to and not be embarrassed about staying in it."

I met my next-door neighbour and she was a lovely Christian woman. She had been praying for a Christian person to get the house next to her and she was happy to meet me. I moved my things in with my parents' help and could sleep in a new bed given to me by charity, one that is run by the Catholic Church.

I was happy that they supplied me with something to sleep on and a cupboard, as well as some things like a table and chairs that I still have ten years later. It seems that in my life of prostitution, addiction, sex workers and dirty massages, I had spent my income in all sorts of ways. I had spent my income on wasteful things trying to dull the pain in my heart.

It seems that although I had wasted all my money, God was still there with His grace, able to give me an affordable place to live. My mother worked out that just to maintain her house and pay the insurances and the rates, she spends almost the same amount of money on a house she owned as I was paying rent per week.

I was happy and encouraged since I have been at the house. I have had no problems with anyone. The government wrote me a letter after the first couple of years saying that the apartment is mine for the rest of my life so long as I do not break their rules. I am happy that God provided.

Sometimes we may doubt God, and one of Satan's main agendas is for us to think that God is not there and is not being fair to us. His agenda is to make us think others have things right with God and things are going well for them, and our lot in life is not right and God does not care enough for us compared with others.

I can say in this sense and in this subject that God did look after me and has provided for me, providing inexpensive government housing, affordable to live in on a low-income because I am on a disability income. It comes in handy and gives me enough money to spend on producing books and doing other things with my income rather than paying all of it for rent.

Chapter 58

First Prophecy Website

I was lying in bed in my new apartment one night after I had been there about six months when Jesus told me to write a website offering free prophecy online.

I said, "When?" He said, "Now," and I got up and loaded a website based on healing your life from sexual abuse. I had developed that website so I added a page to it offering free prophecy. When I started to receive a few requests, the Lord told me to write a website dedicated to free prophecy. The sexual abuse part was putting people off.

I did that. I loaded up a website offering free prophecies and the requests started coming in. People started to request prophecies by email and I could start writing prophecies for people. People started arriving at the website who wanted the gift of prophecy and I prayed for them and mentored them.

I could get them up to speed with prophesying over others. Within a couple of months, I had a few pages of five or six people who could offer prophesies and a home page. People were able to read the biographies of the six people making prophecies. They could choose who they wanted to make the prophecy and write directly to them.

We were making between 15 and 20 prophecies daily, and soon, we became number three on Google, number one on Yahoo, and back then, I think there was also MSN. The site went well and the Lord looked after it well. People were blessed. I spent many hours a day making the prophecies. At that time, it took me about an hour in prayer to get into the anointing and preparing myself to be able to prophesy.

Sometimes, it is difficult to prophesy straight off the bat. You need preparation with the Lord. You need the anointing of the Lord to come upon you so you can prophesy. It is not as straightforward as saying, "God says," then writing something. It is actually God who is saying what you say so it takes some preparation.

In those years, it took me an hour in prayer to prepare. I would read my Bible and pray. Then I would prepare and make prophecies. Back then, I used to get about 10 scripture verses from the Holy Spirit and references. I would look up the references and it would all form a message. I would come home after having a cup of coffee down at my local cafe.

I would come home and I would copy and paste the scripture references all into a document, then, Jesus would give a commentary on each scripture verse and how it applies to the verses. The prophecies ended about three pages long and they were full of scripture and edifying messages. I spent about an hour on each. Early on, I reached a stage where only one in five people was giving feedback and saying thank you for the prophecy.

I would write at the end of the prophecy, "Please give us feedback, whether good or bad on this prophecy and let us know how it influenced your life. We have taken the time to send you this prophecy, please spend five minutes sharing with us how this prophecy has affected your life." Even with that at the end of each prophecy, only one in five people were writing back to say thank you and how it affected them.

I became angry, but it is part of the spiritual warfare attached to making prophecies. I became angry that only one in five people was responding. I thought that this was selfish of Christians to expect a prophecy for free, then not spend even a minute or five to actually say thank you.

I asked the Lord and told Jesus that I was going to quit doing prophecies if He did not give me a straightforward answer. I was going to quit doing prophecies because He had told me to start the website. He reminded me of the scripture where He healed ten lepers and only one leper came back to say thanks to Him. He said with a smile and a laugh that I was getting twice the responses than He did in that instance because I was getting one in five, and He got only one in ten.

I laughed at that and I continued to make prophecies. I did not know at the time, but I had a Jesus talking to me who was not a real Jesus. I think I have mentioned this before and at that time I just believed it was Jesus talking to me. He said, "You don't need your medication anymore. You're healed." So I stopped taking my antipsychotic medication, my mood stabilizer medication, and completely went off my medication.

Things started to unwind in my life. I am sure at this stage, as I was starting to influence between 15 and 20 people a day with prophecies, Satan was not too happy. He intervened and told me through a false voice that pretended to be Jesus that I was healed, that I could stop my medication, and I would be right and I would be healed.

Many Pentecostals are happy to suggest that people go off their medication and that they are healed. There are so many cases of people who think that they are healed and still end up in a hospital. I went off my medication, which was a foolish thing for me to do, but I did it by faith. Again, my heart was right. If you were convinced that Jesus told you to go off your medication, you know it is a matter of faith. I acted in faith and I went off my medication. We will discuss what happened to me in the next chapter.

Chapter 59

Outreach Preaching

I obtained some experience in ministering in an outreach in Sydney, Australia when we went to Sydney's Central Business District (CBD) with a band where we would play Christian and secular songs with modified lyrics (to sound more Christian) before preaching to people. However, the message always remained the same – you are a sinner and you need to change your ways or you are going to burn in hell – not many positive user-friendly statements in that message. From that experience, I learned that it was best to share the Gospel and the good news with people. The word *Gospel* means "good news" or as Andrew Wommack would often say, "It is the too good to be true news."

The Gospel of the kingdom originally meant that we would create it ourselves, but we started to fall away from God's Word. Jesus came and gave His life on the cross so we could all be forgiven and receive an indwelling spirit to rule our lives; to empower us to conquer the ills of life and conquer the problems we have in life. The Christian message is a good one, but it often becomes distorted by people who presume they are "witnessing and sharing the good news of Jesus," but who are in fact causing damage.

While I was starting an outreach by myself, I met a guy from England who was preaching using a megaphone. During his six-week visit, I became acquainted with him and he eventually sold me his megaphone and said I should go out and witness on the streets. What I found myself doing was turning on the megaphone and singing Billy Joel songs, among others. When a crowd gathered, I would change and explain the reason for liking the song and how Jesus is the answer to our lives by making things much more bearable for us in life and give us understanding of why we were born, what we are here for and what life is about. I would spend an hour in one spot singing songs and sharing messages, then I would have a break at the Burger King with a hamburger and a Coke. Then,

I would move on to another area and spend another hour there.

I did that for a few hours a week. The problem was, I had stopped taking my medication thinking that I was healed by Jesus who was going to make up for my medication and supernaturally provide me with the medication I needed. I was slowly falling into a situation where the chemical imbalance in my brain was starting to take shape and work against me, although I still enjoyed sharing the message of Jesus on the streets.

A few Christians came up to me and congratulated me. Once, a guy gave me five dollars and asked me to sing "Happy Birthday" for his girlfriend when she came out of the bookstore – an interesting and an enjoyable interaction. I quickly discovered what songs I should sing and the format I should choose. So when I do an outreach in the future with a band, I could coordinate the messages I would preach or allow to be shared with people.

People are continually harassed by life and have enough problems and struggles occurring in their lives. They do not need to be told that they are sinners or that they are going to hell unless they turn and follow Jesus or that they will spend an eternity in hell when they die. Although that may be the truth, there is still plenty of good news in the Gospel and in the Christian life.

Many people have no idea that they were created by God and that He cares about them. God holds the keys to their purpose in life and the reason they are alive. So many people could find fulfillment in life, a true purpose, and a way to walk in their destiny – what they are created for by discovering Jesus Christ, discovering His voice, having Him talk to them, and sharing His ideas, His instructions with them, and His directions for their lives.

I became determined during those few weeks I was sharing and doing outreach by myself about what I would particularly like to manage or control one day in the future when I get a band together and we start witnessing.

Chapter 60

Third Breakdown

As I mentioned earlier, I had been told by what turned out to be a false Jesus' voice that I was healed. This Antichrist spirit told me I do not need my medication anymore because as I am healed, God would supply all the chemicals I need for my brain. I had gone many weeks without my medication and slowly, the wheels started to fall off. I had a friend called Yianni who reported me to the police, and phoned my mother to have her report me to the police. What topped it off was they had police reports and psychiatric reports on my life. Once, when I was at home, I believed there was going to be a tsunami in Sydney and it was going to come while we are having a high-spirited Mardi Gras and people were going to drown.

At about two in the morning, I wrote to a local Sydney newspaper telling them about the forthcoming tsunami and they must cancel the Mardi Gras because many people would be killed. About six in the morning, there was a knock on the door and I opened the door to find the police there. They asked whether they could come in with some mental health people who said I had been reported for writing an e-mail to the Telegraph and asked whether I believed there was going to be a tsunami. They said perhaps it would be better if I went with them to the hospital.

I asked them to wait while I packed a bag full of clothes. Most of the time, when you go to psychiatric wards, you do not have time to take clothes with you. I took the time while they had me in my house to pack a bag, and off I went to the psychiatric ward. I understood I was off my medication, although I still fully believed that I was healed. I thought the people taking me to the psychiatric ward were mistaken – I was the one who was sane and they were out of their minds because they thought I was insane. That is a "typical" response from someone mentally unwell – thinking that they are okay and everyone else is out of step. Thankfully, as if Jesus was there on the wall of my home, He was watching and overshadowing me, and leading the course of my life.

Around that time, I had been running a prophetic website and many people had quit the site because I had been writing strange and frightening messages to them, and they did not want to talk to me anymore. When I came out of the hospital, a few did talk to me but I frightened a few people as demonic spirits were speaking through me in my e-mails and the messages I was writing.

As I went into the hospital, I became angry with the nurses so they gave me a sedative. It took a day and a half for the sedative to wear off. I was terribly drugged. Yianni, my friend, came to the hospital the next day, but I was too sedated to even speak to him. He came in the next day when I was feeling better, and I could talk more coherently. Yianni was a true friend. He came to the hospital every day of my stay, which lasted for a month. I had an idea that demons were talking to me, but I had no idea there was a false Jesus talking to me. Every time I have mentioned in this book that there was a false Jesus, I have mentioned it for clarity, and for the understanding of the readers. Up to this point, I still had not realized there was a Jesus – a false Jesus – a false spirit pretending to be Jesus speaking often to me. The real Jesus often spoke to me as well, but with this false Jesus speaking to me at the same time, you can understand it became confusing for me to hear Jesus say things that turned out to be untrue.

It was difficult to reconcile a Jesus who was a liar in my mind, but I had managed to handle it, although, it had put me back in hospital again. It is difficult to come to terms with who you are in the hospital yet all you did was to stop your medication because the supposed Jesus, the false Jesus, had told you to stop taking it. When you do not understand it was a false Jesus speaking to you, it is difficult to understand why Jesus would say you are healed when you are not. I was locked up with many psychiatric patients.

While I was there, I did a prophecy for a guy there who turned out to be a backslidden Christian – a person who used to attend church and had given his life to Jesus many years before but had not been walking with Jesus lately. I shared a vision of him sitting on the end of a bridge, drinking a six-pack of beer and that Jesus was there with him and understood him. Apparently, that was a time he was feeling suicidal and trying to summon the courage with the six-pack of beer to kill himself. It touched him and he broke down in tears. I asked him, could he see and he said, "Yeah." Then I asked him could he spiritually see? Could he see the angels that were all around us? I could see them at this stage, but I just wanted confirmation that they were there. I pointed outside of the psychiatric ward and he said, "Yes, the whole park is full of angels." I said, "The ones closer than 50 meters square from us, are they different angels?" He said, "Yeah, they are," and he said that they had their wings open, forming a sort of canopy over us.

We went for a walk and at one stage I said, "What are the names of the two walking on either side of us?" I expected him to say Michael and Gabriel because I had received supernatural experiences with relatively important angels coming down to visit me. On the right side, he said, Michael, and on the left side, he said the angel's name was Daniel. I said, "Is Daniel a man?" He said, "Yeah, he is," and it was Daniel the prophet. It was interesting that I had met a saint on Earth and he was walking with me. It was interesting that Jesus was manifesting Himself and these supernatural beings to my Christian friend. I could prophesy, and share with him deep things that meant much to him in his life through the gift of prophecy. Although my mind was out of control and medication was trying to reel it in, I still had true encounters with God. I could truly hear His voice.

There was a girl there while I was suffering intensely in the first few days; I asked her whether she heard voices. She said yes, she was a schizophrenic. I said, "Can you do me a favor? I am going to ask God to speak to you, and I want you to share what He says to you with me. He has a message for me." She said, "Will He speak to me?" I said, "Yeah, I will pray for you that He speaks to you," and I prayed for her.

She said, "God wants you to know that you are in a safe place and that everything is going to work out. Just enjoy yourself and enjoy the food and the company. Things are going to be sorted soon. You are in the right place with me. You have been obedient and I am going to look after you. Relax." I was amazed and happy with the message.

She said, "Wow! What is that? How can I listen to that voice?" And I said, "Just ask God to speak to you in the future and He will speak." She said, "It is such a pleasant voice. It is so wonderful to hear such a beautiful voice." I said, "It is God speaking to you." Even during a visit to the psychiatric ward, I had helped a Christian recommit his life to Jesus and I had helped a psychiatric patient hear God for the first time and open herself to hearing from God.

Psychiatric medications are important. I believe in divine healing and I have heard testimonies of people who have been healed from bipolar or schizoaffective or both disorders. I know people who have been healed and have not needed medication, but I would be cautious of recommending people stop their medication as I did. It was the second time I had stopped my medication and it was the second time I had landed in the hospital because of it. It is a traumatic experience.

Again, there were several Christians who came to the mental ward once a week to share and do a Bible study. It was wonderful to sit down with them and share Jesus with them. I love people who take the time out to go and talk to mental patients about Jesus. They influenced me and they meant much to me. It reminds me of the sheep and the goats' parable, "I was sick and you came to see me," Jesus said. I applaud those who come to psychiatric wards. Again, I had a breakdown. The medication kicked in after a month and I was put back in my right mind.

Chapter 61

Second Prophetic Website

When I came out of the hospital, I was reminded by Jesus that He had asked me to start a prophetic website and offer a free prophecy online for people. I was well and in my right mind again, and the Lord led me to start another prophetic website and build up an additional team, so I started it.

I did not have to do all the prophecies myself for too long before people started to volunteer to come and work on the website and make prophecies. I had a particular prayer that I used for people who wanted to volunteer to pray and I would pray for them to get the three gifts of prophecy – the gift of Prophecy, Word of Knowledge, and Word of Wisdom. They would pray the prayer and I would ask them to do a prophecy over my life to check that they received the gift. They would do a prophecy over my life and I would give them extensive feedback, sharing with them how they had each of the three gifts and how those gifts had manifested in my life and manifested in the prophecy over my life. They were encouraged. I would send them a request each day and they would send the prophecy back to me. Then I would send the prophecy back to the person and I would give them feedback on the prophecies they were doing.

I felt it was important to arrange intercessors for the prophecies. I arranged a prayer for people to read the prophecy request of people, read the prophecy that one of my team of prophets prophesied over the person. They would read the request. They would read the prophecy, then they would say a prayer confirming the prophecy and encouraging the person to press on, believe in the prophecy and go forward with their life.

It was relatively comprehensive. A person could log in, see my website online, and get a prophecy. They would not only get a prophecy, but they would get a prayer as well. Sadly, I found many people were not so thankful. I used to put on the bottom of each prophecy, "Please give us feedback with a good or bad regarding this prophecy. Did it encourage you? Did it make you feel better? Please give us good or bad feedback on what was shared with you as a courtesy to us."

I found only one in five people we made a prophecy for shared their feedback with us. It was disappointing. I think in this world, when you offer things for free, people are not so thankful even when they get something free. It seems that people like free, free, free and it is only about themselves. I found it was disappointing to see how many people expect something for nothing. I suppose nothing changes.

So many of us go to church, but do not put money in the offering plate or support our pastors financially. So many Christians do not financially support their pastor with a tithe of their income. So many of us are used to just getting things free in this world and that is a shame. I have experience in praying for people and seeing people receive the gift of prophecy. I have experience in building a website. I have experience in managing up to 40 or 50 requests a week for prophecy, managing a team of prophets, building a team of prophets, and mentoring the prophets.

I call people prophets; they are not in the office of prophets but prophesying. For a short reference, I use the word prophet, but it is essentially not a recognized person in the office of prophet, but they are just a prophesier – someone with the gift of prophecy.

I have included this for clarification so you do not get carried away thinking you have become a prophet just because you have prayed a particular prayer. I was encouraged because I was fulfilling God's will. Over a year at a rate of 50 per week would mean about two and a half thousand people were prophesied over each year and you would be doing tremendous work for God. Many people became encouraged for nothing.

Websites were $30 and $40 for a year's posting fee, so it was relatively cheap to do. You need an Internet connection, which you paid for, but it was not much more expensive. So many people's lives were blessed and encouraged. What I found strange was that Satan did not seem to like people being prophesied over. I am not sure if I mentioned it before with my first prophecy site, but I certainly understood it by the time I was running my second site.

All my life, I have had bullets flying past me from the enemy. When I had opened my first prophecy site, I felt as though the bombs were going off around me continually. It was as if I was in a real war, and it was dangerous and frightening. The amount of spiritual warfare that intensified when I started to do personal prophecy online was remarkable! It is true what Joyce Meyer says, "Higher levels, bigger devils." It is certainly true that we are in a real spiritual fire and if you want to encourage fifty Christians a week with a word from Jesus, then you will be in a real battle. Some people might think that it is a remarkable ministry and it is, I suppose. It is just that I never considered it an amazing ministry because I was not educated in ministry. I was never trained to be a minister. I was never trained to be a prophet by anyone else.

I was just doing things as Jesus told me to do them, and thankfully, this time, when Jesus told me to do it, it was the real Jesus speaking. Thankfully, when I spoke with Jesus' voice, it was Jesus speaking through me. That was a tremendous blessing to many people. I learned much by exercising my gift of prophecy and exercising my abilities to manage a team of people doing personal prophecies for others.

Chapter 62

Visit by Mutu

I had an affiliation with a church in Coffs Harbour where my parents lived, and a friend from there used to attend church in Asia when he did engineering projects overseas. Once, he heard a preacher who was anointed by God and had plenty of God’s power and wisdom. He invited the preacher to come to Australia and preach to his church. It was remarkable that he invited the person and it was even more remarkable that the person came. His name was Mutu – the shortened version of his name as he had a much longer name in his Asian culture. He was of Indian descent, but he came from Malaysia. He was a Malaysian Indian, but he was a tremendous man and I met him for the first time in Coffs Harbour.

He requested a private meeting with me a few days later. While I was telling him how I hear Jesus, how I hear God the Father, and how I talk to Mary Magdalene in Heaven, he thought it was all interesting and he listened for a while. Then he asked me, “How do I know that it is Jesus speaking.” I said, “He has spoken to me all my life.” He said, “But how do you know that it is Jesus?”

I did not have an answer for him. He said, “How do you know that is God the Father?” And I said, “Because He has spoken to me,” and he said, “But how do you know it is Him?” He got me thinking, then he told me that the voices that I was hearing – the Jesus voice, the Father voice and Mary Magdalene voice were all demons speaking to me and confusing me, and causing me trouble.

He said to me, “When you want to hear Jesus speak, read the Gospels of Matthew, Mark, Luke and John. When you want to hear God the Father speak, read the prophets of Isaiah and the Old Testament. Read all the books of the prophets. Do not speak to Mary Magdalene.” He said that is what I should do from now on. When I want to hear Jesus speak, read the Gospels. When I want to hear God speak, read the prophets. And, if they talk to you, do not talk back and do not answer them back. Do this and they will soon give up talking to you.

That was sad for me, but I would combine this meeting with other meetings I had with Mutu over the years. I think I only have them in one section here. When I met Mutu, I shared for hours and hours all the angelic visitations and all the visions of angels I had received. We went on a six-hour trip and I shared all my stories with him. He authenticated that all my stories were true and that I was not deceived in any of them.

There were no wrong spirits pretending to be manifested angels. He agreed with me that everything was true and above board. It was encouraging for me to know that someone anointed by God agrees that I had seen, met and conversed with these angels. That it was all true. I had hundreds of questions and it seemed that I asked Mutu at least a hundred questions about particular verses in the Bible. He seemed to know the answer to every question I had, which was remarkable. And it set me free.

At that time, I believed in God's judgement and God's laws, and I believed you had to obey the Old Testament and the New Testament. I had one foot on the side of grace and one foot on the side of the law. Some would call that legalistic thinking. I was into an angry God and a vengeful God, and I was frightened of God. Mutu reinforced that in my life because he was much like that. Although he was a man full of Jesus and His love, he was a man who agreed with the punishments and the chastisements of God, with one foot on the side of law and one foot on the side of grace. Years later, I was to relinquish that way of thinking, but at the time, Mutu reinforced those beliefs in me. Mutu listened for hours and hours to me – story after story, and answered question after question.

Mutu did a teaching on the Fivefold Ministry of apostles, prophets, evangelists, pastors and teachers. It described what each of the five ministry offices did. I remember that while teaching on those Fivefold offices, he taught on the nine gifts of the Holy Spirit, such as tongues, interpretation of tongues, discernment of spirits, the gift of prophecy, the gift of word of knowledge, gift of word of wisdom, the gift of healing, and the gift of miracles.

He explained what the nine gifts of the Holy Spirit were, in addition to the five ministry offices. I remember he was the first preacher who I listened to for more than an hour and not become bored. I just loved to listen to him. He was just remarkable! When he did the teaching on the Fivefold Ministry and the nine gifts of the Holy Spirit, we had questions. We would ask questions in the middle of the teaching. It went on for five hours and we were sad to see it end, but he said we needed a break because we are going to come back that night. We were sad to go, but I had never been in such an enthralling meeting for five hours before. I learned about what the true anointing of God is – that when you have the true anointing on your life, people will listen to you for hours!

It is the same with the anointing on a book. If a book keeps you reading and turning the pages, it has real anointing on it and the person speaking has an anointing. That was remarkable! When it came time for Mutu to leave for the airport in Coffs Harbour, everyone lined up at the window to wave him goodbye as he walked outside. He went past saying farewell at the window, then he motioned with his hands for everyone to move aside. I was standing behind everyone because I did not want to watch him, because I knew I would cry if I saw him leaving. He made everyone move aside and he looked at me in the eyes and he whispered to me, "I love you." It just made me cry. I cried for 20 minutes with gut-wrenching tears on the way home in the car. I said to Jesus as I was crying, "Please tell me, because only you know why he needs to go. Why can I not be with him for the rest of my life?" I just met a person who I thought was Jesus on Earth. He was just a remarkable person.

He had all the answers to all my questions and I felt as if I had met Jesus in a person. I wanted to travel with him for the rest of my life. I was so upset that he was leaving and I will not see him for over a year. I told Jesus that he has to give me an answer so I can stop crying. The next day, Jesus gave me a scripture reference. I looked at the scriptures and there was a story of the demoniac and how he came down to the boat after he had the demons cast out of him into the pigs.

He said that he wanted to go with Jesus and He said, "No, go back to your fellow citizens and share them the good news of what happened to you and testify to my healing powers." The demoniac left and went to share the good news with his fellow citizens. Jesus said, "It is the same with you. You need to leave Mutu, let him go, and go and testify to people that you are being healed."

Mutu solved the major quandary in my life of a false Jesus talking to me, a false Father speaking to me, and a Mary Magdalene who was not Mary Magdalene speaking to me. I was deceived and it finally made plenty of sense to be told there were false voices talking to me. It gave me an understanding of some problems I had received in my life and I had been deceived to this point by voices that were not real when I believed they were.

I followed these voices everywhere and did everything they told me to do. It turned out that I was not always listening to Jesus. That may not come across to you as a big thing but it certainly is. Many people would say, "Well, why not throw out the baby with the bathwater," but if you are going to hear from Satan and his demons pretending to be Jesus, why not just have the Bible and not even listen to Jesus? I can go on to share that I developed a good sense for listening to Jesus and I started to discern when the false voice was speaking to me. You certainly could choose not to ever listen to the voice of Jesus again but that was not the course that I eventually took later in my life.

Chapter 63

Called as a Prophet

I used to attend a church called Newtown Mission in Sydney – a Uniting church. I am not sure whether you have a Uniting church over in America, but it is a combination between a Wesleyan and a Methodist church, but follows the traditions of Wesley, the preacher. I liked this church because they had a drop-in centre where poor people could come for free meals four days a week. I liked the church's outreach there and I liked the church as much as you could like a church. I knew the ministers there and I seem to get on well with them.

One day, Brian, one of the pastors in charge of the drop-in center, was preaching. He called people forward for prayer and I just felt compelled by Jesus to go forward. Remember, I was not listening to Jesus anymore. I was just reading my Bible as Mutu had told me, but I felt an enthusiasm in my spirit to go forward. I got on my knees, which is rare for me to go forward for prayer and go on my knees – but I did. Brian came up to me and said, "You have been on your knees in the prophetic for years and Jesus is calling you to your feet to be a prophet and to move powerfully in the prophetic." Now, I had already been prophesying on my website and managing a team of prophets but Brian was calling me to something deeper.

He prayed for me to receive the anointing of a prophet and be called as a prophet. It was encouraging to have someone in ministry recognize the gift in my life. It is one thing to have a gift – it is another thing to have a minister of a church calling forth that gift in you and not only recognizing the gift in you, but prophesying that. It is going to increase in its intensity and its strength and your ability to exercise that gift in your life.

It was remarkable and made me happy. I became a regular at giving a prophetic word during the corporate worship time. Between songs, I was out of the chair to share a prophetic word, corporately, a message from God to the whole church. I would be given the microphone to share a message. At one stage, Yianni and I could do that by just asking for the microphone. But it reached a stage in church where they wanted us to share with them before we shared with the rest of the congregation. That was okay when it truly came from God and not come from us, as it meant the message was true so we were able share the message anyway. I am not sure if there was ever an occasion where I was going to share a message and Brian said "no" to the message and I was not able to share it.

All I know is when you are operating in the prophetic and you are operating as a person called to prophecy and to prophesy in meetings, I know that you have to be subject to the leaders and come under their authority. You do the prophecy and you operate, and conduct yourself in a way suitable and fitting to the church. So when they changed their rules and you had to share the prophecy before you can share it on the microphone – that was okay.

You still shared the prophecy with the church. The pastor had an idea where to put that prophecy into the meeting and he was happy with it, and you were happy with it. I reached a stage where I became rather tired of doing the prophecies over the church because I did not seem to get a response. No one seemed to give me feedback. I thought it was an important message from God for people to hear but people did not seem too thankful for the message I shared each week.

I do not know when I stopped but eventually it did not move me anymore. I think Jesus understood my feelings and stopped giving me messages to share with people. At one stage we had a visiting apostle to the church and he said that the church was obstinate and did not want to listen to the Spirit of God. He became frustrated with the church because they did not want to move in the ways of God and move with the way the Holy Spirit wanted to move the church.

It lined up with how I was feeling about prophesying in the church too, but I was encouraged that Brian prayed for me to move in the prophetic. Whenever I visit Newtown Mission nowadays, he says, "Welcome back, Prophet." He is encouraged with my appearances at the church from time to time when I go back and visit that church. I do not attend that church nowadays but I was encouraged by Brian.

I have repeated myself often but it bears repeating – it is always encouraging if you are a pastor, to encourage your flock, to move in the gifting and to move in what they are good at. It is good for you to recognize, if you are a pastor, something that one of your flock is good at and encourage him to move in that and to practice the gifting they have been given by God. It was most encouraging to me to have my gift of prophecy recognized formally and for him to be led by the Lord to tell me that I was going to move more powerfully since then.

I also was walking back from church one night when He shared with me and I said, “This is interesting, Jesus. I am not allowed to listen to you and hear your voice but you want me to prophesy, how is that going to happen?” Jesus said, “You only listen to my voice when you prophesy then you do not listen to my voice at other times. Only when you prophesy, I will speak through you and you will be able to hear me speak, and for other times we will just be silent.”

I did that for years where I just prophesied hundreds of times, merely to hear the voice of my Saviour and to hear the voice of God. I fell so in love with hearing them speak through me and I treasured my relationship. I missed my relationship of speaking to God and speaking to Jesus, and have them speak back to me. But I had to go through that period so the false voices had less hold on me and I did not depend on speaking to these false voices all the time.

Chapter 64

Yianni and Phil

This chapter is about Yianni and Phil – you might remember Yianni from when I was staying at the mental hospital after a breakdown. Yianni was my friend who came in to see me spending 11 hours every day with me from about 9:00 in the morning till about 8:00 at night. He stayed with me all the time during my hospital visit even going without lunch. In the parable of the sheep and the goats, Jesus says He commends people who visit those sick and in the hospital. I must say that people who visit others in the hospital are special to those who are sick. I was certainly sick and in a bad way in that hospital. Yianni made friends with people in the psychiatric hospital and would talk to them often. When I went to the toilet or to lunch, he would make friends with people to make them feel welcome, and to boost their feelings. It takes a special kind of friend to go to a psychiatric hospital and willingly choose to spend 11 hours a day with his deranged friend who was saying crazy things – and to love him anyway.

Yianni has always seemed to have loved me whatever condition I was in and whatever I was doing with my life. He is a person who has suffered much rejection in his life and not many people seemed to warm to Yianni and like him. Even if you do not reject him, he sometimes seems to do things that cause people to reject him. Jesus told me to be a friend to Yianni and to stay close to him. It was certainly warmed my heart to have Yianni at the hospital. I had all sorts of visions at the hospital and I explained them to Yianni, and he just listened without arguing.

Around that time, I wanted to get my book, *The Fallen Ones,* published. I had been sitting on the book for about 10 years and Yianni said he had an eccentric friend who was bipolar and had the same mental illness as me. He said he was a good proofreader and editor, and I should be introduced to him. After he introduced us, I got to know Phil well as he proofread my book and we discussed all the changes so we finally reached a position where I was ready to self-publish the book through CreateSpace, part of the Amazon Company. Then Jesus told me to throw the book away – either I could preach in the future or I could publish my book, but I could not do both. It was a big decision for me to throw my book away especially as I had just spent about $500 on Phil editing the book. I had spent all this money and Jesus told me to throw the book away, but through the experience I got to know Phil. He became a friend, and I started writing articles shortly after that, which I will talk about in a future chapter. Phil started to proofread my articles so there were fewer mistakes in them.

I got to know Phil as a friend through the proofreading and I used to go to his place and watch videos. Sometimes Phil was up at night because he could not sleep, and he would to come round to my place, and we would stay up all night watching DVDs. I remember we liked Law and Order, SVU (Special Victims Unit). I bought every series and we would watch Law and Order, talking and drinking up to 5 cups of coffee through the night. Sometimes we would drive into the city in Phil's car and we would have a meal in an all-night restaurant called *Pancakes On The Rocks*. We would have pancakes and ice-cream. It was a wonderful time with Phil as he loved to talk and I loved to talk with him. He used to speak to Jesus, and he could answer my questions.

At one stage, Phil said to me that I was not to question what Jesus already had already told me through him, and I was not to use Phil to check what Jesus had told me. Jesus told Phil that I was to be confident in what I was told by Jesus and not to cross-check. Sometimes Jesus tells you things too difficult for you to believe, and sometimes you want to check them out with another prophet. Phil maintained that he was not a prophet. He just heard from Jesus and did not have the gift of prophecy. Although he was acting in the gift of prophecy, we could never seem to agree that he was prophesying to me. He just maintained that he had a telephone line to Jesus who talked to him. In addition, it was fun to have a friend that could stay up all night and could understand bipolar disorder.

When two bipolar people get together, they become close friends quickly because they understand the depth of depression and the sadness of being bipolar. They also understand the manic highs and staying up for two or three days in a row without sleep. Phil and I spent many nights together all night – sometimes Yianni would join us, but it was mainly Phil and I. He would phone me about 11:00 at night and ask me whether I was going to be up for the night. If I was, he would arrive an hour later with drinks and snacks to eat. We would stay up, talk, watch movies, or as I have said, go out for something to eat in the middle of the night. Phil seemed to always pay for the petrol. He never asked me for petrol money unless he was extremely short of money. I often wanted to go out and he might say he needed five dollars for the petrol which I would give to him, but he never pressured me for money. He always seemed generous with his money and shared his money with me buying snacks and other things. Phil was a good friend to me.

I had met Yianni in the city in 2000 and I have known him all this time, about 13 years in all. Yianni has always been a prophetic person and a prophet of God. He could certainly do with some maturing just as all of us could. Yianni merely needs some counselling and healing in his life, yet he is a loyal friend. He has also been generous with his money to me. When I do not have any money, he is always the first to open his wallet and pay for things. If I had to pay Yianni back for all the expenses he had spent on me, I would need to be rich because I need more than $500 before I could start to repay him. Yianni did not demand money back. Like me, when he gives money he does not lend it. He does not use his money to manipulate you or to have power over you as some do. He has been a good friend. Yianni, Phil and I have been good friends for a long time. I hope that gives you a better understanding of my life.

Chapter 65

Feels Rejected at Newtown Mission

I attended Newtown Mission Church, a Uniting church, in Sydney, Australia where Pastor Brian prophesied over me and declared I was going to move in the prophetic and become a prophet. The church allowed me to speak in their church and share prophecies in their church. Initially, they allowed me to speak, then they progressed to where I had to give them an idea of what the prophecy was before I could share the prophecy. However, I eventually started becoming a little tired of Newtown Mission. It seemed as if I almost needed to use my prophetic gift just to talk to people. I seemed to have to tell people about what God was saying to them and use my gift of prophecy to talk about their lives. Just keeping conversations going was proving difficult. It seems as if I was so hurt, broken, and unhealed that I just did not seem to harmonise with the church. Phil, my friend who had gone to Newtown Mission before, had left saying he did not like it. He said he was in a better mood when he came to church, but he felt so rejected and misunderstood at church that he would leave feeling more depressed.

He said to himself that he feels depressed enough much less going into a church and being rejected and feeling even more depressed. Both Yianni and Phil had homosexual experiences in their past as I had, but for many years Phil was a practicing homosexual and Yianni for a few more years than I. Yianni had a learning disability although he did not have a mental illness.

Phil felt rejected at Newtown Mission and just did not seem to harmonise. Phil took a long time before allowing himself to be drawn out. He is a private person and it was difficult for him to communicate. He was at his best with someone who did plenty of the talking so he could make comments and converse, but he was not particularly good at starting conversations. He did not understand women. He had spent all his life sleeping with men and being with men. He did not know how to interact with women so life at Newtown Mission Church was difficult. When I initially heard about Newtown Mission, I had heard good things from Yianni and bad things from Phil. I initially went to the church just to see who was right, and after a while at the church I was not developing any friends.

At Newtown Mission I only made one friend who I saw outside the church services. I only saw that friend once because I had said that no one is friends with me outside church hours. He made an appointment to see me outside church hours to prove me wrong that I was being rejected. I think many people go to churches and they just do not seem to harmonise. They do not have a good job, a good car, an iPhone, or all the modern conveniences. They did not have iPhones in 2002 but they do not have the latest mobile phone. They do not have a good job, a good Apple computer, a normal life and they certainly do not have a mental illness as I did. In addition, they may have found it a little weird that I was always talking about Jesus, how Jesus talks to me, meeting angels, and some of the other things I did. I suppose I was rather like Yianni feeling and being rejected, but perhaps I said things that made people reject me. I was confused, hurt, and broken. If you have been reading my book so far or watching the videos, you will have realized that I had a dark and tortured life.

I was not a particularly pleasant person to know, but I had plenty of heart, emotion, and love to share. Although I was not given the opportunity, I just did not seem to harmonise. I remember Yianni and I went to a Bible study at Newtown Mission once, and we seemed to dominate the Bible study answering the questions and commenting on all the questions. Next week, we were told by the Bible study leader we were not welcome back. That was my experience with Bible studies. I often go to Bible studies and I seem to have an answer for every question. Many people when asked questions hold back with their answers because they are unsure of themselves and I seemed to have a go at every question and seemed to have an answer. Often my answers are correct or my answers often sound correct and plausible. I seem to dominate conversations in Bible studies but people do not like others continually speaking or who seem to think they have an answer to every question. I know myself when I find people continually talking in a meeting, you sort of rise up and you get upset about them continually speaking. I can imagine people getting upset with me continually talking in that meeting. It was difficult.

I went to Newtown Mission for a year or two, but the longer I went, the sadder I was becoming. Merely because I wanted friends than mentally challenged Yianni and bipolar Phil. I wished I had a normal friend – a friend who did not have anything wrong with them, and had a normal life and a good job. I wished for friends who were more real, more together and with a more ideal life, rather than those who the world consider "losers" and unwise. I remember in Corinthians it says

1Co 1:27-29
But God has chosen the foolish things of the world to put to shame the wise, and God has chosen the weak things of the world to put to shame the things which are mighty;
and the base things of the world and the things which are despised God has chosen, and the things which are not, to bring to nothing the things that are, that no flesh should glory in His presence.

I remember that passage speaks well of Yianni and I. Yianni might be mentally challenged but sometimes the Lord moves on Yianni and gives him words to say. The wisdom that comes out of his mouth is profound and astounds people. The sad thing is that many times what he has to say is not so profound and people do not hang around long enough to get the pearls out of everything that is said.

I felt rejected at Newtown Mission as I have said, and I started to experience what Phil was experiencing every week – making it more difficult for me to go. The more I tried to make friends, the more I tried to impress people and say things that would make them like me – the more rejected I felt and I seemed to receive the wrong responses. You know how it is when you are talking to someone, they make an excuse saying they have to talk to someone else, and they walk off to talk to someone else, and never return to talk to you.

That was happening to me often.

It was sad. I was sad. I was not in a good place. It is not (or it should not) be difficult to ask to go to a church and make friends. But it seemed after a year or two at Newtown Mission the only friend I had was the friend I had walked in with. I was starting to agree with Phil that the church made me more upset than it made me happy.

Chapter 66

Full of Pride and Rebellion

While I was going to Newtown Mission, one of the pastors received an invitation to a prophetic meeting at another church. The meeting was a paid meeting where people had to pay but they were given two free passes to go. The pastor approached me knowing that I was prophetic and said to me that I could go if I liked and he gave me the passes. I went to what was a fabulous meeting and I enjoyed the preaching. The preacher, who was a prophet, asked people to come forward who wanted a prophecy and prayer. I went forward and I was happy. I was butting in and answering his questions as he was teaching and often talking during his sermon to which he had invited the audience. I had a good time.

I went forward for prayer and the prophet said I was full of pride and rebellious spirits. I was possessed and I needed to learn how to submit and listen to my pastors, and do what my pastors say and I needed to humble myself. He did not cast out any demons. He did not say anything other than my prophecy. He said nothing encouraging and he just left me feeling bad. So I had a name to a couple of the demons in my life. I had a spirit of pride and rebellion. I had no idea how to get rid of those spirits. I had no concept of how to deal with them. I was just told that I needed to submit to my pastors and humble myself. It is one thing for a person to say to you that you need to humble yourself. It is another thing to understand how to humble yourself. I have never read a book or heard a good teaching on how to humble yourself, and I still do not understand how to humble myself. It turns out in my life I have been humbled by God when He wanted to humble me, but I never seemed to have humbled myself. Pride and rebellion sounded as though they were serious spirits. I know it said the spirit of rebellion is similar to witchcraft in the Old Testament.

I knew that was powerful and bad. I felt bad. I felt shameful and condemned out of that meeting. I am not sure as a prophet I would deliver that message to a person but it helped to know that I had these spirits in my life. Around the time, I did some research. I came across some research on the teachings of the Jezebel spirit and the more I studied the more I realized that I had many characteristics of the Jezebel spirit. So here I have pride, rebellion, and Jezebel. I seemed as though I was a serious head case, a serious spiritual dummy, a spiritual enemy of the Lord God, and there were some serious spirits in me. I was rather worried. I went to a healing meeting once and asked for healing of the Jezebel spirit. I wanted them to cast it out but they did not cast out the Jezebel spirit. I remember my friend, Phil, could not only talk to Jesus but he had the gift of being able to discern and cast out spirits.

I came home after the healing meeting and asked Phil whether he could he cast out the spirit of Jezebel out – which he did. The problem with spirits is that you have to be sick of the behaviour of that actual spirit and you need to repent the behaviour and not conform to the behaviour of that certain spirit anymore or the spirit will not come out. I did notice when Phil cast out the Jezebel spirit that my prophecies changed. The tone and the language of the prophecies I was doing online by e-mail changed. There was dramatic effect in my prophecies so I believed the spirit had come out, but pride and rebellion are terrible spirits. Someone who is proud cannot be taught anything. They cannot be told that they are wrong. They will not listen to instruction. They think they are right about everything. They think they are good at everything. They think they are better teachers and better preachers and pastors. They think they could run a church better than the pastor. They think that they could teach a sermon better than the pastor. They think that they can go up to a pastor and tell him what is wrong with him and how he could have preached better. They have got all sorts of advice for all sorts of people. If only people would come to them and ask them for advice. I was finding people were asking for prophecies through e-mail.

I could prophesy but I did not seem to have any influence at Newtown Mission and people were not coming to me for advice. It is frustrating when you are a "know-it-all" and you think you know everything. The pastor of the church will not ask you to preach when all you want to do is preach and teach people the things of God that you think you know, and they will not invite you into the pulpit and preach. It is frustrating and annoying!

These are all signs of the spirit of pride and the spirit of rebellion. Rebellion is thinking you are better by saying you are better than your pastor, complaining about your pastor, and pulling your pastor down in front of others. These are all signs of rebellion and Jezebel, and the spirit of pride. I was infested with demons and I was not in a good way. It is remarkable that God can make a difference in a person's life and heal them emotionally well enough so they can become effective ministers for the Gospel and be a good witness to everyone who comes to them in the future.

Chapter 67

Burnout

As I was ministering online, about 40-50 prophecy requests were coming in each week and I was ministering a team of prophets. A team of people prophesying who I called prophets but who were not necessarily prophets; just people with the gift of prophecy. As I was ministering it became draining. I reached a stage where I just totally burned out so I had no energy left for prophecy requests, to manage the incoming e-mails, and to manage the team of people doing the prophecies. I ran out of steam, became tired of doing prophecy, and faced burnout.

I remember six months before I had done a prophecy that I had written out for Yianni and gave it to him. It said he was going to help me in my ministry soon but he did not seem to agree with it at the time. When I faced burnout, I asked Yianni whether he could he take over the prophecy group and manage it. Yianni took over the prophecy group and managed it for a year, making it a prayer and prophecy group. Many people would come in for a prophecy and he would write them that he was going to pray for them, and he would write a prayer for them. He managed the requests and the website for a year.

It is important to know that one of Satan's most strategic weapons is to come against effective ministering Christians and allow them to burnout or run out of steam. It is one of his most effective ways of taking someone out of the ministry: by making him ineffective by getting them to a stage where they have run out of energy, and becoming tired of doing ministry for the Lord. It may come as a surprise that I have been burned out several times with prophesying and ministering. Nowadays, I do not do personal prophecies over the Internet – I only do them face to face with people where I can get feedback and be assured that my prophecy hit the mark.

It seemed when I did personal prophecies over the Internet, only one in five people said thanks or gave any sort of feedback to say the prophecy hit its mark. When you are doing prophecies face to face, you can see straight away that the person is affected. Most often because they are in your presence they will give you feedback on what the prophecy meant to them. That is exciting.

I was burned out. When you are in ministry, many people are attacked by Satan with this and you just need to find rest in the Lord. You need to go back to your first love and fall back in love with Jesus, and get the real reasons that you do ministry and come to grips with serving Jesus. Get the right motivations and the right attitude to get back up and start to minister again.

After a year I could restart my prophecy website and minister again but Yianni faithfully ministered for the prophetic website and took the requests. He did not have an Internet connection so he used to go to an Internet café where he spent the money to do the ministry. That was good of him. If you have experienced burnout, I pray that God restores you to your first love and you come into a deeper relationship with Jesus. I pray you understand He loves you and He does not need you to minister for Him to love you. He loves you for you being you! I just want you to understand that you are precious to Jesus and you are not the first to have been attacked in this way.

Chapter 68

Prophetic Evangelism

In the year I took a break from doing prophecy, the Holy Spirit gave me a new interest. He introduced me to the talent of walking up to total strangers and giving them a message or prophecy from God. It was a real unique ability and a great talent, and fast became something that I enjoyed doing. Essentially, it means walking down the street and having someone highlighted in your spiritual senses so they seem to stand out for some reason. Just as an attractive girl might stand out to a guy walking down a street or an attractive guy stands out to a girl. A person can just be highlighted and stand out. It seemed sort of special. Then when you realize this, you can ask the Holy Spirit or ask Jesus whether He has a message for that person. He will give you one or two sentences of a message or the understanding of a message to take to the person. The Holy Spirit taught me to go up to the person and say, "Excuse me, I have a gift and occasionally I receive a message for a person and today I have got a message for you."

Then I share the message with them. At the end of the message, I tell them that, "I might have seemed as though I am a clairvoyant but I am not. I am a prophet and I received that message of God for you. I hope it blesses you." I leave them with that and that is called prophetic evangelism. I have since written a published book called *Prophetic Evangelism Made Simple* or will be by September 2013. The book merely explains how to evangelize people by using the prophetic gifting. It is an exciting gift to go up to 10 or 15 people a week and give them a personal message of God. When you walk up to a person and share things about their personality and the gifting in their life that you do not know, and things about their life you could not possibly know, it blesses them. It surprises the person and fills them with wonder about the "sort of gift that enables you to walk up to me and just share all these things about me and you do not even know me." They take notice of what you have to say and the advice that you give them through your prophetic word. There are elements of prophecy because they are Words of Knowledge.

The Word of Knowledge is information about a person who you would not ordinarily know, as Jesus said to the woman at the well in Samaria, "You have had five husbands and the one who you are currently living with but to whom you are not married." That was called a Word of Knowledge. After that she said, "I can see you are a prophet." That rocked her world and she knew she was speaking to someone remarkably gifted and spiritual.

Well, today it has the same effect on people when you say, "You have got two brothers and a sister and your older brother is a mechanic." That gets the person's attention. Or telling a person they are gifted in business and always had a mind running with ideas for business, and always had creative ideas about what to invent and what to start, and what to do. That surprises a person. It gets their attention.

After the Word of Knowledge, you can move on to prophecy, things God wants to say to people and things about their future. You can go into Words of Wisdom. Words of Wisdom are directions that God wants to give a person to "Hold on," or "Be patient," or "Try harder," or just "Don't worry about your finances, things are going to work out for you. Just don't worry and just put your trust in God and everything will work out."

Prophecy is a remarkable gift and I talk more about it in the book I mentioned if you want to do the gift of prophecy. Around the time I had burnout from the website, God released me order to give prophetic words to strangers walking in the street and to talk to them.

I am not sure if I had used that introduction line before about having a gift and "I have got a message for you today." I think the Holy Spirit only gave that line to me in the last year or so. I think I used to walk up to a person and just say that I had a message from God for them and I used to deliver the message to them. Yianni was not always happy with me delivering the messages to people.

He used to stand aside and wait until I had finished, then keep on moving. He was not comfortable with me sharing prophetic messages with strangers, and that is okay. It is good to have a friend who will be with you and stand by your side as you deliver the messages. But it is okay. Yianni loves and has always loved me for who I am, and has not judged me.

It is good to have a friend like that. I was remarkably blessed that although I was not giving prophecies online, I was giving prophecies face to face with people. I found that an effective and enjoyable way to witness that Jesus is alive. A person would truly understand when you told them the message came from Jesus. That Jesus gave him the message and understands that Jesus is still living and He is supernatural, and He gave you the information about their lives that you could not possibly know.

It is something dramatic and effective, and persuasive for a total stranger. It is an enjoyable lifestyle. I recommend you my book if you want to move in that. Everyone who is a Christian can move in the gift of prophecy. Since I started 11 years ago, I have done between 7,000 and 10,000 prophecies for strangers and I enjoyed every one of them. I did five of them tonight with a friend called David with whom I go into churches.

We got out before church sharing prophetic information and messages with people.

Chapter 69

A New Church Called Streetlevel

As I spent time witnessing and doing outreaches on the streets, I had many opportunities to share my faith. I would open the Bible and teach the Christians around me doing the outreach and handing out tracks trying to influence people in the path and the message of Jesus Christ. I would preach to the Christians and if someone stopped to listen to my preaching, I would convert my preaching into a passage that I was sharing into an evangelistic message. While they were listening, I would preach to them and share the message of faith with people standing around and listening assuming they were not Christians. If they left then I would continue preaching a message to the Christians. The leader of the outreach liked my preaching although he did not realize I was bringing a message to the Christian followers who were part of the outreach.

Around this time, my friend Yianni, who had visited me in the psychiatric ward, started to disappear on a Friday night and only return about nine thirty at night. Eventually, he started to ask me to come to the other church he went to on a Friday night. Although this was my first opportunity to preach, I was preaching weekly on the streets, normally once or sometimes twice on a Friday night. I was hesitant to forego this opportunity to preach to go to a new church. I have seen churches before and I was not too impressed. I was currently doing what I perceived as God's will in my life, and I was not open to visiting a new church.

Yianni took about six months of talking to me weekly saying, "You will achieve more in one talk at this new church where they let you stand and share how your week has been than you will achieve in six months down here." I was impressed with what he had to say. So eventually, one Friday, he took me to this new church. When I entered, it seemed like an exact copy of the Newtown Mission. It was full of people like the Newtown Mission's clients who were fed in their drop-in centre. It was full of people who did not look like church people, or even like well-manicured or well-dressed church people. Half of them looked as though they were down-and-out and in a desperate situation. They were my sort of people. The church opened with songs and worship, then they opened the floor to the congregation with what they called "Care and Share."

Essentially, Care and Share was somewhere anyone in the audience could stand and share what God had been doing in their life or what had been happening in their life in the past week or two. It was an open format and unless you swore or said something unkind or unpleasant, they allowed you to speak for at least five minutes without taking the microphone from you. If you did become offensive or continued to swear after you had been warned, they would take the microphone from you, but it was an open church and it had an open format when it came to sharing. On the first night, I stood and shared something. I was impressed that people listened to me. They had a habit of clapping when you stood to share and clapping when you finished sharing, and I found it encouraging. Since then, I would not go to the outreach until after the church services at Streetlevel run by the Salvation Army. It is part of the Salvation Army group of churches in Sydney, Australia but it is also entirely different from the typical Salvation Army church.

The Salvation Army was originally started by Catherine and William Booth who wanted to reach the drunks and the outcasts of the city of London and wanted to take the Gospel to the streets and clean up the streets of the broken-hearted. His original mission was to help the broken-hearted people of the world but in recent times they seemed to have drifted to include the more middle-class sections of society.

At Streetlevel, we have drunks, we have street children, we have homeless people, we have transsexuals, we have lesbians, we have gays, and we have all sorts of people. If you can imagine it, we have it at Streetlevel. We have people at Streetlevel who have normal jobs and we have normal people. They love the atmosphere and they love coming to a church where they can be open and share what is on their heart.

The normal people like to mix with people who are open about their life and are transparent as I am with what they are going through with their life. Not all the so called "normal" people stand and share each week. It seems mostly the broken-hearted who stand and have a voice each week. The original pastors who started the church are called Robbin Moulds and Paul Moulds. They started Care and Share with the understanding that every person needs a voice and needs to know they are heard.

Every person needs to express themselves and know that they are loved. So they started Care and Share with that intention that the most broken of the individuals who visit Streetlevel can stand and have a voice each week, and have something to share and get something off their chest. Along with many others, I find it so encouraging to listen to the stories and what people say each week.

Often the sermon is the second most popular thing of the whole night besides praise and worship. Sometimes the sermon has been already preached in the messages that people have shared in Care and Share, as they shared their heart with people of the church. It is a welcoming church. It is an open church. It is a church full of transparent people. It is an eclectic mix of people. It is a sort of church that Jesus likes to hang out in. I found his presence was strong at Streetlevel the first time I visited. I soon became a regular visitor of Streetlevel on a Friday night.

Chapter 70

Leave Newtown Mission

After about six months of attending Streetlevel on a Friday night and attending Newtown Mission on a Sunday night, I managed the courage to leave Newtown Mission. I found that when I arrived at Newtown Mission, I had only Yianni as a friend. I found as I left Newtown Mission, I only had one other friend called Rob Harding. It is sad that during my time at Newtown Mission I had to use my prophetic gifts to carry out conversations with people and use messages from God for people to have them continue to listen to me.

The pastors were friendly and sorry to see me go but I was a little upset. I still had demons in me rumbling and causing me problems. I was upset generally with not having friends. I am rather different, as you can see from a testimony. I am frank and honest. Sometimes that turns normal people away from listening to you. I was intense and believed in a God of justice and a God of judgement. I was difficult to listen to and difficult to agree with. I did not agree with people and I always thought I was correct. I was self-centred, although I followed Christ and tried my best to do things that Jesus told me to do. I was certainly difficult to get along with and opinionated. People seemed to stay away from me. After six months of going to Streetlevel I finally made the decision to leave Newtown Mission and just attend Streetlevel Mission on a Friday night, which left my Sundays open.

Occasionally, I visited Hillsong Church in Sydney for some fun on a Sunday because I enjoyed their worship and I enjoyed their messages. Other times, I just had Sundays free and attended church on a Friday night at Streetlevel, which was amazing! I used to go out after church on a Friday night with Yianni for a cup of coffee and something to eat. It was a normal practice for me to stay out to about midnight on a Friday night or to early Saturday morning, then catch a bus home in the early hours of Saturday morning. Newtown Mission helped me develop my prophetic gift. I could prophesy over people at Newtown Mission. I could give corporate words of prophecy at Newtown Mission.

I was called in to the office of prophet by Brian, the pastor at Newtown Mission. I was happy it had happened but I also was disappointed that I had not made friends. I did not have friends to go out with during the week between church services. I did not have friends with whom I could go out for a cup of coffee or spend time with.

It was disappointing to me. Things changed when I started to attend Streetlevel. I started to get on with people, have more friendships with people, and develop conversations with people that went on for more than five minutes. I did not have people making excuses to go and talk to someone else when you knew that they just did not want to talk to you. I seemed to have more in common with people at Streetlevel on a Friday night. It was certainly a good place, much like therapy, to share your heart weekly for five minutes with everyone listening. I had much pain inside as you can imagine from my testimony so far. I was still addicted to prostitutes and I was still addicted to pornography, and still had many problems in my life.

I had a tremendous amount of pain that I was processing and it helped me stand each week and share at Streetlevel. Robbin and Paul Moulds became close friends of mine. The pastors at Streetlevel Mission were exciting to talk to and the most compassionate and loving people that I have ever met in my life. They were up there with Mutu. They have proved over the years repeatedly that they love me whoever I was, whatever I said, however judgmental or closed-minded I was – they loved me for the long term. They had an invested interest in just showering love on me.

They believed differently from me. They believed in the Gospel of grace. They believed things differently in the Bible than I did but never let on except in their preaching, when they preached on grace and on the love of Jesus. They never seemed to argue with me or contradict me in what I believed or said to them. They just showered love on me and shared with me their love and their understandings of Jesus, and the love that He has for all of us sinners. So Newtown

Mission was an essential part in my life but as I grew more and more in love with Streetlevel, I got the courage to leave that part of my life behind.

Chapter 71

Freedom from Prostitutes

Somehow I became aware of a ministry called Elijah House Ministries. I think it came up when one of the people prophesying on my prophecy site suggested Elijah House Ministries to me to help handle some of my pain. I had it confirmed that Elijah House Ministries was a good place to go to learn and to be counselled. I had it confirmed a few times with people so it had become apparent that God wanted me to move in that direction and get counselling through this worldwide ministry. I went to a one-week course on life and the position we are in as people who have grown up with pain and suffering in their lives. A few months later, I went to a second week of courses in which they did a teaching on true repentance and what true repentance looks like.

They compared King David with King Saul and showed that when King David was confronted by Nathan that he would steal the sheep of a man who only had one sheep. He repented straightaway and was sorry for his actions and repented toward God. When he had his baby taken by God and his baby died as recompense for his sin, he was quick to wash his face and clean himself up, and goes back to God and carry on with life knowing that God was a God who would handle him as He saw fit.

They compared it with Saul who made a sacrifice when Samuel had said to wait for him before he did the sacrifice. Saul, when he was confronted with his sin made excuses and said people were depending on him. A few times that Saul sinned, he made excuses for his sins. They said that that was not true repentance.

True repentance is not saying sorry to God. True repentance is coming to grips with your sin and saying to God, "If you give me the power, I will never do that sin again." True repentance is a total turnaround in your behaviour towards God. When you repent fully, you have to consider never doing that sin again.

It was an amazing teaching and I am sure you could look up the full length video called *True Repentance* by Elijah House Ministries and see what the video has to say. I watched the video, then spent some time with a counsellor downstairs after the video. I said that it had influenced me and shared with the counsellor my addiction to prostitutes.

He listened to me talking about my addiction to prostitutes and he said that, "All I can see here is a level of boasting where you seem to think you are a good client to these prostitutes. In fact, you are abusing them as their father or their stepfather had done. You are essentially raping these girls. Just because you were paying for them, you thought you were a good client. You are never going to find repentance while you believe this. You are only going to find repentance when you truly come to understand how much pain you have caused these girls by using their services … how much pain you have caused God by doing this act and how much pain you are causing yourself by abusing your body and spirit in this way. Until you can come to realization that you are abusing these girls, disappointing God and abusing yourself, you will never reach a stage where you can truly repent. So you need to do some thinking about that, Matthew. When you are ready and emotionally fit and emotionally capable of understanding the pain you are causing then you can pray the prayer for repentance, and God will hear your prayer." Well, I spent a week thinking about that.

As a writer and a poet, I can emotionally feel things and for the first time I felt how bad my sin was. I felt how it was affecting prostitutes and the girls with who I had dirty massages. As I was considering it, Jesus said, "When you say you repent in church, I want you to say aloud that your righteousness is of filthy rags and nothing you do is righteous before God."

I went to church that week and I repented aloud during the worship service. That week I was set free! On Tuesday when I got paid, when I normally went to see a prostitute or went to a dirty massage, the temptation was normally a hundred percent and strong. I used to get dragged by my collar by a demon down to do the sin. I repented on the Sunday and on the next Tuesday, the temptation was only 10%

of its strength. It is as though the demon of lust had left me when I repented before God and the whole church for my sin, and I had been set free. So thankfully I walked for many years afterward without an addiction to dirty massages, prostitutes, or the services of sex workers.

I was happy that I was set free – after what had been a 20-year addiction, I was finally released and set free. I certainly had a joy in my step and in my spirit that I had been released from this bondage to sin that had taken all my money for years on the services of these girls.

Chapter 72

Writing Articles Begins

I found, on a website promotion, an e-mail broadcast on how to advertise your websites. I discovered you could write articles on it using an article database site and put a link at the end of your article for your website. Over time with a few hundred articles, your website would be lifted in the keyword search to a high place on Google's search page. This was the motivation for me to write my first article and God used that motivation to put me in the habit of writing articles. I started my first article with the subject on *Ten Tips on How to Witness to Strangers.* I sat and wrote four pages on the subject. It was a good article.

Then day after day I sat and started to type articles. I would think of a subject and write them. At that time in my life I spent plenty of time in the Old Testament prophets and I thought I was one of the two witnesses, as I have mentioned before. I thought I was going to judge the world. It was heavily based on the Old Testament prophets who believed in an angry judgemental God, who was going to pour His wrath out on the world. Much of that theme and much of the character of those articles I wrote in the early days carry this judgemental attitude. I remember one article I had about four parables that indicated that Christians can go to hell. I believed quite sincerely in those days that Christians could be in such a position that would send them to hell. Although I do not totally dismiss that, I feel quite confident that Christians should not or could not be in a position that would take them to hell anymore.

Although I wrote many articles and I continued to write articles right from the start, many of those articles were tainted with a mixture of law and grace. The apostle Paul teaches that we should not have a mixture in our life as a mixture is sin and an error. We should not have a mixture of the Old Testament law and a New Testament grace. Paul shares that if the old law was okay then a new covenant would not have needed ratification or put into existence. That a new covenant was created meant the old covenant has passed away and something had been found lacking in the old covenant. So God in His wisdom brought Jesus to this world and brought in a new covenant of grace. We are saved by grace not by works, lest no man should boast. It is an act of faith that we come into righteousness and Jesus gives us these righteousness to wear as a robe to cover our sin. The Bible says our sinful and lawless deeds are remembered no more and God casts our sins into the sea of forgetfulness.

When I wrote these articles years ago, I was not in that frame of mind. I did not believe in the grace message. I believed in an angry God. If you go back to my articles of years ago on Ezinearticles.com, you will find the articles I wrote were legalistic and judgemental in their tone. Among them, I did write several inspired articles, but essentially, my articles were hard and domineering, critical of Christians and demanded exacting standards on people to live the proper Christian life.

Chapter 73

Sleep Sickness Begins

When I was freed from my addiction to prostitutes, a spiritual attack suddenly happened in my life. I believe it was brought on by Satan – from where most illnesses and sicknesses come. I would go to bed at 9:00 or 11:00 at night, and when I wake at 8:00 in the morning, I would be so tired, I would go back to sleep. When I woke again at 11:00, I would still be so tired that I would go back to sleep again. It was not until about 3:00 or 4:00 in the afternoon that I would wake, after sleeping for 19 hours.

After sleeping 19 hours, you would think that you would wake refreshed and happy to face the day. What actually happens is you wake depressed and tired. Within a few hours, I was tired and wanted to go to bed again. I would go to bed again and went through the same process – sleeping for 19 hours, waking depressed, sad and tired, and I could not wait to get back to bed again. This sickness was something sad. I called it the sleep sickness. It was something that came in to my life and it seemed as if it was a reward for breaking my addiction of prostitutes. I had a friend who told me I had been addicted to prostitutes for so long that this new sleep sickness was a way my body was spending time digesting the trauma that had happened in my life. I was now handling my situation head-on without that addiction to self-medicate my pain. Whatever it was, it was frustrating and tiring. It went on to last for four years. It was a debilitating sickness. It was sad.

Occasionally I used to break the monotony of the sleep sickness merely by staying up for a whole night and writing articles, and watching movies. I used to invite Phil around to watch movies all night, then stay up through the day till the next night. I would stay up two nights in a row. I would have three days full of energy and fun, then I would collapse into bed for four days and let the sleep sickness take over again. It was a frustrating illness, a sad illness, something that depressed me and made me cry often.

As a manic depressive or bipolar, I was open and susceptible to the depression that comes with being bipolar, so this was a sad stage in my life. I found that I would watch many movies and I wrote many articles. I was writing about four articles a night, sometimes up to 10 articles per week and uploading them to EzineArticles.com. My articles were growing and my movies were growing, and the time I was spending with Phil was growing. I was having some sort of fun for two to three days a week while I was suffering from this illness.

Chapter 74

Meeting Sarah

I was going to Streetlevel church for a while and attended services weekly on a Friday night. I was encouraged by Streetlevel to attend our community centre and to volunteer around the community centre from Monday to Friday. I wanted to volunteer but my sleep sickness was keeping me in bed all the time and it was difficult to volunteer. However, I found by writing articles and staying up at night, I could then go and volunteer the next day. One day I came into the kitchen and there was a young girl called Sarah, whom I had met the year before, taking over as manager of the kitchen. She was preparing about a hundred meals for the homeless and people who visited our centre each day for a lunchtime meal.

I was introduced to her and I was impressed. She was young – around 19 or 20 – just a couple of years older than my son at the time. I was always happy to meet a young girl. Because I had been sexually abused at 14, part of me stayed at that age. Although a grown man, I seemed an innocent young child in the way I behaved and acted with particular people. I had this innocence about me although you have seen that I had a life of sin, I have always remained childlike in my faith and always been attracted to younger people because part of my spirit has been stopped at 14 – just as if an inner child is still part of me.

I had always been attracted to younger people and younger women were attractive to me, as was Sarah was attractive in this state as a younger woman. As you have read through my testimony so far, you can be sure that I do not have a good track record of having female friends. It was interesting to start in the kitchen with a young woman who seemed a little fiery and a little sure of herself. On the first day, I had a busy day talking. When you are a lonely individual and you do not get much opportunity to share your life with others, you find when you are given the opportunity to speak, lonely people can talk plenty and I had much to say. I told her much about my life. I went from story to story as we washed and prepared meals for the hundred people on the first day.

I was impressed with seeing her and knowing that she is going to be in there five days a week. I went home, stayed up the next night, then came in and spent the next day with her, carrying on from where I had finished telling story after story. I was impressed because she listened and asked questions about my stories. Not just listening and saying, "Yes, yes, yes", but she took the time to ask questions about particular things I was saying in the stories; for me to illustrate and expand the story further for her to understand. I found that she had little to say at the start of our meeting, and she seemed quiet and reserved. I was later to discover, as I became acquainted with Sarah, she was a beautiful girl who was understanding and loving, but she was private. It took time for a person to win the confidence of Sarah and to win her affection to where she would open herself and share things about herself with just anyone.

She was personal and private when it came to her affairs. I was doing most of the talking, which I was happy to do because I had someone who was listening and I had someone who could not get away from me, Not like Newtown Mission where a person could make an excuse go off and talk to someone else. Here I was in the kitchen from 9:30 in the morning to 3:30 in the afternoon with someone essentially locked in the kitchen with me for six hours and who had to listen. And listen she did, she took the time to listen to my stories. I have to say that she had tremendous love and grace for me. She was terrific at understanding me and listening to my stories. She could have said, "Shut up! Just work and don't talk so much," which others have felt no problem in doing in my past. People could shut me down and stop me from talking in the past but she was not like that.

She listened and laughed and understood my stories, asked me questions about the stories, and had me speaking more and more. I found out that I had come to enjoy volunteering at Streetlevel. The sleep sickness was causing me untold grief, but I had found that if I stayed up two nights during the week I could come in the two days after. If I stayed up three nights, I could come in for three days so I was working two to three days a week volunteering. Sarah never told her mother about my staying up. Her mother was Robbin Moulds – another loving person and the pastor of our church. With her husband Paul, they led the Streetlevel church of which I was part of. Although they were a loving couple, Sarah never told them that the only way I was coming in two or three days a week was by staying up without sleep. They never became aware I was manic and in a state of mania every time I was volunteering. If I left it to the sleep sickness I just could not get out of bed until three or five in the afternoon, and I could only come if I stayed up all night. So I used to stay up on a Monday night, come in on a Tuesday, then stay up on the Tuesday night and come in again on Wednesday. Then I would have a day in bed so I could stay up Thursday night and come in again on Friday. So I was getting two to three days' worth of work done and meeting Sarah two to three days a week at church. It was all fantastic and it was an exciting thing to do.

I always found Sarah smart and intelligent. A person who has a strong mind, and is strong willed. She was certainly a person who could be a tremendous support to any man. She could lead a family and be strong enough to lead in business or lead in a ministry, and also have a husband with equal abilities to manage a ministry. She could even work to support her herself. She was strong and capable and she was an enjoyable person to work with in the kitchen. I started to become acquainted with Sarah. She just listened and listened and listened to me. Never in my life had I ever met a person who had listened to me for so long. Never in my life had I met anyone I could talk to so much and have them listen, and who was a normal person.

I know my friend Yianni used to listen to me all night, but only Yianni could do it. We would stay up all night talking to each other and we would listen. But besides Yianni, I had found no one who would listen to me for hours.

Sometimes Sarah was in the kitchen listening for six hours a day and three days of that meant plenty of listening. She was spending much time with me and exercising much patience. Often she could have told me to be quiet or "Work and don't talk so much," but she never told me that I can remember. She might have told me, but I cannot remember, and it was not so many years ago that I would have forgotten. All I know is she listened and showed me tremendous love and support. I think all of us need a little Jesus Christ in our life. I often spend time seeing Jesus in visions and meeting Jesus in visions. I often spend time dialoguing with Jesus back and forth in my mind. Yet with all this time spent with Jesus in my mind and seeing Him in visions, all of us need a person who can be a Jesus Christ to us in the flesh. Sarah was that as well as her mom and dad. Robbin and Paul Moulds were certainly models to me of whom Christ was living in the flesh on Earth and their tremendous support and loving to me.

I was an angry person. I believed in the Old Testament prophets and I believed in a judgemental or vengeful God. I certainly believed in an angry God more judgemental than the God that Sarah believed in, but initially she kept her opinions of how wrong I was to herself. She just listened to me. She talked to me and shared things with me about her life occasionally, but usually she just encouraged me to be me and to be comfortable around her.

I am prophetic and often I receive scripture verses for a person or I receive a prophetic word for a person, but I could not get anything on Sarah. Normally the Lord would give me some information about any person I am mixing with if it is His will, and most times He will give me something on a person. I cared about Sarah and she was someone I wanted to know more about and I wanted to be a better friend of. I asked the Lord and all He said was that she was an unbroken stallion – a horse no good for racing until it is been broken. When its will has been broken, it becomes a useable horse that can be used by a rider to win races, then go off and become a stallion and breed racehorses.

God was saying that she had tremendous strength, character, and ability that could do great works. But at present she was unbroken, which sounded as though there was going to be a season of pain or something will happen in her life that's going to model her into becoming a champion. She could become something like a champion racehorse. I had this idea about Sarah from God and it was exciting to hear that. I wanted to know more but God would not tell me more. Sarah did not talk so much about her life but she listened to me as I have already told you ten times or more. It was an enjoyable process becoming acquainted with her more and more as the weeks progressed.

Chapter 75

Crying Many Tears

The sleep sickness from which I was suffering was having a tremendous toll on my life. A year had gone past, I was volunteering in the kitchen with Sarah, often spending time in becoming acquainted with her. I suppose I spent about six or nine months in the kitchen volunteering with her. She was starting to question and object to some things I said. After a few months of knowing her, she was starting to argue with me and tell me I was wrong in particular areas in my life. This was a surprise to me because not many people have ever confronted me and told me I was wrong and was so confident that I was wrong, and that they were right. Sarah had this ability.

But the sleep sickness was taking its toll on me. It was demanding on me just going to sleep whether at 9:00 or 11:00 at night, and not being able to get out of bed till 3:00 the next day after 19 hours' sleep. Then, waking up chronically depressed and tired with no energy but just wanting to go back to bed. I developed an addiction for sleeping tablets. I was taking sleeping tablets to sleep because I was so tired. It was a remarkable cycle. I had gone for prayer at church several times for the sleep sickness to be healed. I believed in the prayer of the sick and the prayer of the righteous healing for people who needed to be healed. I knew it was an attack from Satan because when I had conquered my addiction to prostitutes, the sleep sickness had manifested in the same week and it was trying to force me to return to my old ways.

Perhaps, I was receiving a message that if I went back to my old ways of sleeping with prostitutes, then Satan would relent with this sleep sickness and would not let it continue in my life. After about six months of holding my addiction at bay and not hiring prostitutes or sex workers for dirty massage, I went back to Elijah House Ministries for counselling. I was walking home one day after I had been up for three days and three nights, and the more I was up, the more Jesus would speak to me more clearly. I remember I was talking to God the Father one night and I think the sleep sickness.... perhaps, I am jumping the gun here with some of the story. But in later chapters we will jump back for the sake of the story continuing about the sleep sickness.

I was walking home and talking to God about the sleep sickness. God said, "We're sorry that the sleep sickness is in your life. There's a reason for the sleep sickness in your life. We've put it in your life so you develop perseverance." I shared that with a few friends that God had said the sleep sickness was in my life to teach me perseverance. One friend became angry with me and said that God wanted me healed and all sicknesses are from Satan, and God would not be saying that about a sickness Satan had caused. If I agreed with that statement, it is just me accepting that I am sick and God is not going to do anything about it. He said it was actually Satan talking to me telling me that it is there for perseverance but it is no such thing. He became angry with me. I talked to another friend, and he also did not seem to agree that God was giving me this sleep sickness for perseverance.

So I went to the counsellor I was seeing from Elijah House ministries to handle the grief from some pain in my life, and he had prayed several times for me to get healing from the sleep sickness. He had prayed for others to be healed physically and they had been healed. He did much emotional healing in my life and others' lives so I trusted his prayers. I shared with him what God had said to me that the sleep sickness was in my life to develop perseverance. I asked him, "Do you think that that was God speaking?" He said, "I certainly do." He said, "It's obvious that you don't understand what perseverance means," and I said, "No."

He said, "Perseverance is the ability to press on and go on against impossible odds," and he said, "This sleep sickness has been a tremendous strain and it's impossible for you to go on yet you're persevering with it and you're persevering with life, and you're not giving up on God. But you're pressing on each day with your faith and you're just proving to God that you're a person who perseveres under tremendous trial." I was happy that it was confirmed that God had the sleep sickness in my life for a reason. And if it were in my life for a reason, then when I learned to persevere enough, then the sleep sickness naturally would leave me.

So I spent much time crying tears. I remember once I was at my church Streetlevel. I was at the front and there was a song about crying in the dark times, crying in the pain, and praising God in the storms. The lyrics came up on the projector and Robbin Moulds our pastor, Sarah's mother, saw me. She came over and put her arms around me, and said, "This is when you cry, Matthew, and this is when you praise God." Tears were rolling down my cheeks and I was singing to God that 'I love you and I praise you in the storm and I praise you in the dark times. God, you are wonderful!' It was amazing to worship God even in my pain.

I cannot explain how tremendously difficult it was to live with an illness causing me to be so chronically depressed all the time, and there was nothing I could do to change it. It just came on from the same week I had given up prostitutes. It came out of nowhere. It lasted three years until this point. I was just crying weekly. By the time the first two or three songs had played in church, I would be sitting in my seat weeping. For years, pain was percolating from my body just as though a leach was on my skin sucking blood. Pain was coming out of my body as I was crying the pain out. Tremendous sadness, depression, loneliness, rejection, and all the pains I had grown up with were coming out slowly in the worship in church each week.

So it was tremendous suffering. I think God gave me the ability through suffering this to have empathy for others who suffer from depression, sleep disorders, and other things that they have to battle with that take tremendous perseverance. I thought I would share that subject with you in some depth.

Chapter 76

Start to Record Videos

When the world had the global economic meltdown, we had just elected a new government in Australia. The new government introduced a stimulus package and part of that package was to give money to each person on a disability or other pension, and to people on a low income – a handout was the stimulus package. The idea was that if they gave money, the low-income earners would go out and spend the money on goods and services, which would stimulate the economy. They decided they would put the government in debt to stimulate business and the economy to try to pull ourselves out of the global slowdown. They gave me about $1,300. I remember I bought a computer and I bought a video camera to record videos.

It is only recently in the last three months that the video camera has stopped working and I have started to record videos straight from my Apple laptop. It was not as professional as with the video camera, but it is working. However, I bought a new video camera, and after six months I learned how to work the camera, how to record, how to upload the movies on a computer, how to process them, how to edit them, and how to upload them on YouTube.

I started to preach online as I was not getting many opportunities to preach at church. I decided to start to preach online on things I had been teaching in my articles. At this stage, as this video goes up, I have now more than a thousand videos on YouTube. There have been three books I have recorded so far on video. Each chapter of the book has been recorded and transcribed, and edited, and proofread, and transformed into a book.

A tremendous number of videos go into each book and chapter so I have a large collection of videos. I started to record videos back then. I was excited to map subject titles and I would write titles with some information about what I was going to share, then I would shoot the video. I would do about five at a time, then upload them all on my computer, process them all, then upload them all on YouTube. What used to take maybe an hour to record six 10-minute videos took about 4-5 hours to process and upload on YouTube. It took at least three times longer to get it on YouTube than it did to shoot the video. When you see more than a thousand videos on my YouTube channel, it is an indication that many thousands of hours – at least 3,000 hours – have been put into uploading all those videos on YouTube.

When you are called to be a teacher of the Word of God and you are making articles five videos at a rate of at least five per week, you get this personal satisfaction that starts to reign in your life. I remember before my wife left me, I had a spirit of death hanging around my life constantly trying to talk me into committing suicide. Three times in my life I was serious about committing suicide and each time someone talked me out of it. Twice the people were not even aware that they were talking me out of suicide by the things I said. I think I shared earlier when I was in the shower and my mother sent my younger brother in to save me the first time I decided to kill myself, but there were two or three other occasions that I have not shared in the book.

I remember it saying in one of the Gospels, if everything that Jesus said and did were recorded in books, the world would not have enough space to hold all the books of what had happened. The same is true in when you are doing a biography. You cannot record everything that happened in your life because the book would be too thick and it would be too much for people to read.

I had this spirit of death in my life constantly trying to make me commit suicide. I certainly lived for many years with no desire to live. Once when I was going to commit suicide, Jesus told me through a pastor that I was not to kill myself because He did not want me to end my life and I was to stay alive to move in ministry and do what He wanted me to do. I was not allowed to take my own life. From that time I had lived when I did not want to live – where I would prefer someone to come into a bank and shot me instead of holding up a bank. I would prefer to have someone shoot me or for me to die from cancer or some disease rather than live. For about 14 years, I lived with this desire to depart this Earth and I had no desire to live.

It was while I attended Streetlevel church and started to cry out all my pain that this desire to end my life and not to live anymore started to lift from me. I was now in a state where I did not always want to be dead and in heaven, but I was starting to enjoy life. I was getting inspiration to record videos and to write articles. I was spending time with Sarah more and more in the kitchen and working as a volunteer. And I was giving something back to the broken-hearted and the homeless in our community centre at the Salvation Army.

I was feeling this tremendous sense of purpose and it was exciting for me to be in a position where I wanted to live, and feeling that I was achieving something. On the article website called EzineArticles.com, you can see how many people are reading each article and it would give you a count of how many people were reading your articles each month. I think at the moment I have about 6,000 people reading my articles each month and my YouTube videos are watched by about 4,000 people a month.

So it is impressive that through videos and articles on the Internet, I am reaching about 10,000 people a month. It gives you a tremendous sense of purpose especially when you start to write books and have them published as I have being doing in recent years. It is exciting to see and it is an exciting life. So recording the videos was another step for me and it brought a little joy into my life. It gave me a sense of purpose and direction.

It gave me things to do in the middle of the nights when I was staying up all night. I certainly did not mind spending the three hours processing every hour of video because I had so much time to spare during the night. It is certainly the best thing to do in the middle of the night when no one is using the bandwidth. At peak times it takes longer to upload on YouTube, so the middle of the night suited me well for uploading the videos then. That is my snapshot about uploading videos.

Chapter 77

A Fight with Sarah

After months of getting to know Sarah, I was starting to face some opposition from Sarah although she had built such a tremendous foundation of love and acceptance in my life. She had built the trust and the love for me to start to confront some of my wrong beliefs and thinking patterns. She was the kind of person who did not have to be right about things but merely loved me enough to correct me in my wrong thinking. She started to confront me when it came to things I was talking about in my many long conversations with her that she disagreed with and were lacking foundations in the Bible or seemed at odds with her beliefs and experiences of God.

I believed I served an angry and judgemental God and I did not understand unconditional love, grace or acceptance. I believed I was righteous although I was still addicted to pornography. I still considered myself more distinguished and holy and righteous, someone doing God plenty of favours. I was self-righteous of my own actions. I was doing all these videos articles. I was doing this entire ministry prophetically on a prophetic website. I was a busy and in-demand preacher on the Internet. I certainly had my opinions and my beliefs about things but I was confident that I was right. I was writing about how right I was. I was backing up everything with scripture verses that were not in context but according to what I had been taught by others. Sarah was starting to confront me.

I remember once we were in a car and I started to say something, and she disagreed. I raised my voice and said, "No, you're wrong," and she said, "No, you are wrong, and the reason for this is…" She went into the reason and I argued with her reason. She explained another reason and I argued with that. I started shouting at her saying that she was wrong and that she should not dare speak to me. She was only 21 years old at that time. I told her that she should not be speaking to me like this. She should respect me and if she knew more, she would say less – something I often used to say to others.

I was essentially telling her to shut her mouth because she was wrong. She was wrong this time. "You're not right this time, Sarah, you're wrong. So just shut up because you're wrong." I was becoming angry and agitated.

Sarah started to become angry and agitated with me. Not so much because of my behaviour because she is a loving and considerate and blessed person to know. I think she became so upset merely because she could not break through to me. I was obstinate. I was unteachable and I was proud. I could not be told I was wrong. I think she tried so hard and that is why the argument became so heated. I think she just became so angry with me as I was being so proud and unreceptive to the truth she was trying to present to me. She was shouting at me, and she finally said, "Matthew, you're the most un-Jesus like person I've ever met." I considered myself Jesus like and I considered myself a loving person, extremely like Jesus in His character traits. If you could have slapped me with an insult, then that was the biggest insult you could have given me. I was totally blown away and I said to her, "You can't mean that? How could you say that?" She said, "I'm saying it. Now, shut the door!" She slammed the door in my face and she drove off. I was totally shocked that she had said I was the most un-Jesus like person she had ever met. I was amazed at the heat the conversation had generated. I was surprised that she had closed the door and she had driven off so fast.

Whether she slammed the door, I cannot remember but I was amazed at how angry she was. I had never seen her as angry as that, especially not with me. I had only seen her listening and being patient with me. I had never seen her angry with me. I had never seen her in a heated argument as that. As I went home that day, I was in deep regret because I thought I had lost my true friend.

I always wanted a female Christian friend. I had always wanted a young woman whom I could be close to that I could love and be my friend. She was like a daughter to me, a young friend to me. She was someone so special to me and dear to my heart. Yet I was filled with fear as I went home on the train to my place. I believed I had finally crossed the mark with her. I had finally blown the friendship, and I had just done too much.

One thing with people who have been rejected so much in their lives is when they are not rejected naturally by people, they will do something to provoke rejection in any person. Only people with tremendous grace and love will be able to keep people like me in their lives because they continue to give grace to them and put up with all their bad personality traits. And they continue to love them for years until they finally change and the Holy Spirit changes them.

The next day I went to work with fear wondering whether she would still be speaking to me. She was a bright and sunny and happy Sarah. She said, "Hi, Matthew. How are you?" She gave me a hug and she did not mention the day before and she was acting like nothing had happened. It was totally implausible to me. I think that day I received the first chink in my armour. When a solider gets a chink in their armour, they would get a cut or dent in their armour. If you continue hitting that dent, you could break through with your sword into their armour and kill the person. Well, I had strong armour around myself with my beliefs in this judgemental and angry God. I was so convinced of my beliefs that God was right and we were wrong, and Christians were going to hell if they did not get holy and repent.

I was so convinced of it that I had been preaching it on YouTube in my videos as well as in my articles. I even had an article about four parables that prove Christians go to hell. I was convinced of an angry young unforgiving God yet here was Sarah so convinced that God was full of agape love and unconditional love. We are loved without cause and there is no reason that we should not be loved while we are sinners. Christ died for us, the verse says in the Bible. Jesus loved us so much that He died on the cross for us even while we are still sinning. All the sins we will ever commit in our lives have been forgiven 2,000 years ago. Some people will preach that we have to repent each day and if we have not repented particular sins, we will go to hell when we die. Yet all our sins were forgiven 2,000 years ago. Every sin I will ever commit in my life was paid for by Jesus on the cross. Jesus shouted at the end on the cross, "It is finished."

It was finished, that the penalty for sin had been paid. So whether you repent or you do not repent the sins you commit, the price for those sins has already been paid. This was something I did not understand and I did not comprehend. I was so full of my own righteousness. I was so full of pride and arrogance thinking I was right that it had not dawned on me that I could be wrong.

It was such a fierce and heated argument the day before that someone had to crack. I saw that Sarah had cracked with her anger – getting angry with me for the first time in my life. Yet the next day she was sweet as pie without being contriving or manipulating. But she had genuinely forgiven me and wanted to leave the past where it was, and wanted to continue our friendship, and the love that we shared between us.

I had received the first chink. Grace is true because if the God I served was a God like Sarah's – if the God I served could honestly see me so wrong, bad, arrogant, and prideful, yet forgive me in the next breath or the next day, and be so loving towards me without dealing out punishment or shame or judgement or condemnation for my behaviour, or addressing my behaviour and saying it was wrong before they forgive me. I was just totally blown away and shocked.

I think Sarah showed the grace of God to me and put the first chink in my armour. The armour was soon starting to fall down around my knees, and I was soon naked before God with nothing to hold on to except His true message of grace, love, and unconditional and unmerited favour.

Chapter 78

Reconnect with Son

I was going each Tuesday afternoon to Streetlevel. We have lawyers that visit there and do legal work for the homeless and the disadvantaged. They make their services available pro bono, meaning without people having to pay for it, and they give free legal advice on a whole range of legal issues that the homeless and disadvantaged face.

I sat down with them and asked, seeing as my son had turned 18-years of age, how I could reconnect with him and what was the best strategy to use. They said to reach out to him, search for him on Facebook and see if I can find him there. That is what they suggested. And so I got the child custody payment slip out and looked up my wife's last name because I didn't remember what it was and how to spell it.

I did a search on Google for her name and a multi-level marketing business, one where you have distributors and you build distributors on top of distributors. I found one in Brisbane since I knew she was partial to those sorts of businesses. I found one where she described herself as a pastor and someone who was selling chocolates by Party Plan; meaning she is selling it by having parties, distributing chocolates, and getting 30% of all the sales and profits that's made for invited guests and building distributors.

I said, "Aw, that's the Sharryn I know." So I wrote to her e-mail address and said, "My son is now 18 years of age. I did what you asked me to do 10 years ago. I walked out of his life. I haven't tried to interfere with his life. He's now a man so could you please pass on this e-mail to him and ask him if he wants to write and talk to me?" About three weeks later, I got an e-mail from my son Brandyn.

He said, "It's good to get your e-mail. It's good to hear that you wanted to reconnect with me. Please don't get your hopes up about ever meeting me because to me you're just an older man who I don't know. But I'd be interested to talk to you further by e-mail." So I sent him an e-mail and connected with him on Facebook. He's not a person who goes on Facebook very often. I haven't seen him on Facebook very much over the years since he turned 18.

That was about five years ago that I first connected with him and he's 23 now. So I wrote e-mails to him. I wrote e-mails to his fiancée at that time and we'd talk to each other. He wrote me an e-mail and said, "Please don't share with me what my fiancée's been saying to you. That's private between her and you. I trust you to be a good voice in her life and she's had a tumultuous life with her own father. So I trust that you can be nice and understanding with her and not pass on her private information to me."

I shared that with Paul Moulds, our pastor at the time and he said that it was a very responsible e-mail I was getting from my son. It proved that he had faith in me. It was very encouraging for him to be writing something like that to me. Over the past five years, I haven't had a lot of contact with him. I was going to go up and visit Brisbane, which is a thousand kilometers from here last year.

I wrote to him and asked him if I could meet up with him when I came up and he said, "Write to me a month before you come up and we'll see if we can arrange something." So his attitude had changed over the last five years from the first e-mail that said, "Don't get your hopes up" to a point where he trusted me and was going to make a move to meet me if I came up there. So, I did reconnect with him and it got me excited.

I remember on my son's 18th birthday, we're having a lesson on how to pray for people that come forward at church and to be part of the ministry team that prayed at church. The leader that was teaching the ministry course on how to pray had this five-step program of questions you ask when someone comes forward and how you proceed to say the prayer. He wanted someone to pray for as an example for the class.
He asked for one of us who needs a prayer and no one was going

forward. So I came forward and said that on my son’s 18th birthday, I said that I wanted to reconnect with him. It was only a couple of months later, and there I was with an e-mail from him saying ‘don’t get my hopes up but he’d like to correspond by e-mail.’ So God truly does answer prayers. As I’ve shared in videos, I chat back and forth with God.

It’s not really often that I actually request things from God and ask things from Him. I found in the past when I’ve prayed for other people that many breakthroughs have come for other people and God seems to like answering my prayers. It was a very personal and emotional prayer answered, that within months of me requesting to reconnect with my son, I actually reconnected with him.

It’s an amazing thing to have the redeeming factor of missing a son. I don’t think people fully realize how much the Father gave up when He sent Jesus to earth and how much it cost the Father to see His son die on a cross. I don’t believe the Father ever turned His face away from Jesus dying on the cross. I got taught by a person called John Crowder who said that in the Old Testament days when they didn’t have printed Bibles, they used to remember psalms.

They’d sing psalms and be able to remember it word for word. That’s how they used to sing and repeat them, and read them out at tempo. So a preacher or a priest rabbi would say the first line of the psalm and by quoting it, the people would know that he’s going to start addressing the subject of the psalm and for them to start to run it through their mind because he’s going to be talking about certain aspects of the psalm.

On the cross Jesus said, “My God, my God, why have you forsaken me?” And that was Psalm 22 in the Bible and that’s the very start of the psalm. Later on in the psalm, it says that God wouldn’t turn His face from someone who’s suffering and who needs his God, and God would surely not turn away. That’s later on in the psalm and all through the psalm it says, “My bones are out of joint and they’re casting lots on my clothes.”

It was the whole psalm about the actual death of Jesus prophesying His crucifixion on the cross. People read the psalm to themselves because Jesus had quoted the beginning of the psalm. Anyone there that knew the psalm by rote, by understanding and by memory, would see the psalm getting played out word for word right in front of them as Jesus died on the cross. In that psalm, it says that God wouldn't turn His face away.

So I don't believe God ever turned His face away from His son but not many people understand the personal pain of the Father to have His son come from a perfect heaven down to a dirty, disgusting sin filled earth and then die a massive heart-breaking crucifixion on the cross for our behalf. It's not until you've lost a son that you understand and it is going fifteen years since I've seen my son.

Not seeing my son for 15 years and only corresponding a little bit by e-mail and Facebook is a tremendous pain in my heart. I miss my son but it also gives me a redeeming quality that I understand how much God missed His own Son. I've got an understanding of how God feels and I also got an understanding of how many single dads feel about not ever seeing their children; those that are denied through circumstances, through mental illness or through the wife not allowing him to see his children anymore.

So, I understand men who suffered that in their life. I've got an understanding of how much you miss your children. I certainly miss my son. So, it was so good to reconnect with him even in a small way.

Chapter 79

Musings of a Mad Prophet

The Musings of the Mad Prophet was a book that I first published when I had about 80 articles and I chose the first 67 to go into a book.

I had a roommate who was staying with me that provided me the money to pay for the publishing. I had to pay for the editing and the proofreading of the articles but he paid for the publishing which was $500 dollars. I had helped with it and I am very thankful for it. It was called *The Musings of a Mad Prophet* because I was mad!

I was a person who believed that God was a judgmental God and an angry God of the Old Testament. A God that was never satisfied and never really pleased in the Old Testament unless you were doing everything you could according to what He wanted. I was a person who was confused and mixed up and didn't understand the true gospel of Jesus Christ; as well as the grace that's provided through the cross, the new covenant and spilling the blood of Jesus.

So, I was messed up and pretty angry. A lot of my articles reflected this idea that God was angry and Jesus was angry too and He was angry at the Pharisees. This is what I surmised. I believed that Jesus was just as angry at the modern church because so many of the insults He leveled against the Pharisees of His day could be leveled against the modern church of this day.

So many things are the same. They could be held to be true of the modern day church. They were the same things that Jesus leveled at the Pharisees. So I gathered 67 of my articles and put them together in the first book that I wrote.

Somewhere in the editing process, I lost one of the articles. I decided that I didn't agree with one of the articles that were in there. So I reduced it. I originally started with sixty-seven because I was born in 1967 and so 67 was a number that stood for my date of birth. Then when I reduced it by one number, I ended up with 66 which was the same number of books in the Bible.

So I didn't design it to be that way but that's what it ended up. Today, not many people buy *The Musings of a Mad Prophet*. Not many people have bought it in the past and no one has written a review on the book. Although I did have my friend Sarah Moulds, who I've talked about, I did have her father Paul Moulds read the book and he was quite impressed with what I had to say in the book.

He sat me down for half an hour and had a good talk with me. He wanted to know where I'd studied my theology and where I'd learned my doctrines from. I said that I'd just picked them up going to church and reading the Bible myself. He said he was very impressed. He'd read most of the articles in there.

Paul is a very strong, grace man and very strong preacher of the new covenant of grace. So I'm sure that he was showing me a lot of grace in the way that he treated me and the way that he responded to my book. I know that many of the articles would have had a slant of legalism and the law and a mixture of law and grace in them.

He may not have agreed with many of the articles doctrinally but he showed me his love and acceptance. He proved his grace in accepting the book and saying that the book was good, and it was a good work of mine. I should have got him to sign up at Amazon and write a review for me and that may have led to some more books.

These days, I don't mention that book. I say that I've published two books when in actual fact I've published three. Today, I don't recognize that book as one of the books I've published because I don't want people reading the old covenant teachings and legalism, and the mixed grace message of the book.

I prefer that people understand my new understanding of God, His son Jesus and His grace. That's picked up in *The Parables of Jesus Made Simple*, my second book. It explained in a little dimension in my third book which I'll talk about in the future.

So I was a mad prophet. I was someone who was a fire-breathing prophet of doom and gloom. I believed in tribulation. I believed that Christians weren't going to get rapture during the tribulation but were going to suffer and go through all sorts of hard times with the Beast being on earth and being threatened and killed, and things like that.

I believed somewhat that we sort of deserved it; and that we're so wicked and so into the flesh, and so far from God's perfect will in the churches that we deserve to be judged by God. I knew that I was doing a lot better than most Christians. Well, that's what I believed. That's what a lot of people who preach holiness believe; that they're doing a lot better than others.

They assume that they're holy. I had sinned in my life with addictions to pornography and that caused me trouble. But besides that, I thought I was perfect.

I sort of had that opinion years ago that I was pretty perfect and blameless apart from that masturbation and pornography sin, if you glossed over that one. I was pretty good and pretty perfect in God's sight. So, I had this high opinion of myself and this is expressed in the articles that made part of the book *The Musings of a Mad Prophet*. I wouldn't even go back and read that book now.

I think the same way as some actors who won't watch a film that they've been in. I'm personally embarrassed that I used to feel that way about certain subjects in the Bible, God's grace and His forgiveness. I think that it'll be a testimony in the future for people to be able to see what I used to say and what I used to believe in and compare it to what I say and believe now. It'll be a testimony to the transformation that is taking place in my life.

Chapter 80

Go Off Medication Again

You would have thought I have learned my lesson going off my medication and ending up in the hospital twice from a breakdown or a psychotic episode.

You'd think that someone with a reasonable amount of intelligence in this world would not go off their medication and think that they're alright. But when you've got a voice that's pretending to be Jesus – and you are sure it is Jesus – saying to you that you're healed and that you can go off your medication now, you act out in faith, believe and walk off your medication.

At one stage in my life, I knew Mutu, a visiting teacher that taught me not to listen to Jesus and God the Father and Mary Magdalene. To read only the Word of God, read the gospels when I want to hear Jesus, read the prophets when I want to hear God, and don't talk to Mary Magdalene. I know he'd had those instructions but I spent a few years prophesying and got used to the voice of Jesus Christ and thought I was comfortable with His voice again.

I didn't think that I was being lied to. So once again the Jesus voice of the Antichrist spirit said to me that "You're healed and you need to go off your medication and walk free of this, and you'll have a wonderful testimony for people." Once again I believed that and went off my medication. It took a number of weeks.

I think it took about 10 weeks before I had an incident in the community centre where I went and I spoke to Robbin Moulds, Sarah's mother. I was very upset with her and getting very angry. Her son, Nathan Moulds, came in from another office and was wondering if his mother was okay because of my loud voice.

His mother assured him with a look that things were okay. He left the office and I continued my angry barrage with his mother. I talked to Robbin and she said that she seriously thought I was going to hit her that day, but she was willing to get hit and wasn’t scared of me. She also had laughed even though she thought that I was going to hit her.

I’m not particularly a violent person. I do get angry but I’ve been in few fights in my life. I’ve only been in fights when I’m trying to protect myself. So I didn’t hit her but I went out from her office and she had to go out. I was standing at our reception in the Salvation Army and went behind the reception desk and served customers which I usually do when they’re short of staff.

When I was behind the reception desk, a person who was new to the Salvation Army said I had to get away from being behind the reception desk. I took exception to that and said he had no idea that I’d been behind the reception desk and serving people before; and who was he to be telling me what I could do and what I couldn’t do.

He was the new man on the block and I was someone that had been around and he obviously didn’t know who I was. So I got very angry with him and told him I’d kill him. It got to a point where I was going to be violent with him.

I’ve learned how to be angry and intimidating with my anger because I’d had a brother that had personally beaten me up. I thought that sometimes there were solutions in violence. So even though I wasn’t a violent person, I was brought to a certain stage that day that I was sounding very angry and out of my mind, and totally out of control.

One of the people in the Salvation Army got on the phone and rang the police and told them to come down and pick me up because I wasn’t in a good state. Angela is a good friend and later confessed to me that it was her who rang the police. She was seriously worried for me. She’d never seen me angry before.

I’m a very happy and go-lucky sort of guy. I’ve always got a smile and I always seem to be encouraging to people. It was very distressing for her to see me so worked up and so angry. She knew that I had a mental condition and she knew that I needed to go to a hospital. So she rang the police.

They informed the police that I need to go to a hospital. Sarah came out in the midst of me being angry and took me aside, and was trying to settle me down and trying to get me to leave the premises before the police come. She told me to "Just go home and settle down." I was walking up to leave the premises with her when the police arrived, saw me, and realized that I was the person who was reported to them.

I immediately got angry again with the police and said, "I bet you're here to take me to the hospital." They said, "Is that where you think you need to go?" I said, "You know if I had a knife, I'd kill you," and they said, "Well, we pretty well believe that and it's a good thing you haven't got a knife."

They put me in the back of their paddy wagon and took me off to the mental health unit of the nearest hospital emergency ward. They had me admitted into a hospital. The actual mental health ward of the hospital was full at the time so they had to put me in a ward, a closed room in a ward in the hospital. But once again, I found myself in a hospital.

Chapter 81

Hospital Stay...

I'd freshly arrived from my community centre at the Salvation Army and I'd been reported to the police by Angela, a friend in the Salvation Army. Sarah had been sorry to see me go but saw me loaded up into a police van. When I got to the hospital, they didn't have a place in the psychiatric ward for me.

I was put into a ward and shown into a room and given a newspaper to read. They took blood tests and basically told me to stay in the room. Once again it was boring. I had to stay there for a couple of days. I remember I'd been doing YouTube videos because I was seriously wired or seriously in a state of mania without my medication.

So I asked them for a pad of paper and a pen, and I wrote about 80 subjects of videos that I wanted to do on the Book of Revelation and different things. I got a Bible from the hospital and was researching. Then after each chapter, I was starting to flesh out things to say in each of the chapters and doing scripture verses and stuff. So for two days, I got meals and stuff and regular checkups.

I was busy for two days fleshing out about 80 videos that I was going to shoot when I was able to get out of the hospital and get home. Once I'd been to the hospital, I realized that you only have to stay a few weeks up to a month and you get let out again when you got medication. But only when they feel that you're safe for the environment and for society again.

So I knew the process and the rigmarole. I was upset once again that Jesus had told me that I was well and I didn't turn out to be well but... It's a funny condition and a funny relationship I had with Jesus. Even though technically, you could say that Jesus lied to me if you didn't take into consideration that there was an Antichrist spirit speaking to me. You sort of forgive Jesus. I'm not sure if I realized that the false Jesus had told me that I was healed.

So Jesus didn't really lie to me. I just thought it was Jesus and whatever else it was had lied to me. Whatever the case was, I knew I had to do my time, take my pills and get well. I was thinking about doing the 80 videos that I'd fleshed out on paper to do when I got home with my video camera. So after two days, I was transferred to the psychiatric unit which can be a scary place. They're often full of people that are really crazy.

They're crazier than you in some respects and you've got things in common. You can talk about crazy things and crazy ideas. People in psychiatric wards understand you and can relate to you. Sometimes you can find a Christian in there that you can talk to about pretty intense subjects and you can speak with a level of intensity in your character and in your voice for quite awhile. Someone who's clinically insane can handle that intensity in you.

You're both locked up in a place with no place to go and so you've got the time to talk. You can fill your days by talking and listening. There always seems to be a couple of nurses in each psychiatric ward that you take a shine to. In this psychiatric ward in Sydney's St. Vincent Hospital, there were a couple of nurses that I really enjoyed. There was one female and one male that I really liked there.

I always enjoyed talking to the female and the male nurse who were both nice. I think I've discussed it before that in many psychiatric wards; nurses are burnt out and upset. All they seem to see are crazy people day in and day out. They don't really get to see me when I'm in a good state or in a good mental condition. They only get to see me and other people when we're in a really bad state, when we're saying some really crazy things.

So life for them must get a bit monotonous after a while, that all they're dealing with are crazy people. These crazy people like me think that they're right and they're one of the two witnesses, one of the two prophets who are going to judge the world. They're convinced that they've seen Jesus and they've met Jesus many times in visions and they're going to judge the world and cause a third of the world's population to die, or all sorts of crazy things that they believe that they're going to do.

Which I'm sure I was writing about the two witnesses of Revelation and I was going to do videos on them that I'd fleshed out in the hospital before I'd come into the psych ward. So I'm sure that was a theme that was on my mind and probably what I was talking about. So you can understand nurses thinking that you're a little crazy and giving you a wide berth.

They always have a place in the hospital which is a nurse's station that is behind glass doors; a locked or a security office. So they only come out to do medication, check on things and go up and down the wards once in awhile. But most of the time they spend is in their office locked away safely. They don't seem to like to come out and talk and socialize much with the patients. I can understand that. But it's sad that so many of them are burnt out and have got bad attitudes towards the psychiatric patients.

I don't know if I could really expect much more of people. I know that for many years I did prophecy and I got burnt out. Then now, when people ask me for a personal prophecy online, I politely tell them I've been burnt out and I don't do it anymore. There's a certain state you reach when you're burnt out, you just haven't got the time or energy to deal with it anymore. So I can imagine when a nurse gets to that state and they haven't got any other career prospects or any idea of doing anything else because that's all they're trained for.

I can see that they're stuck in between a rock and a hard place. They've got this job to do but they don't really enjoy the job, so they just go to work and suffer through it. It's a sad thing that psychiatric patients need some care, empathy, concern, and understanding. So many of the nurses in the psych wards don't seem to understand or don't have the empathy to be able to comfort the patients that are in there.

I think I've spoken on that subject before but just for those people out there that haven't got a mental illness, this is to give you some awareness. That a psychiatric ward is a place where you go to get better and they get your medication stabilized. They get you on a medication that's going to deal effectively with your mental illness. You're only there for a short time until everything's stabilized, the medication running fluidly through your blood, you're in a healthy condition and you're no threat to yourself or society.

It's certainly not a nice place to be. It's not a place that I ever want to get locked up in again and it's not a place I want to revisit. I'd certainly revisit psych wards as a chaplain if I was ever allowed to become one. I'd certainly do that as a ministry because I think I'd be very effective in sharing my life with broken-hearted people in those places. Certainly, I'd be good to be able to go in while in my right mind and deal with people, rather than going in there without my mind being in proper control.

It's a scary thing to have your mind out of control. It's something that I wouldn't wish on anyone and it's something that scares people. It scares the average person that you've got a mental illness.

Certain people get this fear of you from that point on. They don't want to socialize with you or they treat you differently. I can understand that they would be fearful of me, that I'm not like a normal individual and not like a normal person to the average person. Yet, I do function well and I do a lot of things like publish books, write articles, do YouTube videos, and do effective ministry on the net a lot better than the average person.

So I have got gifts and talents and yet I can understand people are scared and wary of the fact that I've got a so-called mental illness. So in the hospital, they only allowed me out when I signed what they called a Community Treatment Order and that means that I had to turn up and take my medication. Once a month I had to get a forced injection and pills because I couldn't be trusted to take my medication.

Every month I had to turn up for the forced injection. I had to see my psychiatrist. If I didn't turn up, if I didn't see my psychiatrist, they could ring the police and have me locked away. I had to sign a document that effectively forced me to be on medication and forced me to have blood tests to check that the required medication was always in my system. They keep a check on you. That was the only way to be let out of the hospital so I signed that agreement.

It's sort of a little bit like blackmail but it's a way that the community and the hospital can protect themselves. That this person has now gone off his medication three times and he cannot be trusted to take his medication. So we're going to up the ante a little bit and we're going to step up our control over Matthew Robert Payne, and we're going to make sure that he takes his medication.

I was locked away in the psychiatric ward over Christmas and New Year's Day which was sad for me. I was invited to go to Sarah's New Year's Day party with Robbin, Paul and Sarah at the family house. I got let out of the psychiatric ward and went in to see my psychiatrist five days later and got angry, so I got locked up again two days before the New Year's Day. I was unable to turn up.

They took my mobile phone from me so no one could call me. They wondered where I was but they didn't know what I was up to. I was locked away and because they wouldn't give me my mobile phone, I couldn't contact Sarah and say that I was locked in the hospital. So, it's sad. It's depressing for me. I wished I was at the New Year's party but that wasn't to be. That's one of the things about mental illness – sometimes you suffer things that you're not really happy for. So, it's not good to be lied to by a false Jesus.

Chapter 82

Prophecy over Popular Christians

I was at home. I'd been let out of the hospital. I'm not sure how long it was after that, maybe a couple of months. Jesus led me to do a prophecy on YouTube for a very popular female Christian missionary, public speaker and conference speaker.

For her prophecy, I won't mention who it is but often if it's mentioned in charismatic circles, people are very surprised that you did a prophecy over that person and you'd have the courage to do a prophecy over her. I was really attacked by Satan after I'd done the video and uploaded it to YouTube. I was attacked, with thoughts that said, "Who was I to be doing a prophecy for her and how am I ever going to get it to her? She wouldn't listen. She'd be too busy to listen.

You've wasted your time and you might as well take it off YouTube. You might as well take it down – she's never going to see it. It's not right anyway. You just made it up and you're just trying to impress someone popular in ministry. You're full of yourself, Matthew. You're crazy. You're out of your mind. This isn't God's idea. This is your idea and it's a crazy thought. You're a crazy person. You're out of your mind. So take it off YouTube and don't even try and contact her because you're just a waste of space and a waste of time."

So they're the sort of things that Satan levels at you. Of course he doesn't say, "Hello, this is Satan speaking," and then go on with that barrage. They're just thoughts that you get in your mind that you're crazy, and that you shouldn't be doing this. So how is she ever going to see it? You think that you're boasting and trying to be too proud, and being silly prophesying over someone so important.

The person concerned has been at many churches and so she's not just anyone in the world. God allows us to get attacked and stand our ground. We're told to stand when we put on our spiritual armor to stand strong, so I stood. In the afternoon, I got an e-mail from a friend whom I knew online. It was a testimony of this lady's husband who had been cured of dementia and was doing well. It was an e-mail from him.

It was a newsletter from him that a friend had forwarded on to me. So now I had this lady's husband's e-mail address. So I wrote him a letter and said, "The Lord impressed upon me to do a prophecy for your wife and here it is." He wrote back and he said that it sounds really true and it's got a ring of truth in it. It's very encouraging. She's in Hong Kong at the moment but he'll let her know the address of it on YouTube. Hopefully she'll get back to me.

Well, within a couple of days she'd written me an e-mail and said that she'd been on the ground crying tears and she can't believe that Jesus loves her so much. She's just amazed that I had courage and the obedience to obey Jesus and send a prophecy to her. She said that it means so much to her. Over the course of the next month, she sent three more e-mails – a total of four saying every time she watches the prophecy, she's amazed that God loves her so much and she's in tears every time with the words.

After the first response from her husband and her, the Lord led me to another famous Christian. He had a post that he was sending to 30 famous Christians. He had written a post on Facebook and then sent that post to 30 other Christians and I looked down the list and God just highlighted names of popular Christians that he'd sent his post to.

It was back when Facebook notes were popular things. He'd written a note and then tagged 30 Christians in it that were very popular in the world. Jesus pointed out 25 popular ones and said, "Sit down and do prophecies over them." So over the next two days I sat down and did prophetic words over them. I think one of them was Rienhard Bonnke at one stage and one was Joan Hunter.

So they're a couple of people, one was... anyway, one was Nicky Cruz. So, I sat down and did these 25 prophecies and sent them off with an introduction saying that I'd done a prophecy over this famous missionary woman who'd planted many churches. I included her feedback on the prophecy that I'd done over her and I said, "I hope you'd be encouraged to watch a prophecy from me and please give me feedback if you can."

I think out of the 25, six of them wrote back and said, "Thank you that was very accurate. Thank you for that." Some wrote longer e-mails. Some wrote shorter e-mails. A lot of them didn't get back to me and I credited a lot of that to secretaries that just didn't pass the e-mail along to the person or watched the prophecy and didn't feel it was relevant for the person.

Some would have watched the video or prophecy and didn't have the time to write back to me, or didn't feel led to write back to me and respond. Whatever the case is, I know that six people received their prophecies and were happy with it, and wrote me feedback to say so. Nineteen of them didn't. But what established me in doing that was that I'd now heard from major leaders in ministry that my prophetic words were true.

One thing that Satan attacks you with when you're doing prophecy as a Christian is that you're not accurate and you do not really speak words from God Himself. Satan says that you're actually just making up the words yourself. It's a very vicious and relentless attack on your life to say that you're no good and you're just making up words yourself – you're crazy, you're out of your mind and you're not accurate.

The best thing anyone could ever do for someone who prophesies over them is to give them good honest feedback. If there's anything wrong – sure, bring that up. Often when a person brings up something I've said wrong, often they'll misunderstand what I said and I'm able to clarify it. But sometimes I'm simply wrong. Part of a prophet's job or someone who prophesies is to accept that sometimes you hear something wrong.

You pass on something that can come from your own flesh or it can come from a false spirit. Whatever the cause, your prophecies aren't always true. New Testament prophets aren't like Old Testament prophets. Old Testament prophets were God's source of talking to people. Today, we've got the Holy Spirit and Paul says in Thessalonians not to despise prophecy but we're to test all things and keep what is good.

He was essentially saying to go through a prophecy and the things you agree with, keep and stand on and agree with God that it is going to happen in your life. But the things that don't seem to be true, the things that don't seem to be good in a prophecy – just leave them aside. So He's saying don't despise prophecy, don't stop prophecy from happening but certainly if there's elements of a prophecy you don't agree with – just put them aside.

So, we've all got the Holy Spirit now to discern whether God's speaking or not and God can speak to all of us. So prophets don't need to be essentially as accurate as they were in the Old Testament times when that was the only voice for God. I was really encouraged to have leaders of the faith write to me. Getting an e-mail from Nicky Cruz was very exciting and saying that he accepted and received the prophecy that I'd sent him.

He was one of my favorite people from my childhood. I saw him live one time giving his testimony and it was fabulous. It was really, really especially good to send him a 10-minute prophecy and impact his life with something God had said to him. It was really amazing to be used. The missionary couple was really a blessing. Since then, I've become friends with the husband of the missionary couple and we've become fairly close.

He said three or four times on Facebook so far that every time I talk to him I'm very encouraging to him. He finds me so encouraging. It's such a blessing to be able to be just a little person like myself and yet encourage someone who's doing such a mighty work for God in the world.

Chapter 83

Blog Calls Me a False Prophet

When I sent out the prophecies for the popular Christians in the world, some of my prophecies came up when people search in Google and YouTube under those Christian’s names. People were intrigued and watch a prophecy that I do over someone important.

Someone who had a Christian blog watched one and he noted that I said that God was boiling up a cauldron, like a witch’s cauldron and doing something with it. I had an image of a cauldron and God doing something. I had a meaning for what that meant in the person’s life. The blog post said that I was saying something pretty evil about the person’s life.

He made this blog post and it came up on the front page of Google. In fact, it is still on the front page of Google when making a search for Matthew Robert Payne. In the blog post he says, “Perhaps Matthew isn’t the prophet that he thinks he is and maybe he’s showing his true colours here.” He then explains the prophecy and puts a link to the prophecy on his blog post so people can listen to it themselves.

I made the mistake of commenting on the blog and defending myself. It got into a real argument with people on the blog attacking me. I kept on posting there with my website address and my full name. The more you do that, the more it positions the post higher up on Google. So even though I was arguing my point, I was making the person’s blog post even more popular on Google and rank higher up on the Google search.

I learned my lesson that there can be no reasoning with some people who have already decided that I am a false prophet, They have hundreds of verses that they can use as ammunition to prove that their claim is correct. They seem to know the Bible a whole lot better than I do. I just can't seem to win in an argument.

I made what I thought were convincing posts in the comments section but when you read it, it is like a barrage against me. You can go and read it if you like, see what I had to say and compare it with what other people had to say. It was certainly scary to have my name up on Google and someone calling me a false prophet. But apparently, that's par for the course. It is something that's expected for anyone who's anointed and anyone that God is going to use in the ministry.

Satan will urge people to call us false prophets and false teachers, and that just goes with the territory. Jesus was said to be ministering under the power of Beelzebub. When Jesus cast out the demons and healed the deaf and dumb guy; that was essentially proof that He was the Messiah. The people who cast out the demons in those days had to ask the person for the name of the demon and then cast the demon out by name. Because the person who had the demon was deaf and dumb, the possessed man couldn't hear and couldn't speak. That means they couldn't get the demons' names. So the person was forever trapped with a demon, but Jesus was able to ask the Holy Spirit for the name of the demon and cast it out without help or cooperation from the person. It proved that He was the Messiah. It was one of the evidences that the Pharisees were looking for, one ability that the Messiah needs to possess to prove that He was indeed the Messiah.

They actually accused Him of doing it by getting in touch with and getting the name of the demon from Satan, and then casting it out. Jesus was accused of being out of His mind, being a crazy person, and using the prince Beelzebub. We should expect the same thing when we go into ministry and that people will level things against us. In ministry, we make mistakes and we say things that aren't right and have ideas and scripture references that aren't properly supported.

We can make mistakes in our sermon like any pastor or any preacher but when a prophet does it, they call us a false prophet. When I set myself up as a prophet, said that I was called to be a prophet or perhaps when I get a prophecy wrong, this person saw this prophecy with me mentioning a cauldron that I could see. He couldn't understand the spiritual message that was getting conveyed in the prophecy. He just construed it to say that I was a false prophet and that's it.

People in the Christian world see my name, see the word "false prophet" and they immediately click on there and read what it has to say. If the blog post has got a convincing argument, they will believe it and will not make an effort to read anything else about me. Or they will decide to stay away from me because apparently I am a "false prophet" who will lead them into mistruth.

I think prophets can be wrong and prophets can make an error in their own life, in their personal life, and in their Christian life. I don't think that a prophet's sinning or a prophet being in error essentially makes him a false prophet. I believe the Old Testament's definition of a false prophet is someone who leads the people he's influencing to serve another God. So if a prophet leads people away from God, away from revering and fearing the Lord and serving the Lord with their whole life; that is what I would call a false prophet.

If a prophet's message is leading people away, he could be false. If he's leading people to serve money, he could be false. If he's leading people to serve him rather than serve God, he could be false. But a prophet who was just wrong in the doctrine or wrong in the prophecy is not a false prophet. That is why I was hurt by this person's post and I was especially hurt to be caught up in the arguments that went on in the comment section of the post.

Some of the comments are no longer there but there are a number of them still there on the post. It's upsetting when you first experience it, like your first girlfriend breaking up with you. It's hard the first time a girl breaks up with you in the same way that it is hard the first time that you've been insulted. The first fight you've been in was a hard thing too. So because this one is a first, it was especially hard on me.

I was soon to learn that to be an effective witness for God, I had to get ready to be called a false prophet. I've been warned that Part 1 and Part 2 of this book is going to cause me to be called a false teacher and a false prophet more loudly than anything else that has ever come before it. So I've had to be mentally prepared for the barrage of insults and posts that will happen on the Internet because of what I'm saying and sharing in my life's story.

Chapter 84

Called False Prophet and Teacher on YouTube

I made the 25 videos over certain people's lives and, as I have discussed in the last chapter, someone made a blog post saying that I was a false prophet because I'd included some things like I could see a cauldron. They said that I was seeing something dark and I wasn't even aware of the fact. They were saying that I didn't even know what I was talking about and calling my name into disrepute.

I saw a post online by a person saying that Rick Joyner was a false prophet and that he wasn't true to God. I made a video response to the actual video saying that Rick Joyner was a true prophet of God and this is an error, that the person saying that he wasn't of God is in error. That attracted the attention of the person who made the video of Rick Joyner and he went onto to make a video about me – calling it "Matthew Robert Payne – A False Prophet and Teacher."

He went on to make another video called "Matthew Robert Payne – What spirit is this guy coming from?" Both of those videos are removed now but for awhile they caused me quite a bit of distress and they were made up of scenes from my videos. What the person did was get about 20 of my videos and take a whole lot of things I said out of context and make a movie out of it. He made it laughable, made people laugh at me and made me seem really twisted and silly.

It had an effect that at one stage, three and a half thousand people had watched one of them.
So a lot of people who were searching under my full name in Google to find out more about me had seen it on YouTube. A lot of people were finding these videos because these were number three and number five on the Google search page under my full name. That is why these videos caused me a lot of distress.

People who wanted to get to know me better and do their research on me were watching these videos and found it disturbing. I'm sure that many people who watched these videos never want to have anything to do with me again. They didn't write to me and ask questions like, "Are these videos true?" Or "Have you got anything to say about these videos?" I never heard from any of the three and a half thousand people who watched one of those mean videos. I didn't hear any questions.

I only heard a question from Yianni about the videos and what I thought of the videos. It's a shame that people search a person's name and then straightaway will go to something that talks about that person being a false prophet or a false teacher. I think it's something built in us that likes to respond to negative news. I think that we're trained by the people who run the media in this world to look at people through the lens of false information and believe scary warnings about certain people.

I think it's a shame that people focus on that sort of thing, and it was certainly destructive to my life and caused me a lot of distress. The videos were up for about a year until I found a person who helped me have them removed. I found the rules for posting videos on YouTube. I found that the person had breached my copyright and that all the videos were copyrighted to me because they were videos that I uploaded. Because he'd used all of my videos, he breached my copyright.

We had to go through each of his videos and find the timestamps that were in my videos, when it started and stopped and which video of mine he'd used. A friend of mine over in Perth found all of those places and we sent the report in to YouTube and YouTube thankfully took the videos offline. But I'm sure as this book gets produced as Part 1 and Part 2, many people will write blogs and do videos to say things against me. They will be saying that a Christian can't blatantly sin and he can't be proud about the sin.

So I think when this person did this video and the other person did the blog about me – I think that was just the Lord's preparation for me to get used to being attacked and having my name pulled down.

I think that it's something that's going to happen in my future and I've got to be used to it. Not all bad things originate from people. I want to say that there are many people like the person who posted this video who have ideas that they should warn the public about people like me.

But their original ideas and their motives sometimes come from demons but they're not aware that the demon speaking to them sounds like the Holy Spirit. They feel like Jesus has directly told them to do a video defaming my name, calling attention to me, and warning people about me. So they can't be fully held accountable for what they did because they, in their best knowledge, are doing something that they feel the Lord has called them to do.

When I posted chapter 83 about a blog calling me a false prophet, a person wrote to me and said, "Don't worry about those blog posters. It's often those false prophet busters that you go to find out who's truly anointed and get a list." I had to laugh at the idea of being on the list of people to be warned about, to be one whom people need to steer clear of, a warning given by blog posters.

Chapter 85

Videos for Second Book

It turns out that the videos that I recorded for this second book were going to be for my third book. But at the time when I recorded the videos, I wasn't aware of it.

I had made a few hundred videos so I was comfortable at recording and uploading them to YouTube. I'd decided that I'd flesh out chapters of a book, name chapter titles of a book, name the book, record each chapter of the book as a video, pay people to transcribe the videos and make the videos into a book. So I had the idea of doing a book called *The Prophetic Supernatural Experience* and that was a book about the gift of prophecy and the office of prophet. I sat down and I recorded on a piece of paper all the chapter titles in a sequence of going one after the other, moving further and further into depth about what prophecy and the office of prophet is. I sat down over the course of three days and made the 54 videos that made up the book.

Sometimes I can stay up at night and work all night and all day. In this process, it only took two to three days to get the 54 videos made and uploaded. When you consider that it takes about an hour to make each video and a half hour to an hour for each video to upload; that was plenty of time that I spent uploading videos. It's easy to record six videos at ten minutes each and it will take an hour to record one after the other. But uploading those six videos takes about two and half hours.

So uploading 54 videos in three days meant that it was a positive effort and I was constantly working at the effort. I recorded the videos with the full intention of getting them made into a book. When it came to the point, I had a friend, Phil, who decided to help me make the videos into a book and pay for part of it.

He decided that he wanted another set of videos that I've recorded to be made into a book. He wasn't happy about this book and it wasn't a book that he wanted to support. He wanted to support another book that I'll talk about in the future. So I recommend to a lot of people that they can make videos and make each chapter a video in a book. Then, they can get them transcribed by a good transcriptionist.

It's certainly an easy way to do things. I've been blessed by the Lord that the person who works on my videos is a wonderful lady called Maria. She felt called by the Lord to transcribe my videos free of charge. Every time I send the videos and she sends me back the transcripts, it truly blesses my heart that God raised up such a person to transcribe my videos.

God is a good God and He's a tremendous God at providing what we need. This has saved me hundreds and hundreds of dollars, having someone who freely types up the videos and spends all her time doing that for me. Each time a video is played, it takes five times the amount of time the video is to type it up. So, a 10-minute video takes about 50-60 minutes to type up. You can just imagine 54 videos and how long that takes to type up. I have to say that I'm very impressed with Maria and I think that she should get a mention in this book. So *The Prophetic Supernatural Experience* was a book based on my experience in the prophetic, my experience with the gift of prophecy, and my experience as a calling to be a prophet.

It was an exciting book and it was one that I was certainly happy to make. I had to change it due to some changes in my beliefs when it came to grace and salvation and God's new covenant through Jesus Christ. But I didn't have to make too many changes to it.

Chapter 86

A Grace Explosion

I was in my community centre at Streetlevel one day in Surry Hills in Sydney and I was talking to Sarah. She was sitting down and I remember her saying, "I've got something in a book I want you to read." I smiled and she got out the book, turned to a certain page and said, "Read that paragraph."

I started to read that paragraph that she showed me. It was a paragraph about the older brother in the prodigal son story, how the older brother was indignant and didn't want to go in to the party because his brother was a loser. I read about that older brother and it was all about me. I got a tremendous shock because I'd done teachings on the fact that the older brother wasn't going to go to heaven.

I assumed that the party he didn't go in to was heaven and anyone who's acting like the older brother isn't going to heaven. So when I read this paragraph that was outlined by Sarah, it really hit me really hard that I used to see myself as a prodigal son who'd been redeemed and I'd never seen myself as the older brother. This paragraph was certainly explaining the sort of person that I was and it had me square between the eyes.

It snookered me! I was like a deer caught in the headlights of a car. It was amazing how it totally arrested me. She gave me the book to read and I don't know if I read the whole book. I was certainly just surprised that she was a person who wasn't afraid of me and she's someone who willingly stood up to me, willingly said things to me that would stir me up and challenge me. In all my time with Sarah, she's always challenged me since she's got to know me and we built a relationship. This time was no different, but this was a catalyst to change. And the change that was coming upon me was an understanding of grace. I'd like to call it a grace explosion because I'd certainly got challenged. I was at home a few weeks later and there was a Joyce Meyer featured article on a website – *"Seven Signs of a Legalist"*. People had challenged me in the past and called me a legalist and I had no idea what they were talking about. I used to just say I'm not a legalist but I wasn't really sure what a legalist was or what it was defined as. This day, I was searching on Joyce Meyer's site and she had this teaching called something like *"Seven Signs of a Legalist"*. I switched it on and it was for half an hour. I found out that I had six of the seven signs of a legalist and I was certainly a legalist.

That stunned me too just like the paragraph about the older brother. Once again, there was a chink in my armour and I felt truly exposed before God. I felt truly guilty before God, not guilty but convicted that my attitude and my beliefs were wrong and they needed changing. The Lord led me on to find a teacher called Andrew Wommack and I started to listen to his teachings. Andrew Wommack was challenging.

I got led early on to a man named Joseph Prince and he had a book called *Destined to Reign*. I'm not sure how I came across it. All I know is the Holy Spirit led me across Joseph Prince and I read his book *Destined to Reign* and it really challenged me. It showed me that we're not guilty and we shouldn't suffer condemnation. That all of us who are Christians should not suffer condemnation – that we're free. We're free and forgiven and God loves us and He's not a condemning God. It teaches about not mixing the Old Testament law with the New Testament grace. That we're to walk in love and not walk according to the Old Testament laws and rules and regulations, and we're to be free and walk in that freedom. That was tremendous for a person who was bound up with the law and the teachings of the law.

I was certainly a person who was misled and not knowing how to conduct myself. The legalism and the law that I believed in as well as the mixing of law and grace kept me angry and frustrated. I was angry that people weren't obeying the law and angry that people had this slack attitude when it comes to God. But I was angry also that I couldn't keep the law myself and I was still sinning.

I was frustrated inside myself that people wouldn't listen to me but when it comes down to it, I was preaching a mistruth, something that didn't resonate with the average person. I'm aware as I say this that there are many people who believe in the law and believe in the holiness, and God believes in holiness too. He loves people to be holy but these people approach life with a whole lot of rules and regulations.

All it is basically is a spirit of religion and people have got religious spirits that allow them to obey the letter of the law. Jesus said that the letter kills and the spirit gives life. It's the Holy Spirit that leads us into what we should do with our life. It's the Holy Spirit that shows us what we should be doing. We should obey the teachings of Jesus but we shouldn't use it as a law. We should be walking in love and always obey the lessons of love and the promptings of love in our life – not a set of rules.

You can look at the teachings of Jesus, which are beautiful teachings and things that I suggest people walk by. But you can even look at the teachings of Jesus and set them down as rules.You can even be legalistic about the teachings of Jesus and where He didn't want us to be legal about it. He didn't want us to be legalistic about it. He wanted us to flow in love and this is a definition of love that is described in His commandments. So, I was arrested by Sarah. Once again I remember only too clearly the time Sarah got upset with me in the car.

Then the very next day she was all happy as anything, like nothing had happened. I was proved through Sarah, her mother, father and her brother of what a proper demonstration of grace looks like, what unconditional love looks like. So, I was around people who were demonstrating the love of Christ and the understanding of Jesus Christ. I soon started to change my views.

There was a DVD series by Joseph Prince called *Condemnation Kills* that was interesting and I gave a copy to my brother. I need to get a copy again because it has so much wonderful teachings in it. So I'm not totally free of the religion and the rules and the regulations. I still have ways to go but I know that Jesus loves me and I'm a work in progress. I hope that you understand that there is a better way than just rules and regulations.

Chapter 87

The Parables of Jesus Made Simple

Shortly after doing the videos called *The Prophetic Supernatural Experience*, I had an idea in my mind to do a series of videos on *The Parables of Jesus Made Simple*. I think originally, I did the videos of *The Prophetic Supernatural Experience*. I'm not sure if I knew that I was going to make them into a book. I think I had an idea of making them into a book but it became definite when I started *The Parables of Jesus Made Simple*.

When I started the 54 videos for that, I was only on the third video when Jesus said, "You're going to transcribe these. You're going to have these videos transcribed and made into a book." As I was doing *The Parables of Jesus Made Simple* videos, I definitely knew I was going to make them into a book. I was thinking of a book and thinking of the order of the book as I did the videos one by one.

The Parables of Jesus Made Simple had a good explanation of the grace that I'd received and a good understanding of the grace that I was learning about. I'd spent a lot of time watching videos and reading books by Andrew Wommack and learning about grace. My whole life was infused with stories of Andrew Wommack and ideas about the New Covenant of Grace that I was living in.

So the book is filled with examples of grace and examples of the teaching of freedom through the new covenant that we all have as believers. God wants you to know that you're loved and that He loves you no matter what you do and what you've been doing. He loves you. He wants you to know that there's nothing you can do to stop Him loving you and loving you more.

That's a hard statement for someone who's religious to accept. People who have got religious spirits or trained up in religion think that they're loved more by doing acts of service for the Lord. They certainly believe that they're not loved as much when they disobey Jesus or do things that are sinful. So, the statement is a tremendous one. *The Parables of Jesus Made Simple* was started because I'd searched for years for books on the parables of Jesus and haven't really found any teaching that described the parables of Jesus for me.

I looked in book shelves for years and hadn't found any books that really described it. So the Holy Spirit put it on my heart to do my own book. Essentially, I got an alphabetical list of titles of parables and I went from that list from A to Z. I started and I'd pick out the scripture reference and read it. I'd read the parable and understand what it was saying.

Then I'd get my Bible, I'd put it down, I'd turn on the video and I'd start a teaching on that parable. So most of the ideas for the parables or most of the understanding of the parables that I covered in that book were fresh to me. The Holy Spirit sort of revealed the understanding to me as I sat down and recorded the video. I'm still pretty unaware of the meanings of the parables.

If I was going to preach on one of the parables, I'd get out my book and I'd read on the parable, and possibly use the parable that's written in the book to teach on it if I was ever going to teach people face-to-face. *The Parables of Jesus Made Simple* was simply a book, simply like prophecy. When you give a prophecy, the prophecy comes from God. So, the next day if the person says 'thanks' for the prophecy and starts talking about the prophecy – you really have no knowledge of what you've said, because the original thought for the prophecy didn't originate in your mind.

It originated with the Spirit of God, with the mind of God. So you were just a conduit for it to come through and you're just a person that God spoke through. But because you didn't come with the original thought, you've got no memory of what was said. You were just like a piece of pipe that water flowed through, and you are there and conscious but you're not sure what water flowed through you. *The Parables of Jesus Made Simple* was simply a book like that; the

Holy Spirit used me to speak some truths to people and gave them some understanding into the parables. I have to say that the *Parables* book sells about 50 copies on Kindle each month and I'm very happy.

Chapter 88

Quit Striving Says Sarah

I was in a position where I was listening to Sarah and what she had to say. Sarah had a good look at my life and she came to realize that I had an *Internet* site doing free prophecy online. I was writing a lot of articles and I was doing a lot of videos.

She had come to realize that all of my efforts were a form of striving. I was striving to be accepted and loved by God and I was sort of trying to earn my salvation through works. She saw right through this and she said to herself "Matthew does not need to be doing this." She told me to stop making the videos, stop writing the articles, and stop working on the website.

That was a real shock to me because I got my self-esteem that way. I was feeling important in the body of Christ, feeling like I had a ministry and I was ministering to God by doing all these activities. When you look at it in the Christian life, many of us are busy doing Christian activities to please God.

Often, we're doing it to please ourselves and to make up for a lack in ourselves. We're doing a lot of things in the flesh and with the spirit of striving. Here, we are striving to earn our way to heaven and we're doing good works to make ourselves feel approved.

Sarah was putting her finger in my life and she was showing me that these things were not good and it was not healthy for me to be doing these things. I think it took me about six months before I had ceased all activities but God certainly arranged my life for each of them to drop off.

As I learned more and more about grace, I realized that I was loved and I was loved for who I was. I do not have to strive and I do not have to do things to earn love. The more I learned about grace and the more time I spent learning about grace, the more I realized that

I didn't have to strive and do these things to earn His grace; that I was loved for who I was and I was not loved for what I did.

I simply stopped getting inspiration for videos. The Ezine website where I had posted my articles had changed their rules so much that it was impossible for me to post articles without serious editing. I could not afford to get an editor to edit all my articles. I didn't want to pay editors to edit my articles to simply post to a website for free.

So my articles stopped. I stopped the free prophecies simply because I got burned out and God allowed the fact that I got burned out to stop me. Within six months to a year, I don't know how long it was, but within a certain time frame, I had stopped all activities and the only thing I was doing was learning and walking in the grace of God.

Once again, Sarah was integral in this part of my life and she was pleased to know that I had stopped; though not necessarily pleased that it had taken me so long to stop. Sarah is a very confident woman and she knows when she is right and she knows when I'm wrong. She certainly was aware that I was doing things wrong and trying to earn my way to heaven.

Although she was happy when I had totally stopped, she was confident that she was right and so it was no big news to her. Even telling her that I had stopped was a form of striving, trying to gain acceptance from her like "See, I did what you asked." So she was not copping that, she was just happy that I had obeyed but was not giving me true credit for stopping because she knew it had taken me a while. She knew that it served me no good to make her happy about me stopping when God had told her to tell me to stop.

Do you feel the same? Do you find yourself striving and doing things to please God? Is your life about earning love from God and doing things to earn His love? The proper position that we should be coming from is to love God and love people.

We should be loving God and loving people, but we should not be in the process of doing things in order to win the approval of God. So many people are religious and believe in the law and mixing the covenant of Old Testament law with the new covenant. They are busy doing things being right and being good.

They think all these things are earning their way into heaven and they think all these things count. It is not until we stop, enter into rest, start to praise God and be happy to be loved for who we are rather than what we do that we are truly happy.

Chapter 89

Some Visions of Mine

I want to include here some of the visions I've had because people like to hear about these sort of things. This happened years ago so it is not in chronological order of the book but it was the time when I was still sleeping with prostitutes. Of course, I have already given up the habit of sleeping with prostitutes.

This is what I was thinking of when I was writing this part of the book. There was this time when I was on the toilet and I had a song playing from Hillsong Music. The chorus sang, *"I could sing of your love forever. I could sing of your love forever,"* and it just keeps going. *"I could sing of your love forever,"* the chorus keeps on going with that same line.

I was praying to Jesus and I said, *"I could sing of your love forever, Jesus,"* and He said, *"I could sing it to you."* The next time the chorus came, I heard Jesus singing the song. I was crying and I couldn't believe He'd sing that song for me.

I said, "That's amazing!"

He said, "One day, I'm going to sing that song in front of the hosts of heaven. I'm going to sing that song and dedicate it to you." I thought that was going to be when I die.

Two weeks later, I was getting counseled by a prophetic person and was told that I was going to see something in my mind. I saw myself in heaven and Jesus was standing opposite me and the counselor asked, "Where are you?"

I said, "I'm in heaven."

He was shocked! He said, "Tell me what Jesus is doing."

I said, "He's giving me a robe," and he said, "That's good."

I said, "He's giving me a signet ring," and that was good.

He put the ring on my finger and a crown on my head which made me think like I was the prodigal son.

But I didn't tell the counselor everything. The counselor asked, "So what is Jesus doing now?"

And I said, "Jesus is saying come and meet my Father."

I hesitated at that time and the counselor said, "Why?"

I said, "I don't feel worthy," and the counselor said, "Jesus has got you by the hand and you are worthy because if you weren't worthy, He wouldn't be asking you."
I still didn't go and the counselor said, "Why aren't you going now?"

I said, "I feel scared" and he said, "Well, nothing is going to hurt you. Jesus has got your hand. You're going to be okay."

So I entered through these throne room doors. As I entered, a sea of people parted. Jesus and I walked to the middle of the throne room through the people. As I walked up, I fell over about eight times. I think the number of new beginnings is eight. I got to the front and I heard the Father say, "Come up here." I walked right up to the throne as it was up some stairs.

I sat down on Jesus' throne and the Father said, "Have a look here." I looked and He opened the roof of the throne room. Kat Kerr says she's never seen the roof but I saw the roof open and I saw planets really close to heaven. It looked like it was right in the middle of a galaxy and there seemed to be planets about a hundred miles from heaven but gravity was not sucking them in.

I saw the galaxy, saw all these stars and it was amazing! They were moving as I watching them.

The Father said to me, "See all of this, Matthew?"

I said, "Yeah."

He said, "I control all of this," and I said, "Yeah."

He said, "I could grab any one of these planets and stars and send it down to earth, and that would be the end of earth."

I said, "Yeah."

He said, "If I can control all of this, don't you think I can control your life?"

I started crying and I said, "Yes, I believe you could."

He said, "Well, let me control it."

Then Jesus looked like He got a microphone and He said to the people in the throne room and the angels, "I'm going to dedicate this song to Matthew." He started to sing the chorus of the song I'd heard two weeks before, "I could sing of your love forever." You can only hear what your mind can remember and I only remember the chorus.

Jesus sang the chorus to the people in the throne room and I became quite emotional. Then different saints of the Bible started to walk up and stand in front of me and I'd get a name. I'd tell the counselor the name of the saint and then the counselor was saying this was a sign of honor, "Jesus is honoring you with famous saints from the Bible." Abraham came up and a few other saints. Elijah came up. John the Baptist came up.

The final person to come up was Joseph and he stood there and didn't move away. The counselor said, "What color is the robe that Jesus gave you?"

I said, "White."

He said, "No, I don't think it's white. Have a look down."

I looked down in the vision and it was a coat of many colors. Once again, my eyes filled up with tears because the coat of many colors was a sign of promise. It was given to the favorite son and it was a gift from Jacob to his son Joseph.

It really stirred me emotionally. I walked out of the throne room that day with the coat of many colors as my robe of righteousness. That was my first vision of the throne room

.

Another time, I was writing an e-mail to a girl and I was explaining heaven. I was taken to this wall in heaven. I think it’s in heaven. There was a wall and Jesus said, “Take one of the stones out of the wall, Matthew.”

I took out a stone. It was a diamond and it was as big as a soccer ball. It was really shiny and bright, and reflected the light well. God the Father said to me that the stone I had in my hand could fund the U.S. Government for 200 years. That was a really expensive stone, you know. Earth could not afford to buy it. The wall was hundreds of feet high and it went off into some glory mist.

I did not know how long that wall was but it was made up of these diamonds. The Father said, “See how big the wall is?”

I said, “Yeah.”

He said, “And that stone is worth 200 years of U.S. Government funding,” and I said, “Yeah.”

He said, “That is what money means to us up here, Matthew.” That had a profound effect on me at that time. That money, expensive things and riches did not mean anything to God.

I’m not sure if you captured that idea in this book when you read this but it had a tremendous effect on me.

I had another vision of heaven: one day I went to heaven and I was confronted with a whole park full of children. They were doing handstands and playing skip and rope, and there were carousels on the park. It was all green grass and the kids were all playing. This girl called Natalie came up to me and said, “Hello Matthew.”

I said, “How do you know my name?”

She said, “I played with your child when he’s having dreams. I used to play with your child when he was young and I got to know him. I used to show him your life.”

And I said, “That’s amazing.” It was really sweet to meet her. I was looking at all the children and there were no adults. I was afraid for them. Jesus said, “There are no child molesters up here, Matthew. The children are safe and they play better without adult supervision.”

I believe that was true, that children always play a bit fiercer when there are no adults around. Besides, they’re in heaven. They can’t really break their arm or anything of the sort. Natalie asked me if I wanted to go to her favorite place and I said, “Sure.” She grabbed my hand and next thing I know, we’re overlooking some stables. She said that’s where they keep the horses and she rode horses in heaven.

It was one of the things that she liked to do. At that time, I have not read any of the books by Kat Kerr, *Revealing Heaven – Part 1 and Part 2*. I had no idea that they had horses in heaven and little girls went and played on them. But now, I’m aware of those things through Kat Kerr’s books. I was really happy. She was about 14 years of age. Coming from the country, it is the sort of thing I knew: that young girls liked to ride horses at that age when they’re living in country towns.

It was a tremendous thing for that girl to have. I was told by the Lord that all the children in the park were victims of abortions and that every child that’s aborted in the world are taken straight to heaven and they grow up as children. Kat Kerr says they grow slowly in heaven so that when their parents die, they’ll be able to raise them as children in heaven. I’m pretty sure that’s probably how it works. It was amazing! The children were really nice and they are having fun.

I've got a friend, Yianni, who I've mentioned before. At one time, while we were at McDonalds, he asked me, "When you're in heaven, did you see my son?" And immediately, I saw his son in heaven and I described his son to him and his eyes filled up with tears. Apparently, his wife had an abortion and I saw his son. Yianni was very happy that his son was up there and living okay. In the next chapter, I will tell you more of the visions that I've experienced.

Chapter 90

More Visions of Mine

One day, I had been up all night which I often am. I was with a friend. We were having breakfast in this eatery in Sydney City and it was Valentine's Day. My friend was going on about how this was the first Valentine's Day since he had broken up with his girlfriend and that the Valentine's Day before, he was still going out with her.

He was very sad, lamenting and having memories of her. He was getting pretty sad. All of a sudden, the hall of the cafeteria and all of the eatery place with about a hundred chairs, filled up with angels. I was quite shocked and I said to my friend that the whole place had filled up with angels. He looked around and said, "I can't see anything," and continued to talk.

I said, "If you don't mind, I just want you to be quiet for a second. I want to see why they are here. They would not turn up for no reason." He stopped for a second and started talking again. I sort of just pretended I was listening to him and I said to Jesus, "Why are all the angels here, Jesus?" He said, "It's Valentine's Day, Matthew. I wanted to surprise you." I was surprised and really happy.

The angels bring the glory of the Lord and they bring joy. I was not only happy that they were there but overjoyed that they had come to visit me. I always like to meet angels and interact with them.
Jesus said, "See the angel on the left-hand side, on the aisle row, four seats back on the left?"

I said, "Yes," and he said, "He is my cup bearer."

I understood a cup bearer is like a personal valet or a personal servant to Jesus.

I was really happy and I discovered that it was a job that I would like to do. I would like to be the person who travels everywhere with

Jesus and gets His suits ready, gets His clothes ready, makes Him cups of tea, prepares things for Him, and always travels with Him. Someone who is always with Him and is always at His beck and call. That would be a tremendous job to have in heaven. I realized that this angel had a job that I would not mind having.

I had always wondered what I would like to do in heaven and this was very surprising. It was something that I thought would be very enjoyable. As we got up to leave that day, I walked up to the angel, hugged him and said to him, "I love you." He said, "I love you back, Matthew." It was really amazing that I had met Jesus on earth quite a number of times and Jesus understands.

Somehow, meeting that cup bearer angel was even more exciting than meeting Jesus Himself. I have said a lot of strange things in this book and I'm sure that many people will forgive me. Some people who are religious will think, how could you say that you loved meeting an angel more than meeting Jesus? And I will say, "Well, meeting that angel is one of my sweetest memories of visions," and I will just leave it there.

As we were walking out, the angels followed us and John kept on saying to me, "Can you see that person? Do you see that person?"

And I kept on saying, "Why are you asking if I see that person?"

He said, "They are all looking at you, Matthew," and I said, "Ah, that is because all the angels are walking with me. It is making my face shine."

He said, "I can't see your face shining."

I said, "You can't see it but they can see it and that is what all the angels are doing." There were a number of times in my life when people had commented that my face was shining. This is probably achieved with a lot of angels coming and manifesting around you and bringing the glory on your face. Isaiah 60 says that "in the last days, certain people will have the glory of the Lord rise upon them," and on that day, the people were certainly surprised while looking at me.

Another time, I was with my friend Yianni at McDonalds and a few angels turned up and he could tell the angels were there. Then he said, "Is that Jesus?" Someone walked behind us and I said, "No, that's not Jesus but it's a similar anointing isn't it?"

He said, "Yeah, who is it?"

I said, "That's Michael the Archangel," Michael sat down and then he said, "Well, who is that?"

I said, "Well, that's Jesus," and Jesus sat down.

Apparently, there are two cup bearers and the other cup bearer angel sat down too. We were sitting with a friend called Michael and he's an older gentleman. He was saying, "These guys are crazy. You think Jesus is here."

I said, "Yeah."

He says, "If I ever met Jesus, I'd rebuke Him in Jesus' name."

I said, "So you say that you could meet Jesus and not know it's Jesus and you'd rebuke Him in Jesus' name. And if He stayed, He'd be Jesus, but if he left, he'd be an impostor?"

He said, "Yeah."

I saw a tear roll down His cheek so I said to Jesus in my mind, "What's wrong, Jesus?"

He said, "Some people are so full of disbelief that you can't take them very far." I was really shocked and amazed that Jesus would be crying over my friend. He was upset with my friend's disbelief. That was a tear of emotion that He had for Michael that Michael didn't believe.

That was a good day. Another day, I was with Yianni and a whole lot of saints appeared from heaven. Abraham turned up, Mary and Martha turned up and Isaiah turned up together with a whole lot of saints from heaven. I was asking each of them questions and Yianni was giving me the answers that they were giving. I was talking to each of the saints and asking them specific questions; and every time I asked a question, Yianni would hear the question and then bring the answer from the saint.

That was a tremendous time. That time, his son came down from heaven and Yianni was able to hear his son talk to him. I brought his son's voice to him, which was amazing.

I had met with Jesus quite a number of times and one time, I asked Him to bring someone from heaven with him the next time He comes.

He said, "Who do you want me to bring?"

And I said, "I like surprises. Surprise me."

He says, "So it does not matter? I'll just bring whoever I want."

I said, "Yeah, bring whoever you want."

A couple of weeks later, I was in McDonalds, Jesus turned up and He said, "Can you see her?"

I said, "Yeah," and my eyes filled up with tears because the name that came to my mind was Mary Magdalene. Whether you believe she was a prostitute or not, whether that tradition is true or not, I knew that Mary Magdalene was one of the friends of Jesus.

Actually, it says in the Bible that she supported Jesus with her money. So, she was a very close friend of Jesus and because of that, she was someone who I admired a whole lot. I was emotional and Mary comforted me and said some things to comfort me. I was really amazed that of all the saints in heaven, Jesus picked her. It was tremendously emotional for me and it was amazing.

I will never forget that first experience. I did not see a lot but I saw she had long dark hair, down past her waist. She is very pretty, although I did not look too much at her. Apparently, Mary Magdalene and Martha were sisters. It does not say that in the Bible but in the second vision, when Martha came down, Martha said to me that she really admires me.

I said, "Why, when you do not even know me?"

She said, "You have never lusted after my sister Mary."

And I said, "How could I lust after her. I love her. She is a friend of Jesus."

She said, "I hear the thoughts of every man in Heaven and you are one of the few men who has never lusted after my sister." It was amazing to hear that from Martha and it is very encouraging

.

I normally stay up all night to get things done. One day, I was going down to my local service station to buy some milk in the middle of the night. I was buying some milk to make coffee. I was pretty sad. I was in a depression. As a manic depressive, sometimes I'm in periods of depression. As I was walking, Mary and Martha turned up and Mary said, "Stop here," and I stopped. I saw lines on the ground and Mary and Martha started to do hopscotch though I'm not sure if you know what hopscotch is in America.

Squares are drawn on the ground and the girls jump in the squares with feet together and feet apart, and feet together and on one foot, then on two feet. It's very funny. I think the game is played in America too. I imagine it would be. It is a very entertaining game. They kept on finishing the end of the squares and coming back, running back to the start and doing it again. It was amazing to see two attractive women with long dark hair jumping in fits of laughter. It sort of pulled me out of my depression.

A lot of people may be thinking by now that Mary comes to visit me a lot and I'm not talking a lot about Jesus. What I'm doing is talking about some of my favorite experiences. Jesus has been with me and visited me many, many times. Yet, I want to show that there's a breadth and a depth of Jesus and that He shares friends with His friends. We do not have to talk about Jesus all the time.

Another time, I was on a ferry on the way back from Manly Beach, a suburb of Sydney. I was on a ferry coming back across the water on about a 40-minute trip. Mary Magdalene turned up next to me and said hello. I said to her that ferries are a very romantic place for me and I get especially romantic in water. She said, "Well, we're brother and sister and we're both the bride of Christ. So nothing like that can happen."

I laughed and I was just emotional. I was just myself and saying that it was a very romantic place for her to be turning up. She said, "Watch this!" Then, she jumped off the ferry and was sailing through the air like Superman, about two meters or six feet from where I was standing on the ferry. She was about a hundred feet above the water and just parallel to where I was standing.

She was just flying through the air and she said, "You'll be able to do this on the new earth."

I said, "That's amazing!" So that was a really exciting time.

About three months ago, I was walking out of my house and I saw Jesus. I normally see His coat flying in the wind when He arrives. I said to Him, "I'm seeing you every second day now."

He says, "I'm with you every day. It's just every second day that I manifest," and I said, "Where's the scripture in the Bible for that?"

He said, "Lo, I'm with you always."

Jesus is always with us. We just need to open our spiritual eyes for us to realize it. I hope you've been blessed by my stories and I hope you're blessed by my book.

Chapter 91

The Parables Book Published

I had a video recording of *The Prophetic Supernatural Experience*, a series of 50 odd videos that I planned to make into a book. I had a friend, Phil, and he had decided between the parables that I recorded on *The Parables of Jesus Made Simple* videos that I wanted to make into a book.

My friend decided that he wanted to pay for the publishing of the *Parables* book and not the prophetic book. So, I went ahead with the *Parables* videos. I hired a freelance typist on oDesk.com to transcribe the videos. I hired editors on oDesk to do the editing. I had an editor edit it and I had another editor edit it. Then I had a proofreader read it.

I went through the process of publishing it on CreateSpace.com where they allow people to self-publish books and I paid them money for the *Parables* book to be typeset by them. I found an online freelance graphic artist who designed the cover of the book and she did a tremendous job making a very attractive cover for the book. Self-publishing a book is a hard, long and tiresome process.

It is not for the faint-hearted. Trying to do things and get things done can really wear on your patience especially if it is a long process like this one. It is not an easy process, especially getting all the errors out of the book. I think I had seven different people go through my book and up to this day, people still find errors in the book that I just have not gone back and fixed. I respect anyone who gets a book out there with hardly any errors in it. The *Parables* book has got very few, if any, errors.

I totally respect authors who self-publish, they are called Indie authors. I totally respect Indie authors who can self-publish these days. So I uploaded the book to Amazon. At that time, I did not know that you could hire people to do reviews. Apparently, you are not allowed to pay people to do reviews but I did not know that and I hired people on oDesk to do reviews for me. I got a few reviews done.

When I was up online, I uploaded it onto Amazon Kindle and made a digital format for the book so I had a program that wrote the program to put it into a file format that can be uploaded onto Kindle. I had my book published on Kindle. The book started to sell fairly well. I was happy that it was selling about 10 copies. I may not be a famous author but they're selling about 10 copies per month in print and about 20 copies in digital.

About a year ago, my brother asked me the question: what do I prefer? Do I want to make money on Kindle or do I want more people to read my book? I said, "I want more people to read my book," and he said, "Well, take it from $3.99 and make it .99 cents and more people will buy your book at .99 cents." So I did, and the people buying my book went from about 22 to about 50 per month so it more than doubled the number of buyers and readers.

It went two and half times more, sales were getting done at .99 cents a book, which made me happy. It only allowed me to make .30 cents a book but I was quite impressed. I found out that with Kindle Select, a program on Kindle, you can give your book away for free at certain times and you are allowed to make your book for free for five days out of every 90 days. So you can make your book free for two days one month, two days the next month and one day on the third month.

I only found that out in December 2012. I gave my book away for five days and 1850 people downloaded it for free. I got REALLY excited so I had a website made up with the full *Parables* book and I made links to all my Ezine Articles. At the bottom of the articles, you can click a link to my Parables website so people could read my book for free.

On the *Parables* book website, I have a picture of the book that said "Click to go to Amazon." This is so people could read a few chapters or read the whole book on the Parables website. But if they chose to buy the book, they could go to Kindle and buy it for 0.99 cents or get themselves a hard copy of the book. I have come to a point where I just totally want to get things out there for free. I will be giving this current book away for free for five days every 90 days.

If you go to the Matthew Robert Payne author page and become a subscriber there or on Facebook, you will find that I give the book away and I announce it on that page or on the main Facebook page of the Matthew Robert Payne Facebook Page. If you go there and become a friend, I will always announce on my main page that I'm giving my book away for free. So you do not always have to buy this book.

You can tell your friends to become friends and get their copy for free rather than pay 0.99 cents. Or you could become a friend of mine on Facebook and, when I advertise that I'm giving this book away for free, you can post it on your Facebook post page and have all your friends download it free for themselves; which would be good and would help everybody.

I was talking to my pastor a couple of weeks ago and he asked me, "If you had known the hassles that were involved in publishing a book, would you have gone ahead with it?"

I said, "No, I probably would not have," and he said, "But your life is in a tremendous position now that you have published your book. You are a lot further ahead in life and a lot happier person now that you have published books, wouldn't you say?"

I said, "Yeah."

He said, "So, it is a good thing you did persist," and I said, "Yeah, it is a good thing I persisted."

I encourage you to get in touch if you want to publish a book and maybe I will help hold your hand as you go through the process. Maybe, I could get you in touch with my graphic artist, my proofreaders and my editors and save you the hunt for a good people like them.

So, that is a little bit about me. A lot of people say that they want to write a book and never get around to actually writing it. Today, with Kindle, eBooks and self-publishing through CreateSpace, any person can publish a book. Once again, I will have to say that getting errors out of the book is the most important thing. Having a good editor to rewrite your words, polish your words and getting the errors proofread out of your book is very important.

I would encourage you all to get something together and put it out there for your friends and family to read at least. I was very happy with the *Parables* book. Even today, if I wanted to know the meaning of one of the parables, I will pick up my *Parables* book and read to see what I had written then. I feel that the Holy Spirit was very much involved in the writing, the making of the videos and the publishing of that book.

I feel that the book is very inspiring and it is a really good book. I was very happy and still am happy today to watch the sales click through at 50 per month. It is a great experience.

Chapter 92

Growing in Grace

The more I read about the grace doctrine and the grace preached by Andrew Wommack, Joseph Prince and others, the more I realized that I had a lot of changes that needed to be made in my thinking. It was tremendously challenging to accept that I’m loved for who I am and not what I do.

It is still challenging today as I live not to concentrate on sin in my life but concentrate on Jesus and His finished work. He said on the cross, “It is finished,” and He paid the price for everybody’s sin on the cross. A lot of people say that we have to stay holy, to stop sinning and to live a life with no sin in it. It is true that we should strive to be holy and strive to live a sin-free life, but some of us cannot do that for various reasons and so we are having a struggle.

It is good to know that Jesus loves us for who we are and He enjoys our company. He enjoys us and loves us despite what we do. Some people will say that we need to repent and continue to repent. I do that with certain sins in my life and I know that Jesus loves me, although sometimes it is a struggle to remind myself of that. Satan likes to condemn me, fill me up with guilt, and bring sin to my mind and keep me condemned.

Joseph Prince and Joyce Meyer teach that while we are concentrating on sin and we have a consciousness of sin in our life, conscious thought about sin and condemnation keeps us in a cycle of going back to the sin and doing it again. It is only when we are set free; it is only that when we believe that we are the righteousness of God in Christ that we are righteous and holy in God’s sight. It is only when we believe that we are set free and we can walk in the miracle of grace.

So I started to walk and move in grace. Over time, I did what Sarah had suggested and I gave up writing articles. Part of the reason I gave it up was what I mentioned before: that the articles were too hard to get approved,I needed an editor to edit my articles and it cost too much to pay for.

I gave up doing videos and articles but if I still thought that I needed to earn a living, I would pay the proof-reader to do my articles. I was doing that for a while but as the message of grace started to settle around my shoulders and started to permeate me, I realized that I was loved for who I was and not for what I was doing. So many people are caught up doing things for the sake of religion.

It says in the Bible that "We are saved by grace, not by works, lest no man should boast." This is a very important scripture for people to realize that we are saved by the grace of God and nothing else and it is not our works. We all have work to do. There are all things that God has prepared before we were born for us to walk in and for us to do, but they should be motivated by love.

So many people live a life of trying to do righteous acts and do good things to sort of earn God's approval and earn God's love. These people are very vocal about being holy, lying to themselves and walking in righteousness. Yet, Jesus says that all these self-proclaimed works are motivated by a desire to be loved more and desire to be holy is what He calls self-righteousness. He says 'Your self-righteousness is like filthy rags.'

The verse in the Bible that mentions filthy rags can be interpreted to mean menstrual cloths that women have during that time of the month. When we said that our self-righteousness and our righteous acts are like menstrual cloths, then we get a picture of how disgusting they are for God. So it is important to understand that doing things for God have to be motivated by your love for God; not the motivation of trying to buy favor with God and get some sort of "life insurance" for heaven, so that you do not get cast into hell.

It is a fine line. There is a really fine line in between self-works and works that are motivated by grace and love. That is a fine line that I'm still learning to walk in. I retired from writing articles. I stopped doing videos. My motivation for doing videos used to be to do things for God and do videos for ministry. I just stopped – totally stopped for about a year. I stopped doing videos and hardly made any videos now.

I had an online prophecy site which I mentioned in another book. I took that site down and stopped doing anything on that site, but I did continue to witness on the streets through prophetic evangelism. I used to continue to give messages to people on the streets that Jesus loved them and give them specific messages from God about their life and things in their life; which totally blow people away and spin them out.

It comes as a shock to people that God would know about their life and want to talk to them. So, I continued in doing that. At one stage, after about six months of having given up my prophecy site, I started a Facebook group of online prophecies. The Facebook group brought me a lot of pressure and after about three months, I handed the management of the Facebook group over to someone else and the group continues to this day. It is called Personal Prophecy Group.

If you want to search it on Facebook, they give free written prophecies to people who ask for it. I started that group and I think the Lord inspired me to start the group, but He knew in advance that I was going to reach a stage in my life where I was not going to be able to handle it anymore. He wanted to launch a ministry which is still running today and I'm very happy that it is still running today.

Sarah told me six months or a year before to stop striving to earn my salvation. She told me that I was loved for who I was and who I was with God and I do not have to prove myself to other people. I do not have to earn my salvation. I do not have to earn my right to live. I was loved for just being me. I was not loved because I was writing articles. I was not loved because I was doing videos. I was not loved for doing personal prophecies for people.

I was loved because God loved me from the start, from the beginning of my life right till now and He will love me right until the end of my life. I do not need to do anything to impress Him or make Him happy. That was a very encouraging message from Sarah. After six months or a year, I ground to a halt and I ceased all activities. I just spent my time reading books and watching videos on grace and learning about the message of grace.

I do not know a tremendous amount about the subject of grace. I certainly could not write a book on the subject of grace unless you consider this book with a subject about the love of God and the grace of God which I'm sure it is. But I could not write a non-fiction book about the subject of grace and explain it too well.

I do know one thing for sure: that is the passage in the Bible where it says the woman came and washed Jesus' feet with her tears, wiped His feet with her hair and then put perfume on His feet. I know what Jesus said about her, "one that has been forgiven much, loves much." I use that quote at the beginning of part one of my book and I believe that is true of Jesus and true of life. I believe that is true of the message of grace. The more grace that you have been shown by Jesus, the more times you have been forgiven by Jesus, the more you understand how much He loves you and how precious His love is to you.

His love is very precious to you and you will do anything for Him. I will have to say that it takes tremendous courage to share a book and share all your sins with the public. It takes tremendous courage to go into great detail about your sins and the past life that you had, as well as the current life that you have. This can only be done because you are obedient to God and you are telling the full story. You want to be transparent with people, share the true message with people, and the true life that you lived with people.

This is done so that people can be encouraged and say to themselves, "Hey, I'm not that bad. Matthew was worse than me." Or people who may have been worse than me can say, "If God loves Matthew, show certain visions to Matthew, encourages and loves Matthew like this, then perhaps He will accept and love me." I hope that my life and this book is a testimony to the grace of God.

The grace of God is something that is unmerited, undeserved and unwarranted, but it is certainly something that has saved my life,

"His Redeeming Love" a Memoir of Matthew Robert Payne made me happy and made joy spring in my life.

Chapter 93

Voluntary Work in the Salvation Army

After a while, I got offered the chance to get out of the kitchen. Actually, I had experienced working in the kitchen at the Salvation Army where I met Sarah.

Managers changed from Sarah's time onwards. We got a manager in the kitchen who seemed to think my only use was to wash dishes. I left a dishwashing job where I got paid $17 an hour, which is a lot of money in American money, but in Australian money that's what it was paid. You get about $20 an hour now.

I left a job washing dishes and I said I'd never wash dishes again. I come to the Salvation Army and was volunteering washing dishes and doing other food preparation in the kitchen, but I didn't mind doing the dishes half the day. But when this new chef came, she just delegated me to washing the dishes all the time.

For a person who has done food prep and worked with chefs and assisted chefs, I wasn't very happy. I just started to get depressed again that I wasn't having fun washing dishes. I got the opportunity to go and work in our Opportunity Shop like our OpShop. That is where we get donated second-hand clothes, knickknacks, all sorts of stuff, furniture, and we sell it there and make a profit.

The profit from the shop pays for our homeless center. I worked in the Opportunity Shop and I learned to work on the cash register. I learned to sort stock and do different jobs in the shop. My favorite position in the shop was to serve customers. I was a people person as were in the days of driving taxis. I love to engage with people and talk to people.

I enjoyed working in the shop. There were people that came in every day in the shop and I soon developed a relationship with all of them. In our suburb, we had all sorts of people come in the shop. The trendy people came to our shop. Gay and lesbians came into our shop. Transsexuals came to our shop.

If you are a person who is very judgmental about people, you'd have a hard time working in our shop. It is actually staffed with one paid staff and volunteers that in the past have been gay. Salvation Army has this tremendous ability to hire and attract volunteers who are from all walks of life.

They don't seem to discriminate against people. One of the workers in the shop was named John and He was gay. He was a tremendous friend and I really loved him. I worked in the shop and I learned how to work the register even when they got bank card transactions as well.

I'm not sure what you call it in the United States, but these are automatic fund transfers so you can use cards with the computer and stuff. Even when they got that in the shop, I could do that besides cash and I was surprised with myself that I could do that and do it well. I had a tremendous relationship with the people in the shop, except one thing came up.

Apparently, I was talking too much to customers in the shop and sometimes, my wanting to chat prevented people from wanting to leave when they wanted want to leave. So, after about a year of working in the shop, they wanted me to stop and move me somewhere else. The thing that attracted me to the shop was that Sarah got a position to manage the shop, and she asked me to come and be her cashier.

Sarah worked in the shop for about six months and we're together most days. She did a lot of sorting out the back, but she spent a lot of time out the front at the cashier with me talking and doing things at the front. Sarah was the huge attraction why I left the kitchen of washing up and moved up to the shop and started to work in the shop.

Everyone seemed to know that I loved Sarah and I mentioned Sarah a lot. I've mentioned her quite a bit in this book. She's one of my favorite subjects and one of my favorite friends. People really know that I left the kitchen because I didn't like washing up anymore. We got a new manager in the shop eventually.

I was told that I was working too many hours for a volunteered person. A volunteer wasn't allowed to work over 20 hours a week and that was one of the reasons they said I was going to change in the shop. Another reason was that I started to produce this book, and I also left the shop because I was talking to people too much and distracting them too much.

They thought that there'd be a better job for me downstairs making coffee for people. So that's it!

Chapter 94

My Ministry Duplicates

As I discussed before, I said I started a Facebook group concerned with personal prophecy where people could write in for a personal prophecy, and personally make requests at a certain place on the wall where requests were received.

We had a team of prophets there or people who were gifted in prophecy that we call prophets, just for explanation sake. This team used to take two to five requests per week each and prophesy over the people and post the prophecy on the group wall. In that way, the person who got the prophecy was tagged in it and was edified. Then, they could read their prophecy and leave feedback for the person who prophesied over them.

It also gave the whole group of members something that was inspirational and edifying for them to read. A lot of people were entertained coming to the wall each day and reading the prophecies of other people because often, when God speaks, He speaks to more than one person. People could come to the group and read prophecies on the wall and be edified themselves and claim prophecies and parts of prophecies for themselves as though God was speaking to them too

.

It was a good idea that I had set up and I think I discussed that it all got too much for me. I was going through some healing at the time and was getting outbursts of anger. I had an attack from a person with a Jezebel spirit and I responded by swearing at her on her wall. The administrators of the *Personal Prophecy Group* – that’s what it’s called, *Personal Prophecy Group* – on Facebook; found out about my swearing and asked what was happening.

One of the administrators asked me to step down from being an admin. He became an admin in the group that I’d started, a group that I was the head of and then, he asked me to step down from being an admin. I effectively lost control of my *Personal Prophecy Group*.

At the time, the person who illustrates my books for me, Bjarki Clausen, was a good friend of mine and he took over control of the Personal Prophecy Group.

Since that time last year, he did a tremendous job in maintaining and keeping order in the *Personal Prophecy Group*, allowing new prophetic people to come in and minister on the team, and saying good-bye to certain people in the *Personal Prophecy Group* as they left. I got to a stage where I was a little burnt out by doing personal prophecies, and so I was glad to step down from the ministry and take some time to recuperate.

From time to time, I go on there. I'm still listed on the team of prophets and respected by Bjarki. He's in a position where he could reinstate me as an admin now, but I don't feel called into being an admin nor in running that ministry. I was happy to step down and I just jump in there from time to time and do a prophecy over a person. For the last year or so, I haven't accepted personal prophecy requests online.

So if people write to me and know that I'm a prophet, I will kindly tell them that I've been burned out by doing too many prophecies and decline their request for a free prophecy off myself. Not only will I decline prophecy requests for free, but I don't feel inclined to do a prophecy even for money. When we started the Personal Prophecy Group, two or three people started as prophets on our Personal Prophecy Group and then went off and started their own personal prophecy groups on Facebook.

As of today, I know of five groups that have started five personal prophecy groups on Facebook that originally had something to do with the one that I started. The ministry that I started last year – in say, October – has grown about fivefold and each of those ministries has people requesting personal prophecies every day. Each of those ministries has a team of prophetic people handling the requests.

Each of those personal prophecy groups does free prophecies. One group that I really respect was a person who still ministers on our *Personal Prophecy Group* and she started the dream interpretation group. That was a good group that she started. You can post a dream that you had with the dream interpretation group they will interpret your dream.

I've been happy to use that webpage a couple of times for them to interpret dreams. A couple of the dreams I have had in the past were interpreted to say that the spirit of lust still had a control on my life. Although I had intercessors praying for me to break free, it was still a strong force in my life and it would take a decisive effort to get rid of. The spirit of lust causes an addiction to pornography that comes and goes.

That gets me down. I'm going to talk further about that later on, but I had periods of being free of it and then falling back into it. I seem not to like getting my dreams interpreted, because the last two dream interpretations have said that the stronghold and the spirit of lust are still staying in my life. I seem to want it to go. I'm repenting for my sin. I turn away from the sin and I try my best. I depend on God's grace and I get some freedom, and then, it seems to come back to me.

I have weeks at a time. At one stage, I had six months freedom from the sin and then something happened and it came back. It actually happened during the subject of my next video, my next chapter in the book. I had a ministry trip that I took to another state in Australia, on a five-hour flight. A letter was read by a person who I believed was a pedophile in a car that I was in, a letter that was written to a mother from a pedophile who was trying to date her and see pictures of her daughters was read.

It was horrific and disgusting! I'd had a six-month break from pornography and the services of dirty massages, and I was going really well. After that letter was read in the car, I came back with both the habits strong and raging in my life. I think a spirit came upon me as that letter was read in the car. With that subject set aside and will be dealt with that later on, what was really encouraging is I feel like a little boy.

I've had it prophesied over me a couple of times, once about 10 years ago and once recently, two weeks ago. It said that I was a little boy who gave his two fish and five loaves of bread to Jesus and Jesus multiplied the bread, and the five thousand men, women and children were fed. I had it prophesied that I'm that little boy and God is doing duplication supernaturally from even the little effort I've put in my ministry.

He's going to duplicate and expand widely, and my ministry will have far reaching effects. This is an example: there are hundreds of people being serviced by these personal prophecy groups and they all started. The first one was the one I started on Facebook and everyone seemed to see its success and seen how it was maintained, and how it was operated.

They all seem to carry on with the same systems, the same setup and the same structure that I set mine up with, that we had team problems with and we sorted out structures of ways and rules. All of them seemed to operate the way I worked out to operate. It seems that I'm called to be a bit of a forerunner in ministry. I seem to go out ahead of the pack, break new ground and start new things.

This is what some people have called an apostolic sort of an anointing on my life for me to be like a spiritual father who breaks new ground and does new things. I certainly did that with the Personal Prophecy Group and it has been expanded and my ministry has grown through the other ministries. It's tremendously exciting to know that there is a ministry currently with about 125 prophecy requests waiting on their page to be prophesied over.

That's just one of five groups that I operate in that were spawned by my first obedience to the Holy Spirit to start a prophecy group. It is so exciting to be used. It's exciting to do things and to see God move, use and do the things that He can possibly do because of your obedience. Despite the pornography lingering in my life and of God interpreting dreams for me and saying that it's here to stay for the moment, I have lots of success and happiness in my life.

I certainly was pleased with my idea to start a personal prophecy group. Four or five years ago, I started an online website called Personal-Prophecy-Free.net. Under the search words ‘*personal prophecy*’ or ‘*free personal prophecy*,’ it came up number one on Google. You’ll remember that’s why I started to write all my articles,: to get a personal prophecy group up to number one on Google and I did get to be number one on Google.

I know of about five different ministries that run personal prophecy groups and that are still running today – personal prophecy websites that do personal prophecies via e-mail. I know of about five today, ones that I know of that were people who started with me and were mentored by me. God is into duplicating. He’s into obedient people stepping forward and doing what He tells them to do. Then He can use that, multiply that and make a rich harvest come from the simple steps of a simple man. One just like me.

Chapter 95

First Ministry Trip

I have videos on YouTube that are popular and, at the moment, are watched by3,000-4,000 people on YouTube each month. A couple of years ago, I was contacted by a person whose name was Alan. He contacted me and said that he liked my videos, so he went to a website and got my phone number.

At the beginning of 2012, he rang me and said he'd be interested one time for me to fly to Perth, which was a four to five hour plane flight from New South Wales in Australia to another state. Right across the country just like the East Coast is from the West Coast of America, it's about that far on a plane. He said that he is interested and that he runs a small home group and that he ministers to people in certain locations.

He'd be interested in me coming over and doing a ministry trip. We talked on the phone a few times. We exchanged e-mails and round about August-September 2012, I took a break from the Salvation Army OpShop and went on a one-week or close to two-week ministry trip over to Perth. It was exciting for me because the trip was paid for, return tickets were paid for, my accommodation was paid for, and all the meals were paid for.

I could eat what I wanted. Home meals were cooked for me and takeaway meals were given to me. I was taken on sightseeing trips of the city and got the chance to minister three times whilst I was over there. It was a big thing. I thought that this was an open door and something that God was starting in my life. All my life, as you know from my story, I have always wanted to preach. I thought that this was the beginning of my preaching, travelling, speaking, and doing ministry.

It was all very exciting for me. I remember catching the plane over and watching two movies onboard. I watched an Australian movie called Red Dog and it was an exciting movie about a dog that was a friend of a guy and used to travel in cars and trucks and everything, and they became best friends. It was a really memorable movie. When I got over there, I spent about four days with Alan and we got to know each other.

We talked a lot and spent some time together. He cooked some nice meals and we shared some nice chocolates. Then, I had my first ministry experience at a house and we had a certain number of people come over and I preached a sermon to them. What I didn't realize was that Alan wanted me to prophesy over everyone in the room. So I launched off. I think there were about 11 people in the first room.

I launched and did about a 10-minute prophecy and recorded it on my video camera over each person. If you add up about eleven 10-minute prophecies, it comes to 10-minutes shy of two hours that I spent prophesying. It was a tremendous test for me. I'd never done that before. I felt sort of worn out, but that's what happens when you do a ten-minute prophecy over one person and you record it. Then I had my transcriptionist type the prophecies up and hand it to the people a couple of weeks after their prophecy.

They could have like a five-page written prophecy of their life. So I did everything professionally, but it certainly took a lot out of me. I went to the next meeting and, once again, there were about 10-12 people and they wanted me to preach and prophesy over everyone. I remember when I prophesied over this group, I had two hard words for people.

One of the words I gave a woman was that she continually asked for prophecies and goes from person to person seeking prophecies. She's got all these ideas and plans that she wants to do for God, and yet God keeps on telling her to do certain things and she refuses to do these things. She wants all the good stuff out of life and wants to do all the good things, but she refuses to do the things that God has told her to do more than once. He said to her that, "The good things aren't going to happen until you obey Me, and do what I told you to do."

"You and I both know what those things are that you've been told to do and so you can wait as long as you like, but you're never going to get the good things until you've done the things I've told you that you have to do." She wasn't very impressed with her prophecy, that woman. It's one of the first hard prophecies that I've given before. Then, I had another prophecy for another woman and that was a hard prophecy. I said that she's in a testing time and God is going to test her, put her through a refiner's fire and give her a trial, and refine her like gold.

Although it's inspiring, it's not the sort of prophecy you want because you want good things coming to yourself and you certainly don't want a trial. So, I remember that. I remember the message I gave people that I've preached was a good message, but I didn't record that video. I wish I had recorded it. I would have liked to replay that for myself. So before that happened, I rang my mother.

I said, "Can you pray for me to have the grace to be able to prophesy over the people today? I feel the pressure that they want me to prophesy after I preach." It was a bit of a stress to me. Then the third time, we had about 15 people and I had to prophesy over all of them. This time, they told me they didn't want a sermon, but they just wanted me to prophesy over the people. But this time, I was encouraged because 10 of the people were young girls who had come from abusive situations such as drugs and coming out of foster homes. They were staying at a shelter for girls who had been abused or in serious conditions.

It was like a Christian-run rehabilitation center. A couple of the girls weren't Christians and so it was very exciting to prophesy over ten girls who were in a position of hardship and who really needed a lot of hope in their life. I was really pleased that I was able to record those prophecies on video, have the videos transcribed and given to the girls with their names on the top of the full-page prophecy typed out for them.

It made me happy that I was ministering to them and the girls were very appreciative and very happy. On that ministry trip, I felt sad that they wanted me more for the prophecies than to preach. I think that I had some interesting messages to preach and I think I've got a lot to offer people in sermons.

I don't think I'd like to go and just simply go to a church and prophesy over everyone in there. I think that I just felt that I'd been used and I'd been misrepresented; that they basically flew me over to this state to have me prophesy over everyone. I even had about 10 requests given to me for people who didn't make it to the meetings, and they wanted me to upload prophecies onto YouTube so those people could get prophecies too.

I just felt after all my years of prophecy and my prophesying on a personal prophecy group that I started on Facebook – I just felt that I was used and abused when it comes to doing personal prophecies. I think there's a lot more to life than getting a visiting speaker to come and just prophesy to everyone. Not every prophecy in a person's life comes true. Prophecies only really come true if you do the things that God tells you to do with the prophecies.

You can never become a great Bible teacher or a great teacher of the Word if you don't read your Bible. If you've got no interest in reading books and reading the Bible, you can never become a great preacher or a great teacher of the Word. If the prophecies tell you that you've got to spend more time on the Word and spend time with God; but you don't do that with God, well then, He just has to delay the time that it takes for you to become a preacher because you're not doing the hard yards.

You're not doing the homework that you need to do to become that successful preacher that He wants you to be. A lot of people listen to the prophecies and like all the nice things in the prophecies, but they don't do the things that God tells them to do. Some people run from prophecy to prophecy, but don't really achieve much and some of the prophecies don't really come to reality in their lives.

I felt saddened by the trip. I certainly realized that this is par for the course – this is part and parcel of being a prophet and being known as a prophet. I certainly realized that if I'm going to have to face going from face-to-face and ministering as a prophet, I'll have to spend time prophesying over people. But it was a bit of a shock to me. If I was ever invited back to Perth to prophesy again, I’d be prepared this time and I’d have to be mentally prepared to prophesy over everyone in the building.

I think they wanted me to come to a church with about fifty people and give a prophecy to everyone. Well, fifty people, even if you only do a prophecy for one minute, it’d be 50 minutes. So five minutes each person, it’d be about four or five hours you’d spend prophesying. It takes a lot of emotional and spiritual energy to speak on behalf of God for five hours straight.

A lot of people can’t do one prophecy and let alone speaking on behalf of God. It’s a tremendous responsibility to come before a person and say that God is saying what you’re saying and you’re not making it up yourself. The ministry trip was exciting and I was glad that I went and that God had opened a door and given me an opportunity to be paid for a trip to another state and be looked after and shown around and treated nicely.

Yet, I was saddened by the fact that I’m called to be a prophet and sometimes that will mean that I’ll feel like I’ve been abused.

Chapter 96

Produce the Prophetic Supernatural Experience

As I've shared before, I got the idea first of all to make a series of videos that was going to make up a book on the gift of prophecy and the office of a prophet.

I certainly had come into the office of a prophet three or four years ago. It takes sometimes 10-15 years with the gift of prophecy for God to work in your life and develop you into a position where you can actually take up office and be recognized as a prophet; and not just a person who prophesies.

I was in the office of prophet. I understood the elementary basics of what it took to be a prophet. So I did a series of videos like I discussed before on the gift of prophecy and how the gift of prophecy operates, and what the life of a prophet really entails. It was an exciting book. I was glad to write the book.

I had a friend on Facebook who I knew was also a prophet, and I encouraged her and asked her if she'd like to be a co-writer of the book. I had the book transcribed from video and was getting those transcriptions professionally edited so that they read better and looked better.

I asked her if she could read each of the chapters that I gave her and could she add in her own words, some information about the subject of each chapter, and so she did that. She actually chose a verse to start each chapter with and so we started each chapter with a verse. Then, we had my explanation of the chapter and we had her explanation of the chapter.

It was a well-worked book. It was an exciting book to work on and certainly my videos were only part of the book now. A good half of the book was what Laurie Hicks had produced and, if you're interested in the gift of prophecy and you think that you’d like to minister in the gift of prophecy, it’s a very handy book to read.

If you think that you’re watching or reading this and you feel that you’re called to be a prophet, then the book is a very simple book about the life of a prophet and what the calling entails and what sort of things you can expect to go through in the life that you need to live to become a prophet and minister as a prophet for the Lord.

I was happy with the way that the book came together with my and Laurie’s part, as well as with the way that the book reads. For an essentially a simple person, I think that you can tell by the way I explain myself that I share things that are pretty simple to understand And I share things in a pretty simple way.

I’m not impressed when people write really dry and theological books. I certainly don’t get past the few chapters in a book and sometimes get very disappointed when I come across a book that’s very theological and dry. It’s a waste of money and I haven’t got a lot of money to waste on a book.

I told myself that if I ever wrote a book, I’d write it simply so a simple person could understand. I’m pretty simple myself. If I can understand something even if it’s a complex subject, then I know that I can explain it simply and let other people understand it.

Some people who read my books say that even though my explanations are quite simple, they’re also very deep and profound. That’s a very good compliment and something that makes me really happy to hear feedback from people saying that something I’ve written or produced is deep and profound.

I think it’s a little bit like Jesus when He spoke His parables on earth. He spoke simple stories that even children can basically understand the stories. They’re entertaining stories in the Bible, and they’re very deep, very rich, and very profound. There are many levels through the parables of Jesus and they’re very complex to understand.

The first book I produced was *The Prophetic Supernatural Experience*. It was the first lot of videos I produced, but my friend Phil, who was paying for the first book to be produced, didn't want *The Prophetic Supernatural Experience* to be produced with his money. He wanted the parables book to be produced.

So I produced the *Parables* book and it was a very simple but also rich and profound. It has 28 reviews on Amazon now and people are quite impressed with it. I'm also very impressed with it. It's a best seller for me! It sells very well for me. I'm very happy with it. The second book I produced with Laurie was *The Prophetic Supernatural Experience*. That doesn't sell as well as the parables book, but it's a very good book.

I think Amazon Kindle allows you to make your book free for five days every 90 days and *The Prophetic Supernatural Experience* I think has been downloaded by about a thousand people since December last year. I think maybe it might only be about 700 but that's 700 people who are interested in the gift of prophecy or are interested in becoming a prophet. 700 people who've got a very simple and easy to understand book about the gift of prophecy and the office of prophet.

I've said it a few times before that I like things simple and I've found that the book was a very good book for what it was. When I entered the realm of prophecy, when I started to realize that I had the gift of prophecy in my life, I wanted to learn about the gifts of prophecy. It wasn't very easy for me to find a simple book about the three gifts of prophecy.

I found a bit of information here and a little bit of information there. I had to piece things together from a number of sources. I essentially wrote the book so that I could have a simple book on the gift of prophecy and the office of prophet. There are some good people out there that are very experienced – James Goll is very experienced and there's also a great teacher called Graham Cooke.

They're a lot better writers and they've got a lot better books on the prophetic, but I find even some authors can be a little bit too complex and a little bit too smart. I find that like I've said before, I'm simple. If I can't understand it or if I can't get my head around it, well then, I don't really like it.

Even the people who are a lot more experienced, more mature and have been in the prophetic business longer than me make books that aren't meeting the need of, I believe, what the prophetic supernatural experience is offering.

Chapter 97

Community Treatment Order Lifted by Doctor

When I went off my medication three times in my history of being mentally ill, the doctors enforced upon me an agreement called a Community Treatment Order. I think I've shared that in a previous chapter.

Essentially, the Community Treatment Order said that I had to come in and see the doctor once a month. I had to come in and get an injection once a month for my medication. I had to take my oral medication every day. I had to submit to blood tests to test the levels of the oral medication in my blood. I hate needles so I don't like getting my injection.

I certainly don't like blood tests when you're drawing blood. So this was a traumatic thing for me and something I didn't really like. For a number of years, they kept on doing a six-month review of the Community Treatment Order. My doctor and my case manager would say that they're recommending that the Community Treatment Order be continued. They used to invite me in for an interview with the Magistrate over the phone.

They'd conduct an interview with me and ask my opinion of what I thought. I got to the stage where the last couple of times they invited me to the interview, I told them I wasn't coming. First, there was no use coming to the interview to talk to the Magistrate because they simply believed that I needed the Community Treatment Order. They also didn't trust me, and my word wasn't enough that I wasn't going to go off my medication again.

They could have all the same things enforced without having a piece of paper saying I have to do it. I was obeying it and had been obeying it for a couple of years. I was doing everything they wanted me to do and it was just a piece of paper, forcing me to do these things. I said, "It's no use having a piece of paper, why can't you just trust me?" They wouldn't trust me and they kept on enforcing another legally binding Community Treatment Order every six months.

Essentially, that said that if my blood test showed that I didn't have enough medication in my system, they could put me back in a psych ward. I know that getting locked up in a psychiatric ward is a very traumatic experience. You're locked up with people that are really sick and out of their minds and having bad episodes. It's no fun getting locked up in one and it's certainly not fun having a Community Treatment Order hang over your head.

It's like a sentence over your life. It was certainly not enjoyable to not be trusted by your doctors. It came as a tremendous relief when one of my psychiatrists left and got replaced with another psychiatrist. I had the new psychiatrist for about six months and been seeing a new case manager for about a year. When it came to the next six month Community Treatment Order application, they told me that they weren't going to request another Order.

They were happy with my progress and they're happy with the way things were going, and they weren't going to ask for another Community Treatment Order. The day they told me, I walked out of the psychiatrist's office with such a joy in my step. I think I filled up with tears. I was quite emotional that finally, here I was a psychiatric patient that had gone off his medications three times and couldn't be trusted – finally, I was trusted by my psychiatrist.

I was trusted by my case worker again and they believed that I was going to be trusted to take my medication. I still went in once a month to have my injections and I still saw my psychiatrist once every three months. I still went through all the processes, but there wasn't a legal binding document over my head anymore. I was so happy! It's hard sometimes to suffer with a mental illness.

The depression involved with being a bipolar sufferer is tremendously tormenting and can be really traumatic to a person. I've suffered a lot with the depression. There are certain stages of depression, as you've heard in my story, that gets you into a very suicidal state. A state of being when you don't wish to be and don't want to be alive. You wished you could just die in your dreams, be in heaven and not wake up in the morning.

Depression is just a tremendous suffering. So many people say to someone with depression, "Just get over it," and "Lift your spirits," and "Just smile and be happy!" Yet, they don't understand that it's the same as having cancer or it's the same as having diabetes, or it's the same as any other disease. It's something clinically wrong with the person. It's not that they're having a bad hair day.

It's not that they're feeling particularly sad on certain days and just can't get themselves out of it. There's an actual chemical in the brain that is missing that needs to be replaced by another chemical for them to feel good and for them not to be depressed. Mental illness is a tremendous burden on a person's life. Of course, there's the other part of a bipolar which is the mania – which is the "highs."

The mania can work for you or it can work against you. Some people in mania will spend a whole lot of money. It's not uncommon for me to have my whole pension, my two weekly pension payment, spent within two days and for me to have food in my fridge for the fortnight, and then have $20 in the bank for milk for the fortnight. But all the rest of the money will be spent and sometimes I can spend it on the wrong things. But I just seem to blow my money.

This is a result of mania due to my bipolar disorder. I found recently that I've been spending money on producing books and getting things done that are constructive. But for many people with bipolar, when money becomes available when they're high in mania, they'll spend a whole lot of money and put themselves in positions where they end up mentally ill. Or worse, they end up homeless, or end up with the power getting cut off, or having mobile phones disconnected.

Someone in mania can get a three and a half thousand dollar mobile phone bill just talking to a whole lot of people and building up a bill. Someone bipolar does actions and doesn't have any concept of the consequences of their actions. So they make decisions and do things that are crazy for a sane person to do, and yet they don't have any recourse. They don't have any reaction built into them to stop doing crazy things.

Mania can really wreak havoc on someone with bipolar. Of course, I've got bipolar and I've got schizophrenia. The main part of schizophrenia that affects me is the false antichrist spirit voice that speaks to me and pretends to be Jesus That voice can trip me up and cause me all sorts of grief. I'm getting better at being able to discern that voice, but it still comes to me and still causes me grief from time to time.

It's a good thing that Jesus speaks to me so clearly and He can correct things. Mental illness is a hard cross to carry. Of course, in mania, you can be very creative. In mania, you can stay up for two nights in a row. It's just like you're on an amphetamine or on speed. The longer you stay up – the more creative you get and the more spiritually anointed you get.

You can sit down, turn on the computer and do ten 15-minute videos in a row for hours. I was tremendously happy that the Community Treatment Order was lifted by my doctor. I walked home that day with a real spring in my step knowing that God had seen the way for me to bring myself to a position that I had a good reputation with my doctors.

Chapter 98

Receive Vision for New Website

I had a vision to start a new website. I had *The Parables of Jesus Made Simple* and *The Prophetic Supernatural Experience*. When I wrote *The Parables of Jesus Made Simple*, I made a website with the whole of *The Parables of Jesus Made Simple* on the website where you could read each of the chapters for free.

I had all my contact details; my YouTube address, my Facebook address and my email address, as well as all sorts of things about me so anyone can contact me. The Parables website had links at the bottom of my 800 articles. When someone reads an article, they can see that I wrote, "If you enjoyed the article, how would you like to read any one of the 54 parables of Jesus for free? Read them today on my website." I had a link leading to *The Parables of Jesus* website.

When I had *The Prophetic Supernatural Experience*, I wanted to write another book for free. I got to a stage where I wanted to have a website with both *The Parables of Jesus* and *The Prophetic Supernatural Experience* books for free to read, but I wanted both to be on the same website. In the book, *The Parables of Jesus Made Simple,* there's a link to *The Parables of Jesus* website.

At the bottom of *The Parables of Jesus* website, there's a link to the new ministry website that I made which was the one I had the vision for. I had someone create a WordPress ministry website and put both the books there. I put a link on the bottom of *The Parables of Jesus* website that says, "You want to know more about Matthew, go here."

I will have to get to the stage where I opened up the file for *The Parables of Jesus* book and get the website address that I recommend to be changed to my new ministry website. So people don't have to go to *The Parables of Jesus* website to get a link to my new website. They can actually just go directly to the new website. There we go! I hired a person to design a website with the two books on it for them to be read freely and with links to the pictures of the books to Amazon's so they can buy the books.

If they've read enough chapters and they were happy with my writing, then they could go to Amazon and buy the books. On Amazon, I made my books 99 cents so it was an easy decision to buy. I would have made them 30 cents if Amazon allowed Kindle to have a book for for that amount, but the minimum price you can charge is 99 cents. So I have to have them at 99 cents.

On Kindle, we're allowed to have the book free for five days every 90 days like I've shared before about *The Prophetic Supernatural Experience*. I think from December 2012 until the present, I've had about seven hundred to a thousand people download my *Prophetic Supernatural Experience* book. The good news is that when I first made my *Parables of Jesus* book free on the 26th of December, 2012 like a Christmas present, I actually had 1,850 people download the book for free.

When that happened, I got so excited because I was only selling about 50 copies a month at 99 cents, but in five days, 1,800 people downloaded it. A whole year at 50 is 600, so it was like three years' worth of books all downloaded in five days. I quickly knew I was on to something and couldn't wait until the next period after 90 days so I could make it free again.

I made *The Parables* book free again and only 350 people downloaded it. I was sad and I said, "Well, they must have all downloaded it the first time," but I only did it for two days then. I did it for another two days the next month and 1900 people downloaded it. I was happy. I realized that Kindle had a search engine. It depends where your book came up on a search engine when people were searching for free books.

It depended where on the search engine. If it came up on the first or second page – that determines how many books were downloaded. If your book was on the 20th page of ten books per page and you were the 200th choice of a free book in that category, you might not get many downloads. But if you're on the first or second page and the 20th or the 40th book, you might get a lot more.

I realized that each three months when you make your books for free, it's kind of a lottery whether it's only going to have 300 or 400 people download it or 1800. As I'm speaking now in July 2013, as I record this video – I've had over 6,000 people download my *The Parables of Jesus Made Simple* book. That makes me so excited! I've now got the website. Around December 2012, I was working in the OpShop and I got an idea to write a book.

I got a pad out and started to write the name of the book and to write chapter titles out. A friend of mine came into the store and saw me writing. She did not actually see "chapter one, chapter two and so on," she just saw me writing on a pad and said, "You're going to write a new book, Matthew?" I was so happy that someone else could hear directly off God and God had told her that I was prepping out the chapters for a new book.

I was happy that God had told her that because it means that God wanted me to write the book I was prepping out and preparing the chapter titles for. I wrote all the chapter titles out as I serve customers that day. Then got the pad out again and re-wrote the chapter titles and ended up with 113 chapter titles. I think as I've gone through the book, I've combined different chapters together into one.

I think the book is going to end up about a hundred and five chapters that I'm going to finish tonight. This video and the rest of the book will all be done by then. It's a tremendous thing to have a website online where you've got your book for free. It's a tremendous thing to have your books for free on Kindle five days every three months and have thousands of people download your books.

Chapter 99

Produce His Redeeming Love Part 1

I got the ideas for the chapters of *His Redeeming Love* and I started to record *His Redeeming Love*, Chapter One. Around the same time I started to record the chapters of *His Redeeming Love*, I got an idea to do a book on *Prophetic Evangelism Made Simple*.

It was going to be a book about how to go and witness to strangers on the streets by using the gift of prophecy. Essentially, that’s just walking up to a person and saying, “Excuse me, I have a gift and from time to time that gift allows me to get a message for a person and today I’ve got a message for you.” Then, I’d launch into a specific message about who they are as a person and what stage they were in their life, and something God wanted them to know.

It always takes people by surprise and really blesses them. In my life, I’ve done about 7,000 prophecies like that in the last 10 years. I have gotten good at it. I had the idea to record videos to write *Prophetic Evangelism Made Simple*. There’s another book online called *Prophetic Evangelism* by Mark Stibbe and it is a very good book.

I’ve read the book twice and thoroughly recommend it to everyone who would like to witness with the gift of prophecy. But I decided and God decided that the world could do with another book on prophetic evangelism. So I started to record that book the same as my *His Redeeming Love* book. I used to do five chapters of one and then five chapters of the next, and five chapters of one and five chapters of the next.

It was around December 2012 when all this was happening, I was told that I was volunteering for too many hours and they also had an issue with me being in the shop talking to people too much and wanting to interact with people too much. They wanted to limit my hours in the shop and they said they had a new job for me downstairs. I got a bit upset with the fact that they thought I was talking too much.

I love to talk and I am a people person. Reading this book and seeing how many pages there are of Part 1 and Part 2, you'll see that I don't mind talking and I don't mind sharing things. I was a bit disheartened that I was told that I was talking too much. But anyway, I was yet to find out the new job they had for me.

I had new pastors who had been pastors of the church for the year and their names were Mitchell and Robyn. Both Mitchell and Robyn became my good friends. When I got downstairs the next day, they told me about the new job. They said that they had arranged with head office for me to do a coffee station where I would serve coffee, tea and hot chocolate to the people that come into our community center.

People who are homeless and disadvantaged come into our center for welfare assistance and a shower. Homeless people get cheap meals for lunch for two dollars. They're all just disadvantaged people. They said they want me as many days of a week as I can to serve hot chocolate, coffee and tea in the afternoons. I decided that I wanted to spend some time making my videos for my two books.

I told them that I will work three days a week rather than five and have four days a week off and they agreed to that. The next week, I started to serve coffees. They have a blackboard at the front of the coffee station and they have written, "Chat with Matt." That's what it was called and everybody had seen the sign with a "Free coffee, tea and chocolate" written there. A lot of strangers came up to me and would say, "Are you, Matt?"

I said "Yes," and they would get a coffee. About 10% of the people would stay and just stand there and chat. I had the ability to talk to broken-hearted people about their lives and serve them coffee and just chat with them. I used to enjoy talking to strangers in my taxi. You will understand if you have read my book, *His Redeeming Love*

– *Part 1*, you'll realize that I really enjoyed talking to people and talking to strangers.

I enjoyed chatting with people and a lot of the people in our community center come back every day or a number of times per week. As I serve them coffee, each of them stands there and talk to me and I developed good relationships with these people. It gives me a tremendous opportunity to minister in God's love and compassion to everybody. It got me emotional. I shared in a previous chapter when I got my Community Treatment Order lifted that I walked home in tears.

I think I've been emotional a number of times as I've thought about the job that Robyn decided that she would create for me. The Matthew that they had in the shop who was talking too much, they decided that 'Matthew could never talk too much serving coffee to homeless people and as long as they wanted to chat and stay there at the coffee station, he could chat to them all day long.' I was so happy that Robyn decided to create a job just for me.

I was so emotional. I'm emotional, even as I share this. I lost my taxi license and wasn't able to drive taxis again because of an act of indecency that happened to the girl at Tamworth. I wasn't able to have a taxi license. I thought I'd never find a job that was as satisfying as driving a taxi, talking to strangers and talking to people. I found that 'Chat with Matt' was the second best job that I'd ever done in my life.

It's amazing! If you ever go to my website, you'll find that Mitchell, my pastor, has got a reference there, an endorsement for me as a person. He writes from the heart about me and says some nice things about me. Mitchell and Robyn have been tremendous pastors. I shared once before when I was talking about Sarah, that it is all very well to know, talk to and have visions of in heaven.

But Jesus is up in heaven and when He comes, He looks like a ghost and you can't fully interact with him like a human. It is good to have a human Jesus. It's good to have a human touchstone where you can just touch God Himself. Mitchell to me has become a human Jesus.

You know, when I’m struggling with porn and I told Mitchell about it, there was no condemnation from him. There was no judging me. There was just, “How can I help you with this?” He wanted me to become accountable to him and tell him how I was coping with it. At one time, I took the computer that I access porn with to his office. I’ve got two laptops. I wouldn’t access porn on my Apple because I don’t want to destroy the program with viruses. That means I would never access porn on my Apple.

I took my PC in there and he had it for six weeks. I didn’t view any porn because the computer I use to view it on was in his office, but I needed Microsoft Word and I needed my PC to process my books and do my editing. I couldn’t do them at the community center. I got my PC back and porn started again, but Mitchell just loves me.

I could tell him that I went to see a girl and had a dirty massage where they perform masturbation at the end of the massage. I could tell him clearly that’s what I had done the day before and his reaction wouldn’t be a judgment. It would be a hug. If my eyes filled up with tears, with the shame and the guilt for doing it, his own eyes would fill up with tears.

When Mitchell preaches, he doesn’t look at me because when he’s preaching, my eyes often fill up with tears. He knows if he looks at me and sees the tears in my eyes, he’ll start to tear up and it’ll affect his preaching. He doesn’t want to be crying when he’s preaching. Mitchell is a tremendous friend and one who simply just didn’t have the time to write the foreword for this book. I pray that he’ll be able to write a foreword for me in another book one time, but I encourage you to visit my website and read his endorsement. At least, you’ll see something he’s written.

So I started to produce *His Redeeming Love*. I started to produce *Prophetic Evangelism Made Simple* and I started to serve coffee with my own ‘Chat with Matt’ in December 2012.

Chapter 100

Publish His Redeeming Love Part 1

It took about seven months of uploading videos and having each of the videos transcribed. Then, I have to check and edit each of the videos that I transcribed. I also sent them to a professional editor. The copy editor would rewrite and polish all my words, and convert it from what sounded like speaking in a video in what looked like writing on a book. He did a very professional job. Then it will come back to me and I will read it and edit it. Then, I sent it to a proofreader and he spent 10 hours proofreading at $170 all up. Then, I arranged to have friends on Facebook, five friends so far, to write a review for me. I sent a pre-advanced copy of the book as it was getting proofread off to them. When I published it last night, I wrote to the people who made reviews for me and asked them if they could post their reviews on Amazon.

I'm happy to announce that *His Redeeming Love* has been published today. I didn't realize that *His Redeeming Love Part 2* would have its videos finished tonight. The process of having the videos typed up, paying for the editor at $17 an hour to edit each of the video transcripts, and the process of paying a proofreader cost a lot of money.

There's at least $600 left that I have to pay. Then I have to pay another $350 to get it typeset and get a cover designed. It's a hard process to get book two done. When I get book two done for all the people who had downloaded book one for free or for 99 cents, they'll be able to download book two.

I'm very excited tonight to be sitting here recording the videos that will make up the chapters that are the conclusion of my life story up until now.

I have five reviews so far and there should be more reviews by the time you buy this book on Amazon. The five reviews I have on *His Redeeming Love Part 1* are very good. I couldn't have written better reviews for myself. They all seem to say that I was very transparent, very candid, very honest, and very revealing in this life story about myself.

This is a very exciting time. There's nothing like being a writer and publishing a book. It comes with tremendous happiness to publish a book. At present, a book proof-copy is getting printed up and within two weeks, I'll have my first copy of *His Redeeming Love Part 1* as an actual book.

I've got a friend at my church called Ibby who used to be a Muslim and got converted to Christianity. When I got *The Prophetic Supernatural Experience*, I gave him the proof-copy that the publisher sent to me. I gave him the one and only proof-copy of the book. Part of the publishing process is that they send you a proof-copy of your book. You go through the book and see if there are any errors.

Then you come back to them and tell them what errors are in the book and then, they re-print the book. They don't print up another proof. They just print the book from that point on when you've pointed out the errors. I've gone through the book myself twice. I've had a professional editor and proofreader check the book.

I was very comfortable to just press Publish and let him send the proof, but I already have the book published on Amazon. Publishing a book is very time-consuming and somewhat a complicated process to be able to come up with the concept of the book, design chapter titles, write each of the chapters or record videos, get them transcribed, get them edited, get them proofread, and to arrange with people to write reviews for your book.

To finish the whole publishing process is a long process and it tests your patience. It's a hard process to do. It's very rewarding to be at this stage where your book is online and you've got five favorable reviews. At present, I'm waiting for two days for Kindle to have my book on their system, and for Amazon to link my published print copy of the book and the Kindle book on the same page.

You will have an option to buy my book for $9.40 or to buy the Kindle edition of *His Redeeming Love Part 1* for 99 cents when it's all linked up and the reviews are on the same page. Regardless of whether you see the Kindle book or the printed book, the same reviews will appear on both pages when all are linked up.

I'll be a very happy Chap as you can tell once you read the book. Let me assure you that tonight, as I record the videos on my second night up in a row – I'm very excited and very happy, and in very good spirits. Part of being a writer is the exceptional happiness of having your book in print. When I receive the proof-copy, I'll spend some time looking at it and savoring it.

Then, I'll take it to the church on a Friday night and give it to Ibby and sign the copy. Ibby will have two out of my three books, signed editions of the only proof-copy in the world of the books. One day, if I'm ever a famous author, international world-recognized speaker, traveler and writer, he will have the only proof-copies of my book signed and autographed by me.

He'll have something worth a whole lot of money. I'm just dreaming here, but we all are allowed to dream.

Chapter 101

Write Kingdom Nuggets Book

I've been preparing *His Redeeming Love*, going through the process of having it professionally edited from the videos. Then, having it proofread. Then, reading it and arranging for the cover to be produced and for it to be typeset by CreateSpace and then the publisher. Then, arranging for the cover to be fitted to the typeset manuscript and all the process for it to be uploaded and published, and made into a book that's available on Amazon.

It takes a couple of months for me to go through all that process. In the last couple of months, I've been writing a book of devotionals called *Kingdom Nuggets*. I sat down about six weeks ago and fleshed out another book of ten major subjects. I fleshed out each of the ten major subjects into about 15 sub-subjects on each of those subjects' titles.

I had 150 or so chapter headings. Then, I started to write a series called *Kingdom Nuggets* which were just little nuggets of wisdom about the Kingdom of God. I got to the sixth heading out of the ten. I decided that at the end of the sixth topic, I was going to end my book on *Kingdom Nuggets* and make the first edition.

I realize that there are a lot of essential basic things I can talk about on the Kingdom of God. I've got the other four subjects that I haven't covered till ten. I can add a couple of subjects and have a *Kingdom Nuggets* book one and *Kingdom Nuggets* book two. I've been posting them on Facebook. I've created a Facebook group called *Kingdom Nuggets* and invited a whole lot of my friends to the group, and posted the kingdom nuggets in there.

I've been having some tremendous feedback from some of my friends on Facebook saying they really enjoy the *Kingdom Nuggets* and I've had some good discussions about some of them. People post on Facebook what they think of it, and they like and comment on what my posts are saying. So tonight is also a celebration.

I think I've got about eight kingdom nuggets to write and finish, but I think I've got to finish with three. I'm going to pick the best three and write three more kingdom nuggets. By the time I've uploaded all these videos, which will finish this book, I will have finished the transcript for the *Kingdom Nuggets*.

At present, I have someone who's editing and proofreading the *Kingdom Nuggets*. They're working on two-thirds of it. Then, by the time morning comes around in seven hours, I will have sent off my file with the last third for editing.

Through a freelance website called oDesk.com, I have a freelance editor who I've hired to proofread the *Kingdom Nuggets*. Once the person is done editing my *Kingdom Nuggets* and has gone through it with a fine-toothed comb, I'll send all her work off to this other editor and I will have this editor run through it and proofread it again.

It's been double-checked and free of all error and the *Kingdom Nuggets* book will be ready. Yesterday, I published *His Redeeming Love Book One*. Today, I've got the five reviews put on Amazon, and next week I am going to make *His Redeeming Love Book One* free on Kindle.

I'm going to offer some of my friends on Facebook that if they download *His Redeeming Love Book One* for free on Kindle and they write a review and post it on Amazon, I'm going to send them a free autographed book of *His Redeeming Love Book One*. I will autograph it as a reward – as a way of saying thanks for writing a review.

I hope that I can gather another five or ten reviews of *His Redeeming Love Book One* by doing that. By the time you read this, it will be *His Redeeming Love Book Two* or this will be the completed book. By that time, you'll have probably read some of the reviews that have helped you make the decision to buy this book.

In the process of going through things, I hired a graphic artist who did *The Parables of Jesus Made Simple* book cover which I really love. I've hired her again as a freelance graphic artist from oDesk.com. I had her design the two covers for *Prophetic Evangelism Made Simple* and for *Kingdom Nuggets*. She has done a tremendous job on both covers.

I've got the covers ready. *Prophetic Evangelism Made Simple* has been edited and been professionally proofread, and now has a cover ready. All I'm waiting for is $350 for the book to be typeset and then have the cover fitted to it. *Kingdom Nuggets* will be written tonight when I will finish the last three chapters.

It will be sent off to the editor to edit the last third of it. Then, it will go through the process of going to the proofreader to proofread *Kingdom Nuggets* a second time. Then, the $350 will be paid for the typesetter and it will be typeset. Then, the cover will be fitted to it and it will be published.

Prophetic Evangelism Made Simple will be published and then I'll be in the process of getting *His Redeeming Love Book Two* transcribed, edited, proofread, typeset and then uploaded. So *His Redeeming Love Book Two* will come right at the end, but before the book can be made, I will have to save about $600 every fortnight and spend that amount to get it edited.

The total process of doing all of that is about $1500 and it will take me about 20 weeks to do all of it. It takes three to four months before all that can be done with my budget. I just thought I'd share all that to say that it's a very enjoyable life that I'm living and as you can see, I'm very busy. As you can read, I'm very happy. I'm living a successful, happy and an enjoyable life at the moment.

Chapter 102

Still Struggle with Pornography

As I've mentioned in former chapters, my life is tremendously exciting at the moment and I'm in the process of having three books produced – *Kingdom Nuggets, Prophetic Evangelism Made Simple* and *His Redeeming Love Part Two.*

I'm in the process of having all those books produced and go through the project line like a conveyer belt, and the money be spent for them to be all produced, available for sale and for free download. Even though all of this is happening, Satan has still got a little bit of a hold in my life when it comes to pornography.

I know that I can easily solve the pornography problem by installing Microsoft Word on my Apple computer. If I do that, then perhaps I could do all my processing and writing on my Apple computer. It's just that Apple is really hard for me to understand and I don't understand downloading and a whole lot of things on Apple. It's hard to use. So I have this problem.

I want to share with you guys that I'm moving in ministry, in the prophetic – even witnessing to people on the streets every week. I see 10-20 people every week and share a message from Jesus with. I'm producing three books at the moment and I'll have a total of six books when I'm finished. I seem to be really successful. I've got a ministry with a website that gets about a thousand or more visitors a month.

Six thousand people are reading my articles per month, four thousand are watching my YouTube videos per month, and over six thousand have read my Parables book so far since December last year and in the last six months. Even though I'm having all this success, I still have a struggle in my life. What I want to share with you is that this struggle really gets me down and there's a lot of shame and guilt, and condemnation that is involved in this struggle.

I was talking to a pastor of the church tonight that I met for the first time. He said God has already forgiven me and Jesus forgave me on the cross for all my sins, and I've got to learn to forgive myself. He told me that we are commanded to love God with all our hearts and to love others as we love ourselves. He said, "How can you love others if you don't love yourself? The first step to loving yourself is forgiving yourself."

"You need to obey God, love yourself and forgive yourself. If God can forgive you, who are you to disobey and not forgive yourself?" That was tremendously refreshing for me to hear. I walk around in shame and guilt so much. I think of those dreams that were interpreted that said lust has still got a hold on my life. And even though intercessors are praying, it still has a strong hold in my life.

I know if God wanted lust to be gone, those dream interpretations wouldn't have come out like they did. I would have had a dream that said I'm finally free of this lust. I had a prophecy come to me last week, which said that I'm in the waves and I'm in the boat with Jesus, and I'm not to look at the waves of the storm but focus on Jesus.

Like Peter walking on the waves when his focus was on Jesus, the waves didn't worry him. But when I look at the waves of circumstance and distress, I get carried away and sink. The prophecy was saying essentially that the waves are placed there by the enemy, and I'm not to concentrate on what the enemy is doing in my life but to concentrate on Jesus. Essentially, the message of the Bible is that 'We're saved by grace through faith, not by works. Lest no man can boast.'

We all know that scripture verse, but how many of us live it? See, the answer to my addiction isn't trying harder. The answer could be found by putting my computer away and installing Microsoft Word to my Apple computer. If I can't conquer it in the next six months, perhaps that's what I might do. Apple's just so hard and so complicated to use. I only use my Apple computer to play my iTune music and to record videos on.

But if that's what it takes then, within three to six months, that's what I might do and learn to use Microsoft Word on my Apple computer. But we don't achieve things through works – we achieve things through faith in Jesus and through His grace. It's not until we reach a stage where we come to the end of ourselves that we're truly ready to be set free by Jesus. If we could save ourselves from our own sins, if we could redeem ourselves, then Jesus wouldn't have had to die.

It's only through the death of Jesus Christ that we have the freedom to be forgiven. It's only through the death and resurrection of Jesus Christ that we come into a place where Jesus can give us the grace and the power to overcome through the anointing of the Holy Spirit. So it's with my focus on Jesus, my focus on the supernatural, and it's by me giving up my striving not to sin that I reach freedom. And I have reached freedom.

I have reached freedom for six months before I went on my ministry trip. I reached freedom for six weeks when I gave my computer to Mitch. I reached freedom recently for six weeks when I had my computer at home, when I could actually sin but I conquered it! I got up in church and said to the church that I had finally conquered a sin I have had in my life for 35 years. The church applauded and was happy. The next day, I fell into sin and the addiction was back.

I want you to know that I'm not afraid to finish a book or have one of the last chapters of my book saying that I'm still suffering in sin. There are statistics out there that say up to 50% of Christian males are addicted to pornography. There are statistics that are published that say 30% of pastors have viewed pornography in the last month. There are statistics that say 20% of Christian women have a problem with pornography.

There are statistics that say 48% of Christian marriages have been reported to be affected by the effects of pornography in the male or female's life in the marriage. All of these statistics are statistics that I've read. I do not have the sources for them, but you can easily look up the sources and quote the website addresses. I'm the sort of person who hears something and doesn't need evidence to hear it.

All of my testimony has been my testimony. All of my biography has been my story. Whether you choose to believe that I've been on a ferry and met Mary Magdalene and have her fly through the air like Superman – that's your choice to believe it. I was there on a ferry and I saw Mary Magdalene flying through the air like Superman. Some of you might think to yourself, "Matthew's just making these statistics up about pornography."

I don't need to make anything up. I think I've been extreme enough. I think I've been candid enough. I think I've been honest enough – to be able to earn the right by the end of this book to be respected for someone who tells the truth. Although I do not have the statistics on a page in front of me, I certainly know that this is a problem. Now, if 50% of Christian males have a problem with an addiction to porn...

That means 50% of the males reading this book currently have an issue with pornography. The only answer to the solution of pornography is resting in the grace of Jesus Christ and moving in the grace. The only way through the addiction is supernatural healing – a supernatural revision from God through His grace.

There are also underlying problems that may have happened in a person's life. Many times, a person has a root of rejection in their life and these underlying roots need to be addressed in healing. It has to be addressed in counseling because it's no use treating a big injury and putting just a Band-Aid on it. Proper medicine and proper bandages have to be used on a proper injury. If you just put a Band-Aid or a sticky plaster on a serious injury, you'll get an infection. It will rot and it will just bust. All the blood will flow out and it will just flow over the seams.

Pornography is simply a Band-Aid or a simple solution to an underlying problem that's in a person's life. For many years, I've sought counselors and been meeting with counselors, but God has still chosen not to open up a counselor for me to get the final ends of my pain dealt with so that I can conquer pornography. I'm very close to conquering it. I've had success, but I still have shame and guilt when I fall into it.

I want you to know and to be encouraged that I am having success and I am happy. I think there's a lot of attacks in my life because I'm producing three books at the moment and I'm going to do damage to Satan's kingdom with this book. So if you have a problem with pornography, please recognize that you have a problem. Please recognize that you can't do it by yourself – that you've got to come before God and walk in His grace and His enabling power.

God bless you in your struggles and if you have that problem, feel free to contact me and have me pray for you.

Chapter 103

Visions of My Mansion in Heaven

If you are struggling with the sin of pornography – you will constantly be assailed by the thought that you're committing fornication and you're committing a sin that can't be forgiven; that you're committing some form of spiritual adultery.

Your thoughts will depend on your upbringing, on whether you believe in the New Covenant grace doctrine or you're brought up in a legalistic sort of judgmental God. Depending on what you believe, you may believe that you're going to hell. You may believe that as a Christian, you will go to hell if you don't get on top of your pornography addiction.

I've been fortunate recently for God to start to convince me that I'm not going to hell. How Jesus has done that in my life is He's given me prophecies in the past saying that He loves me with an everlasting love. An everlasting love is a love that lasts for forever. Where it said in John 3:16 that, "For God so loved the world that He gave His only Son. Whoever believeth in Him shall have everlasting life."

Everlasting life means eternal life and life that lasts forever on earth and in heaven. When Jesus says He loves you or God says He loves you with an everlasting love, that means that He's going to love you all the way through earth and He's going to love you all the way to heaven. It's comforting to know that you're loved and you're going to go to heaven.

About a year ago, I was in bed talking to Jesus and I suddenly ended up having a vision in my mind, in my mind's eye where you see a memory. Or where you remember a movie and you see the movie in your mind's eye. I saw myself on a back deck of a house and Jesus was having a drink with me, and we're in heaven. Jesus said this was the back deck of my house. It was overlooking a sea or a lake in heaven.

There was a wharf on the lake and there was a nice breeze blowing. It seemed like dusk. It didn't seem light, but it may have been dark because of the fact that it was night time for me. Anyway, I got the word in my mind that we're drinking a Pina Colada and at that time, I didn't know what a Pina Colada was. Later, I found that it was Malibu rum and pineapple juice. But when Jesus said I was drinking a Pina Colada, I could taste pineapple juice in my mouth.

I could taste pineapple juice even though I wasn't physically in heaven drinking pineapple juice in my body. In my mind, I was drinking it and having sips of it, and it manifested in my body so I could taste the pineapple in my mouth. That was the first trip to heaven, but over the last three weeks, Jesus has been taking me to heaven and showing me my mansion. The first time I went into my house besides the back deck.

I went into my house and right up the sides of the walls and into each of the rooms, there were fish aquariums. Fish were swimming through all the walls in these glass aquariums from room to room. I noticed when I went into a room with Jesus, the fish would follow. That was very exciting for me. I found out I had a pool outside in the backyard. The fish swam from the pool, in through the aquariums into the house.

I could go for a swim in the pool and swim with the fish that were in my house. It was very exciting. The next time I went on a trip to heaven, I saw the cat that I had when I was a small boy. This was the same one that I mentioned in *Redeeming Love Part One*, that I lost my cat and became a Christian because I missed it. It was in the house and the cat spoke to me and prophesied that my roommate at the time was going to move out, but there will be no problems with my roommate moving out.

One of the fish in the aquariums spoke to me and said everything's going to work and life is going to start getting exciting for me. Both of the animals spoke to me, spirit-to-spirit. The third time I went to my mansion in heaven, I saw a picture in the lounge room downstairs and it was a picture of a lion and a lamb. It was about nine feet by six feet. As I looked at the picture, the lion and the lamb came alive.

I was told by Jesus that if I walked into the picture, I could go to the park where all the abortions lived – which I mentioned in my other visions. It was a portal. The picture would come alive, but if I walked amongst the lion and the lamb, it would take me automatically to where the abortions lived. I know the future in heaven when I lived there. The abortions may not be in the park anymore, but it can still take me to a place where there are young children that live.

There's another picture in my lounge room of the woman washing Jesus' feet with her tears. As I looked at that picture, it came alive and I could smell the perfume. The smell filled the lounge room. Jesus told me when I looked at that picture that it was a portal to that woman's house. If I walk through that picture, I will end up there. I firmly believe the woman who washed the feet of Jesus with her tears was Mary Magdalene.

That was her act of repentance. I believe that even that interaction may have been the time that Jesus casts the seven demons out of her simply by saying her sins were forgiven. I can't prove that it was Mary Magdalene. I just think that it is a portal to her house. I always ask Jesus, when I was in heaven, if I could visit Mary Magdalene often and have coffee with her. Even if it is not a portal, certainly the woman in that Bible story has always encouraged me and I still would like to hang out with her.

I was taken to the second level of my house on another visit. I was shown a 25-meter heated pool in the house. That was tremendous and I was starting to realize that it was a big house. It wasn't just a house. It was a mansion. At the end of the pool, there was a coffee shop with tables and chairs that sits about 50 people.

The tables and chairs spilled out onto a deck on the second floor. The deck looked out onto the ocean or the lake and it is built with exposed beams and polished wood. So people would be served coffee. I've been told by Jesus that in heaven I was going to be a teacher of the Word, a writer and I was going to serve in a coffee shop like my 'Chat with Matt' down here on earth. I believe I might be serving in the coffee shop in my house, but there might also be one in the city that I'll serve in where I can chat with and communicate with people.

I went further in the house that day and there was a library. It's a library of all the books I've ever read. I've read a lot of books in my life. I'm sure by the time I get to heaven, there will be a lot of books in that library. I went further in the house and there was an office where I wrote all my books and I managed. I had secretaries and people working with me, producing my books, videos and all sorts of teaching aids that I was using in heaven to teach the people in heaven the things of God.

I went further and there was a picture theater that seats a hundred people and it had benches so you could serve food. We've got picture theaters here on earth where you can go. There are luxury picture theaters where you can get alcoholic drinks served to you and hot chips and salads, and all sorts of sandwiches and stuff. It's fully catered and you can have a meal there while you're watching a film.
This is one of those full-service picture theaters. In there, I was told that I was going to be watching films that I enjoyed, but with actors in heaven that have acted in the films and people I know in heaven acting in the star roles of the film. You can have 10 versions of the film with different people acting in the role of the lead character and it's the same film but with different actors.

You can watch the film ten different times and enjoy different people's take on the character. I was told also that some of the films in heaven were films that I had written and had people acting. Currently, I've already written two screenplays that have been shot and acted in heaven, have scores, and were professionally made in heaven. These are two films I wrote earlier in my life.

One was based on my book, *The Fallen Ones* and the other was based on my book, *The Chosen Ones*. Both films were successful. That's all I've seen of my mansion in heaven. I've actually seen more on the back where there's a dock and a boat that which has eight berths in it. There are eight bedrooms where you could let eight people sleep on the boat.

It has a fully functional kitchen and everything needed in the boat. It's a very big cruiser. We go out onto the sea or lake and take a cruise. Around the front of the house was a long table that sits about 60 people. I had seen that table in a film with an extended Italian family and had always thought, "Gee, I wish I knew enough people that I could sit down at a table like that and have a meal with all my friends and family there."

The kitchen downstairs is a fully commercial kitchen. It's a center-console kitchen with all the bench space in the middle and all the implements, ovens and everything on the outside. There's a walk-in cool room with all sorts of meats in it already cooked, ready and prepared. Apparently, I've been told by Kat Kerr that they don't kill animals in heaven to provide the meat, but meat is made out of pure light.

They just produce meat in any flavor that you used to like on earth to eat in heaven. That's a bit of an example of my mansion in heaven. I've seen two stories of the three-story mansion. I haven't seen the third story of my house so far, but it is exciting to know over the ten visits I've had that I definitely have a mansion in heaven and all those things.

It excites me to know things like being a writer, having my films produced, having books I've written, books I've read, having a coffee shop, serving in a coffee shop in heaven, being a teacher, having an office with staff to produce all my teachings in heaven. Knowing that I've got a whole life ready in heaven means that I'm going to conquer pornography. It simply isn't going to take me to hell – if I die tonight, I will go to heaven.

You as a reader, if you're saved and you're a born again Christian, you have to believe that no matter what sin you're in, if you're truly sorry and upset about being in that sin, God's going to take you to heaven. Jesus' blood was sufficient for everyone to be forgiven and washed clean and pure in God's sight. I pray that this has encouraged you and my vision of my mansion in heaven has blessed you.
If you become a friend of mine on Facebook, perhaps you can see an update of my mansion in heaven in the future.

Chapter 104

The Keys to Happiness

If I was to share what is the overarching message of this book – what is it that I'm here to share with you? What's the message that I want to leave you with as we finish this last chapter of the book? I want to say that true happiness is built on a number of things.

First of all, you have to know that you're created by a God. You have to know that God the Creator has a son called Jesus Christ. His son came to earth. He died and bled for you on a cross and His death provided the solution for your sins to be forgiven. If you don't believe that your sins are truly forgiven by Jesus –if you believe that you're going to be punished for your sins, even if you're a Christian, this doesn't lead to happiness but to a lot of torment.

You have to understand that there's a God. That He provided a way for you to live in freedom through His Son, Jesus Christ. You have to get to know Jesus Christ. You have to understand the message of grace and that everything is finished. When Jesus said on the cross, "It is finished," truly everything was done to bring you into the kingdom of God and into a life of happiness and freedom.

One of the major things in life is to have people to love. I know many people reading this book might live a life like me. You might have people that you see at work, if you go to work. You might have people that you see at church, if you go to church. But you might not have many people who truly are your friends when you go to these places. I'm fortunate that at Streetlevel Church, I have people who love me.

When I go to church, I can go from conversation to conversation after church and be loved. When church finishes, we can go out for coffee or a meal. There are people to go out with and people to talk to. But when I come home for four days, if I didn't visit other churches, I will be alone. I know all about being alone. This is why Facebook is such a good place.

I'll introduce you to friends on Facebook if you want some friends to talk with online. Facebook is a good medium, but one of the keys to happiness is to have people to love. If you do not have people to love and people who love you, then you can be sad. I'm pleased that I have some people like Mitchell and Robbin in my life. I have Sarah. I have Ibby. I have friends who love and appreciate me like David and Judy on Facebook, and other Facebook friends.

This leads me to a life of happiness. I know Jesus died for my sins. I know God. I know Jesus personally. I've met Him many, many times. I have people who love me so I have people to love. The third building block that's a very important key to happiness in life is to know your purpose in life.

If you're living a life and you have no idea why you were born or what your purpose is in life, then you have no idea what is the meaning for your life. This can stop and rob you of happiness while you live on earth. There's a teacher called Andrew Wommack and when he preaches on God's purpose for your life, he tells people to put up their hands if they don't know their life's purpose.

He says without fail whenever he preaches that message in a church, 80% of the people in the audience put up their hands to say that they don't know their purpose in life. He invites them to the front and prays a prayer that God will reveal to them what their purpose in life is. Not everyone who's a Christian or born into God's family has the ability to be an apostle, prophet, evangelist, pastor or teacher. They're called the Fivefold Ministry.

Not everyone who's a Christian will have a job ministering full-time in a position in the church. If you're not ministering in a position in the church – what can you do for God? Well, God gifted everybody with certain gifts on earth. There are certain things that if you could do it and get paid for it, you would be so happy. What can you do that will bring you so much joy?

That's what you should be concentrating your time on. That's what you should be putting your effort into. That's what will truly make you shine. If you're happy with painting, paint; if it's fixing people's computers, you fix people's computers; if it's doing stage lighting for plays, you do stage lighting for plays; if its acting, then act; if you're a writer, you write screen plays or you write books.

Whatever it is that you're gifted in, it is what you're meant to do. You're not meant to work in a nine-to-five job and be bored and not fulfilled. You're meant to be doing that thing that turns you on. If you won the lottery, if you won $20 million dollars in the lottery and you had to fill in your time – what is it that you would do to fill in your time when money is not a problem? That's what you should focus your time on.

It's what God gave you as a gift and a natural ability in. That's your purpose in life. You're meant to do it to the best of your abilities and shine brightly for Jesus and bring Jesus glory. You know the more you do it, the more successful you are at it. The more of a witness you are to Jesus. Jesus needs people to serve coffee. Jesus needs people to clean trains. Jesus needs people to be a florist. Jesus needs dressmakers.

Jesus needs fashion designers and graphic artists. Jesus needs editors, copywriters, and proofreaders. Jesus needs transcribers. Jesus needs all sorts of people involved just in the publishing process that I've talked about. Now, I've got a gift of encouragement. My gift allows me to prophesy to people. It also allows me to see good things in people and always encourage them.

When I move in the gift of encouragement, it encourages people, but it also makes me happy. I have the gifts of prophecy. When I prophesy, it makes people happy. It also makes me happy to be able to bless people. I have a gift for writing. Even though some of my books are made from videos, my *Kingdom Nuggets* is proof that I can write a book. When I wrote screen plays and two novels, I sat down and typed them and I didn't make them on video. I wrote them.

I wrote for the movies. I'm a gifted writer. I'm not a gifted singer. I'm not gifted at typing very fast. There are a lot of things I'm not gifted at, but you need to do the things that you're gifted at. You need to pray to Jesus to show you what your purpose in life is.

Essentially, you need to know Jesus, your Creator. You need to have a personal relationship with Him. You need to be able to talk to Him and hear Him talking back.

You need people in your life who you can love and who can love you. If you're unlovable, find other people who are unlovable and make friends with them. You need to know your purpose in life and to be it. I hope that this book has encouraged and inspired you to become a better person. This is my life so far. I'm 46-years of age. I believe *His Redeeming Love Part One* and *His Redeeming Love Part Two* will be published by the end of 2013 at the latest.

I'm only 46-years of age. My grandmother lived till age 96. I believe I have at least 40 years left to live. I have a lot of things to live for. I'm sure that there are many more books and many more things I'm going to do in the next 40 years. I pray that you have the courage to send me a friend request on Facebook and become my friend. I pray that you find my Author Page on Facebook, Author Matthew Robert Payne.

If you 'Like' that page, you can be always updated on when my books are free. I pray that you enjoy my ministry website which is at http://www.matthewrobertpayneministries.net.

I pray that if this book has blessed you, I pray that you can take five minutes out and write a candid and honest review of this book. I pray that you can get copies of this book for your friends. I pray that you can encourage your friends to buy this book.

I pray that you can post a link of this book on your Facebook page and recommend it to all your friends. I pray that you're blessed. I pray that you get in touch with me, write to me, and tell me how I've blessed you. I pray that you become everything that God designed you to be.

Update on my life as of October 2014

As you can see, I missed my goal of publishing part 2 by December 2013. A lot of this has been due to the money it costs to produce books and the massive editing costs. I have written a number of books in the past year. It looks like when this book is ready to be published, my books will be in order of when they were published:

The Musings of a Mad Prophet
The Parables of Jesus Made Simple
The Prophetic Supernatural Experience
Your Identity in Christ
Prophetic Evangelism Made Simple
Kingdom Nuggets
His Redeeming Love

The books coming out over the next year will also include:
Living for eternity
Coping with your Pain and Suffering
Interviews with the Great Cloud of Witnesses

My books in print can be found at my author page on Amazon: http://www.amazon.com/Matthew-Robert-Payne/e/B008N9R896/ref=sr_ntt_srch_lnk_3?qid=1401994248&sr=1-3

In the past year, I have started a successful Facebook Ministry group called Open Heavens and Intimacy with Jesus. As of writing, today the 10th of October 2014, it has 13,300 members and it is a really nice place to hang out and where I oversee it as a kind of pastor.

On Kindle, you can click on this link to join: https://www.facebook.com/groups/OpenHeavensGroup/

On the 5th of June 2014, I was taken through a personal deliverance and the spirits of Rejection and Fear and other spirits were cast out of me with much coughing and dry retching. Since the 5th of June, have had great success with porn. It seems that the personal deliverance had a lot to do with my addiction. I am so happy to be free of my addiction and I hope my freedom will encourage many more to be set free.

I initially was going to publish Book 1 and Book 2 of His Redeeming Love and I did publish book 1 and yet now have decided to put the content of book 2 in one whole book and publish that so people only have to buy one thick book. I have not gone back in the files and edited what has been said about that as it would have taken too much time, and the book was written a year ago when that is what I thought I would be doing.

I have recently found a publisher and so all my books will be released by them in future.

It takes a lot of courage to publish a Christian book that has so much darkness in it. It is published so that other people who have had hard life might be encouraged that our God is a loving God full of grace and mercy. I want people to see that even people in "ministry" can have sin issues and that God can use people in an effective manner even when they still have personal struggles.

As you can see, I have been honest in this account of my life. I have held nothing back. I want people to know that it is okay to be real and transparent when it comes to sharing your personal stories. The fact that I can put this story out there, the fact that I can release it without great victory in my life that overshadows my fallings proves that I am not full of shame and condemnation like many people in churches currently are.

It is time that people get honest and confess their sins and be truthful with each other. It is my hope that any men and women caught in addictive sins might feel better for reading this account of mine. like to confess that I, like Jesus, have not come to speak to the pure and righteous but to the sick people that are in need of spiritual medicine

If you still feel like judging me let me close with a quote out of Joshua Graham's book "Beyond Justice":

"You'll never know how great God's love is, how great His forgiveness is, until you've been as guilty as me."

Be blessed,
Matthew Robert Payne
10th of October 2014

PS If you have been blessed by this book, please consider writing an honest review on Amazon of it.

Lightning Source UK Ltd.
Milton Keynes UK
UKOW03n1407260517
302095UK00002B/36/P